# International and Development Education

The *International and Development Education Series* focuses on the complementary areas of comparative, international, and development education. Books emphasize a number of topics ranging from key international education issues, trends, and reforms to examinations of national education systems, social theories, and development education initiatives. Local, national, regional, and global volumes (single authored and edited collections) constitute the breadth of the series and offer potential contributors a great deal of latitude based on interests and cutting edge research. The series is supported by a strong network of international scholars and development professionals who serve on the International and Development Education Advisory Board and participate in the selection and review process for manuscript development.

Titles:

*Higher Education in Asia/Pacific: Quality and the Public Good*
Edited by Terance W. Bigalke and Deane E. Neubauer

*Affirmative Action in China and the U.S.: A Dialogue on Inequality and Minority Education*
Edited by Minglang Zhou and Ann Maxwell Hill

*Critical Approaches to Comparative Education: Vertical Case Studies from Africa, Europe, the Middle East, and the Americas*
Edited by Frances Vavrus and Lesley Bartlett

*Curriculum Studies in South Africa: Intellectual Histories & Present Circumstances*
Edited by William F. Pinar

*Higher Education, Policy, and the Global Competition Phenomenon*
Edited by Laura M. Portnoi, Val D. Rust, and Sylvia S. Bagley

*The Search for New Governance of Higher Education in Asia*
Edited by Ka-Ho Mok

*International Students and Global Mobility in Higher Education: National Trends and New Directions*
Edited by Rajika Bhandari and Peggy Blumenthal

*Curriculum Studies in Brazil: Intellectual Histories, Present Circumstances*
Edited by William F. Pinar

*Access, Equity, and Capacity in Asia Pacific Higher Education*
Edited by Deane Neubauer and Yoshiro Tanaka

*Policy Debates in Comparative, International, and Development Education*
Edited by John N. Hawkins and W. James Jacob

*Curriculum Studies in Mexico: Intellectual Histories, Present Circumstances*
Edited by William F. Pinar

*Increasing Effectiveness of the Community College Financial Model: A Global Perspective for the Global Economy*
Edited by Stewart E. Sutin, Daniel Derrico, Rosalind Latiner Raby, and Edward J. Valeau

*The Internationalization of East Asian Higher Education: Globalizations Impact*
Edited by John D. Palmer, Amy Roberts, Young Ha Cho, and Gregory Ching

*University Governance and Reform: Policy, Fads, and Experience in International Perspective*
Edited by Hans G. Schuetze, William Bruneau, and Garnet Grosjean

*Mobility and Migration in Asian Pacific Higher Education*
Edited by Deane E. Neubauer and Kazuo Kuroda

*Taiwan Education at the Crossroad: When Globalization Meets Localization*
Edited by Chuing Prudence Chou and Gregory Ching

*Higher Education Regionalization in Asia Pacific: Implications for Governance, Citizenship and University Transformation*
Edited by John N. Hawkins, Ka Ho Mok, and Deane E. Neubauer

*Post-Secondary Education and Technology: A Global Perspective on Opportunities and Obstacles to Development*
Edited by Rebecca Clothey, Stacy Austin-Li, and John C. Weidman

*Education and Global Cultural Dialogue: A Tribute to Ruth Hayhoe*
Edited by Karen Mundy and Qiang Zha

*The Quest for Entrepreneurial Universities in East Asia*
By Ka Ho Mok

# Curriculum Studies in India

## Intellectual Histories, Present Circumstances

Edited by
William F. Pinar

palgrave
macmillan

First published in 2015 by
PALGRAVE MACMILLAN®
in the United States—a division of St. Martin's Press LLC,
175 Fifth Avenue, New York, NY 10010.

Where this book is distributed in the UK, Europe and the rest of the world,
this is by Palgrave Macmillan, a division of Macmillan Publishers Limited,
registered in England, company number 785998, of Houndmills,
Basingstoke, Hampshire RG21 6XS.

Palgrave Macmillan is the global academic imprint of the above companies
and has companies and representatives throughout the world.

Palgrave® and Macmillan® are registered trademarks in the United States,
the United Kingdom, Europe and other countries.

ISBN: 978–1–137–47717–0

Library of Congress Cataloging-in-Publication Data is available from the
Library of Congress.

A catalogue record of the book is available from the British Library.

Design by Newgen Knowledge Works (P) Ltd., Chennai, India.

First edition: February 2015

10 9 8 7 6 5 4 3 2 1


Transferred to Digital Printing in 2015

# Contents

# Series Editors' Introduction

We are pleased to introduce another volume in the Palgrave Macmillan International and Development Education book series. In conceptualizing this series we took into account the extraordinary increase in the scope and depth of research on education in a global and international context. The range of topics and issues being addressed by scholars worldwide is enormous and clearly reflects the growing expansion and quality of research being conducted on comparative, international, and development education (CIDE) topics. Our goal is to cast a wide net for the most innovative and novel manuscripts, both single-authored and edited volumes, without constraints as to the level of education, geographical region, or methodology (whether disciplinary or interdisciplinary). In the process, we have also developed two subseries as part of the main series: one is cosponsored by the East West Center in Honolulu, Hawaii, drawing from their distinguished programs, the International Forum on Education 2020 (IFE 2020) and the Asian Pacific Higher Education Research Partnership (APHERP); and the other is a publication partnership with the Higher Education Special Interest Group of the Comparative and International Education Society that highlights trends and themes on international higher education.

The issues that will be highlighted in this series are those focused on capacity, access, and equity, three interrelated topics that are central to educational transformation as it appears today around the world. There are many paradoxes and asymmetries surrounding these issues, which include problems of both excess capacity and deficits, wide access to facilities as well as severe restrictions, and all the complexities that are included in the equity debate. Closely related to this critical triumvirate is the overarching concern with quality assurance, accountability, and assessment. As educational systems have expanded, so have the needs and demands for quality assessment, with implications for accreditation and accountability. Intergroup relations, multiculturalism, and gender issues comprise another cluster of concerns facing most educational systems in differential ways when one looks at the change in educational systems in an international context. Diversified notions of the structure of knowledge and curriculum development occupy another important niche in educational change at both the precollegiate and collegiate levels. Finally, how systems are managed and governed are key policy issues for educational policy-makers worldwide. These and other key elements of the education and social change environment have guided this series and have been reflected in the books that have already appeared and those that will appear in the future. We welcome proposals on these and other topics from as wide a range of scholars and practitioners as possible.

We believe that the world of educational change is dynamic, and our goal is to reflect the very best work being done in these and other areas.

JOHN N. HAWKINS
*University of California, Los Angeles*

W. JAMES JACOB
*University of Pittsburgh*

# Acknowledgments

Again I express my gratitude to Professors John Hawkins and W. James Jacob for their willingness to include this volume in their International & Development Education Series at Palgrave Macmillan. *Curriculum Studies in India* is the fifth volume to appear.

I am grateful as well to my editor at Palgrave Macmillan, Ms. Sarah Nathan, for her professionalism, courtesy, and support.

My thanks go to Professor Ashwani Kumar who suggested the names of possible participants.

My thanks especially to each of the scholar-participants—Poonam Batra, Mary Ann Chacko, Suresh Chandra Ghosh, Manish Jain, and Meenakshi Thapan—as well as to the two distinguished members of the International Panel: Lesley Le Grange and Hongyu Wang. Without your willingness and work, there could be no *Curriculum Studies in India*.

Thanks too to Fu Guopeng for his help with editing.

# Acronyms and Abbreviations

| | |
|---|---|
| AIPMT | All India Pre Medical Test |
| AISSCE | All India Senior School Certificate Examination |
| APA | American Psychological Association |
| APU | Azim Premji University |
| ASER | Annual Status of Education Report |
| AUD | Ambedkar University, Delhi |
| BEIEd | Bachelor of Elementary Education Program |
| BGIS | Bhaktivedanta Gurukula and International School |
| BJP | Bharatiya Janata Party |
| CABE | Central Advisory Board of Education |
| CBSE | Central Board of Secondary Education |
| CCE | Continuous and Comprehensive Evaluation |
| CFL | Centre for Learning |
| CIE | Central Institute of Education |
| CSIR | Council of Scientific and Industrial Research |
| CSISC | Council for the Indian School Certificate Examinations |
| DAV | Dayanand Anglo-Vedic |
| DIETs | District Institutes of Education and Training |
| DPEP | District Primary Education Program |
| DU | University of Delhi |
| EC | Education Commission |
| EFA | Education for All |
| EPW | Economic and Political Weekly |
| FRC | Friends Rural Centre |
| FSU | Friedrich Schiller University |
| HRC | Human Relations and Communication |
| HSTP | Hoshangabad Science Teaching Program |
| IB | International Baccalaureate |
| ICSE | Indian Certificate of Secondary Education |
| IMF | International Monetary Fund |
| IOE | University of London Institute of Education |
| ISC | Indian School Certificate |
| ISKCON | International Society for Krishna Consciousness |
| JNU | Jawaharlal Nehru University |
| KB | Kishore Bharati |

| | |
|---|---|
| KCF | Kerala Curriculum Framework |
| KFI | Krishnamurti Foundation India |
| MACESE | Maulana Azad Centre for Elementary and Social Education |
| MHRD | Ministry of Human Resources Development |
| MLLs | Minimum Levels of Learnings |
| MP | Madhya Pradesh |
| NCERT | National Council of Educational Research and Training |
| NCF | National Curriculum Framework |
| NCFSE | National Curriculum Framework for School Education |
| NCFTE | National Curriculum Framework for Teacher Education |
| NCTE | National Council of Teacher Education |
| NDA | National Democratic Alliance |
| NEP | New Education Policy |
| NGO | Nongovernmental Organizations |
| NIOS | National Institute for Open Schooling |
| PISA | Program for International Student Assessment |
| RIVER | Rishi Valley Institute for Educational Resources |
| RSS | Rashtriya Swayamsevak Sangh |
| RUSE | Research Unit in the Sociology of Education |
| RVEC | Rishi Valley Education Centre |
| SC | Scheduled Castes |
| SCERT | Kerala State Council of Educational Research and Training |
| SDW | Self-Development Workshop |
| SOE | Sociology of Education |
| SSA | Sarva Shiksha Abhiyan |
| SSTP | Social Science Teaching Programme |
| ST | Scheduled Tribes |
| TCS | Tata Consultancy Services |
| TISS | Tata Institute of Social Sciences |
| UGC | University Grants Commission |
| UPA | United Progressive Alliance |
| ZHCES | Zakir Husain Centre for Educational Studies |

# Introduction

## William F. Pinar

What are the present circumstances in which our curriculum studies colleagues in India work? What intellectual histories inform the categories through which they address these circumstances? What is the current state of the field? These are among the questions[1] I posed to Poonam Batra, Mary Ann Chacko, Suresh Ghosh, Manish Jain, and Meenakshi Thapan.[2] Knowing that knowledge is not free-floating but crafted by actually existing persons, I started by asking a series of questions concerning each scholar-participant's intellectual life history.[3] My summaries[4] (Berman 2001) of these interviews appear briefly; they introduce the authors of the essays that comprise chapters 1 through 5.

These essays concern curriculum studies in India. To the authors of these essays members of an International Panel—Lesley Le Grange of South Africa and Hongyu Wang of the United States[5]—posed questions. In chapter 6 I summarize the exchanges[6] (Luxon 2013; Pinar 2011a) among scholar-participants and members of the International Panel.[7] In chapter 7 I summarize what I learned from the interviews, essays, and exchanges.

Why is *clarification* a crucial concept? The internationalization of curriculum studies invites dialogical encounter across difference.[8] Disputes may arise, but we must first try to understand each other and appreciate each other's intellectual histories and present circumstances. Despite having similar vocabularies, "deliberation" is, for instance, an important concept in curriculum studies in India and the United States; however, the concept's histories and present circumstances differ in both countries (Block 2004).[9] We cannot assume we understand how they circulate outside our own orbit; we must seek clarification, or even appreciate the differences (Pinar 2011c).[10]

In general terms *internationalization* indicates the *recontextualization* of concepts imported from elsewhere.[11] Recontextualization (Pinar 2010; 2011a; 2011b; 2011c; 2014)[12] translates globalization into *localization*, a recasting of concepts crafted abroad for reformulation and sometimes unintended uses in what can be distinctive domestic circumstances. Remembering the past, recognizing its traces in present projects—in India, it is among other things an ongoing struggle between colonialism and indigeneity (Pinar 2009)[13]—confers upon curriculum studies its cosmopolitan cause (Pinar 2009; 2011c).[14]

Having long ago (Pinar 1981)[15] rejected any interest in the "scientific" study of education, I have here emphasized the perspectival character of knowledge, its crafting by actually existing persons. I place this fact at the forefront. Particularity is the substratum of generalization. While facts and events specific to India remind me of issues in North America—corruption (Noponen 2011)[16] for instance—the details differ, the functioning differs. Emphasizing the particular is, however, no intellectual compulsion, an unconscious recapitulation of my socialization as a gradate student.[17] In another historical moment, or in a different academic field, I might proceed differently. But given the cultural, political, and educational standardization that globalization enforces and the homogenization that "proceduralism" (Pinar 2011c)[18] in US curriculum institutionalized, I work here to contradict contemporary trends. Consider it an effort of "counter-socialization," to invoke Krishna Kumar's concept.[19]

Methodologically—more a fascination toward the social science than the humanities—I make a mosaic, each chapter affording a different glimpse of curriculum studies in India. The very first glimpse occurs through the introduction of the scholar-participants; the second through the essays they composed; the third through their exchanges with members of the International Panel; the fourth through my summary of these; and the fifth through the epilogue where the scholar-participants have the "final word" in this protracted dialogical encounter.[20] Having always relied on paraphrase (Pinar 2006)[21]—it is, I suggest, the methodology of the synoptic tradition so central to curriculum studies in the United States (Pinar, Reynolds, Slattery, and Taubman 1995)[22]—I absent myself in the epilogue where only those who might have been obscured in my "recontextualization" reappear, with clarity.

Seeking clarification respects the autonomy of the other as it suspends—sometimes by stating—one's own necessarily perspectival knowledge (Luxon 2013).[23] Situating the self (Pinar 2010)[24] clarifies where one "is coming from." That "place" is simultaneously subjective and social, each domain informed historically. The particularity of *place* becomes personified in the actually existing person engaged in this labor of internationalization that seeks understanding across difference. While occurring through email, this project itself could be considered a "place," not a physical one obviously, but a "site" to which we returned in communication with each other, projecting some sense of "affiliation rooted in place and experience" (Berman 2001).[25]

This volume introduces curriculum studies in India to students in North America, but, as the scholar-participants would I think agree, it does not exhaust the subject. This volume represents an invitation to seek additional clarification. As the term's secondary definition suggests, the process of internationalization requires that "distillation" dialogical encounter can create. Replying to the specific questions members of the International Panel posed, the scholar-participants explained how the past has informed the present circumstances they and their colleagues face. While the influences have been multiple, one through-line is *colonialism*. For almost a millennium, India has undergone the unwanted "importation" of knowledge—including the curriculum taught to children—from elsewhere. At least from the times of the Islamic occupation during the Middle Ages through eighteenth, nineteenth, and twentieth-century British colonialism to the neocolonialism associated with globalization today, India has been subject to occupations of differing sorts, intensities, and durations. The duration and complexity of these historical facts and their continuing consequences require clarification.

This stance of seeking clarification can support the *cosmopolitan* cause of internationalization. I encouraged a diplomatic tone that harmonizes what could be a cacophonous confrontation across incalculable cultural complexity. Clarification and appreciation can be reciprocally related. *Nonviolence* is central to the internationalization of curriculum studies, as Hongyu Wang has demonstrated (Wang 2014).[26] Acknowledgment of difference, assumption of ignorance, courteous requests for additional information, and considered judgment: these are among the practices (Noponen 2011; Pinar 2011c)[27] structuring nonviolent democratic dialogue across difference: my very definition of internationalization.

Why organize these international studies by "nation"? Because curriculum studies fields take form within certain countries, are often profoundly structured by the politics of national "school reform," and become the priorities of national ministries of education. Also because curriculum specialists often reside and work in specific countries with their own distinctive histories and present agendas, organizing efforts at "internationalization" by *nation* is obligatory. It hardly disqualifies other organizational forms of association and affiliation, and of course "exchanges" among scholars occur globally, usually linked by intellectual and research interests, but never free—how could they be?—of the imprinting national history and culture confers.

The final volume in this series concerning the internationalization of curriculum studies, *Curriculum Studies in India* demonstrates the potential of democratic disciplinary dialogue across national boundaries, cultural differences, and generational locations. "Democratic" denotes an "open" discussion, relatively unencumbered by deadlines, demands, or predetermined outcomes. That is not the say we worked "out of this world." Each of us worked, I suspect, by *making* time out of daily circumstances that pressed down on us. Certainly in North America faculty are now inundated by a myriad of often-miniscule obligations that take away time for even their most basic professional duties: reading the scholarship of colleagues. I can't think of a more sinister plot devised by anti-intellectual enemies of the university than what has been accomplished by the time-consuming bureaucratic protocols of what gets called "accountability."

In making time—consciously dilating the present moment so that its temporal structure[28] is unmistakable and so that it does not coincide with what we face—we can discern the persistence of the past. It structures the present. Any present project contains traces of the injuries and injustices characterizing colonialism, now evident in economic and cultural globalization. The presence of the past means that I could be accused of complicity with colonialism, as the questions I posed to the scholar-practitioners could be recoded as "cultural." They presume the presence of a "person," now a contested concept in the West, as decades of discussions focused on the "death of the subject" and the emergence of the "post-human" testify (Weaver 2010).[29] From the chapters that follow, it is clear that the concept—the *person*—still resonates among scholar-participants, if with cultural differences and memories of its disregard and assertion during colonial rule. But democratic dialogue means that anyone can eschew the concepts and contest the conceptual grounds of our discussions (Pinar 2011a).[30]

Especially in education one feels the emergency of the moment, as there are children who must be kept waiting not an hour longer to be addressed: as students, as children, as human beings vulnerable and precious, as plenitude, and not lack as colonialism connotes.[31] Parents can appreciate the primacy of the person; they can feel keenly the emergency of education. So do many schoolteachers and professors of education. Not only in the West do teachers face the sometimes deafening demands for "what works," and not merely in quantifiable terms. Debilitating, even deforming, this demand has also meant that the academic discipline of education has not always been at the forefront of the study of intellectual history. There are many histories of the intellectual "object" of our discipline—the *school*—and of those larger forces and institutions that have said to structure the schools. There are fewer intellectual histories of the concepts—like "forces" and "structures"—in the vocabulary we use when thinking about the school. The net effect is the positioning of an organizational form—the school—as the central concept of the field and in "reform." It is not only children who disappear in such organizationalism.

On occasion—often at the end of a career—there are biographic accounts of individual scholars and educators, but these are often celebrations or remembrances of colleagues who have retired or died (Waks and Short 2009).[32] As someone nearing retirement, I appreciate these acknowledgments of service. But I also feel keenly that despite the emergency of the moment it is always time to acknowledge the persons of whatever age who are struggling to respond to that moment.

It is the presence of the person in her or his research that imprints scholarship as *professional*, as *craft* not *mechanical reproduction*. Professional shcolarship is not merely communication of information; knowledge bears, however indirectly, the traces of the author's lived, educational experience, her or his presence in the words that are sometimes somewhat idiosyncratically coupled together. It is no simplistic expression of our subjectivity either; research expresses our commitment to the actually existing child, as the field of education—and its centerpiece concept *curriculum*—as that ethically accented complicated conversation among children and adults regarding the past, present, and future. Meet the scholar-participants.

## Poonam Batra

> *Intervention in school curriculum can be meaningful only when the socio-political context is understood and made part of intervention strategy and design.*

For the past two decades Poonam Batra has been working in the field of elementary education. As part of the Indian Central Government's scheme for upgrading existing departments of education (VII Five Year Plan: 1987–1991), the University of Delhi (DU) created a "niche space" within its Department of Education for "research" and "intervention" in elementary education. Batra reports that this was "the first time ever" that a university in India has engaged with questions of elementary education.[33] Taken in 1989, following the National Education Policy of Education of 1986,[34] this initiative led to the establishment of the Maulana Azad Centre for Elementary and Social Education (MACESE), a section of DU's Department of Education. "It is important to know," Batra explained, that the Department of Education had the legacy of being "an autonomous institution—called the Central Institute of Education (CIE)—that had been established under the Ministry of Education soon after independence in 1947." CIE became affiliated to DU in 1979 and was henceforth known as the Department of Education.

Batra joined the faculty of the MACESE in the summer of 1991, moving from her parent institution, an undergraduate college, also affiliated with DU. Trained in psychology with an honors graduate degree and a postgraduate degree, Batra reports that she made "a conscious move" from the specialized study of clinical psychology to the field of educational studies. Such a move enabled her to "elaborate my interests and passions both pre- and post- my formal joining of the department of education." Batra attributed her interest in psychology to "good teaching." The questions that have preoccupied her "revolved around issues of discrimination in society, in families, especially the question of fewer spaces and opportunities for young girls to learn and grow."

Coming-of-age in a "middle class family that aspired for mobility," Batra writes, "my parents brought their children into the fold of education through the best known institutions of the time." Educated in English, Batra grew up "like many of my generation, to value education that was 'de-contextualized' and 'objective.'" She had learned that the "1857 revolt" against the Government of (British) India was waged by "traitors." History books had been written by British writers whose perspectives, Batra and her classmates were assured, were "correct" and "objective." British rule in India had contributed to thinking that the written word is "sacrosanct," a view, Batra explained, also aligned with "Indian brahamanical" thinking, as only texts worthy of being read were considered religious texts. As a family, she continued, "we belong to a caste lower than the highest caste (brahmin), but because we had access to education in an English medium school we assumed a 'high caste' status and hence achieved social acceptability." Even in 1989—40 years after independence, Batra reminds—"my entry into the community of school teachers in parts of rural India, who are largely Brahmins, was possible because I had pursued doctoral studies and had therefore become worthy of the company of higher caste brahmins!"

Postgraduate study was, Batra reports, "novel in my family," as "my father had had to bear the burden of financially supporting his several siblings. My mother was a graduate but could not continue her study for similar reasons, as the family had to support the elder son's education." Both Batra's parents had "escaped the brutal fate of the country's partition that had brought them to Delhi from Lahore which, after having become part of the new nation called Pakistan, suddenly became a land alien to those who were born there, as it was no longer part of India." Despite—and also perhaps due to?—these circumstances, "love for knowledge and the desire to seek was a natural part of our family. This seeking was always a seeking within ourselves. Being a girl I was brought up with the idea of pursuing higher education to learn and grow wisdom, and not necessarily to develop a professional career."

It was Batra's "continuing urge" to "understand the human mind and psyche and the interface between the individual and the social" that persuaded her to pursue a postgraduate degree in psychology. As a student she discovered a voluntary organization dedicated to providing psychological support to those who were unhappy, even suicidal. Batra began to volunteer for this organization—Sanjivini—and she quickly discovered that "this was my calling at that time... to reach out to people in distress." During the course of her work at Sanjivini, Batra found that her perceptiveness and sensitivity developed further. This educational experience helped persuade her to undertake a career in educational research at Jawaharlal Nehru University, Delhi.

The psychology Batra had studied had been formulated in the United Kingdom and in the United States, forcing her—and her fellow students—to grapple with concepts, constructs, and entire theories severed from the settings wherein they had been formulated. Although questions of family socialization and other constructs in psychology fascinated Batra, she could not always associate them with her personal circumstances and social conditions. Few of her teachers seemed to think it was important to relate constructs in psychology to the social realities around them, a consequence of the view, Batra appreciated, that "formal knowledge" is essentially "decontextualized." Without these characteristics, presumably knowledge cannot be "scientific" and "objective."

There had been one exception to this rule. During her postgraduate study of clinical psychology, one professor engaged her and her fellow students by teaching English literature. By doing so he was providing, Batra recalls, "vibrant opportunities to study human psychologies through literary characters—imaginative and real." She and her fellow students studied the poetry of W. B. Yeats and the philosophical writings of Jean-Paul Sartre, which encouraged them to "delve deeper into questions of a disintegrating human psyche/mind/being." The work of R. D. Laing[35] and Berger and Luckmann (Berger and Luckmann 1967)[36] "brought a whole new perspective of psychology for me." Batra was "moved," she reports, "from reading research that merely confirmed American Psychological Association (APA) classifications of human behavior to reading literature that prompted the need to question the norm." Such "independent reading opened the realm of interdisciplinary enquiry for me."

It was teaching undergraduate courses in the University of Delhi that provided Batra opportunities "to relate what I read to the specific realities in which my students lived and grew." Indeed, "I learnt more psychology as a teacher than as a student!" Now able to "discern the difference between psychology as a 'scientific pursuit' and as 'an art,'" Batra taught Fukuaka's *One Straw Revolution*, Schumacher's *Small Is Beautiful*, Carl Roger's *Freedom to Learn*, and Stephen Gould's *Mismeasure of Man*. Teaching—as professional activity and as an academic field of research—provided occasions for Batra's "individual sensitivities to reach out," including her "passion for children and the need to assert herself as a woman in a patriarchal milieu." These "led me to choose the field of education for research."

Growing "fairly dissatisfied" with her MPhil. research (1980) that had been prompted more by the professional pursuits of her supervisor than by her own interests, Batra decided to withdraw from the doctoral program. Her "activist orientation" moved her to search for "a meaningful area of research that would enable change rather than become a mere theoretical pursuit." Batra decided to work with a nongovernmental organization to undertake research in education. The choice she faced was to work either with Mirambika, a school based in Delhi based on the philosophical framework of Sri Aurobindo,[37] or with Eklavya, an organization that operated in the municipal schools of Madhya Pradesh, a state of Central India. While the former afforded Batra the opportunity to work through Sri Aurobindo's vision of integral education, the latter appeared to her to be "a more compelling reality."[38]

"Eklavya provided me the much awaited opportunity to test many of my ideas on the ground," Batra remembers, "to undertake research that would involve action by way of intervention in the formal system of primary schooling." Eklavya's agenda was the design of primary curriculum. "Using the newly designed curriculum as a tool," she tells us, "my doctoral work focused on understanding processes of child thinking with a view to look at some of the well established theories of children's development critically from the lens of a socio-cultural context."[39]

After a short tenure as faculty at the Centre for Educational Studies in Jawaharlal Nehru University (JNU), Batra joined DU's MACESE at the Department of Education (CIE), writing the Perspective Paper (MACES 1991)[40] for the unit's future agenda and its role in the university. One of the key agenda items was the development of a teacher education program for prospective elementary schoolteachers, the only such initiative housed in a university in India in 1994. Typically, elementary teacher education was a certificate/diploma program requiring a maximum of two years and offered by district-level institutions. Known as District Institutes of Education and Training (DIETs), established post-NPE (1986) with Five-Year Plan funds, these institutions operated—operate still, Batra adds—in isolation, without linkages with universities or other institutes of higher education.

Since Batra's research agenda became focused on curriculum and pedagogy, gender studies, and elementary education, including public policy and teacher education for elementary school teachers. Batra was instrumental in developing the Bachelor of Elementary Education Program (BElEd), a four-year integrated program of teacher education (Batra 2009).[41] Prior to the design of the program, she had led a feasibility study (MACESE 2001)[42] to assess the desirability of instituting a degree program for the preparation of elementary teachers. That study documented not only the need for professionally qualified teachers, Batra reports, "but also the need to create opportunities in higher education to promote research in elementary education with the aim to develop a knowledge-base that is contextualized and rigorous."

The BElEd, Batra tells us, is "one of the most important initiatives in curriculum development of teacher education in post-independence India." Other innovations concern the school curriculum. Among the early interventions include Gandhiji's Nai Talim, which integrated ideas of work and education, bearing resemblance to the work of George Herbert Mead; Tagore's experiments with Shantiniketan, a school where children were encouraged to grow in natural environments; Aurobindo's integral education that integrated the mental, the physical, and the spiritual in the development of higher consciousness; the Ramakrishna Mission schools that also attempted to integrate the spiritual with the material; and the Krishnamurti[43] Foundation schools that continue to make their mark in India as well as internationally. Since the 1980s, Batra continued, "innovation" in school curriculum has been supported by nongovernmental organizations (NGOs). "Foremost" among these has been Eklavya (see above). Batra cited Digantar as another organization engaged in school curriculum development.

There is, Batra reports, "a deep hiatus" between university departments offering liberal program in educational studies[44] and departments providing teacher education. In India, she explained, "we have not been able to create legitimate spaces for formal institutionalized engagement with education as a research pursuit and a discipline." Part of the intent in establishing the BElEd was the establishment of "institutional spaces within the university for engagement with questions of research, enhancing disciplinary discourse, policy and practice in elementary education." Batra credits her involvement with the conception and development of the BElEd as deepening her thinking on those issues of curriculum, pedagogy, and children's learning that she had experienced "firsthand in varying contexts of social realities in India." This thinking informs her current commitments to teacher education and social change, as she explores "the policy-practice interface while engaging deeper with social science perspectives in education; understanding pedagogic shifts from a gender lens; deepening discourse on structure and agency in education and social change."

# Mary Ann Chacko

*My understanding of the discipline of education and the field of curriculum studies in India is in its nascent stages.*

Mary Ann Chacko has been disappointed that while universities in the West projected themselves as "global," often they exhibited "very little engagement with the global in terms of course contents or faculty research." At the time of this project a PhD student at Teachers College, Columbia University, Chacko chose her current research topic—NGO-School partnerships for Youth Leadership in India—after noticing "the exponential increase" in youth leadership programs not only in the United States but in India as well. Her research question became: "What prompted and nurtures now this 'globalization' of youth leadership programs, especially in India?" What she suspected—what was in fact a "missing link in youth leadership discourse"—is the "likely connection between youth leadership discourse and neoliberal restructuring of nation-states."

India is a "fascinating case" for an empirical study of globalization, Chacko reminds us. No discussion of globalization occurs without acknowledging the economic rise of India. The story is by no means that simple, as "the mix of colonial modernity, postcolonial nationalism, and liberalization has led to intense debates about the meaning of India under globalization." These various circumstances make India a "compelling case to study the intersection of the local and the global in youth leadership discourse."

Professor Nancy Lesko of the Department of Curriculum and Teaching at Teachers College, Chacko acknowledges, has proved "invaluable." Lesko deploys a "poststructural lens" to critique the "construction of youth as a universal and stable category," foregrounding those "rationalities" that represent youth in "particular ways" at "particular historical junctures" and the ways in which these representations "govern youth and adults." Lesko's work has enabled Chacko to appreciate that "youth is a deeply ideological category."

For the present project Chacko explored the contributions of Krishna Kumar, "one of the foremost educational thinkers in India today,"[45] and one who has been "actively engaged" in the "revamping" of the school curriculum in India. He has been a "vocal opponent" of efforts to "Sanskritize" the curriculum by the Hindu right. Chacko is grateful to her "friend and colleague Ashwani Kumar[46] for pointing me in this direction." Krishna Kumar's work—which "actively engages with the entanglements of curriculum with the socio-political, cultural, and economic specificities of India"—will inform Chacko's depiction of the movements, issues, and controversies in curriculum studies in India. As a doctoral student, Chacko feels free to undertake "independent" research irrespective of the institutional and larger political circumstances, and "I intend to take full advantage of this 'space.'"

Having completed her BA and MA in English Literature, Chacko's "only exposure" to a systematic study of education as an academic discipline was when she undertook her teacher training, a one-year program. "I remember that my curriculum studies text focused on individuals who had exerted a prominent infleunce on curriculum development worldwide, including Maria Montessori, Pestalozzi, and John Dewey." Two Indian educationists were also discussed: Mahatma Gandhi and Rabindranath Tagore. In Chacko's view, the field of curriculum in India has been "extremely porous," borrowing "heavily from developments in the West." Given these circumstances, Gandhi and Tagore "stand apart as two, among what might only be a handful of individuals, who have attempted to fashion curricula that are organic and responsive to the socio-political, economic, and cultural specificities of the country."

In Chacko's view, a "cohesive" field of curriculum studies is "yet to take shape in India." The study of curriculum in India resembles more "a map of curriculum development in the West, particularly in the U.S." The Indira Gandhi National Open University's module on *Curriculum: The Concept*—its reputed long-distance teacher education course—allows, after discussing "the evolution of curriculum as a field of study," that it may have given the "impression" that curriculum studies as a discipline is an "American gift to the world of education" (p. 15). For Chacko, these quoted lines illustrate the American-centric nature of the extant field of curriculum studies in India.

Chacko's own work focuses on the "increasing role" played by organizations outside formal educational institutions, such as NGOs, in producing new "imaginings of childhood, youth, nation-state, and citizenship," imaginings with "repercussions for our conceptions of schooling and curriculum." Her research is located at the intersection of three global trends in education: (1) the increasing presence of non-state entities in the educational sector, (2) a shift in priority from educational access to improving educational quality and innovation, and (3) an acknowledgment of youth as legitimate sociopolitical actors. NGO-school partnerships for youth leadership education constitute a site of confluence of these three trends. At the same time, Chacko continued, such study will "enhance our understanding of how the global ideal of youth leadership is inflected in different local contexts and under the influence of specific cultural, economic, historical, and political forces, produces different meanings."

As she undertakes her doctoral dissertation research, Chacko finds that "globalization," while a "contested term," remains "useful" for examining why and how "initiatives, influences, and aspirations travel across differences." The challenge, however, is to locate "the global" not only in the West, as doing so would cast youth leadership discourses in other parts of the world as "mere translations" of the "original idea." Chacko will examine the "globalization of youth leadership as an educational ideal" as well as the "roles played by non-governmental organizations not only in designing and implementing youth leadership programs but also in *producing* youth leadership as an educational goal." Rejecting "dominant conceptions" of youth leadership as "ahistorical, developmental ideals," Chacko studies it as "a *commodity* that is fetishized in an era where nation-states are increasingly undergoing neoliberal restructuring to meet the demands of the global market." It would be "misleading," Chacko cautions, to study youth leadership programs "as though they are purposefully designed to produce neoliberal subjects to serve the demands of the market." Youth leadership programs, Chacko points out, are designed and implemented by NGOs with "varied goals." With their "specialized expertise, readiness to innovate, and decentralized structures," NGOs have been at the "vanguard of developing and disseminating new ideas and practices in education." One must, however, resist the temptation of characterizing NGOs as the "champions of public interest and agents of democracy," as their roles are embedded "within the neoliberal project itself." The "proliferation" and "complexity" of youth leadership programs in the context of "neo-liberalization and the state's contested partnership with NGOs"—including "the active role" played by NGOs in the "design and delivery" of youth leadership programs—form the focus of Chacko's research.

As a discipline, Chacko reports, the academic field of education occupies a "marginal place in the Indian academic landscape." In fact, few universities in India have a faculty or department of education, a concern for Chacko who intends to return to India to teach in a faculty of education. The situation is gradually changing, she believes, and more universities are housing education departments. With that future in mind, Chacko is concerned that her present research focuses exclusively on "non-formal spaces of education." In her post-PhD career "one of my goals is to work closely with schoolteachers in order to study teacher knowledge." Chacko believes that "theoretically and methodologically rigorous research conducted within formal spaces of education such as schools is essential for the advancement of the field." Moreover, a "deep engagement with teacher knowledge can have a positive impact on the status afforded to practicing teachers whether by policy makers, experts in the field, or by the parents and the community." This is, Chacko emphasizes, "crucial at a time when teachers are increasingly being targeted for what is deemed to be the failure of public schooling in different parts of the world."

Chacko acknowledged three "experiences" as influential in her present "position." The first was her "teacher training," the second her "experiences as both a school teacher and teacher educator," and the third her "involvement, though peripheral, in a teacher inquiry group at Teachers College, Columbia University." "I believe that teachers possess specialized knowledge," she told me, and "that an engagement with teacher knowledge is essential in the preparation of teachers, professional development, and for the advancement of the field of curriculum studies." During her teacher training, Chacko recalled, "no attempt was made to help me link what I was learning in teacher education to my own assumptions about the role of the teacher or of teaching." Nor was there any effort to "link the content knowledge to the training in pedagogy or teaching techniques that I was receiving." "We were urged to make our lesson plans interactive," Chacko remembers, "but we were never given the space to reflect on the possible benefits and challenges of an interactive teaching style. This inability to make personal meaning of what I was learning led to a very precarious learning experience."

To correct this deficiency, Chacko recommends that "examples of teachers' daily experiences" become a part of the "knowledge base" of education and curriculum studies. The point of these examples, she cautioned, is not "to make claims about what teachers should or should not do, but to investigate issues that arise in trying to teach." She recalls "meetings where teachers came together to learn, plan, and share the inquires they are conducting in their schools and classrooms." Facilitated by university-based personnel, this New York–based "inquiry community" was "a space where teachers shared their dilemmas and anxieties, shared formal, practical, and organizational knowledge, chose the issue they want to explore or problem they want to solve, shared ideas and resources for data collection and shared their findings." Disbanding was not easy; participants wanted to meet again. "These communities," Chacko reflects, "became sites that embodied Freire's notion of praxis wherein theory and practice exist in dialectical relationship with each other. My personal educational experiences and my interaction with this inquiry team has made me a staunch though cautious supporter of knowledge-of-teacher practice."

# Suresh Chandra Ghosh

*For me, freedom is the most invaluable, the most precious and the most cherished object on this planet.*

Ghosh identifies six important landmarks in his intellectual life history. The first was his entry to college after the school-leaving exam at standard 10 in 1954; the second occurred when he left for London in 1963 to conduct his doctoral research after obtaining a masters degree in history from Calcutta University; the third was when he returned to India from London in 1966 and joined Jadavpur University, Calcutta, as a lecturer in History for a short period before leaving for Edinburgh University in 1968; the fourth was when he returned from Edinburgh University and joined Jawaharlal Nehru University (JNU), New Delhi, as an editor of Educational Records of the Government of India and was promoted to associate professor in History of Education in 1971. The fifth landmark was in the year 2000 when he took leave from JNU for a year to join the faculty of Friedrich Schiller

University (FSU) as a visiting professor. The final landmark was when, two years after his return from FSU, Ghosh retired from JNU in August 2002 and embarked on his current project, investigating "very critically" religious history, a discipline, he points out, "never taught and researched in our universities since their birth in India, and this may perhaps be described as the sixth and final phase in my intellectual life history."

Ghosh entered college in 1954, seven years after India had achieved independence, two years after the country had become a republic. After the departure of British officials in 1947, there was, he reports, a shortage of personnel in the civil and military administrations. "The rush was on," Ghosh recalls, for colleges to offer programs in the liberal arts and sciences. While there were institutions of medicine and engineering, there were few offering programs in management. Moreover, admission to the commerce programs in the arts and science colleges was regarded as "the last refuge" for those students unable to obtain admission to programs leading to bachelor degrees in the arts and sciences. Students "flocked" to arts and science colleges "knowing fully well that job opportunities for them were limited only to teaching and government services." Ghosh's intention was to become a secondary school teacher.

It was while studying at Chandernagore College in West Bengal that Ghosh met Mr. Sankar Dutta, a "brilliant teacher" of History, who had studied at Presidency College. He inspired Ghosh to pursue a degree in History at Presidency College, Calcutta. The college had originated as a Hindu School in 1817, then recast as Presidency College in 1855 by Dalhousie (1848–1855), who dreamt of it becoming a university.[47] When Ghosh studied there the college was regarded as "one of the best colleges of Arts and Sciences that admitted only the most brilliant students."[48] Admitted to the History (Honours) course,[49] Ghosh was encouraged to become a historian. Ghosh was inspired by the example of Dr. Amalesh Tripathi, who was one of the first after independence to obtain a doctorate degree in History from the University of London. After graduation from Presidency College in 1958, Ghosh was admitted to Calcutta University to study for a masters degree in Modern History,[50] which was conferred on him in the year 1961. Ghosh took up a position as lecturer in History at a college at Silchar, in the state of Assam.

The second landmark was Ghosh's admission, in October 1963, to the PhD program in History at the University of London where he expected to conduct research on Modern Indian History. Ghosh was interested in British Social Life in Bengal, a subject he discovered was not prominent in the history in Modern India. Assigned to "Major" Harrison,[51] Ghosh was advised to model his doctoral dissertation after a paper entitled "The British in Benares in the Late Eighteenth and the Early Nineteenth Centuries" by Bernard Cohn, an anthropologist at the University of Chicago. Ghosh recalls: "I was immediately thrown into the deep sea. I had no academic knowledge, qualifications, or formal training either in Sociology or Anthropology. However, I did not lose heart and after a great deal of difficulties and hardships in collecting data on the subject I began to write my chapters." Harrison was not enthusiastic. Discouraged, Ghosh considered leaving for the University of Alberta, but recovered after his chapter on the Anglo-Indian Community was "tremendously appreciated" by the South Asian History Seminar.[52] He received his doctoral degree in 1966 and his dissertation was subsequently published in 1971, titled *The Social Conditions of the British Community in Bengal, 1757–1800.*

While it had been "a wonderful transformation for me (from a historian to a sociologist)," the shift in disciplines "spelt hardships" when Ghosh was unable to obtain a position in Modern Indian History in any Indian university upon his return home in 1966. Complicating the question of professional identity was the prerequisite of political connections. "Ultimately and with great difficulty" Ghosh obtained a position as a lecturer in Modern Indian History at Jadavpur University "with the help" of the Council of Scientific and Industrial Research (CSIR) of the Government of India, an agency established "to stop the flight of brains from India to abroad." Soon, however, Ghosh himself left for a postdoctoral fellowship in Edinburgh where he assisted Mr. V. G. Kiernan in his teaching of a course on Indian history. At the same time Ghosh conducted research on Dalhousie in India—a subject both sociological and historical. That research was subsequently published by Munshiram Manhorlal in New Delhi in 1975 under the title, *Dalhousie in India,1848–57.* In 1977, Ghosh edited and published "a very interesting historical manuscript with sociological overtones" by James MacMurdo, a Scottish official of the East India Company, which he discovered at the Scottish National Library. It was published under the title: *The Peninsula of Gujarat in the Early Nineteenth Century.*

The fourth landmark was when Ghosh returned from Edinburgh to India in 1971, this time working at the National Archives in New Delhi. The government was then establishing the prestigious Jawaharlal Nehru University in the capital, and Ghosh applied for an associate professorship in History. He was interviewed but was not appointed, as the position went to a protégé of Professor S.Gopal, a former Oxford don who was the son of the President of India, Dr. Sarvapalli Radhakrishnan. About this time *The Social Condition of the British Community in Bengal, 1757–1800* had been published, and Ghosh was appointed to the post of editor of the Educational Records of the Government of India at the JNU.

A year and a half later, he was designated as an associate professor in History of Education when the Center for Educational Studies was formed. At this center, he started teaching and guiding research at the MPhil and the PhD levels in Educational Studies. History of Education became one of the four disciplines supported by the center, the other three being Sociology of Education, Economics of Education, and Psychology of Education. The center was named after a president of the country, Dr. Zakir Husain. It was there that Suresh Ghosh was gradually initiated into a discipline in Education and, he notes, this transition was as smooth as it had been when the discipline was moved (over a decade before) into anthropology as an area of social history. History of Education is likewise a subset of the wider history of society with elements of politics, economics, and religion.

From 1971, Ghosh then undertook research on the history of education, publishing articles in the *History of Education* (London), *Modern Asian Studies* (Cambridge), *Minerva* (London), and the *Journal of the American Oriental Society* (Pennsylvania). In 1976 he published his edited works on the educational records of the Government of India 1859 to1896, titled *The Development of Educational Service* C2 volumes. The next year saw the publication of *The Development of University Education, 1916–1920* as well as another of his edited works, *Educational Strategies in the Developing Countries.*[53]

In Paris in 1981 Ghosh presented a paper on the formation of the British educational policy—later published in *The Supply of Schooling* (Paris, 1983)—that was
highly appreciated by late Professor Emeritus Brian Simon and his wife the late
Professor Joan Simon. From this first meeting, "I became very close to Brian and Joan,
and we regularly corresponded with each other until they finally left this planet."
After Simon's death, a chair in the History of Education was named after him at the
Institute of Education at the University of London, where his papers[54] are archived.

In 1983 Suresh Ghosh became a full professor and held the chair in History of
Education at the JNU. In 1985 was published his *Indian Nationalism*[55], followed
in 1989 by his *Educational Policy in India since Warren Hastings* and, in 1991, *The
Freedom Movement in India, 1857–1947*. In 1995 appeared *The History of Education
in Modern India*; by 2013 it had undergone four editions and a reprint in 2010. In
2000 appeared his *History of Education in Medieval India* followed in the next year
by *The History of Education in Ancient India*. These three volumes on the history
of education were published as a single volume in 2007 by Rawat Publications in
Jaipur under the title *History of Education in India (3000 B.C.—1999 A.D.)*. In
August 2002 Suresh Ghosh retired.

The next landmark in Ghosh's intellectual history was in April 2000 when he
served as a visiting professor at the Friedrich Schiller University, in Jena, Germany.
The FSU was closely associated with celebrated German intellectuals and philosophers, among them Goethe, Schiller, Hegel, and Marx. Scholars there—prominent
among them Professor Martha Friedenthal-Haase—were "very keen to know about
our education system in ancient India." Their interest, Ghosh writes, "was justified,"
for "very few" have "any understanding" of education in ancient India.[56] "What
scholars both in India and abroad know," he observed, "is the present system of education introduced by the British in the nineteenth century." And so Ghosh lectured
on ancient education in India, its emergence from religious scriptures, its adaptations
to changing conditions, and its contributions to "the prosperous and spiritual civilization that has become India's proud heritage." Ghosh's lectures were subsequently
published in 2002 as *Civilization, Education and School in Ancient and Medieval
India* by Peter Lang, a well-known European publishing house at Frankfurt.

"Religion has not been a program of study and research in our universities,"
Ghosh explained, presumably in the interest of "maintaining harmony in a plural
society like ours." He continued: "I find our knowledge about the subject has not
extended beyond what we have learnt about it from the British Orientalists and the
European Indologists of the late eighteenth and the early nineteenth centuries. My
present preoccupation with our religious history from 1500 B.C. to the first decade
of the present century may be regarded as the sixth and the final landmark of my
intellectual life history."

Until the choice of religious history, Ghosh's choice of research subjects was, he
writes, informed more by "extraneous factors than by myself or by my own interest."
His interest in history was piqued "by my teacher at the undergraduate colleges, first
at Chandernagore College then at Calcutta Presidency College." His interest in history shifted to an interest in sociology and anthropology at London at the doctoral
level, "again at the insistence of my supervisor." While Ghosh did choose the subject
of his doctoral research—British Social life in Bengal—the research itself would be

"converted into a socio-anthropological study." Unable to obtain a position in the JNU History Faculty—due to the dominance of Marxist historians determined to admit no one who was not Marxist—Ghosh was pushed into an unexplored area, for example, history of education in India. "As religion formed the basis of education in ancient India," Ghosh reflects, "I have enjoyed a very smooth graduation after my retirement in 2002 to a study of our religious history. This interest in our religious history may be regarded as the last and final change in my curriculum vitae."[57]

"I must state here," Ghosh offered, "that I was lucky that I chose History as my first curriculum for my smooth transition later from one discipline to another. History is the backbone of all disciplines."[58] Why? "History borrows from all disciplines but no discipline can do without History. At every stage of the change of my curriculum, I was able to make substantial contribution to learning due to my grounding in History." Historical research, however, is for Ghosh spiritually informed. "I find my joy and happiness in such humble creative work," Ghosh explained. "I think the moment I shall cease to work I shall cease to exist. As our *Bhagavad Gita* says, the life of inaction is a life of death. I have a thirst for knowledge, and knowledge can be acquired from learning not only from educational institutions, as we all know, but also from the whole world outside these institutions. The whole of life is a process of learning, and the whole world is ready to teach us. We are the navigators of knowledge in a vast and boundless ocean, and for all of us, knowledge continues to remain as 'a sinking star beyond the utmost bound of human thoughts.'"

# Manish Jain

*I am interested in understanding how multiple histories of colonialisms have shaped the epistemology and history of school disciplines, education and educational experiences of people across different geographies, social locations and periods.*

Manish Jain was born in Delhi. Due to the availability of educational facilities in the city and being a third-generation educated person in an upper caste[59] Jain[60] family, where both the parents were graduates afforded him (in his words) "a certain privileged position," especially "given huge disparities with regard to educational access and continuation among different caste groups and regions." Unlike many of his relatives who were engaged in business, Jain's parents had limited resources, a situation that did not support domestic bliss. "While my entire schooling was in a government school and that too in Hindi medium till class ten," he reflects, "being largely brought up by unmarried aunts who were schoolteachers meant some cultural capital was available to me." As being an unmarried woman is stigmatized in Indian society, Manish observed gender biases faced by these aunts from close quarters.

During his primary schooling, Jain was friends with classmates whose parents had menial jobs. Many of these friends, he recalls, "failed from class six onwards and were lost." Others worked with their parents and/or sold goods on the streets during festivals. Jain remembers envying the wages these former classmates were earning at such a young age, but as he came of age, he grew increasingly conscious of the inequalities of Indian society. Even as a young child, Jain had become conscious of the caste and religious geographies of his neighborhood, conscious of those from *Valmiki* community (an untouchable community who worked as scavengers) and of Muslims who lived in certain areas and streets named after different caste groups. In the areas of old Delhi,[61] in the early 1980s Hindus and Muslims still shared a neighborhood. Boundary demarcation on the basis of religious affiliation and ghettoization, Jain recalls, began to occur in the mid-1980s and intensified in 1990s with the communal campaigns by the rightist Hindutva.[62] Riots ensued.

In November 1984, while studying in class 9, Jain witnessed the brutal massacre of Sikhs following the murder—by her two Sikh security guards—of the then prime minister, Mrs. Indira Gandhi (Chakravarty and Haksar 1987; 1992).[63] "Hiding on the roof of my house," he remembers, "I saw Sikhs running for their lives as blood-thirsty crowds chased them. Three days of burnt bodies and scooters and smoke everywhere was to leave an indelible mark on my adolescent mind." As he listened to his young neighbors boast of looting, he was left making "simplistic correlations between education, low economic and caste status, and this greedy and communal behavior," correlations that would be challenged in future years. "When we returned to school, two of my Sikh classmates had cut their long hair," Jain recalls, a radical move given that long hair is one of five religious requirements for male members of the Sikh community. These classmates had lost family members in the riots. "One of them," Jain recalls, "asked me why one wouldn't become a terrorist after this massacre and loss. I didn't have any answer but the meanings of identity and nation was no longer a settled issue for me."

In 1981, Jain and his family moved from a rented house in Delhi to "an irregular and illegal colony in '*yamuna paar.*'"[64] This colony had open sewage drains.[65] Jain recalls:

> We used hand pumps for all our water needs and lit candles/kerosene lamp to light the house on most evenings, unlike our old rented house in Delhi that had tap water and regular supply of electricity. During rains, we carried shoes in our hands to cross the muddy roads of the colony to reach the main road to catch the only public bus that connected our area and our school. In all seasons, we used to run on the crossings and road to board and change buses to reach school and walked about two kilometres to return home. With introduction of private buses in the public transport system, we had to run even harder to catch the overcrowded buses. The owners of these private buses didn't want school students with subsidized bus passes to board the buses, as it meant loss of ticket-paying passengers. But we did not have option of safe school buses unlike students of private schools. In the later years of our school life, when the tie was made part of our school uniform, it didn't change our identity and self-esteem as most of us did not speak or write English like students of English medium private schools. This English/vernacular divide was to resurface in different ways and while pursuing Ph.D., I was to be accused of becoming an "elite" for having acquired better proficiency in English than other friends from Hindi medium.

At college Jain recalls falling under the influence of the student wing of a leftist parliamentary political party, English was the language of discussion. That and the class background of the core members left him feeling like an outsider.[66] "I felt that to do socially relevant work," Jain realized, "I needed to pursue social sciences and so I dropped B.Sc. (Zoology)." That decision took him to Political Science and to a different college. Almost 300 years old, Zakir Husain College had both Muslim and Hindu students. Especially during a campaign by Hindutva political forces to construct a Ram temple at the site of a historical mosque in Ayodhya, the birthplace of the Hindu god Ram, "pursuing Political Science at that college in that location[67] meant intense attention to questions concerning the place of religion and secularism in modern nation, and specifically the meanings of heritage and history and the latter's deployment for political mobilization." In 1992, emboldened by the mobilization of women and lower castes, Hindutva forces demolished the mosque, precipitating riots and, later, demands for a uniform civil code to replace Muslim Personal Laws. These events, he recalls, also resulted in "intensive soul-searching and debates" among liberal, leftist, and feminist scholars. Interest in the politics of Hindutva forces has also led scholars to question their "large network of educational institutions, curriculum, textbooks and socialization of the young into communal hatred."[68]

When, in 1989, the prime minister announced that a certain percentage of government jobs would be reserved for the Other Backward Castes (OBCs), upper caste students, especially in northern India and Delhi, protested. Several of Jain's college classmates joined the "movement." While he believed in equality, Jain faced a dilemma, "not from my own upper caste location but from the liberal belief that caste should have no place in modern society." That position left Jain concerned that the reservation of government jobs for any caste would divide the student community along caste lines. Instead the government should reserve jobs for all.[69] In this view, caste was considered "a relic of the pre-modern era," and modern government should be "based on reason and devoid of any operation of power and special interests." "Later in the course of my research work, I was to engage with the emancipatory potential and silences of the idea of unmarked universal individual in the history of liberal individualism and how colonisers and nationalists viewed caste and were challenged by non-Brahminical[70] movements."

The downfall of the Union of Soviet Socialist Republics and other states in Eastern Europe, Jain recalls, "brought questions about socialism," as the first US attack on Iraq in 1991 led to "fears of unipolar imperialist domination." In 1990 Jain participated in the people's march organized by Narmada Bachao Andolan (NBA) forcing him to focus on the "realities of rural India," for example, "tribal life and latter's repeated displacement by the mega projects of development including dams undertaken by the postcolonial Indian state." The questions posed by NBA concerning the politics of development—benefit to whom? at whose cost?—and its critique of the Western model of development (whether capitalist or socialist) with its focus on industrialization functioned, he recalls, "to rattle my middle class, educated and urban socialization." During the subsequent year Jain spent two months with the rural and tribal youth in the mobilization against the Sardar Sarovar Dam. He traveled to "remote areas," learning about "the other India" and the "divide" that separated the privileged India from the dispossessed Bharat. "Later, in 1995, I was to attend a meeting at Manibeli, the first tribal village to be submerged by the upcoming dam." This meeting was attended by educationists, researchers, school teachers, NBA activists as well as tribal people, all discussing about the future of the eight schools named *jeevanshalas* or schools of life, "about making them more functional and more creative amidst the increasing height of the dam and the looming threat of drowning."[71]

These events left Jain acutely aware of "the divide within the student community," and the need for "political, mobilizational, and cultural work within the city itself." In 1992, Jain joined a small student's organization that was leftist in its orientation but open to learning from new social movements like NBA and to questions of gender and caste.[72] "We were to work with students and young people from resettlement colonies, slum areas and dalit[73] habitations." Jain and his fellow activists networked with student organizations from northeast India, where, he explained, "different ethnic groups have made demands of self determination, brought awareness of debates about colonial policies/colonial occupation of/by the independent Indian nation-state and the need to develop nuanced and sensitive policies for constructing a democratic federal polity and nation-state." While engaged in this activism Jain was studying postgraduate courses on political economy of development and political thought. This was a time when the Indian economy was opening to the global market and, he recalls, the World Bank and the International Monetary Fund (IMF) "imposed structural adjustment policies was to help in making interconnections between local, national and global."

After obtaining an MA in Political Science, Jain joined the BEd program at University of Delhi, "as getting a job was necessary with imminent retirement of my mother and a professional degree could help." Professor Krishna Kumar taught a course on the philosophy and sociology of education. As this volume testifies, Kumar was—and remains—an "eminent figure" in the field of education in India. Jain referenced his "wide array of work in the field of colonialism and education, educational theory, sociology of education, curriculum theory, analysis of history textbooks in the nation-building project in India and Pakistan, pedagogy of language, identity formations, modernity, and conflict." Jain continued: "With his ability to draw interconnections between mundane examples from daily life, classroom and larger historical and social forces and his pedagogy that encouraged students to reflect on their experiences and question the received wisdom, he made [a] deep impression on me." Jain's classes with Kumar—along with studying the works of Michael Apple, Paulo Freire, Henry Giroux, and the sociology of curriculum in India—"directed" Jain's concerns to the "politics of knowledge and representation and attracted me to the field of curriculum studies."

After obtaining the BEd degree, Jain started teaching history, civics, and political science in a private school in Delhi. While studying for the MEd, Jain conducted a content analysis of civics textbooks taught during the first decade of Indian independence. He hoped to understand the profiles of and expectations from "the citizen" in the nascent stage of the Indian nation-state. This focus on civics textbooks, Jain explained, followed from "my interest in the subject I taught as a school teacher." More generally it followed his appreciation of "the dominant hold of textbooks in Indian schools, as well as the influence of the critical scholarship that conceptualized curriculum and textbooks as political texts that legitimize existing power relations in society." During the course of this research, Jain found citations of colonial civics in two writings of Krishna Kumar. From these Jain was able to locate the first textbook of colonial civics.

Jain was introduced to the works of Franz Fanon in a course on political thought in the third world. As well he studied the writings of Ngugi wa Thiongo (1994), Gauri Viswanathan (1990), Judith Walsh (1983), and Bernard Cohn (1996)[74] that dwelled on the cultural aspects of colonialism, including the embeddedness of colonial knowledge and education in colonial conquest and domination. Krishna Kumar himself, Jain notes, had examined the colonial and nationalist agendas of education. "These insights, influences and my interests," he remembers, "laid ground for a doctoral research that would examine the colonial roots and trajectories of civics curriculum."

Jain's commitment to study civics and conceptions of the citizen was informed "to a large extent" by the intellectual histories of the disciplines of curriculum studies, postcolonial studies, history, and political science in India and worldwide.[75] Studies by Michael F. D. Young, Pierre Bourdieu, Basil Bernstein, Michael Apple, and Henry Giroux were, he recalls, influential: "my work is in the tradition of such studies." Research papers edited by Ivor Goodson (1985) and Thomas Popkewitz (1987)[76] helped him understand the social significance of disciplinary knowledge as a school subject: "My work was influenced by their argument that history of a discipline is embedded within and shaped by the dominant discourses, the state and other structures of power and the power relations among subordinate and dominant social groups at a particular historical moment. Reading research in the area of histories of curriculum in Canada[77] made me aware of the absence of such work in India and the need to do something in this regard."

Other historical studies of "modern knowledge systems" and their "embeddedness within colonial discourses provided significant theoretical and methodological ground" for Jain's research. The establishment of departments of Women's Studies in various universities—along with the emergence of the field of dalit studies—have underscored how "gender and caste pervade social life and knowledge production." Histories of women's education in colonial India have examined "the gendered nature of the 'suitable' curriculum prescribed for girls."[78] Additionally, research from various theoretical perspectives on citizenship education outside India have also "helped me form my own perspective and questions for study. I have already discussed the influence of my teacher Professor Krishna Kumar's work on my own research."

"The foregoing account of my research," he concluded "makes it quite clear that colonial experience and its impact on education has had a considerable impact on my research interests and research." Even in the initial stages of the conceptualization of his doctoral research, Jain remembers, "I was interested in comparatively studying how colonial experience, historical conditions and processes shaped the epistemology of civics and the idea of citizen in different British colonies and in Britain." To engage in such comparative study, he coupled Marxist, feminist, and subaltern studies of India's colonial history with histories and accounts of the First Nations in Canada. Doing so, he recalls, "ruptured the binary of colonizer and colonized in India and Canada." No static or unchanging phenomenon, colonialism had, Jain reminds, "multiple meanings, practices and experiences and at the same time." He added: "despite multiple histories of colonialism," we must not forget "the global operation of capitalism." Attentive to "marginalized groups" and questions of "gaze and perspective that challenge the silences and dominant accounts of national and colonial histories," Jain realized that "in my research, I needed to take simultaneous note of colonialism as an economic phenomenon, political relationships, ideological construction, and cultural project that has not only shaped the past but continues to operate in present from metropolis centres as well as through the practices of nation-states having peripheral position in the global order."

Jain referenced postcolonial scholar Dipesh Chakarabarti's insight that Western knowledge is itself "provincial" and is in fact a specific way of thinking "locally." He noted that the "contemporary postmodern and cultural turn" had "destabilized categories," among them "woman" and "feminism," neither of which operates now and "a singular sign." Acknowledging that "the rich tradition of women's movement and feminist research in India has drawn on Western experiences and scholarship," Jain cited "the emergence of the dalit women's movement" and those questions of "religious identity that animated rightist Hindutva politics and women's participation in it has generated debates that cannot be reduced to global concerns. These have had a bearing on my own research."

Manish Jain self-consciously situates himself and his research in history and place. "Being citizen of a developing country which is the largest democracy in the world and one that is following neoliberal policies resulting in dispossession and accumulation, expressing itself in huge inequalities amidst growth of [a] huge middle class with 'global' aspirations as a potential consumer for national and multinational corporate houses," he writes, "forces me to engage with meanings of citizenship, colonialism, globalization, education, citizenship education and curriculum and decide about my own location and role as a researcher and teacher." Jain references India's "ambitions of a greater role in the regional/global politics," its "increasing closeness to the U.S.A.," its engagement in "a suicidal nuclear race with its neighbor Pakistan," and its "uneasy relationship with China." As well he acknowledges that India is "guilty of the genocidal slaughter of Muslims in Gujarat in 2002," but that the term nation does not "denote fixed locations and relationships." Specifically, the meanings of "citizenship, democracy and nation-state" cannot be contained by "discourses emanating from [the] West which self-designates itself as global." But nor can these communicate "cultural essentialism" functioning to "demarcate the developing countries or the peripheries within them as 'local,'" denuded of "the historical experience, agendas, concerns, contexts and struggles that shape this local." Jain concludes: "Thus, as a researcher located in a developing country, I need to constantly take note of the 'global' discourse and researches on education, curriculum and citizenship education and keep asking, how they relate to postcolonial India."

## Meenakshi Thapan

*I knew I had found what interested me most:*
*to understand what life at school is all about.*

The genesis of Meenakshi Thapan's present intellectual preoccupations and research agenda lies in her encounter with the Indian philosopher J. Krishnamurti in October-November 1973.[79] "I was a very young undergraduate student, read-ing for Psychology (Hons.) at the University of Delhi with an interest in questions about life and the possibilities of transforming the self through investigating one's own thoughts, beliefs, and actions. In many private sessions with him, spread over Delhi and Chennai, over two-three months, Krishnamurti addressed many ques-tions arising from my dilemmas about the nature of existence, and asserted that it was education alone that had the power to change individuals and thereby, society. At the end of my time with him, when I returned to Delhi to complete my studies, Krishnamurti invited me to teach in his schools, with a particular emphasis on the Rishi Valley School in rural Andhra Pradesh, run by the Krishnamurti Foundation in India (KFI)."

In June 1974, Thapan went to work in the Rishi Valley School as a "young teacher-helper" in the primary sections of the school, "assisting" in the transcrip-tion of Krishnamurti's audio talks. "One year at this school," she reports, "provided insights into the functioning of schools, the minds of very young children, my own abilities to find novel methods of working with them, and the difficulties of work-ing with the older, and more conservative, teachers and with other, like-minded col-leagues." After this experience, Thapan spent some six months working at another KFI residential school in northern India located near the city of Varanasi. "This experience," she recounts, "was to open up my own interest in education and its possibilities although I was not necessarily aware of it at the time."

Thapan returned to the University of Delhi to pursue a masters degree in Sociology.[80] It was then she decided to write her MPhil thesis on a topic that helped her realize "how much those early experiences had shaped my intellectual endeav-ours." In the PhD program "I knew I had found what interested me most: to under-stand what life at school is all about, including how schooling takes place, what students and teachers bring to school from their own socio-cultural worlds, how they inhabit the structures within schools, in what processes they engage to negoti-ate with those structures, manipulate them to their advantage, or submit to them. How do they interact with one another, with processes and of course with the ideas that frame schooling in a larger sense?"[81] And last but not least, Thapan wondered where she should study these questions.

"Without a doubt," Thapan chose the Rishi Valley School.[82] She had two rea-sons for this choice. First was size: "It is a small school, shaped by particular ideas, and with a worldview that I was curious to explore in the setting of an institution." Second were theoretical concerns. Thapan reports she was influenced by symbolic interactionism, wherein actors were regarded as "makers of their reality, construct-ing the world through their everyday interactions and engagement with schooling processes." There was "a disenchantment with the Marxism" due to the exagger-ated importance ascribed to "structures" and their presumed "influence over human action." Structures "no doubt" shape human action, she allowed, but they are "not necessarily of overriding significance if we were willing to take into consideration the social worlds of actors themselves as they seek to construct, deconstruct, mod-ify, re-build them in their daily lives of struggle, strife and change." Among those whose work influenced Thapan were the British sociologists Peter Woods, Martyn Hammersley, Sara Delamont, and Paul Atkinson. She was also influenced by "an understanding of institutions as 'social facts' (Durkheim) and in terms of [an] interpretive understanding (Weber) of what went on inside them."

Thapan's interest in "an alternative educational framework" also derived from the writings of M. K. Gandhi, Rabindranath Tagore, Swami Vivekananda, and Sri Aurobindo. "I was interested in understanding how an alternative educational perspective that sought human development above all else could benefit humankind and social institutions in a changing society like India."[83] Thapan cited colonialism[84] as "undoubtedly" shaping education, including Indian responses to it, like the works of Dayanand Saraswati, who, Thapan explained, "sought to revive an 'Indian' way of education, based on a kind of Hindu revivalism as a response to the colonial onslaught and the overwhelming use of the English language in educational institutions." "How did the work of J. Krishnamurti on education differ," she asked, "from these other thinkers? In what ways is it possible to bring about a different kind of education in a country as large and diverse as India?"

At the time Thapan was a doctoral student in the Department of Sociology in the Delhi School of Economics. There were no professors working in the field of sociology of education or in educational studies generally. Thapan chose to work with Professor T. N. Madan who, while and not a specialist in education, nonetheless, allowed her "to pursue my research interests with complete autonomy. I must add that in the winter of 1984, after I had submitted my doctoral dissertation, I was fortunate to meet and spend time with Professor Basil Bernstein when he was a visitor to a university in New Delhi."[85]

In 1985, Thapan was granted a Commonwealth scholarship to spend a year at the University of London Institute of Education (IOE). At the IOE, Thapan worked with Basil Bernstein understanding his work "in depth and detail." Bernstein was "keen that I also read and understand the work of the French sociologist Pierre Bourdieu whom he considered the greatest authority on the sociology of education. In fact, I was packed off for a week in March 1986 to the Centre for European Sociology, headed by Pierre Bourdieu, in Paris." Thapan found Bourdieu's work "very engaging, challenging and anthropologically grounded."[86] Bourdieu's work, she continued, "shaped my interest in understanding educational practice, and human engagement, from a completely different perspective that also sought to surpass the subjectivist/objectivist divide, but now from a point of view that was not located in one field alone."[87]

Now Thapan works in the Department of Sociology at the Delhi School of Economics, a premier social science institution in the University of Delhi. She is the only scholar who researches and writes about the field of education. The department is different from other departments as it is a Centre of Advanced Study in Sociology, enabling professors to undertake independent research and study in fields of their choice. There is no dominance of any one research field over another. It is an institution that values scholarship, research, and intellectual pursuit. Recently she has been studying issues pertaining to problems that beset youth globally and the increasing development of a culture of violence across societies.[88] Toward this end, Thapan has conducted fieldwork in a secondary school in Vancouver[89] in 2007 and in a middle school in Paris during 2006.[90]

Thapan has conducted fieldwork among Indian immigrants in northern Italy, focusing on secondary students of Indian origin. She has been interested in understanding not only their experience of migration, but also their relationships with members of the host society, with their peers as well as with adults with whom they are in close contact, such as teachers and other service providers.

Recently Thapan has compiled a series of essays by young scholars focused on different kinds of schools in Delhi, Ahmedabad, and Andhra Pradesh. Titled *Ethnographies of Schooling in Contemporary India* (Sage, forthcoming 2014), Thapan hopes that this edited volume will enrich our understanding of what goes on inside schools. Additionally, Thapan has edited a reader on *Education and Society* in the prestigious series on the Sociology and Social Anthropology of India edited by T. N. Madan (Oxford University Press, forthcoming, 2014). Thapan's important work seeks to emphasize the need for a more humane education that is not only alert to pervasive inequality and injustice but also seeks to consciously encourage awareness among young people. Thapan believes it is only when educators themselves feel the urgency of such education that they can support the unique individual growth and social transformation schooling promises.

\* \* \*

You have now "met" the scholar-participants in a project predicated on nonviolent inquiry dialogically conducted across difference, reminding each of us how situated—personally, culturally, nationally, politically—we are, however uniform might be our commitment to curriculum research and development. In the chapters that follow the important work referenced in the preceding introductions will be detailed. Intellectual histories and present circumstances will be clarified. You will, I believe, come to appreciate the profundity of what is at stake in curriculum studies in India.

# Notes

1. This work could not have occurred without the generous support of the Social Sciences and Humanities Research Council of Canada (Project 410–2009–0953).
2. These discussions were conducted over the Internet over a three-year period. Except for Mary Ann Chacko, I had met none of the scholar-participants. Restricted to the print of email and documents, virtual relationships form slowly and partially, here related to ideas and perhaps even more sensitive to subtle expressions of tone. While the Internet made the project possible, it also tended to restrict us to the protocol, as face-to-face meetings might have allowed impromptu ideas and events that answering email does not. That cuts both ways, as restricting our exchanges to email also kept us focused on the task at hand.
3. These questions appear in the index.
4. Discussing Virginia Woolf's *The Waves*, Jessica Berman (2001, 153) cautions that "the maiming action is the summing up itself." Quoting constantly may provide no insurance against "maiming," but the practice does underscore the dialogic composition of summarizing statements, however unified they imply the narrative is. I trust my summaries show the marks of the conversations embedded within them.

5. Both Le Grange and Wang had worked with me—and this project—before: Le Grange (2010) was a scholar-participant in the project on curriculum studies in South Africa in which Wang posed questions. Each scholar contributed a chapter to the second edition of the *International Handbook of Curriculum Research* (see Le Grange 2014; Wang 2014).

6. Exchange, I have suggested (2011a, 21, n. 12) is a more modest concept than "dialogue," but here I offer a more dignified definition, as also a "metaphoric extension of gift-giving...exchanges that refuse equivalence, are disjointed in time (rather than immediately reciprocated), and that culminate in wonder." In this phrasing Nancy Luxon (2013, 70) is contrasting that—Iris Marion Young's—conception with a psychoanalytic one—for example, exchange as including "combative collaboration"—I prefer to juxtapose the two as supplements. After all, nonviolent protest could be conceived of as "combative collaboration," a "gift" to both colonizers and the colonized.

7. Manish Jain did not participate in the exchanges. When I represent him in chapter 6, I quote his chapter.

8. Whose "internationalization" is it? It is everyone's of course, but the presumably damaging implication of the question is that "internationalization" is a project of scholars in the "first world." It is precisely these legacies of power—self-opaqueness, self-enclosure, even narcissism—that renders "internationalization" so urgent a moral and political project for scholars in the "first world." For India, "internationalization" occurred thousands of years ago; it remains ongoing.

9. Regarding its significance in India, see chapters 2, 6, and 7; in the United States see Block 2004.

10. The word "even" may strike readers as strange, but given the contemporary cult of critique in North America its use is an acknowledgment that for some my efforts to appreciate on its own terms the work of colleagues in other countries will seem "uncritical." Criticism may occur—I agree it is central to advancing the complicated conversation that is the field, as my own work (2011c, for instance) testifies—but only after understanding, "even" appreciation. Nonviolence is important throughout, even during disputation.

11. I'm using "imported" in both official and unofficial ways, here as an intellectual process. Here it also has a more reciprocal meaning that the one-way process the term denotes, as there is "an exchange." In clarifying concepts to others—in other words, through teaching—one can gain additional insight about the subject and its communication.

12. *Recontextualization* is a subheading in chapter 7, but its appearance here reiterates its importance in understanding internationalization elsewhere, including South Africa (Pinar 2010, 82, 151, 165), Brazil (Pinar 2011a, 13, 14, 21), in Mexico (Pinar 2011b, 12, 32, 96, 224, 233, 238), and in the United States (Pinar 2011c, 27, 77). See also Pinar 2014, 1, 7, 12, 13, 80, 96, 301, 305.

13. Here the term denotes the affirmation—in part through study—of cultures and histories internal to what is now India. It is no simple contrast to colonialism, as you will see, as scholar-participants acknowledge colonialism's "blessing" as well as the "curses" of indigenous cultures. When "indigeneity" obscures internal differences, it becomes totalizing (see Pinar 2009, 22).

14. This cause is furthered by dialogical encounter across difference defined as not only cultural and political but also historical. The intellectual—indeed subjective—expansiveness prerequisite to the ethical engagement of alterity is structured not only by knowledge and lived experience, but by temporality as well. See Pinar 2009, 2011c for fuller theoretical expositions of cosmopolitanism.

15. Referencing Bauman, I point to the incommensurable differences between natural land social science, affirming the study of curriculum as one of the humanities (Pinar 1981).

16. In its ordinary sense, Noponen (2011, 109) points out, "corruption" means "acting in institutions or institutional settings are very often able to use their status, privileges, or resources in unjust ways to gain private profit at the expense of others." For Aristotle, Noponen (2011, 108) reminds us, moral corruption was parallel to political corruption; each can be attributed to the "scarcity of relevant good." One consequence of colonialism could be corruption. The ancient vice of greed can adapt to nearly any circumstance.

17. I came of intellectual age during the era of New Criticism. While shedding its disdain for authorial intention, reader response, and historical context, I have kept its commitment to close reading.

18. Procedures can be important of course. When they obscure the process they are formulated to expedite—as they did during the Eight-Year Study (see Pinar 2011c, 77–91)—"reform" becomes reproduction not reconstruction.

19. See chapter 2.

20. As "complicated conversation," referencing what has been said before is compulsory, and not only for the sake of courtesy but for continuity as well. That ethical imperative of erudition has always encouraged me to quote extensively and, as noted before, in chapters 6 and 7, I do so. Here I want to acknowledge the significance of *endnotes*, opportunities to reference antecedent and associated "conversation" that also address issues of continuity, for example, memory and remembrance without which an academic field cannot proceed. The *index* is another traditional scholarly practice that is hardly extraneous but in fact translates the text thematically and in the process acknowledges the persons who perhaps most prominently participated in the ongoing conversation one is presuming to participate in. Often regarded as an annoying obligation or even as expendable altogether, the index in my view is an important opportunity to recode intellectual histories, present circumstances, and the persons who have lived through each. In addition to relying on the index to pinpoint occurrences of concepts and persons in the text, I advise reading it through from beginning to end, as if it were a cryptic code disclosing what the main text might be withholding.

21. See Pinar 2006, 11–12. As I argue there, the juxtaposition of synopsis and quoted assertion encourages appreciation of the perspectival character of knowledge and understanding.

22. See Pinar et al. 1995, 11.

23. "Those occupying the position of 'educator' must suspend their existing knowledge," Nancy Luxon (2013, 72) points out, "so as to investigate new situations unhampered by previous authoritative judgments.... [R]esearchers adopt the position of 'student' and resist received wisdom so as to develop new insights." Luxon is here discussing the authority of the analyst in psychoanalysis, but the point is relevant here. Internationalization means suspending one's expertise—certainty inevitably embedded in national history and culture—in order to understand (clarify and appreciate) the work of colleagues working within different national histories and cultures.

24. See, for instance, Pinar 2010, 231–234, 237, 240.

25. See Berman 2001, 166. Here Berman is discussing Gertrude Stein's *The Making of Americans*, but the emplacement of participation, even when virtual, structures the exchange; it bears the imprint of the project even as its rewrites its contours and content, here exchanges almost lost given the time between them but retrievable through the records email programs provide.

26. Wang (2014, 67) starts her essay with an epigraph from Gandhi.

27. Referencing MacIntyre, Noponen (2011, 102) tells us that "the essence of any practice is the internal relationship between its ends or products and the acting or practicing itself." Means and ends enjoy reciprocity as the character of the exchanges builds character (see Pinar 2011c, 10–11).

28. Namely that the present moment becomes present only as we discern its relation to the past that imprints it and the future we imagine might supplant it. Submerged in minutiae we disappear into an endless present without presence.
29. See, for instance, Weaver 2010.
30. In Brazil that occurred (see Pinar 2011a, 11, 14).
31. Manish Jain makes this point: see chapter 4.
32. See, for instance, Waks and Short 2009. What is missing in the North American literature are volumes that acknowledge "leaders" in non-North American fields. The volumes in this series contribute to correcting that absence.
33. Elementary in India refers to grades 1 through 8, spanning the primary and upper primary (middle school) stages of education. (Batra's note).
34. For "the first time," Batra explained, the Education Policy (NPE 1986) had "articulated the need for a perspective on 'child-centered' education and the assertion that education must be looked at as a critical agent of social change, especially in the context of achieving gender parity and equal opportunities for the marginalized in India."
35. Despite the distance of continents and culture, I too was introduced to R. D. Laing during graduate study. His work informed much of the analysis of my doctoral dissertation research, later published in "Sanity, Madness, and the School." See Pinar 2000.
36. Berger and Luckmann 1967.
37. "A revolutionary during the freedom struggle," Batra explained, "Sri Aurobindo later chose the path of spirituality to contribute to India's freedom, proposing a national system of education known as Integral Education. A number of schools across the country follow this frame of education. All of these are established under Sri Aurobindo Education Society and are intimately linked with Aurobindo Ashrams."
38. Batra reports:

    Ashram rituals had converted Sri Aurobindo's philosophy into a "religious" pursuit, much against the warning mentioned in his own writings. This ritualisation influenced how the school conducted itself in terms of both children's development and learning and teachers' practice. However, Mirambika became a favorite choice of progressive parents in Delhi, who largely belonged to elite sections of society. The hiatus between some Mirambika children who were residents of the Ashram (many of them were workers' children and orphans of destitute families) and those who came to study in Mirambika from elite families could not be bridged, and often led to conflict and tension. The 'social' and the 'psychological' remained in tension mainly because the Ashram did not as a matter of policy address the social. The idea of a commune was foremost in the running of the Ashram but with complete denial of its dynamics. The premise was that the inward journey which is the key to higher consciousness (which in turn is the sole aim of the evolution of humankind) will by itself resolve social tensions. I was not quite convinced. For me, issues of inequity in the material world were important to address materially as well as through deep reflection and higher consciousness. I therefore chose to work with the 'larger reality' so to speak, so that my work could impact the larger state system of education where children come to school with aspirations but learn precious little.

39. In addition to conducting research, Batra was engaged with the local community, making three interventions. First, "I assumed an active role in helping a family seek justice for the injustice meted out to a young daughter by her in-laws, which led to her death. The community was entrenched in patriarchal ways and resistance came only from some of the women of the community who received support from others only because I was able to provide the legal support required." Her second "intervention was with regard to

severe paucity of water in the village as a result of faulty development policies and unfair distribution practices. Most of the village area was left dry since a few years as a result of the installation of water pumps that left the wells dry. Soon the control of water supply became centralized as a result of laying of pipelines for distribution. This led to an unequal distribution of water, more for the small towns and block and district administration units. Even though the pipelines ran through the village, the pressure was too low for people to access water through the few community taps that existed. The panchayat head was summoned as a result of mobilization of the women in the local community." Batra's third intervention in the local community concerned the mid-day meal program for the primary schools of the Betul district. Corn-soya milk packaged as powder and distributed by CARE, a US-based agency, was distributed in schools every day. This product was infested with insects but was nevertheless being distributed. While the hungry children ate, the others would often throw it away. I held several meetings with the concerned officials and teachers to investigate the issue. On the basis of complaints, the issue was raised in the Indian Parliament through the Voluntary Health Association of India (VHAI). This food program of CARE India was later withdrawn by the Government of India." "These experiences," Batra concluded, "facilitated my understanding that intervention in school curriculum can be meaningful only when the socio-political context is understood and made part of intervention strategy and design."

40. See MACESE 1991.
41. See Batra 2009.
42. See MACESE 2001.
43. For a review of Krishnamurti's conception of education see Kumar 2013.
44. And even when offered, Batra reports, such programs suffer diminished status. She explained: "Students and faculty of the University of Delhi for instance, have typically perceived Departments of Education as 'second rate' institutions where the usual activities of a university, such as knowledge generation, research and providing for an intellectually stimulating environment were conspicuous by their absence."
45. See Chacko's chapter; see also the introduction to Manish Jain.
46. See, for instance, Kumar 2013.
47. At that time there was no university on a Western model in India. Ghosh's note.
48. Among its graduates, Ghosh reported, was the Nobel Laureate in Eonomics, Amartya Sen.
49. Ghosh recalls that tuition was, in 1956, 20 rupees a month.
50. In answer to my question regarding "Modern History," Ghosh explained that the program "emphasized modern British and modern European history along with modern Indian history which was in fact a history of an extension of Britain in India" (Ghosh, interview).
51. Called "Major" to acknowledge his past service in the Indian army, Harrison was also a first class graduate in History from Cambridge University, Ghosh noted.
52. Most appreciated, Ghosh noted, was "my originality in using unexplored sources and in interpreting them on the basis of the data collected on Births, Baptisms, Marriages and Burials of the officials of the East India Company between 1757 and 1800, sent home to London from the East India Company's headquarters at Calcutta."
53. This second volume consisted of papers presented at an international seminar held in New Delhi in 1974.
54. "Some of my handwritten communications to him are also there," Ghosh suspects.
55. To my question—"Do you think nationalism—or is the plural more precise?—in India still contains within anti-colonial sentiment?"—Ghosh replied:

> I think if there are some traces of anti-colonial sentiments which still exist among some of our people... [despite the fact that] our government with its English

nomenclature of departments and positions, and its mode of working, our laws and regulations with a few additions or alterations after independence as in the passing of the Hindu Marriage Act, our education system and its mode of functioning are all either copies or derived from British models. If with a knowledge of all this fact, people still show anti-colonial sentiments, they cannot but be dubbed as hypocrite.... I think the English language is now not only in India but also in most parts of the world a great civilizing and modernizing force. What is disturbing in Indian society today is not anti-colonial sentiments but evidences of parochialism as practiced by some political parties in some of our States as in Maharashtra and this, I think, is the result of the failure of our educational planners and thinkers to plan a curriculum at the school level to instill in the mind of the children a mutual respect, understanding and admiration for each other belonging to different States and thereby creating a sense of bonding among themselves and a sense of belonging to the country.

56. That "system," Ghosh writes, "dominated our lives and actions till the coming of the Muslim invaders and conquerors in the eleventh century."

57. In answer to my question—"would you say that religion—in contrast to the earlier interests—is very much your own, not stimulated by others?—Ghosh answered:

Yes. It has not only come from my mind but also from my heart. Nobody ever asked me to study or investigate the subject. In Indian universities religion or religious history is not a subject for study and research in the name of secularism since the days of the British. In this context, I must also say that when I was a child, my mother had a tremendous influence in instilling in my mind and heart a belief in our religious ideas and practices. As a child I had not questioned them but now in the twilight of my career and life, I must look at them when searching for the emergence of our education system out of our religious scriptures in ancient India. I have been able to discover a historical and scientific basis for them. And this I have been able to record in my lectures delivered at FSU, Jena, in 2000–2001 and published next year in the form of a book by Peter Lang at Frankfurt.

58. "I agree," I interrupted. "That is why I forefront history in this project, both in terms of individual intellectual life history but also in terms of the intellectual history of curriculum studies in India." Ghosh expressed his appreciation for this emphasis.

59. "In the four varna caste system of Hindu society," Jain explained, "Brahmins (the priestly class) stand at the apex, followed by Kshatriya (the warriors), Vaishyas (engaged in business), Shudras (service class, engaged in farming and different artisan groups). Outside these four varnas are the Panchamas, the untouchable groups, who are excluded from religious, political, economic and social spheres under the bane of the ideology of purity and pollution. Brahmins, Kshatriyas and Vaishyas are considered upper caste. I was born in a Vaishya family. Some scholars have pointed out that the system and structure of dominance laid out in the varna system was not always followed in practice. They argue that jati was/is the lived reality of caste system and represented relations of dominance and subordination at the local village level."

60. The Jains, Jain explained, are "followers of Jainism that emerged as a critique of Brahminical Hindu practices. It is a religion of asceticism. It emphasizes nonviolence and its followers practice vegetarianism. Jains are amongst the smallest religious community in India (about four million followers in India). About 95 percent of Jains who enroll for education reach graduation plus levels in comparison to 20 percent from Christians who stand next in the educational status of different religious communities in India. Jains have significant presence in business and professional community."

61. Old Delhi, the walled city of Delhi, Jain explained, was founded as Shahjahanabad by the Indian emperor Shahjahan in 1639. It was the capital of the Mughals until the end of the Mughal dynasty. It lost its capital status to Calcutta during British rule. In 1911 the capital was moved back to Delhi and New Delhi was constructed, comprising official buildings and residences of colonial officials. The wide roads, Western-style buildings, and the power status of New Delhi contrasted with the narrow lanes, historic monuments, and places of religious worship of old Delhi. In earlier periods different religious communities lived in old Delhi, but in last two decades it has come to symbolize Muslims, even if people of other communities also inhabit it.

62. Hindutva is distinct from Hindu, Jain explained. Hindutva refers to "political-cultural efforts to construct Hindu identity, to create the 'non-Hindu' *other*, namely the Muslims and the Christians and build Hindu Rashtra as opposed to secular India. Rashtriya Swayamsevak Sangh (RSS) (literally Association of volunteers for the Nation) with its various organisations, including its political wing Bharatiya Janata Party (BJP) that also led the coalition government at the center from 1998 to 2004, leads Hindutva brigade. RSS was formed in 1925 during [the] colonial period.

63. See Chakravarty, Uma and Nandita Haksar 1987; 1992 (Jain's note).

64. "*Yamuna paar*," Jain explained, "literally means across the river Yamuna that passes through Delhi. While geographically, this would mean that both the parts are *yamuna paar*, it is northeastern Delhi which was designated as *yamuna paar* in common parlance. While *yamuna paar* is also part of Delhi, in the 1980s and until the mid 1990s, people traveling from east Delhi would say that they are going to Delhi. Delhi marked a different socio-geographic space, denoting power, development and centrality, whereas *yamuna paar* symbolized lack of power, development, distance and marginality. During the last decade, a large number of middle and upper class colonies and housing societies have developed in Eastern Delhi. But they do not constitute the symbolic universe of *yamuna paar*."

65. The open sewage drains continue despite promises of a sewer system by different political and elected representatives. Now these open sewage drains are composed of concrete, unlike those in the 1970s and 1980s (Jain's note).

66. Research on colonial and postcolonial Indian society, Jain explained, has documented that "colonial rule created a public sphere and civil society in India which was restricted in its membership. Ease with English was one of the gatekeepers for entry in this restricted domain where the 'cultivated, leisurely, unthreatened elites' (Kaviraj 1997, 235) indulged themselves on issues of 'public' importance."

67. While science classes were taught in a new building, humanities and commerce classes were still held on the old historical campus located in old Delhi (Jain's note).

68. See Kumar1990; Lall 2005; Sundar2004; Sarkar 1996; Froerer 2007; Bhog 2002 (Jain's note).

69. "All the left political parties supported the government's decision," Jain notes. "In the Delhi university campus, all left-leaning student and teacher groups, though numerically weak, collectively opposed the anti-reservation stir and arguments."

70. The challenge to the ideology of varna system and caste dominance from the shudra and untouchable groups is characterized as non-Brahminical (Jain's note).

71. "My teacher Prof. Krishna Kumar," Jain recalls, "also attended this meeting and was to examine the platitudes about education in this context." See, Kumar 1997.

72. "I left this organization within next three years," Jain recalls, "due to differences between what it professed and practiced on gender question."

73. "Today," Jain explains, "the untouchable communities use the term *dalit* to address themselves. *Dalit* as a category points to not only domination inherent in caste system and untouchability but also dalits' own knowledge of this oppression and desire

to overthrow it. Thus, it is used with a subversive potential to signal the experiences, desires, dreams and struggles of these people."

74. Thiongo 1994; Viswanathan 1990; Walsh 1983; Cohn 1996 (Jain's note).

75. A doctoral fellowship by the Shastri Indo-Canadian Institute provided Jain the opportunity to study in the Centre for the Study of Historical Consciousness at the University of British Columbia. There he examined the history of civics curriculum in another British colony, namely Canada. The time in Canada provided Jain "opportunities to reflect on newer questions, reconsider my earlier theoretical positions in the light of different historical experiences, and support for some previous hunches." Studying imperialism, nationalism, and racism in Canada and British Columbia specifically "destabilized the conceptual categories of colonizer, colonized, nation, nationalism and imperialism." Study of contested conceptions of Canadian citizenship and the nation led him "to rethink issues of culture, race and heritage and pay attention to historical specificity." The reciprocal relations between discourse and materiality were analyzed in the four seminar courses he attended: *Race and Nation in the History of Education*, taught by Professor Jean Barman and *Curricula in Historical Context* taught by Professor Penney Clark. On the suggestion of Professor Barman, I also attended the courses *First Nations and the Educational Change* and *The Social Context of Education Policy* taught by Professors Michael Marker and Leslie Roman, respectively (Jain's note).

76. Goodson 1985; Popkewitz 1987 (Jain's note).

77. These include the following: Tomkins 1979; 1981; 1986; Barman 2003; Brummelen 1986; Stanley 1990 (Jain's note).

78. "I am grateful," Jain notes, "to Nandini Manjrekar for pointing out that I should use my awareness of such feminist historical studies to underline their contribution to the field of curriculum studies."

79. In a follow-up question, I couldn't resist asking if Professor Thapan had "experienced any dissonance between Krishnamurti the person you met and with you talked and his ideas? Did he seem congruent with his ideas?" "No dissonance," she replied emphatically. "He lived his life as he spoke. He was very austere, serious but also had a terrific sense of humor. My parents introduced him to me. I realized very quickly what a fantastic mind I had the privilege to be with."

80. In North America, I pointed out, sociology as a discipline would tend to be antagonistic to Krishnamurti's ideas. "Not so at the U of Delhi?" I asked. "Sure," Thapan replied, "they were antagonistic. But I am a very independent person. I didn't receive high marks for my M.Phil. research but my Ph.D. experience changed all that. I showed how one could use sociological analysis to study a school in depth. My book received excellent reviews in the popular as well as academic press, in the former because of the overwhelming interest in Krishnamurti and in the latter because it was at that time the only ethnographical study of schooling in India.

81. In North America, I pointed out, "we would characterize these interests as 'phenomenological.' Did that term have currency there?" "Yes, Thapan replied, "that is what I did, a phenomenological study; we called it symbolic interactionism as well.

82. Thapan's doctoral dissertation on the Rishi Valley School was later published in 1991 by Oxford University Press as *Life at School: An Ethnographic Study*. (A second edition, with a new introduction, appeared in 2006.) This was a landmark event in the studies of schooling in India, both in terms of method and in content. (For the most recent review see http://tkpi.org/people/life-at-school/) No scholar in India had attempted an indepth sociological study of a school in the rich, ethnographic detail that this study provides. In this work, Thapan tells us, I sought to "transcend the intellectual divide of the structures/agency debate as well as draw on the nuanced details that the study of interaction

in the multiple settings of the school provided." It constitutes a major contribution to the ethnographic study of educational institutions; it is widely taught and encouraged scholars to study schools ethnographically, such as *Life at Mirambika* by Anjum Sibia (published by NCERT, Delhi, 2006).

83. At this point I asked Professor Thapan if she thought that such an educational perspective could also benefit countries that are very different from India? Or are there certain cultural and historical prerequisites to specific educational theories and practices? She replied: "There are definitely cultural and historical forces that shape educational perspectives and practices. Mahatma Gandhi's writings on education say this all so clearly. But there are voices in very different cultures that say something similar, if in different vocabularies. I'm thinking of the 'small is beautiful' material, and calls to return to the humanities and the arts. I think cultural specificity is important, but one must not overlook commonalities and shared perspectives. Do you agree?" I agreed.

84. Does not inequality precede colonialism, I asked? "Sure," Thapan replied, "but colonialism is the most significant form of inequality that changes a nation's way of connecting to itself and to its cultural and social roots. This has far reaching consequences that last for generations and affects, among other things, the way in which education is conceptualized, planned and organized. In other words, it has a devastating outcome for future generations."

85. I asked: "Did Bernstein's work influence you intellectually? If so, how?" Thapan replied: I was in awe of him, and scared of him too as he was caustic, even scathing in his comments, reducing people to wrecks in minutes. Intellectually I wasn't influenced by his work as much as by the ways he opened my mind to the ways in which pedagogical discourse is the ruler of consciousness. He also pushed me to reading Bourdieu. We had many discussions about Bourdieu, the ideas of the thinkable and the unthinkable, and this was so significant for understanding educational knowledge. Years later when I was in England I visited him; he had become a shadow of himself. He was an inspiring, if frightening, teacher."

86. To my question—"How did Bourdieu and Bernstein sit with Krishnamurti in your mind?"—Thapan replied: "I guess I kept them in different compartments. Krishnamurti was a lot more about my inner life, although what he said about education was absolutely essential for a different kind of world to happen. Bourdieu and Bernstein helped me grow as a scholar who could critically examine educational thought and practice.

87. "My early work (on the Rishi Valley School)," Thapan reflected, "sought to do this as well, but it was too grounded in ideas and people's perspectives and perhaps did not pay sufficient attention to the inequalities that prevailed in everyday life." Thapan published a paper examining Bourdieu's key concepts titled "Some Aspects of Cultural Reproduction and Pedagogic Communication" (1988). She acknowledges Bourdieu's work as continuing to shape her research, citing *Reading Pierre Bourdieu in a Dual Context: Essays from India and France*, 2006, as well as her "Introduction. The Uses of Bourdieu's Social Theory: An Interdisciplinary Perspective" (with Roland Lardinois, in the same volume).

88. "Do you find comparison helpful," I asked Professor Thapan, "or do you tend to focus on particularity and contingency, if associating these with other particularities and contingencies in other countries?" She replied: "I do focus on particularity, but I find it fascinating that the issues are so similar in a general sense, although true each context is very different."

89. While I was in Vancouver in 2007, Professor Thapan and I did not know each other and we did not meet.

90. Conclusions based on the fieldwork in the Vancouver school have been published in "Why Do I Not Belong? The Struggle for Integration across Barriers of Race and Language

in a Canadian School," published in *Contested Spaces. Citizenship and Belonging in Contemporary Times*, edited by Meenakshi Thapan and published by Orient Blackswan in Delhi in 2010. Thapan completed a comparative study of similar problems, reported in "Schooling Processes, Student Practices, Youth Culture: Citizens in the Making in France and India" (2008), published in *Cultures of Governance and Conflict Resolution*, edited by Balveer Arora, Peter Ronald deSouza, and Angela Liberatore, and published by the European Commission. Thapan has also been "deeply interested in issues pertaining to girls' and women's education in India and has attempted to document some of the prevalent problems as well as identify the sources of resistance and struggle among young and adult women in very differing social and cultural contexts." See her "Cultures of Adolescence: Educationally Disadvantaged Young Women in an Urban Slum," in *Educational Regimes in Contemporary India*, edited by Radhika Chopra and Patricia Jeffery, and published in New Delhi by Sage Publications in 2005. See also her "Adolescence, Embodiment and Gender Identity: Elite Women in a Changing Society," in *Urban Women in Contemporary India: A Reader*, edited by Rehana Ghadially, and published in 2007, also by Sage.

# References

Barman, Jean and Mona Gleason. eds. 2003. *Children, Teachers and Schools in the History of British Columbia*. 2nd Edition. Calgary, AB: Detselig.

Batra, Poonam. 2009. "Teacher Empowerment: The Education Entitlement-Social Transformation Traverse." *Contemporary Education Dialogue* 6 (2): 121–56.

Berger, Peter L. and Thomas Luckmann. 1967. *The Social Construction of Knowledge: A Treatise in the Sociology of Knowledge*. New York: Anchor.

Berman, Jessica. *Modernist Fiction, Cosmopolitanism, and the Politics of Community*. Cambridge: Cambridge University Press.

Bhog, D. 2002. "Gender and Curriculum." *Economic and Political Weekly*, April 27:1638–1642.

Block, Alan A. 2004. *Talmud, Curriculum, and the Practical: Joseph Schwab and the Rabbis*. New York: Peter Lang.

Brummelen, Harro Van. 1986. "Shifting Perspectives: Early British Columbia Textbooks from 1872–1925." In *Schools in the West: Essays in Canadian Educational History*, edited by Nancy M. Sheehan, J. Donald Wilson, and David C. Jones, 17–37. Calgary, AB: Detselig..

Chakravarty, Uma and Nandita Haksar. 1987. *The Delhi Riots: Three Days in the Life of a Nation*. New Delhi: Lancer International.

Chakravarty, Uma and Nandita Haksar. 1992. *1984 Carnage in Delhi: A Report on the Aftermath*. Delhi: PUDR.

Chopra, Radhika, Patricia Jeffery, and Helmut Reifeld. 2005. *Educational Regimes in Contemporary India*. New Delhi: Sage Publications.

Cohn, Bernard. 1996. *Colonialism and Its Forms of Knowledge: The British in India*. Princeton: Princeton University Press.

Froerer, Peggy. 2007. "Disciplining the Saffron Way: Moral Education and the Hindu Rashtra," *Modern Asian Studies* 41 (5): 1033–1071.

Ghadially, Rehana. 2007. *Urban Women in Contemporary India: A Reader*. Los Angeles: Sage Publications.

Goodson, I. Ed. 1985. *Social Histories of Secondary Curriculum: Subjects for Study*. London: The Falmer Press.

Kaviraj, Sudipta. 1997. "The Modern State in India." In. *Dynamics of State Formation: Europe and India Compared*, edited by Martin Doornbos and Sudipta Kaviraj, 225–50. London: Sage Publications..

Kumar, Ashwani. 2013. *Curriculum as Meditative Inquiry*. New York: Palgrave Macmillan.

Kumar, Krishna. 1990."'Revivalism and Education in North-Central India," *Social Scientist* 18 (10): 4–26.

Kumar, Krishna. 1997. "A Memory for Democracy," *Seminar*, March: 47–51.

Lall, Marie. 2005. *The Challenges for India's Education System*, Chatham House, April. Briefing paper.

Lardinois, Roland, and Meenakshi Thapan. 2006. *Reading Pierre Bourdieu in a Dual Context: Essays from India and France*. 1st edition. London ; New York: Routledge, India.

Le Grange, Lesley. 2010. "South African Curriculum Studies: A Historical Perspective and Autobiographical Account." In *Curriculum Studies in South Africa*, edited by William F. Pinar, 177–200. New York: Palgrave Macmillan.

Le Grange, Lesley. 2014. "Curriculum Research in South Africa." In *International Handbook of Curriculum Research*, edited by William F. Pinar, 2nd ed., 466–75. New York: Routledge.

Luxon, Nancy. 2013. *Crisis of Authority. Politics, Trust, and Truth-Telling in Freud and Foucault*. Cambridge: Cambridge University Press.

Maulana Azad Centre for Elementary and Social Education (MACESE) (1991), Perspective Paper, Department of Education, University of Delhi.

MACESE (2001) Feasibility Study Report, Department of Education, University of Delhi.

Pinar, William F. 1981. "Whole, Bright, Deep with Understanding: Issues in Autobiographical Method and Qualitative Research." *Journal of Curriculum Studies* 13 (3): 173–88.

Pinar, William F. 2000 (1975). "Sanity, Madness and the School." In *Curriculum Theorizing: The Reconceptualization* edited by William F. Pinar, 359–83. Troy, NY: Educator's International Press. Originally published in *Curriculum Theorizing: The Reconceptualists* Berkeley, CA: McCutchan.

Pinar, William F. 2006. *The Synoptic Text Today and Other Essays. Curriculum Development after the Reconceptualization*. New York: Peter Lang.

Pinar, William F. 2009. *The Worldliness of a Cosmopolitan Education: Passionate Lives in Public Service*. New York: Routledge.

Pinar, William F., ed. 2010. *Curriculum Studies in South Africa*. New York: Palgrave Macmillan.

Pinar, William F., ed. 2011a. *Curriculum Studies in Brazil*. New York: Palgrave Macmillan.

Pinar, William F., ed. 2011b. *Curriculum Studies in Mexico*. New York: Palgrave Macmillan.

Pinar, William F. 2011c. *The Character of Curriculum Studies: Bildung, Currere, and the Recurring Question of the Subject*. New York: Palgrave Macmillan.

Pinar, William F., William F. Reynolds, Patrick Slattery, and Peter M. Taubman. 1995. *Understanding Curriculum*. New York: Peter Lang.

Popkewitz, Thomas S. ed. 1987. *The Formation of School Subjects: The Struggle for Creating an American Institution*. London: The Falmer Press.

Sarkar, Tanika. 1996. "Educating the Children of the Hindu Rashtra: Notes on RSS Schools." In *Religion, Religiosity and Communalism*, edited by P. Bidwai, H. Mukhia, and A. Vanaik. Delhi: Manohar Publishers.

Stanley, Timothy. 1990. "White Supremacy and the Rhetoric of Educational Indoctrination: A Canadian Case Study." In *Making Imperial Mentalities: Socialisation and British Imperialism*, edited by J. A.Mangan, 144–62. Manchester: Manchester University Press.

Sundar, Nandini. 2004. "Teaching to Hate: RSS' Pedagogical Programme," *Economic and Political Weekly* 39 (16) April 17: 1605–12.

Thapan, Meenakshi. 1988. Some Aspects of Cultural Reproduction and Pedagogic Communication," *Economic and Political Weekly of India* 23 (13): 592–96.

Thapan, Meenakshi. 2010. *Contested Spaces: Citizenship and Belonging in Contemporary Times*. Orient BlackSwan.

Thiongo, Ngugi Wa. 1994. *Bhasha, Sanskriti Aur Rashtriya Asmita*, edited and translated by Anandswarup Varma. Delhi: Saransh.

Tomkins, George S. ed. 1979. *The Curriculum in Canada in Historical Perspective*. Canadian Society for the Study of Education, Sixth Year Book, vol. 6, May.

Tomkins, George S. 1981. "Foreign Influences on Curriculum and Curriculum Policy Making in Canada: Some Impressions in Historical and Contemporary Perspectives," *Curriculum Inquiry* 11 (2) Summer: 157–66.

Tomkins, George S. 1986. *A Common Countenance: Stability and Change in the Canadian Curriculum*. Scaraborough, ON: Prentice-Hall (Canada).

Viswanathan, Gauri. 1990. *Masks of Conquest: Literary Study and British Rule in India*. London: Faber and Faber.

Waks, Leonard, and Edmund C. Short, eds. 2009. *Leaders in Curriculum Studies: Intellectual Self- Portraits*. Rotterdam and Tapei: Sense Publishers.

Walsh, Judith E. 1983. *Growing up in British India*. New York: Holmes and Meier.

Wang, Hongyu. 2004. *The Call from the Stranger on a Journey Home: Curriculum in a Third Space*. New York: Peter Lang.

Wang, Hongyu. 2010. "Intimate Revolt and Third Possibilities: Cocreating a Creative Curriculum." In *Curriculum Studies Handbook: The Next Moment*, edited by Malewski Erik, 374–86. New York: Routledge.

Wang, Hongyu. 2014. "A Nonviolent Perspective on Internationalizing Curriculum Studies." In *International Handbook of Curriculum Research*, edited by William F. Pinar, 2nd ed., 67–76. New York: Routledge.

Weaver, John. 2010. "The Posthuman Condition: A Complicated Conversation." In *Curriculum Studies Handbook: The Next Moment*, edited by Malewski Erik, 190–200. New York: Routledge.

# Chapter 1

## Curriculum in India
### Narratives, Debates, and a Deliberative Agenda

*Poonam Batra*

## Context

The early period of British colonial rule witnessed a long and sharp debate between the Anglicists and the Orientalists about the validity and utility of classical and indigenous systems of knowledge in the Indian subcontinent. The adoption of Macaulay's minute by the East India Company in 1835 led to the ascendance of the Anglicists and the establishment of a colonial system of education with the goal of creating a new class of English-proficient petty public servants. This in time led to the displacement of vernacular systems of education based on classical and "folk" curricula derived from a plurality of educational traditions.

The British "essentialist" view of knowledge of the nineteenth century emphasized the individual, scientific, universal, and moral aims of education ahead of the social and cultural. This, combined with the colonial construction of Indian society, designed to preserve the ideological lead of the Empire post-1857,[1] helped shape the official nineteenth-century school curriculum. The rejection of nationalist Gopal Krishna Gokhale's Bill (1911) to make primary education free and compulsory by the colonial administration and English-educated and often upper-caste elite further helped sustain a curriculum that focused on colonial objectives. Holmes and McLean (1989, 151) argues that despite tensions between the colonial view of education and the nationalist postcolonial aims of education, British essentialism grew unassailable roots in India partly because "colonial values coincided with those of indigenous traditions."

The rejection of indigenous knowledge and the sociocultural context in shaping curriculum in the diverse subcontinental landscape of India created a deep conflict between education and culture (Kumar 2005). This is still in contest in contemporary South Asia. Thus "school-based knowledge became isolated from the everyday reality and cultural milieu of the child."[2] This isolation characterizes the bulk of educational practice across India even today and lies at the root of the country's poor performance in universalizing critical education, well over half a century after the close of one of the largest mass emancipation movements that led to India's independence in 1947.

From the mid-nineteenth century colonial education came to be associated with an urban elite, severed from the culture and economic realities of the rural masses. In 1901, Rabindranath Tagore founded Shantiniketan[3] as a concrete response to his fervent critique of colonial education. In his view, the British system was inadequate as it failed to resonate with the people of India. His aim was to create a learning environment inspired by nature and a curriculum that was responsive to the culture of the people. Tagore was convinced of the goals of modern education but was equally convinced that these be achieved through the language and culture of the people. Tagore's views on education influenced the articulation of nationalist ideas on education, but were not accepted by many political leaders of the Swadeshi[4] movement.

Gandhi's "Nai Talim"[5] was conceived as a national system of education—an alternative to colonial education as part of the nationalist struggle for freedom. It was adopted by many states in 1937, about the same time when Tagore popularized science through his idea of *loka-siksha* (popular education). Although Tagore acknowledged the convergence between his idea of popular education and Gandhi's basic education, he felt that the scheme of basic education placed undue emphasis on practical training at the cost of artistic creativity (Bhattacharya 2004). Shantiniketan remains to this day a symbol of Tagore's conviction that the "object of education is the freedom of mind which can only be achieved through the path of freedom... (where) children should not have mere schools for their lessons, but a world whose guiding spirit is personal love" (Tagore 1921, 147).

Gandhi's "Nai Talim" tried to address several critical aspects of the social and economic realities of the 1940s, especially of rural India. School curriculum was designed to use local languages and local cultures in training people in traditional crafts such as spinning and weaving. More importantly, "Gandhi was proposing the allocation of a substantive place in the school curriculum to systems of knowledge developed and associated with oppressed groups of Indian society, namely artisans, peasants and cleaners" (Kumar 2009, 11) The attempt was to break the frames of knowledge associated with dominant castes. Gandhi's "Nai Talim" was a response to both—the elite system of colonial education perceived to be culturally and economically irrelevant as well as to the upper caste hegemonic control over who can be educated. In doing this the "problem" of curriculum was to become an act of "deliberation" rather than one based on "an intrinsic view of knowledge." This powerful idea of Gandhi was much ahead of its time, when Western debates on curriculum of the 1950s and 1960s were circumscribed to either articulating the "scientific principles" of developing curriculum or turning toward the philosophers' claim of identifying knowledge that had intrinsic worth.

The distinction between the colonial curriculum and the curriculum of the countermovements initiated by nationalist leaders lay in the *purpose* of the educational project of the time. While the British aimed to develop subservient colonial citizens, the aim of the nationalist leaders was to liberate the Indian people from the shackles of colonial English education and create free citizens who could emancipate an India rooted in the diverse cultures of its people.

Gandhi's idea of basic education was an attempt to make curriculum democratically accessible by making it socially and economically relevant. However, his proposal met with resistance from the upper-caste elite in whose interest it was to preserve the colonial system of education and an essentialist view of knowledge. Holmes and McLean (1989) show how the obstacles to basic education also lay in the shifting nature of economic activities from rural to urban areas and the government's focus on industrial development in the first national five-year plan. The idea of making education productive both for the child in terms of developing appropriate skills and capacities and for making the school an institution that could sustain itself economically was deeply contested. As a result, Gandhi's proposal to replace colonial education was experimented only in small pockets of India and never really became part of mainstream education. The National Curriculum Framework (NCF 2005) attempted to revive an interest in reestablishing this link between work and education. This is yet to generate a sustained interest among curriculum developers.

Curriculum in contemporary India is bound to vary across the diverse terrain of Indian society and polity. It would therefore be a fallacy to talk of school curriculum in India as a homogenous entity. We could perhaps talk of a wide set of curricula that operate across different parts of the country. This diversity could, as many would argue, be associated with the diverse ideological hues reflected in the governance of different states. However, there are several other dimensions along which the basic tenets of school curricula in Indian society have been designed and implemented as in the case of Gandhi's "Nai Talim." Some of these may be driven by ideologies rooted in movements of social reform,[6] others in philosophical traditions, and still others in spiritual traditions of Indian society. For instance, schools that follow the philosophical underpinnings of J. Krishnamurti or Vivekananda are distinct in their approach as compared to schools that follow Sri Aurobindo's approach of integral education. These in turn are distinctly different from Gandhi's Nai Talim or Tagore's Shantiniketan. However, the essential aim of education in each of these traditions is to develop the inner self along with the ability to reason and acquire other mental faculties and skills—the focus being the whole, integrated person. Each of these operates with a curriculum that aligns with the vision of education of its founders.

The diversity of these and other school curricula in India is indeed daunting.[7] However it cannot be said that these different orientations have impacted mainstream school curricula in India—state or private—in any major way. The underpinnings of each of these diverse curricula are philosophical, sociological, educational, spiritual, and ideological in nature. Central to the educational vision of Krishnamurti, for instance, is the idea of the transformation of individual consciousness through an education that regards "relationship" as the basis of human existence. The process of education must therefore include "an understanding and deep cultivation of psychological processes as much as academic excellence" (Thapan 2007, 64). The Krishnamurti Foundation of India (KFI) schools focus on giving children several opportunities to reflect and understand, through deep engagement with nature and community, with the aim to develop an awareness of life and themselves. In Krishnamurti's (1953, 46) words, "Education must help students to recognise and break down in themselves... all social distinctions and prejudices, and discourage the acquisitive pursuit of power and domination." Foregrounded in many of these perspectives is a view of the curriculum as a process of engagement of the learners with nature, self, and their social milieu. Alternative schools in India, following various persuasions, coexist and struggle to sustain their vision via negotiating spaces within the formal education system that require qualifying public examinations. However, mainstream curriculum remains largely impervious to their influences.

The key ideas that shape curricula in mainstream schools in contemporary India are best understood in two ways: through a detailed study of national curriculum documents and through a close examination of prevalent school practices. A study of the national curricula documents prepared in postindependence India by the apex institution of education—the National Council of Educational Research and Training (NCERT)—gives us an idea of the key aspects that have defined the contours of school curriculum since independence.

# The Modernization Project

Critical to the postcolonial context was the construction of a national identity via education, in particular, the school curriculum. NCERT was set up in 1961 as an apex institution in charge of developing curricula and designing textbooks for schools across the country. School textbooks were conceived to play a significant role in the early nation-building years of the Nehruvian socialism of the 1950s and 1960s. Providing good, inexpensive textbooks of uniform quality and content throughout the country was seen as an important part of the welfare state that would contribute toward efforts at uniting the diverse people of India.

Questions of modernity were also crucial for the young Independent India of the 1950s as the aim of education was perceived to prepare the youth to participate in industrialization and technological advancement. The Nehruvian period was thus preoccupied with developing institutes of excellence in science and technology, providing a host of opportunities in higher education. While most of the well-reputed institutes of science and technology were established within the first two decades of independent India, the first serious attempt to articulate the contours of a school curriculum happened as late as 1975, a decade after Nehru's death. The first policy statement on education came post-1966 when the National Commission on Education (GoI 1966) submitted its report on the state of education in the country and proposed several concrete suggestions for educational and social change.

The thrust of the Ten-Year School Curriculum Framework (NCERT 1975) was the modernization project along the lines of the Education Commission report. The commission viewed modernity and nationalism as synonymous. The central role of education was that of "nation-building." Hence, educational objectives were defined within the paradigm of national development. This was a marked departure from the Secondary Education Commission,[8] which in the early 1950s had "laid emphasis on the psychological requirements of the child and the need to relate school subjects to the immediate environment of the child" (Batra 2010, 19). This was to remain an idea until 1986 when the National Policy on Education (NPE) articulated its commitment to bringing the child to the center of educational change.

The aim of school curriculum was to "give up the colonial-feudal system meant for the production of clerks" that underpinned Macaulay's proposal. Stress was simultaneously laid upon creating Gandhi's "Nai Talim" that conceptualized curriculum as "internal transformation" with the aim to relate to the "life, needs and aspirations of the nation" (NCERT 1975, 1).

Modernization meant engaging with the growing body of knowledge in science and technology. Tagore's initiative of popular education had attempted to popularize science among the masses. Gandhi's "Nai Talim" on the other hand was more about developing the self with the aim to minimize gaps between what is thought, espoused, and "lived" in reality. For Gandhi, bringing work and education together provided opportunities to "enable the use of hands to develop insight into material phenomena and human relationship involved in any organised productive work." The aim was to develop in the young "attitudes of cooperation, social responsibility within a frame of equality and freedom of the human spirit." This was the view reflected in the 1975 national curriculum document.

For about twenty years between 1968 and 1986, the modernization project was perceived by the state to help achieve social justice, productivity, national integration, and a rational outlook. Curriculum as an instrument of social change was to inculcate Constitutional values of plurality, an open society that was democratic, secular, and socialist. School curriculum was designed to reflect all this in structure and content thus advocating the crucial role of pedagogic approaches in achieving these curricular aims.

Though the running narrative of the 1975 curriculum framework was one of national development and there was a need to "replace the old with the new," the central role of India's states in addressing diversity along language, culture, and tradition was also recognized. The emphasis however was on the national and not the local. For instance, the specific guidelines for history outlined in the 1975 curriculum document cautioned against the introduction of local history at the school stage, which often runs the risk of promoting "parochialism and regional cultural chauvinism."

The need to create a national identity was accorded a priority greater than the needs of the child and an understanding of its sociocultural environment. The development of national identity in the post-Partition era, which witnessed brutal communal violence, was seen as the most immediate task. It was important that the state accorded respect to the beliefs and practices of minority and majority religious communities and constructed a history of harmonious coexistence and cultural synthesis. This was perceived to be best done through education via well-written school textbooks.

"Unity in diversity" was the "pan-India" historical narrative constructed during the nation-building years that led the common man to take pride in the country's pluralistic heritage. School curricula responded to this by minimizing the projection of conflict and maximizing the portrayal of peaceful coexistence in its narratives. This was possible through a careful selection of history and its treatment. Civics as a school subject played the role of projecting a united India by way of engaging young students with the structures of institutions that promised to sustain a democratic polity and society. Examples of these structures included the electoral and other state systems and the political institutions of democratic governance. Scholars have argued that the civics curriculum was essentially a colonial "narrative of an ideal citizen," constructed alongside a narrative of having "faith in the working of the political system" (Jain 2004). For a young nation, it may have been necessary to develop faith in the governance structures, but this view of civics did not in any way address questions of how ordinary lives are shaped by economic relations and social structures.

Apart from the compelling need to portray a united nation that shaped school curriculum in the early years, the value of intrinsic worthwhile knowledge and curriculum making as a scientific exercise prevalent in the United Kingdom and the United States in the 1950s and 1960s also influenced the shaping of the first curriculum document (1975). Presenting a body of knowledge that concerns the everyday life of people in an abstract, decontextualized manner was a pragmatic pedagogic strategy that was aligned to the belief that education was about transmission of information that was value-free.

The postcolonial Nehruvian modernization project thus focused on creating the secular, socialist, and scientific citizen. The emphasis, however, was on higher education, science, and technology. The school system and the curriculum remained within the clutches of the colonial educational frame and upper-caste imagination that had little reason to support the cause of mass education.

# The Child as Citizen

It took India more than 20 years to re-examine school curriculum in 1988, after the education policy of 1986 was released.[9] At this point in time the academic discourse in India was being realigned to include the prevalent Piagetian frame from the United Kingdom and the United States. The Plowden Report of 1967 in the United Kingdom had laid considerable emphasis on designing a curriculum that was child-centered, in keeping with ideas derived from the theory of Jean Piaget. The second strand of thought came from the Deweyian discourse of progressive education in the United States, the central thrust of which was the child and education as a social process. Both strands originally came from years of theoretical debate and empirical research on the ideas of how to make the child the centee of educational practice. However, in India, ideas of child-centered education made a notional entry into the educational discourse, first, through the NPE, 1986, and subsequently through the District Primary Education Programme (DPEP) of the 1990s. The discourse on "child-centered" education within the domain of preservice training of teachers remained largely rhetoric or was reduced to an oversimplified understanding of the complex and subtle ideas offered by Piaget and Dewey. Opportunities to engage deeper with these ideas through research in institutes of teacher education were limited.

This narrow interpretation of child-centered education was inconsequential to the larger aim of positioning education as a "powerful instrument of human resource development." This was also the time when the Ministry of Education in the Indian government was renamed as the Ministry of "Human Resource Development." The attempt was to standardize parameters along which education could be "defined and delivered" within a "mission mode." This approach of designing school curricula led to the formulation of the Minimum Levels of Learning (MLLs) in 1991 by the NCERT. MLLs were defined for each stage of school education and for each subject. This was an effort to articulate learning outcomes in the behavioristic traditions of the mid-twentieth century. By reducing school knowledge to specified codes of textbook chapters as in the case of MLLs, curriculum was circumscribed to sectarian perspectives and frames. The exercise of curriculum design thus became a mechanical ritual, treating knowledge as a given and "broken down into a hierarchical taxonomy of specific learning objectives," drawn from the curriculum traditions of the 1950s led by Bloom (Sarangapani 2000, 15).

Curriculum reform via the MLLs viewed the child as a citizen, with character building and developing responsible citizens as major thrust areas of the 1988 curriculum framework. Government documents of curriculum and syllabi are replete with examples of "the role of civics to 'train' citizens, develop 'responsibility,' improve their 'quality of character' and inculcate the 'right ideals, habits and attitude' in them" (Jain 2004, 178).

A common scheme of studies for elementary and secondary education was developed with the stated aim to reduce disparities by providing a standardized curriculum. The 1988 curriculum framework went into considerable detail with regard to reorienting the in-service training of teachers, examination reforms, Continuous and Comprehensive Evaluation (CCE), and the integration of mass media and technology with education. One of the major policy shifts that led to a host of other reforms in the years to come was the separate provision of schooling for children who were in sectors of organized and unorganized labor and were thus left out of formal schools. A system of nonformal education first set up in 1975 was institutionalized through policy. This laid the grounds for a two-tier system of education that gained currency during the period of reform in the early years of India's economic liberalization in terms of both a differentiated curriculum and an unaccountable process of primary schooling.

It is evident that the 1988 curriculum focused on the psychological underpinnings of curriculum design with the child at the center. This curriculum was to influence the trajectory of educational practice for years to come. Soon after the first stage of liberalization in the early 1990s, India borrowed aid from the World Bank to undertake a nation-wide process of educational reform at the primary school level. The DPEP led processes of pedagogical renewal in several states between the years 1993 and 2001. Although direct entry into school curriculum was not permitted to international donors, the textbook and pedagogic renewal effort ensured an indirect entry into the field of school curriculum. The decade following the 1988 curriculum thus saw the formulation of MLLs and a serious attempt at uniformization of classroom teaching through focus on an "outcome-based" orientation of the DPEP interventions. One of the key objectives of DPEP was to enhance learning levels of children and to promote ideas of child-centered education among practicing teachers. The belief that a few spontaneously produced ideas about the child and her learning processes, without adequately embedding them in contexts "are enough to construct a notion of quality and can constitute an adequate basis for all pedagogical decisions" was severely critiqued (Dhankar 2003, 8). Batra and Nambissan (2003, 135) argued that "such discourse is bereft of theoretical grounding and perspective. It also romanticises the nature of the child and trivialises the pedagogical significance of the fundamental principles of progressive education."

The major thrust of the 1988 curriculum on developing "productive" citizens found renewed emphasis in the National Curriculum for School Education (NCFSE) (NCERT 2000). This time the emphasis was on developing the "Indian" citizen. The NCFSE suggested in unequivocal terms that the "curriculum is a device to translate national goals into educational experiences." The national goals were to build on "Indian philosophy, cultural and social traditions, needs and aspirations." The indigenousness of school curricula was strongly recommended. This emphasis aligned with the belief that the rich Indian tradition has contributed to world civilisation, hence the need to develop learners who are patriotic and nationalistic Indians. This was to be undertaken by teaching values through a common core curriculum. The agenda of a common core curriculum was to create social cohesion through the inculcation of values whose source lay in religion. Diversity was to be addressed through a passive acceptance of inequity and with the establishment of a clear rationale for a differentiated curriculum for academic or vocational pursuits.

# Cultural Nationalism

The first 50 years of state-supported academic discourse was guided by a secular socialist Nehruvian tenet that sought to delink progress and nationalism from cultural tradition and religion. The narrative of "secular nationalism" reflected in the 1975 and 1988 curriculum documents stood the test of various political forces. It however came under serious threat from the Hindu Right after the Bhartiya Janata Party (BJP)[10] led coalition government came to power in 1999. Scholars, however, argue that history textbooks of the 1960s and 1970s that "critiqued colonial and communal stereotypes and presented a history that was secular and national" came under attack by the Hindu Right for the first time in 1977, during the postemergency years (Bhattacharaya 2009, 104). These textbooks were thereafter withdrawn leading to several protests.

An expanding network of Vidya Bharati schools and Shishu Mandirs of the RSS continued to pose a serious threat to the secular character of school curriculum. An evaluation study of a variety of school textbooks undertaken by NCERT in 1996 (cited in Ramakrishnan, 1998) revealed that many of the textbooks developed by Vidya Bharati, which claim to inculcate knowledge of Indian culture in school children, had strong elements of religious fanaticism. This threat emerged as much from an attempted distortion of the school curriculum as from the special training of the teachers in the Hindu way of life. This continues to be a real threat even post-NCF, 2005, because these books are widely used in schools of the BJP-ruled states and in schools managed by organizations influenced by the Hindutva ideology.

In 1999 when BJP came to power as the lead party of the coalition—National Democratic Alliance (NDA)—at the center, history textbooks became the site of fierce contestation. The new political regime formulated a new curriculum framework that brought curriculum debates into the public domain for the first time. This National Curriculum Framework for School Education (NCFSE) (NCERT 2000) led to the assertion of political ideology in defining school curriculum. It was severely criticised by scholars for violating Constitutional values of secularism, democracy, and fraternity. According to Kumar (2000) the NCFSE presented a different "idea of India" through its undue emphasis on developing a national identity and moving away from the Nehruvian commitment to modernity and secularism. The textbooks that followed promoted a discourse of cultural revivalism and Hindu nationalist movement in India. These textbooks were widely debated in public leading to a withdrawal of the curriculum on judicial intervention. What was missing in these debates was the voice of the teacher.

Issues of equity, inclusion and exclusion, learner diversity, religious identity, and communalism gained considerable significance in the curriculum debates that followed. Scholars argued that history was crafted to reinforce national ideologies and history texts were used as narratives that would inculcate patriotism and develop productive citizens. The school texts presented a narrative of "Hindu nationalism" that glorified India's "Hindu" past and sought to incorporate Buddhism and Jainism into the fold of Hinduism, while debasing Islamic rule during the medieval period (Marlena 2003). History texts were criticized for blurring boundaries between myth and history and imposing a homogenized Indian tradition based on the construct of Hindutva. Several critics saw the NCFSE as an imposition of the Hindutva agenda in the garb of a national identity. "The controversy regarding the content of textbooks brought into direct public scrutiny issues of curriculum content selection and presentation as well as the need to examine linkages between ideology and the state in the design of school curricula" (Batra 2010, 20).

The Hindutva agenda was also seen as a systematic attack on rational discourse in education (Patnaik 2001), indicated by attempts at distorting history through state-sponsored research agendas in social science institutes. Panikkar (2001, 80) argued how "the kind of education proposed would create a strong sense of pride, bordering on chauvinism...would foster a generation incapable of interrogating the problems of society, and would contribute towards redefining the nation in religious terms, more specifically as Hindu *rashtra*." This was also seen as a concerted attack on the plural fabric of Indian society. The popular imagination in the state of Gujarat was systematically communalized over more than a decade through pamphlets, journals, and school textbooks that viewed the Aryan civilization as Hindu civilization, Muslims and Christians as foreigners and Nazism as a glorified construct (Setalvad 2001).

Attempts were also made during the BJP regime to thwart scientific inquiry within the social sciences, undermine the study of history and introduce Vedic astrology as a subject of higher studies. In these attempts was hidden the agenda of striking at the very core of rationality that was Nehru's chosen path to combat communalism in a volatile India that had witnessed one of the worst histories of partitioning its people. It became clearer that India's national education policy having successfully avoided the dichotomy between the indigenous and the Western has enabled "the internalisation of a universal outlook and the location of the indigenous in the wider matrix of human history." However, with a forced dichotomy between the two while privileging the "Indian" and placing an emphasis on religious values, there was an attempt to "redefine the nation in religious terms" (Panikkar 2001, 80) through the NCFSE.

The process of the ideological capture of school curriculum by the Hindu Right is visible through the history of independent India and in contemporary times. In 2006, the BJP-ruled state of Rajasthan redesigned school textbooks within the frame of Hindu ideology, despite the approval of NCF, 2005, by the Central Advisory Board of Education (CABE) committee. Since education continues to be a state subject in India's federal polity except in cases of specific programs and schemes of education led by the central government, school curriculum continues to be vulnerable to such ideological capture. While earlier this process was insidious as in the case of Gujarat that led to the state-sponsored program of ethnic cleansing and ghettoization of the Muslim minorities, post-NCFSE 2000 debates, this has taken the form of asserting state autonomy.

Several scholars pointed out other aspects of the NCFSE that came under close academic scrutiny. Nambissan (2000, 50) has argued how curricular and pedagogic concerns in the NCFSE "fail to be adequately informed by an understanding of the specific context of educational deprivation, particularly where the economically and socially vulnerable communities such as dalits and adivasis are concerned." For instance, research has consistently demonstrated that various forms of discrimination are widely practiced in regular government schools, such as the school day being significantly shorter in schools of SC/ST concentrated villages (Anitha 2000); social discrimination as reflected in teacher attitudes and peer culture (Thorat 1999, cited in Nambissan 2000); and the continued portrayal of marginalized communities in subservient roles in school textbooks (Nambissan 2000). The NCFSE was seen as "a call for 'peaceful co-existence' between religious and caste authorities and elites by permitting each untrammelled control over their flock.... The call for a child-centered pedagogy [was] used to dismantle the authority of professional academic disciplines in school education. Their place would be taken by community leaders" (Subramaniam 2003).

Curriculum in the NCFSE was hence largely seen as an instrument that will develop "capacit(y)ies for *tolerating* differences arising out of caste, religion, ideology, region, languages…" (NCERT 2000, 9), rather than one that would question the practice of social discrimination (author's italics). It was an attempt to accept social difference as a given and education as a process of learning to tolerate this difference.

A major study of school textbooks from a gender lens, undertaken in the states of Madhya Pradesh, Tamil Nadu, Delhi, and Gujarat by Nirantar, attempts to unravel the deep impact of aligning school curriculum with state ideology. Their main critique was that none of the critics of the NCFSE "moved beyond looking at gender as a somewhat isolated and independent marker of social and cultural inequities." In the light of the fact that "the school sets out the notion of the ideal citizen, the ideal woman, the ideal family, the ideal worker..." it has been found that "...the process of gender socialisation is mediated through the category of the nation" (Bhog et al. 2009, 6, 23).

The more recent exercise of curriculum renewal via the NCF, 2005, highlights the crucial role of social sciences in establishing "social enquiry as a scientific endeavour" and in developing a "just and peaceful society" within the larger frame of Constitutional values. It underscores in particular the need to break away from patriarchal frames of knowledge. For the first time in India, the curriculum debate is linked to the professional and pedagogical concerns of the child and the teacher. This was a welcome step away from an earlier observation made by Paliwal and Subramaniam (1992, 33), who have argued how "preoccupation with ideology has impeded the development of the pedagogy of social science teaching."

Historians "submerge(d) their differences and...came together to defend the old textbooks" (pre-NCFSE) as argued by Bhattacharya (2009, 105); they also felt compelled to address several concerns brought into focus by the interdisciplinary knowledge of ecological, gender, cultural, and subaltern histories as legitimate frames within which school histories ought to be written. Before highlighting the key concerns articulated in the NCF, 2005, it would be useful to take stock of some of the imperatives of the curriculum review that derive from dominant educational practice.

## Curriculum and Educational Practice

In his essay *What Is Worth Teaching?* Kumar (2009) argues why curriculum development needs to be intimately related to questions of the "kind of society and people we are, and to...the kind of society we want to be." He challenges the current frame of educational practice in India where curriculum is perceived to be "received knowledge" to be designed in accordance with a predetermined set of principles. He attributes this to the overwhelming influence of Tyler's (1949) idea that the aim of education is to change behavior patterns and the uncritical adoption of Bloom's taxonomy of educational objectives within this frame. It must be noted that this remains the dominant frame within which school teachers are prepared.

It is therefore no surprise that the dominant pattern of curriculum transaction in schools across India continues to rely on lessons planned along the lines of a taxonomy proposed by Bloom in the 1950s. The failure of the Indian educator community to break away from these archaic forms of educational practice can be attributed to several factors. Foremost among these is the archaic institutional culture of the preservice education of teachers. Batra (2014, 12) argues how "the perceived appropriateness of educational psychology as a foundational discipline for the education of teachers led to a major shift from the earlier focus on the notion of a 'child' to the notion of a 'learner.' This shift appears to have further distanced the teacher from the child and her context." This means that teachers are trained to engage with questions of teaching and learning outside context; and knowledge for developing teachers continues to be ahistorical and universalistic.

In Kumar's view, the narrowness of curriculum deliberation in India can also be attributed to the fact that "curriculum designing in the school stage is the charge of the bureaucracy of education (and)...the quasi-bureaucracy of the state-controlled institutions of pedagogical research and training" (2009, 13). School curriculum has never been examined for its selection and treatment of content. Even when the opportunity arose during the DPEP program of pedagogical renewal when several states took the initiative to rewrite school texts, subject content was neither examined for whose voices it represented nor for its epistemological underpinnings or philo-sophical and ideological inclinations. The frame within which new textbooks were written under the DPEP was the *mantra* of "child-centered education." This led to a virtual disappearance of subject knowledge and an overemphasis on activities bereft of content. Issues of the common person and those that brought several critical con-cerns to the fore of social debates were not even on the margins of curriculum design activities. Kumar (2009, 15) refers to this as a "transcendental curriculum" that is not only wasteful but also destructive for it promotes "domesticated consciousness" leading to a deep disconnect between formal education and everyday lives.

A further explanation by Kumar helps us understand why the behavioristic model continues to draw support in the Indian context. First, the model of the 1960s had great intellectual appeal for the Indian planners as they looked up to the West for solutions to the problems of education in India. Second, this appeal had roots in the colonial policies wherein the sociocultural milieu was perceived as "an obstruction rather than an asset for education" in India (Kumar 2005, 72).

The adoption of a system of mass public examinations was another critical factor that determined the trajectory that school curriculum took in Indian society. It cre-ated a textbook culture that eventually led to a nexus with the examination system to create a curriculum that was alienated to the social milieu from which diverse learners came (Kumar 2009).

While mainstream curricula discourse did not deviate from concerns of prac-tice, an alternative space was being carved by nongovernmental organizations that were striving to make a significant difference in the learning environments of state schools. This led to major intellectual shifts in redefining school curriculum within the larger democratic frame of education.

## Curricular Discourse in Alternate Spaces

School curriculum became the subject of enquiry, debate, and alternative vision by the nongovernmental sector of education in the 1980s. Eklavya[11] was one such organization that chose to work on middle-school science and social science with the state schools of Madhya Pradesh (MP), a state in central India. This section[12] highlights the contribution of the Eklavya social science program in developing a discourse on curriculum studies in India.

The social science program of Eklavya was initiated in 1983 in nine state government schools of MP. The aim was to enable teachers and children to address social issues and processes in an active and analytical manner through well-designed conceptual materials in social sciences. A new set of textbooks was created and training methodologies were developed to engage teachers concerning the basic principles and pedagogic approaches of social science teaching. Systematic documentation and evaluation of the effort, including field-trials of text materials, were carried out by the Eklavya team; and feedback from teachers and children was used to continually evolve the curriculum. Many other schools and organizations within Madhya Pradesh and other states have subsequently drawn upon this program to give shape to efforts toward curriculum reform.

While the textbook remained the central source of knowledge, the nature of the school textbook in India changed with the contributions of Eklavya. The textbooks written and designed for the rural and semirural populations of state schools in Madhya Pradesh started an important trend. In particular, the social science texts are considered as unparalleled exemplars that have significantly informed the post-NCF, 2005, textbook writing process. A detailed understanding of the social science curriculum as embedded in the Eklavya texts will give clarity on the nature and design of the social science curriculum as envisaged and implemented.

Debates about social science curriculum have revolved around selective representation of dominant worldviews. Anyon (1979) and Apple (1993), for instance, have argued how selection of content influences curriculum design and textbook writing, where curriculum represents a "given" version of what is perceived as legitimate knowledge. Anyon (1978, 40) has argued how "knowledge which counts as social studies knowledge, tend(s) to be that knowledge which provides formal justification for and legitimating of prevailing institutional arrangements." Apple (1993, 46) has called attention to the "broader cultural messages" of textbooks that "bear similarities to government policy" and how the mere mention of the history and cultural elements of less powerful people renders such knowledge inconsequential.

These and other significant concerns informed the curriculum development process for Eklavya. Textbooks were written in a manner that foregrounded the local cultural knowledge and social milieu of the children they addressed. The aim was to enable an easy connect between what children read as official knowledge and their lived realities. Equally important was the critical meaning that teachers and students derive out of school texts. The demand of texts that make visible marginalized voices and narratives is to engage teachers with these so they can figure how to resist interventions by educational policy-makers in the teaching-learning process" (see Batra 2005).

Social science teaching as normally practiced focuses on information about societies and historical events without any reference to children's actual lived experiences. The Eklavya books provide a pedagogic frame that makes the social world of the learner both an object of study and a process by which learners constantly get to reflect upon their own social and personal experiences. In this way, they resolve the dichotomy often posed between the child and the curriculum. Organizing subject matter in developmentally appropriate ways, interspersed with questions, engages the reader in a dialogical process of meaning making. Children are continuously encouraged to compare the normative with actual experiences. This is made possible through the presentation of diverse viewpoints and an articulated rationale for a position taken. Without impinging upon the autonomy of the teacher, the texts provide useful pedagogical spaces to evoke dialogue during which information is interrogated to engage and reflect.

One of the more important contributions of Eklavya's engagement with the exercise of designing curriculum is to reflect on the disciplinary, pedagogic, and social dimensions of curriculum development. Even though Eklavya had to follow the prescribed syllabus of the state, it was able to negotiate the space available to treat the subject matter of social science critically. The texts were able to redefine the objectives of social science teaching and learning within this constraint.

Presenting complex social realities through the use of various strategies such as stories, illustrations, and sources helps children develop a concrete image of the social world under study. This facilitates the transition to abstract thought and the internalization of concepts. It forms an intermediate stage between learning from physical experience of the social environment, such as the family, village, or town, and learning abstract representations and ideas.

Curriculum for Eklavya was as much about presenting subject matter in a coherent manner as about framing critical questions around it and generating dialogue. The text organization unfolded an inquiry process that provided teachers several cues to frame questions that enhance conceptual engagement. The questions would be around identifying and organizing evidence and analyzing and synthesizing arguments. Questions deliberately posed in the narrative and not only at the end of the chapter gently nudge the teacher to stop, ask questions, and prompt students to think, discuss, and debate. This would lead students to engage with ideas rather than with packaged information. The teacher would become a true mediator between the child and the curriculum and the texts the means and methods of interaction between teachers and learners. The content is woven into this pedagogic structure of the texts, enabling a concrete translation of many abstract ideas such as inclusion, diversity, and identity. What distinguishes the Eklavya textbooks is the attention given to the presentation and organization of subject content, carefully weaving its critical analysis with pedagogic elements that assist in the creation of meaning (Batra 2010).

With a concerted focus on sociopolitical processes and interlinkages between various aspects of society, polity, and economy, the history chapters, for instance, revolve around specific rulers, periods, and themes rather than recount a linear presentation of chronological facts. A critical aim was to demonstrate how the past is reconstructed on the basis of available source material. The Eklavya texts embody the ideas expressed by Dewey on the aim of history in elementary education, that, history for the educator "must be an indirect sociology—a study of society which lays bare its process of becoming and its modes of organization" (1915, 155). This later became the cornerstone of writing history texts post-NCF, 2005.

One of the critical goals of the Eklavya curriculum was to enable a society that fosters individual freedom and enhances human agency. The civics curriculum addressed this by breaking fresh ground in the interpretation of civics as a subject. First, civics moved away from a state-centric portrayal of governance structures and processes to one where people are active agents in everyday life. Second, texts depict the state and society not as smooth, consensual entities, but as arenas of many conflicts and contradictions where people intervene actively in bringing about positive social change (Madan 2010). This approach was possible because the subject matter was drawn from a variety of social science disciplines, including sociology, economics, and political science.

Themes provided the possibility of interdisciplinary engagement with the larger issue of meaning and aims of education. For instance, an exposition of the socioeconomic positions of diverse people and the way it affects their bargaining power in the market helps learners to develop sensitivity toward multiple perspectives and viewpoints. The element of tentativeness in presenting information rather than stating facts with finality conveyed important subtext messages of developing open minds. Much has been carefully left for the children to discover, expecting them to use their own judgment and reasoning capacities. A constant attempt to connect with the immediate and familiar social milieu of learners through appropriately worded questions and activities created interest and an ownership of the process of learning.

Skills such as observation and comparison of phenomena, posing of problems, formulating hypothetical questions, reasoning, drawing inferences, and articulating new questions facilitate the development of children's ability to think critically. In this sense "skills refer not only to discrete techniques but also to complex procedures and methods" that are intimately tied up with the subject matter under study (Wiggins, Grant, and McTighe 2005, cited in Batra 2010).

One of the key aspects of this process of designing school curricula was its emphasis on disciplinary content drawn, involving institutions and academics dealing in frontier research in the concerned disciplines. The objectives of social science teaching, the perspective and framework of subject matter, are thus about the finer nuances of the debates in progress as well as the process of inquiry that brings into focus such debates.

The other significant development in the Eklavya curriculum was a continuous engagement with teachers, which included observation of classroom processes. Teachers of the state schools were walked through each topic so as to engage them with the finer nuances and debates on the issue at hand. For Eklavya, the textbook writing process was a process of developing curriculum along with the teachers' engagement with subject matter. It was as much about developing clarity of various constructs as about engaging with teachers' assumptions, beliefs, and attitudes on a number of social issues of gender, caste, social hierarchies, development, religion, tribal culture, and national identities. There were several daunting moments when teachers were perceived to be steeped in conditioned notions on many of these questions. While it was difficult to persuade teachers to question their deeply held beliefs and reconstruct their ideas and constructs, more often than not, pointed discussions on these themes seemed to yield little result. However, the presence of a diverse set of teachers in the training workshops and their confidence in expressing their point of view often assisted the Eklavya team to view stereotypes critically. Over the years a significant change in the way some teachers started viewing social issues became visible (Eklavya 2010).

Given the fact that curriculum development in India is largely under bureaucratic control, the role of an NGO evinces special significance. The State Council of Educational Research and Training (SCERT) in Madhya Pradesh merely provided a formal organizational platform. There were no systemic mechanisms to receive academic feedback from the government. The implicit and often explicit assumption was that the social science program is that of an NGO, not of the government of Madhya Pradesh. The Madhya Pradesh Textbook Standing Committee approved the textbooks as a formal requirement but did not participate in the development of text materials.

The relationship between the state government and Eklavya was one of patronage. It was neither professional nor systemic. It therefore deterred efforts to set up mechanisms for peer review, evolving methods of evaluation, and developing a vision of plurality in curriculum programs. The challenge lay in garnering political support for departing from conventional frameworks of developing and transacting school curricula. With a change of power equations between the government and Eklavya, the state finally withdrew support and closed[13] the program in the state schools in 2003 after 30 years. Central to this decision was perhaps a lack of conviction among the bureaucracy that school curriculum needs to be engaged, requiring proactive intervention by the academic community. For them the educational agenda ceases at provisioning of schools and teacher training institutions.

The space provided by the state for about two decades had created a major impact on the trajectory that school curriculum was to take during donor-aided educational reform. The DPEP led to a spurt of activity in developing school curriculum materials, in the form of textbooks and teaching aids[14]. This led to the involvement of Eklavya and other NGOs in various states, especially the northern belt of Hindi-speaking states. This continued under India's flagship program of universalizing elementary education, the *Sarva Shiksha Abhiyan* (SSA). More important, the NCERT's initiative at curriculum review, which led to the formulation of NCF, 2005, built on the curriculum discourse created by the Eklavya experiments in developing science and social science curricula. The most tangible example of this is the substitution of the middle school "civics" textbooks with interdisciplinary textbooks called "social and political life," patterned on the Eklavya texts.

# Curriculum for Social Transformation: A Deliberative Agenda

The change of national government in 2004 led to the NCERT curriculum review in 2005. The task assigned by the ministry was one of "detoxifying" school curriculum and textbooks designed under the NDA government that had faced the charge of "saffronizing" education. This underlined a new political interest in the role of education in national development. Under UPA I,[15] NCERT took the opportunity to redefine the role of education in social mobilization and transformation directed specifically at questions of caste and gender asymmetry and minority empowerment.

Deeper than these politically driven initiatives, the professional need for curriculum review emerge(d) from the long ossification of a national education system that continues to view teachers as "dispensers of information" and children as "passive recipients" of an "education," sought to be "delivered" in four-walled classrooms with little scope to develop critical thinking and understanding.[16]

One of the key problems perceived by the NCF 2005 was the burden of non-comprehension highlighted by the Yashpal Committee Report (NCERT 1993). This burden was seen to be a consequence of two critical features: one, an incoherent curriculum and its disconnect with the culture and life of children, and, two, the inadequate preparation of teachers who are unable to make connections with children and respond to them in imaginative and dynamic ways. "This intimate link between curriculum design and the preparation of teachers has been repeatedly demonstrated in successful educational innovations across the country since the 1980s—Neelbagh and the Valley School in Karnataka; Eklayva, in Madhya Pradesh, KSSP in Kerala and Digantar in Jaipur to name only a few" (Batra 2005, 4348). Yet, this link has been missed in the national curriculum documents since 1975. In this sense, the NCF, 2005 too was critiqued for engaging in a futuristic exercise of curriculum design without adequate connects with ground realities including the "disempowered teacher" (Batra 2005).

The NCF, 2005, linked the ongoing debate on curriculum to the professional and pedagogic concerns of the child, even though ideological questions remained central to the public discourse. Through a nation-wide process of consultation the NCF, 2005, exercise involved civil society representatives, university academics, and some teacher practitioners on various aspects of curriculum design and development. Issues of the knowledge-creation process, learners and the learning process, the education of teachers, and examination and systemic reform were discussed at length. These debates foregrounded the intimate relationship between school and society and the critical role of education in enabling social transformation.

Five guiding principles of curriculum reform, emerging from the concerns of existing educational practice, were suggested: "connecting knowledge to life outside the school, ensuring that learning is shifted away from rote methods, enriching the curriculum to provide for overall development of children rather than remain textbook centric, making examinations more flexible and integrated with classroom life, and nurturing an overriding identity informed by caring concerns within the democratic polity of the country" (NCF 2005, 5).

The NCF thus views curriculum as a "deliberative act" that subsumes classroom discourse and processes. Never before in India has a national curriculum document engaged deeply with questions of learning, knowledge, the sociocultural context of learners, and a pedagogic approach. It set itself the task of bridging the yawning gap between home and school knowledge and envisioned pedagogic trajectories that would enable knowledge creation as a process of social construction. For instance, dialogue, meaning making, and developing rational thought were considered fundamental to the democratic practice of schools. "While recommending the need to move away from a 'textbook culture' (where the textbook is seen as the only source of legitimate knowledge) towards a plurality of locally produced text materials, the NCF 2005 makes an important argument in favour of bridging gaps between the lived experiences of children and formal school knowledge" (Batra 2005, 4350).

Several new ideas articulated in NCERT's 21 position papers found prominent space in the NCF, 2005, document. Among these critical ideas were the changing role and notion of citizenship, inclusion of gender as a critical perspective in developing school curriculum, and foregrounding diversity as the key principle in designing curriculum. Bhattacharya (2009, 106) states how this opportunity was taken to "problematise the idea of the nation in a variety of ways... to underline the multiplicity of histories and narratives... and to emphasise that there is no single linear narrative."

The curriculum perspective foregrounded the agency of the child and the teacher in co-constructing knowledge. It brought into focus issues of multiple sources of knowledge and the significance of incorporating local knowledge in school curriculum. Texts portrayed people and children of different castes, class, religion, languages, and communities. The learner was no longer an abstract notion out of a psychology text, but one with an identity and a sociocultural context. The curriculum emphasized learning as social activity and teaching as social practice. Where the individual child was important, the social context from where children came was equally important. The schooling process was to address the knowledge that children bring with them as a legitimate part of classroom discourse.

The NCF, 2005, faced serious debates around ideological positions. While the bulk of the post-NCFSE 2000 debates were targeted against the Hindu Right that claimed legitimacy of religion in the educational space, the post-NCF, 2005, debates pivoted around ideas of local knowledge, child-centered constructs, and the pedagogic frame of constructivism. Many left-leaning objections were raised against the idea of multiple textbooks and the inclusion of local knowledge in school curriculum. This was perceived as obscurantist and likely to run the risk of religious forces entering school curriculum (Habib 2005). Critics of constructivism raised concerns about the notion of constructivism as a homogenous category and more fundamental questions of defining knowledge (Saxena 2006).

The NCF, 2005, vision, it was argued, is based on several assumptions about teachers. First, that schoolteachers would be able to negotiate the challenges of a diverse classroom and "include, excluded social narratives, experiences and voices and make them available in the classroom" (Batra 2005, 4349). Second, that schoolteachers would be able to transcend the compulsions of a "textbook culture" to encourage the use of multiple sources of knowledge in the absence of adequate engagement with questions of knowledge during teacher preparation. Third, that schoolteachers are familiar with the nuanced debates[17] around child-centered education, the frame within which the post-NCF, 2005, textbooks are designed and teachers are expected to transact.

Subramaniam (2003), for instance, recalled "the firmness with which Gondi tribal parents rejected the idea of teaching their children in Gondi language in their first years of schooling." They insisted that their children be taught English and Hindi. This speaks volumes about a community that may not have literacy skills but understands well what is good for their children in terms of social mobility and employment. The problem with school curriculum had been erroneously perceived to be only that of being in dissonance with the developing child. The significant strength of the new NCERT texts is the manner in which knowledge is presented and connected to the lived realities of children's sociocultural milieu. The real problem was one of engaging teachers with the nuanced debates on issues of child-centered and constructivist approaches as well as the politics of knowledge selection and presentation.

## The Cultural Underpinnings of School Curriculum

Undoubtedly one of the more important positions taken by the NCF, 2005, is the critical contextualization of curriculum. While some perceived this to be similar to the position taken by NCFSE 2000, the difference in perspective is critical, as suggested by Paliwal and Subramanium (2006, 26). The NCFSE takes the position that contextualization is to be achieved through curricular materials. The NCF, 2005, places this responsibility on schoolteachers, hence implying a central role for the teacher in effecting a meaningful curriculum. This critical difference indicates a fundamentally different way of conceptualizing curriculum. Curriculum in the NCFSE frame implies "subject knowledge" that is selected and organized in a manner (contained in a textbook) that conveys the dominant cultural viewpoint. The process of contextualization through curriculum materials as in the NCFSE formulation renders knowledge and culture synonymous.

For the NCF, on the other hand, knowledge is central to school curriculum as it resides in textbooks *as well as* the manner in which it is co-constructed in the quotidian of teaching-learning. Knowledge in the NCF implies both the body of knowledge in a given discipline *and* its embeddedness and interpretation in the sociocultural frame of everyday cognition. Culture and knowledge are not one and the same. It can therefore be argued that while the role of contextualization in the NCFSE was to define curriculum in cultural terms, the role of contextualization in the NCF is to enable the construction of meaning in the classroom.

Toward this end the school textbooks developed post-NCF, 2005, present subject matter in a manner that opens up curriculum to the social and personal experiences of the learners. It is in forging this intimate link between textbook knowledge and social experiences that culture becomes a significant practice of meaning and not the dominant precept of thinking. Embedded in the sociocultural milieu, textbook knowledge is constructed, probed, and reconstructed. This is critical pedagogy. In this frame "culture" becomes a means of meaning making as well as an epistemological object for interrogation and reflection.

To translate this vision of school curriculum requires the use of complementary pedagogical processes in the preparation of teachers. This is the more difficult question in view of the fact that in India, the education of teachers has been frozen in the colonial frame. As argued by Paliwal and Subramanium (2006, 48), the only way to circumvent the dangers of the "irrational, the regressive and the unscientific" likely to be embedded in context is to develop teachers who are prepared to engage with contexts within the larger democratic frame. This clearly implies that the curricula and pedagogic approaches for the education of teachers need to be anchored in a discourse of critical theory and not merely in the practice of teaching as is widely believed. The role of teacher preparation in transforming school learning environments is, however, rarely recognized, since curriculum is essentially viewed as subject content and classroom practice as the effective delivery of this content. This chapter presents a counter viewpoint.

## Critiquing the Curriculum of Educating Teachers

As argued elsewhere,[18] teacher education institutions in India function as insular, "private" spaces akin to that of a "family." Elements of feudalism such as the Hindu ritual of invoking the divine to inaugurate academic events coexist with the public posture of a secular academic orientation. Cultural notions associated with childrearing, such as exercising authority and power over children, and the conviction that the aim of education is to change behavior define the contours of teacher preparation. Interactions between teacher educators and student teachers therefore assume the character of a cultural decree in which the "elder" patronizes and controls. The cultural gets manifested in the daily rituals of conducting the morning assembly; the prominent display of slogans and icons, and the formulation of "lesson plans" and "teaching aids" within predetermined frameworks. These rituals structure social relations, deeply socializing the teacher within intellectually insular environments.

In this frame, an effective teacher is one who can "control" children and socialize them in desirable ways of behaving. The larger cultural aim of education is to build character and morals. These popular notions about schooling form the dominant culture of teacher education institutions as they derive legitimacy from Tylerian constructs that dominate preservice education. Most teachers are trained to believe that they need to be judgmental about children and their learning, that they need to be in control. The NCFSE, in laying emphasis on a curriculum embedded in "Indian" culture, was in effect proposing an emulation of and thereby a convergence with the dominant culture of teacher education institutes.

The curriculum of preparing teachers must unfold processes that empower teachers. This necessarily includes engaging with a host of fundamental questions related to the nature of knowledge, the aim of education, and the conception of learners and learning. The capacity to reflect upon oneself, to develop an understanding of the social world, and to recognize the potential role of an educator in cultivating a change of consciousness and creating inspiration for learning are significant elements in this process.

Using the example of the Bachelor of Elementary Education (BElEd) Program, it is argued how teacher education can by design provide "learning spaces" that challenge popular assumptions and belief systems while paving the way for the expression of multitude modes of awareness and varied ways of constructing meaning. The principles that govern the structure of the four-year program can be broadly categorized as follows: interdisciplinary and transdisciplinary enquiry, dialogical interplay between theory and practice, deconstruction and reconstruction of school knowledge, engagement with constructs of human relations, the self and the practice of communication, and hands-on experience with creative and professional skills. Each of these helps engage with fundamental questions about the nature of knowledge, the nature of learner and learning, and the aim of education via critically designed components of the program in the overall aim to prepare teachers differently.

## The Curriculum of Preparing Teachers Differently

In the early 1990s a serious attempt was made by the University of Delhi to fundamentally alter the ways in which teachers are prepared. Extensive and intense engagement with university academics, teacher practitioners, and other professionals in education led to the design of a four-year integrated program of elementary teacher education. The key curricular provisions and pedagogic principles that were applied to design this program are highlighted in reference to the dominant patterns of training teachers.

Dominant patterns of teacher education include a strong emphasis on studying learning theories without adequate reference to who the learner is. Focus on the learner is achieved through psychological theoretical frames that emphasize universal constructs and individual difference. Individualistic orientation is replaced in the BElEd via interdisciplinary engagement of teachers with issues of diversity and social difference. This engagement happens through a simultaneous engagement with children in "real" contexts in and out of school. Systematic deconstruction of universal concepts of children's development is sought via sociopsychological engagement (Burman 1994/2008), and the "neutral" foundations of the practice of teaching are challenged via sociological and feminists' constructs of knowledge and pedagogy (Apple 1993; Weiner 2006). The overarching psychological frame that forms the dominant subculture of teacher preparation is substituted by a deliberative discourse on the social context of teaching and learning. This breaks the false neutrality and "apolitical posture" within which teachers are usually prepared. Student teachers learn that school education is about matters of lived experience. Hence, they are in a position to problematize social realities they may wish to change (Batra 2009).

Typically teacher education programs make no provision to engage with subject knowledge. The BElEd is designed to engage teachers with the epistemological underpinnings of the school subjects they would be teaching. This includes debates about school curriculum and student teachers' assumptions and cultural beliefs about knowledge and learning. The pedagogic approach attempts to establish learning as a social process and teaching as social practice.

Practicum courses of theater, craft, and self-development, in particular, provide opportunities to engage with conflicts and beliefs that are embedded in society and that influence structure and constrain the actions of teachers and children in a learning environment. "The basic conceptual parameter is that drama is education, meaning thereby that it is one of the natural ways available to human species for learning about the world by playfully constructing it" (MACESE 2001, 55). Teacher practitioners who have undergone the BElEd hold that drama has helped them to explore "possibilities" and in creating them where none exists. Drama provides a context as well as a medium of learning for a shift in the notion of pedagogy and the "democratisation of classroom space." "Democratisation of classroom space, likened to Peter Brook's 'concept of space' which theatre creates, encompasses a gamut of dimensions starting from the physical classroom space, to the mental, individual, social and shared space" (Shivapriya 2004, 45). It creates a "learning space" that begins with the breaking down of power equations between the teacher and the taught, the adult and the child. This creation of a democratic learning space entails a shift in the notion of pedagogy and necessarily fosters the idea that knowledge is not transmitted but constructed actively within the shared context of learning. A "learning space" is bound to create, in Dewey's words, "occasions which are not and cannot be foreseen wherever there is intellectual freedom. They should be utilized...but with a discerning ability...to use them in the development of a continuing line of activity and not trusting them...to provide the chief material for learning" (1948, 96).

Exploring the self is a major thrust of drama and other components of the BElEd program. Drama helps to surface, acknowledge, and deal with attitudes, beliefs, and notions that impact learning. These may range from a teacher's personal notion of pedagogy and learning to prejudices and biases in relation to the larger socio-political reality. Drama throws open the possibility of catharsis, which when complemented with personal growth workshops carries immense therapeutic and educative value. Apart from addressing issues deeply personal in nature, these provide nonthreatening spaces for addressing social issues of gender, identity, exclusion, and injustice. These emerge within the processes of dramatic improvisations, text readings, poetry sessions, and personal sharing that enable student teachers to reflect on their own positions and develop deep feelings of empathy and social sensitivity.

Working in groups during drama and personal growth workshops and during presentations of seminars and field reports, students hone their skills of communication, interaction, classroom organization, and teamwork. A mix of theory and practicum, content and context provides teachers the opportunity to creatively negotiate the challenges posed by the education system steeped in tradition, habit, and authority. "Reflective action" begins with an awareness of the self that replaces "routine action." In the words of a student (MACESE 2001, 139), "These [self-development] workshops provided an opportunity to explore the self. We very distinctly understood how the socio-cultural context, in which we have grown up, has shaped our perceptions and attitudes. We became conscious of our biases and other influences, and develop sensitivity to their negative influences on teaching...resolving some of our conflicts, we began to honour each other's differences rather than being content with enjoying our commonalities."

Developing deep insight into the inner self and developing consciousness is a significant aim of preparing teachers differently. These aspects of the self continuously develop through an intense engagement with theory as well. The key factor for the success of the BElEd lies in the careful integration of experiences that challenge the "cultural self," its understanding of society and its envisioning the role of the collective in creating change. The experience of effecting the curriculum of the BElEd and engendering a new discourse led to the articulation of a persuasive National Curriculum Framework for Teacher Education (NCFTE) (National

Council for Teacher Education 2009) and model syllabi (National Council for Teacher Education 2011).

The articulation of curriculum as a deliberative act, reflected in the school curriculum (NCERT 2005) and the curriculum for teacher education (NCTE 2009), has been made possible through a series of deliberate processes that have characterized school education in the two preceding decades. These can be attributed to two momentous developments in the history of schooling in contemporary India. The first was a series of ideological attempts to shape school curriculum along "cultural" frames located in religion that ran contrary to India's Constitutional position on this question. The positive outcome of this was the active involvement of civil society groups in generating a public debate on questions of knowledge, school, and society that led to a judicial intervention in favor of Constitutional values. The second development was the generation of a small but significant community of professionals whose epistemic capacities were honed by progressive educational initiatives and teacher education programs. In response to the NDA government's imposition of the ideology of Hindutva via school textbooks several graduates and faculty of the University of Delhi's BElEd teacher education program participated in developing an elementary education curriculum for the state of Delhi in 2002. A critical discourse that emerged from this exercise[19] prepared the way for the NCF, 2005, influencing the future contours of school curriculum in India.

# The Individual and the Collective: Forging an Interface

That the aim of education is both the individual and the collective is not really a matter of debate. The problem lies in viewing the individual and society as opposing entities. Dewey (1915) asserted that an understanding of the child must begin with psychological insight into its nature that must continually be interpreted in terms of the "social." Recognizing that development does not follow an "isolated trajectory," Vygotsky (1978) believed that children are both natural and cultural entities; learning is grounded in the social medium in which they grow and the classroom is a collaborative community. Inherent in this perspective of a link between education and society is the acknowledgment of the "agency" of the teacher and child. Both Dewey and Vygotsky lay great emphasis on the crucial role of the educator. Looking back on his educational work of the 1960s and 1970s, Bruner (cited in Gardner 2004, 93) acknowledged how "it was taken for granted [at that time] that students lived in some sort of educational vacuum." Reviewing his own thinking on education, he later called attention to a belief in the active agency of the human being in the education process. Apple (2012) has called for the need to redefine the role of education and to bring back the role of schools as agents of transformation. Each of these thinkers carries an underlying conception of education as a process of reconstruction and transformation.

The process of reconstruction and transformation implies a breaking away from the hegemonic control of the dominating and powerful and moving toward an egalitarian social order for the common good. Curriculum for both students and teachers is perceived to be a critical agent in this process. In this perspective, the substantive agenda of educational theory and curricular practice is one of examining closely the relationship between school and society—how schools perpetuate or reduce inequality; how knowledge and curriculum are socially constructed; whose interests are served by education; and how power is produced and reproduced through education. Working on the lived experiences of students, the teacher is perceived to be critical in transforming the experience of domination to make the students "emancipated" participants in a full democracy.

Underlying such education is a conception of knowledge that is characterized by a dialectic between external (social constructions) and internal (reflective/searching within) forces. The assumption that an intellectual engagement with issues of knowledge, power, domination, and control is sufficient to bring about social transformation is erroneous. Theoretical frames of this nature rarely prompt educators to move beyond the intellect toward a wider and deeper engagement with the inner being of the teacher, such as her sense of identity, that also rests on the physical, the psychic, and the spiritual plane.

The idea of engaging with domains other than the mental is inherent in early Indian philosophical orientations to education. "The object of education" in the words of Tagore (1921, 126), "is to give man the unity of truth... (with) the separation of the intellect from the spiritual and the physical, school education puts the entire emphasis on the intellect...we devote our sole attention to giving children information, not knowing that by this emphasis we are accentuating a break between the intellectual, physical and spiritual life....We must make the purpose of our education nothing short of the highest purpose of man, the fullest growth and freedom of soul."

While articulating his conception of "integral education," Aurobindo (cited in Pavitra 1991, 52) stated, "Education to be complete, must have five principal aspects relating to the five principal activities of the human being: the physical, the vital, the mental, the psychic and the spiritual." He believed that a conception of education must necessarily be based on a clear conception of the true aim of human life, both individual and collective. In his words "[the] individual exists not in himself alone but in the collectivity...the free use of our liberty includes also the liberation of others and of mankind." This was the echo in Gandhi's concept of "*swaraj*," which entails the idea of freedom from an oppressive regime and from the fetters that incarcerate our inner selves.

# Conclusion

This chapter has attempted to engage with the changing discourse on school curriculum in India from preindependence to contemporary times. It has argued that the central conception of the school curriculum in each period is closely associated with the purpose of the educational project of the time. The educational project during the British colonial period was to produce clerks and subservient colonial citizens within the frame of nineteenth-century essentialist Anglicist education.

Several countermovements to this were initiated in the early twentieth century by nationalist leaders such as Aurobindo, Tagore, and Gandhi. They sought to liberate Indians from the shackles of colonial English education and create free citizens who could emancipate an India rooted in the diverse cultures of its people. Although these movements took root in different parts of the subcontinent, they were resisted by the colonial administration and sections of the upper-caste Indian elite, whose hegemonic control of the education system continued well after independence.

The postcolonial Nehruvian modernization project focused on creating the secular, socialist, and scientific citizen via an emphasis on higher education, science and technology, and planned development. The school system in general and the curriculum in particular remained within the clutches of the colonial educational frame and upper-caste imagination that had little reason to support the cause of mass education.

The first serious emphasis on mass education grew from the concern in the 1970s of addressing poverty and maintaining national integration through a curriculum narrative of "unity in diversity" and education of the obedient citizen who rises above narrow sectarian and regional concerns in defense of a nationalist state that was increasingly under siege.

The preparation for a modernizing India to transition into the twenty-first century and the first wave of economic liberalization created the grounds for state-led educational universalization along a new educational project of preparing productive citizens to contribute toward national economic development. This gathered momentum with the economic reforms of the 1990s and the entry of multilateral and bilateral agencies into India's school system for the first time since independence. With its focus on the learner as an object and the teacher as an agent of transmission of a state-led curriculum, it posed little challenge to the historical momentum of the now-decrepit colonial educational delivery system.

As the momentum gathered to universalize elementary education, the opportunity to capture ideological space in a polity increasingly fractured on caste and identity lines became clearer. The first serious attempt to create a cultural nationalist curriculum narrative was launched in the late 1990s, to give fillip to a long-brewing experiment of creating cultural nationalist citizens around a constructed homogenous historical, cultural, and majoritarian identity. This was seriously contested and struck down by the courts as violating the Constitution and obscuring the secular plural fabric of Indian society.

Civil society outrage and judicial intervention paved the way for the articulation of curriculum as a deliberative act in 2005. The contemporary educational project is framed in terms of creating an active citizen whose agency is recognized not only in the process of learning but in the process of bringing about social transformation as well. This constructivist curricular strategy uses contextualization to generate knowledge to challenge the regressive and narrow sectarian interpretation of culture.

The epistemological underpinnings of school knowledge and the centrality of the agency of the child and the teacher are seen to be critical to this constructivist curriculum project. It is based on several robust initiatives in school and teacher education that have tested and proved the pedagogic principles and approaches within mainstream education. Together these have created major conceptual shifts in the notions of the learner, knowledge, learning, and the purpose of education that have dramatically changed the process of teaching-learning in India and could be an important international exemplar.

The inherent challenge of this constructivist approach is that it is predicated not only on the agency of the learner, but also on that of millions of teachers who are immersed in the practice of folk pedagogy, and the maintenance of an instrumental system of education in which they have been passive intermediaries in the delivery of a centrally determined educational project. The education of the teacher and the teacher education curriculum has therefore turned a full circle to the early twentieth-century debates on the purpose of education as liberating social practice.

The context of curriculum in India therefore cannot be isolated from the question of the dominant educational project, its challenging countermovements, and the intent to universalize school education. In the contemporary Indian context, where universalization of school education even across gender barriers is underway, critical pedagogy is the first manifestation of the role of active citizenship in enabling much promised social transformation. For the first time, since the countermovements of the first nationalist educators, the curriculum frame allows for the active processes of deconstruction and reconstruction. In doing this it creates the space to challenge popular assumptions and beliefs embedded in culture and establishes its criticality in preparing educators.

This reflective engagement via the curriculum with the cultural self impels a discerning shift from the passive acceptance of social inequity to a syncretic response within a diverse and locally rooted society. The real challenge for contemporary and emerging curricula is to uphold the "idea of India" as a dynamic plural construct and not as a narrow, monolithic, and unchanging reality. To enable culture to act via a continuous process of meaning making requires curricula experiences that enable a dialectic engagement between social construction and inner reflection. India's contemporary school and teacher curricular project is poised at this historical inflection point.

# Notes

1. Marked by the transfer of power from the East India Company to the British Crown.
2. Kumar (2005, 72).
3. Shantiniketan was founded by Tagore in 1901 with the aim to locate a school amid nature.
4. The Swadeshi movement was part of the Indian freedom struggle that challenged the British Empire by following the principles of self-sufficiency (*swadeshi*). Its chief architects were Aurobindo Ghosh and Lokmanya Bal Gangadhar Tilak. This was a key focus of Mahatma Gandhi, who described it as the soul of Swaraj (self-rule).
5. Also referred to as Basic Education or the Wardha Scheme.
6. Jotirao Phule and Savitribai Phule were social reformers in Maharashtra who envisaged a society based on liberty, equality, and fraternity. They fought against the unjust caste system through the education of women and the lower castes, starting with a girls' school in August 1848.
7. Among the several other types are included madrasas based on ideas of Islamic education. Although there has been a process of modernizing the madrasa, several continue along traditional objectives in which religious texts remain the core curriculum.

8. Report of the Secondary Education Commission (1953), also known as the Mudaliar Commission Report was constituted in 1952 to enquire into the position of secondary education in India and suggest measures for its reorganization and improvement.
9. The 1986 policy on education also came 20 years after the first education policy of 1968.
10. BJP is the Bharatiya Janata Party, the political offshoot of the RSS (Rashtriya Swayamsevak Sangh) known for its Hindutva ideology. RSS uses schools and hence school curriculum as the vehicle for taking forward their political, ideological, and social agenda. For instance, the Vidya Bharati Shiksha Sansthan, established in 1978, opened schools in states with BJP in power. The BJP-led coalition government of the National Democratic Alliance (NDA) was in power at the center between 1999 and 2004 and is currently in power at the center since the last general elections in May 2014.
11. Carrying the legacy of the Hoshangabad Science Teaching Program (HSTP) initiated by Kishore Bharati, an NGO, Eklavya spread HSTP across the state of MP. The social science program in middle schools was their second most important educational innovation.
12. This section draws heavily from the documentation of the Eklavya social science program in Poonam Batra (ed) (2010).
13. For details, see Balagopalan (2003).
14. The preferred term used for teaching aids during the DPEP was Teaching-Learning Materials (TLM). A substantial amount of funds was allocated to developing TLMs during DPEP and SSA.
15. United Progressive Alliance (UPA I) refers to the first term of the coalition central government that came to power in the 2004 general elections.
16. This idea is reflected in the perspective outlined by the National Curriculum Framework, NCERT, 2005, pp. 2. Cited in Poonam Batra (2005).
17. Lisa Delpit (1995) for instance offers a nuanced critique of how constructs of child-centered education are of little value to educate children of black communities living in America.
18. See Batra (2014).
19. In response to attempts to impose the NCFSE (2000), the curriculum and textbooks for the state of Delhi were developed under the academic leadership of Krishna Kumar.

# References

Anitha, B. K. 2000. *Village, Caste and Education*. Jaipur: Rawat Publications.
Anyon, Jean. 1978. "Elementary Social Studies Textbooks and Legitimising Knowledge." *Theory and Research in Social Education* 6 (3): 40–45.
Anyon, Jean. 1979. "Ideology and United States History Textbooks." *Harvard Educational Review* 49 (3): 361–86.
Apple, Michael W. 1993. *Official Knowledge: Democratic Education in a Conservative Age*. London: Routledge.
Apple, Michael W. 2012. *Can Education Change Society?* London: Taylor and Francis.
Balagopalan, Sarada. 2003. "Understanding Educational Innovation in India: The Case of Eklavya." *Education Dialogue* 1 (1): 97–121.
Batra, Poonam. 2005. "Voice and Agency of Teachers: A Missing Link in the National Curriculum Framework." *Economic and Political Weekly*.
Batra, Poonam. 2009. "Teacher Empowerment: The Education Entitlement-Social Transformation Traverse." *Contemporary Education Dialogue* 6 (2): 121–56.
Batra, Poonam, ed. 2010. *Social Science Learning in Schools: Perspective and Challenges*. New Delhi: SAGE.

Batra, Poonam. 2014. "Problematising Teacher Education Practice in India: Developing a Research Agenda." *Education as Change* 18: S1, S5-S18. doi: 10.1080/16823206.2013.877358 . http://dx.doi.org/10.1080/16823206.2013.877358.

Batra, Poonam, and Geetha B. Nambissan. 2003. "Classics with Commentary: John Dewey's Experience and Education." *Education Dialogue* 1 (1) Monsoon: 122–36.

Bhattacharya, Neeladri. 2004. "Classics with Commentary: Tagore on School and University." *Contemporary Education Dialogue* 1 (2): 258–74.

Bhattacharya, Neeladri. 2009. "Teaching History in Schools: The Politics of Textbooks in India." *History Workshop Journal* (67): 99–110.

Bhog, Dipta, Disha Mullick, Purwa Bharadwaj, and Jaya Sharma. 2009. *Textbook Regimes: A Feminist Critique of Nation and Identity*. New Delhi: Nirantar.

Burman, Erica. 1994. *Deconstructing Developmental Psychology*. 2nd ed. London: Routledge.

Delpit, Lisa. 1995. *Other People's Children: Cultural Conflict in the Classroom*. New York: New Press.

Dewey, John. 1915. *School and Society*. Chicago: University of Chicago Press.

Dewey, John. 1948. *Experience and Education*. New York: The Macmillan Company.

Dhankar, Rohit. 2003. "The Notion of Quality in DPEP Pedagogical Interventions." *Education Dialogue* 1 (1) Monsoon : 5–34.

Eklavya Team. 2010. "Dynamics of Knowledge and Praxis: A View from the Field." In *Social Science Learning in Schools: Perspective and Challenges*, edited by Poonam Batra, 265–86. New Delhi: SAGE.

Gardner, Howard. 2004. "Howard Gardner on Jerome S. Bruner." In *Fifty Great Modern Thinkers on Education: From Piaget to the Present*, edited by Joy A. Palmer. London: Routledge.

Government of India. 1966. "Report of the Education Commission (1964–66): Education and National Development." New Delhi: Ministry of Education.

Habib, Irfan. 2005. "How to Evade Real Issues and Make Room for Obscurantism." *Social Scientist* 33 (9–10): 3–12.

Holmes, Brian, and Martin McLean. 1989. *The Curriculum: A Comparative Perspective*. London: Unwin Hyman Ltd.

Jain, Manish. 2004. "Civics, Citizens and Human Rights: Civics Discourse in India." *Contemporary Education Dialogue* 1 (2) Spring: 165–98.

Krishnamurti, Jiddu. 1953. *Education and the Significance of Life*. London: Victor Gollancz, Ltd.

Kumar, Krishna. 1992/2009. *What Is Worth Teaching?* 4th ed. New Delhi: Orient BlackSwan.

Kumar, Krishna. 2000. "The Problem." *Seminar* 493 (September).

Kumar, Krishna. 2005. *Political Agenda of Education: A Study of Colonialist and Nationalist Ideas*. New Delhi: Sage Publications.

Madan, Amman. 2010. "Civics Curriculum and Textbooks." In *Social Science Learning in Schools: Perspective and Challenges*, edited by Poonam Batra, 107–26. New Delhi: Sage Publications.

Marlena, Atishi. 2003. "The Politics of Portrayal: A Study of the Changing Depictions of Religious Communities and Practices in Indian History Textbooks." MA Thesis, Oxford: Oxford.

Maulana Azad Centre for Elementary and Social Education (MACESE). 2001. "Bachelor of Elementary Education Programme of Study." New Delhi: MACESE.

N. Shivapriya. 2004. "Drama in Teacher Education: An Evolving Perspective". MEd Dissertation, Delhi: Department of Education, University of Delhi.

Nambissan, Geetha B. 2000. "Dealing with Deprivation." *Seminar* 493.

National Council for Educational Research and Training (NCERT). 1975. "The Curriculum for Ten Year School: A Framework." New Delhi: NCERT.

NCERT. 1988. "National Curriculum for Elementary and Secondary Education: A Framework (NCESE)." New Delhi: NCERT.

NCERT. 1993. "Learning without Burden: Yashpal Committee Report." New Delhi: NCERT.

NCERT. 2000. "National Curriculum Framework for School Education (NCFSE)." New Delhi: NCERT.

NCERT. 2005. "National Curriculum Framework, 2005 (NCF)." New Delhi: NCERT.

National Council for Teacher Education (NCTE). 2009. "National Curriculum Framework for Teacher Education: Towards Preparing Professional and Humane Teacher."

National Council for Teacher Education. 2010. http://www.ncte-india.org/publicnotice /NCFTE_2010.pdf.

National Council for Teacher Education (NCTE). 2011. "Re-envisioned Two-Year Elementary Teacher Education Programme." NCTE.

Paliwal, Rashmi, and C. N. Subramaniam. 1992. "Ideology and Pedagogy." *Seminar* 400 (December): 33–35.

Paliwal, Rashmi, and C. N. Subramaniam. 2006. "Contextualising the Curriculum." *Contemporary Education Dialogue* 4 (1): 25–51.

Panikkar, K. N. 2001. "Whither Indian Education? Seminar Presentation at the National Convention against Communalisation of Education in Nalini Taneja (2001) National Convention against Communalisation of Education: A Report." *Social Scientist* 29 (9–10): 77–91.

Patnaik, Prabhat. 2001. "Seminar Presentation at the National Convention against Communalisation of Education in Nalini Taneja (2001) National Convention against Communalisation of Education: A Report." *Social Scientist* 29 (9–10): 77–91.

Pavitra. 1991. *Education and the Aim of Human Life.* 5th ed. Pondicherry, India: Sri Aurobindo International Centre of Education.

Ramakrishnan, Venkitesh. 1998. "A Spreading Network." *Frontline* 15 (23): Webpage: www .flonnet.com/fl1523/15230100.htm.

Sarangapani, Padma. 2000. "The Great Indian Tradition." *Seminar* 493 (September).

Saxena, Sadhna. 2006. "Questions of Epistemology: Re-Evaluating Constructivism and the NCF 2005." *Contemporary Education Dialogue* 4 (1) Monsoon.

Setalvad, Teesta. 2001. "Seminar Presentation at the National Convention against Communalisation of Education in Nalini Taneja (2001) National Convention against Communalisation of Education: A Report." *Social Scientist* 29 (9–10): 77–91.

Subramaniam, C. N. 2003. "NCERT's National Curriculum Framework: A Review." *Revolutionary Democracy.* http://www.revolutionarydemocracy.org/rdv9n2/ncert.htm.

Tagore, Rabindranath. 1921. *Personality: Lectures Delivered in America.* London: Macmillan and Co. Ltd.

Thapan, Meenakshi. 2007. "Education and the Purpose of Living: The Legacy of J. Krishnamurti." *Contemporary Education Dialogue* 5 (1): 64–77.

The Plowden Report. 1967. "Children and Their Primary Schools: A Report of the Central Advisory Council for Education." London: Crown.

Tyler, Ralph. 1949. *Basic Principles of Curriculum and Instruction.* Chicago: The University of Chicago Press.

Vygotsky, Lev. S. 1978. *Mind in Society.* Cambridge. MA: MIT Press.

Weiner, Gaby. 2006. "Out of the Ruins: Feminist Pedagogy in Recovery." In *The SAGE Handbook of Gender and Education,* edited by Christine Skelton, Becky Francis, and Lisa Smulyan. London: Sage Publications.

# Chapter 2

## Schooling as Counter-Socialization
### Krishna Kumar's Contributions
### to Curriculum

*Mary Ann Chacko*

## Introduction

Krishna Kumar grew up in the town of Tikamgarh in the state of Madhya Pradesh (MP) in central India.[1] He pursued his higher education in the University of Sagar (Madhya Pradesh, India) and the University of Toronto (Canada) from where he earned a PhD in Education. He is a professor at the Central Institute of Education, University of Delhi, where he also served as its head and dean. In 2004, he was appointed director of the National Council of Educational Research and Training (NCERT), an autonomous body set up by the Government of India in 1961 to advise and assist central and state governments in improving the quality of school education. During his five-year tenure he oversaw the publication of the National Curriculum Framework (NCF 2005), a document that provides the framework for the development of school curricula, syllabi, textbooks, and teaching and assessment practices in India. NCF (2005) was unique in its design of the processes of nation-wide deliberation through which this document was developed. During his tenure, NCERT also undertook the publication of textbooks in all subjects for all levels of schooling.[2]

Krishna Kumar was also a member of the Yashpal Committee set up by the Government of India in 1993 to advise on improving the quality of learning while reducing the academic burden on school students. He has delivered numerous memorial lectures, including the Gladwyn Lecture in the House of Lords of the British Parliament. He was awarded the *Padmashri*, one of the highest civilian awards given by Government of India and was conferred an honorary DLitt. in Education by the Institute of Education, University of London. Kumar writes in English and Hindi. His books, which have also been translated into numerous Indian languages, include *Social Character of Learning* (1989), *Political Agenda of Education* (1991), *What Is Worth Teaching?* (1992/2009), *Learning from Conflict* (1996), *Prejudice and Pride* (2001a), *Raj, Samaj aur Siksha* (1978/1991), and *Shiksha aur Gyan* (1991). He has published in journals and newspapers including *Economic and Political Weekly*, *Comparative Education Review*, *Contemporary Education Dialogue*, *Seminar*, and *The Hindu*. Kumar has also written short fiction in Hindi.

# Curriculum: An Act of Deliberation

Krishna Kumar's contribution to education in India is grounded in his conception of curriculum. In *Learning from Conflict* (1996, 18) he describes curriculum as "a series of choices made under the demands placed by the social milieu on education and the constraints placed upon pedagogy by children's psychology and the conditions prevailing at school." This description underscores Kumar's attentiveness to the "power of [local] context," and the "ubiquitousness of interaction," including the interaction of teaching practices with student characteristics, school environment, and the macroenvironment—aspects that, according to David Berliner (2002), are among the distinguishing features of educational practice and research.

For Kumar (1992/2009), one of the disturbing features of India's educational culture is its reluctance to conceive of curriculum as a "problem." What does he mean by curriculum as a problem? It implies the necessity of being cognizant of curriculum's constructed nature, resultant of particular choices and decisions, which in turn can be challenged. In India, however, curriculum and the principles of curriculum development are regarded as "received knowledge" (see also Kumar 1983). Such mystification of curriculum deters us from inquiring into why "a certain body of information happens to be equated with education . . . [and encourages us] to shun our responsibility and allow ourselves to be governed by choices made long ago or elsewhere under very different circumstances" (1992/2009, 1–2). Kumar rejects the pretension of universal principles of curriculum design to insist that we shape an educational culture that is sensitive and responsive to the society and culture of the children we seek to educate.

In order to counter our myopia surrounding the processes and principles of curriculum design, Kumar (1992/2009, 13) proposes that we conceive of curriculum development not as "an act of social engineering" but as "an act of deliberation . . . based on the assumption that no voice will be wiped out." Unfortunately the Indian educational bureaucracy has never treated procedures of curriculum design as an act of deliberation, nor has there been an inquiry into the selective and elitist nature of knowledge embedded in the prevailing curriculum (Kumar 1983; 1992/2009). Kumar (1992/2009) visualizes curriculum deliberation as a "social dialogue" that will enable the curriculum to reflect societal concerns and issues. What is extant, however, is a "transcendental curriculum," marking a dissociation between schooling and society—an aspect that we often attribute and critique as a feature of curriculum in colonial India. The paradox, however, is that even to this day the sociocultural milieu continues to be perceived as "an obstruction rather than an asset for education" (Kumar 1992/2009, 16).

Krishna Kumar's commitment to deliberation was reflected in the process undertaken to develop the National Curriculum Framework (2005) during his tenure as director of NCERT (Srinivasan 2010; Kumar 2012). NCF (2005) was formulated through "intensive deliberations" enabled by the creation of 21 National Focus Groups comprising scholars from different disciplines, NCERT faculty, schoolteachers, and nongovernmental organizations. Conferences were organized to obtain the views of rural teachers, while public opinion was garnered through advertisements in national and regional newspapers (NCF 2005).

While Kumar's work, especially his *Political Agenda of Education* (1991), illustrates that colonial education in India had indeed damaged the interaction between school (dominated by religious instruction) and community that existed in precolonial India, his work also reminds us that if that bridge persists in a state of disrepair today, it is the result of the apathy of the postcolonial nation-state. Deeply inspired by Gandhian values of local self-reliance, imaginative action, and the significance of family and community for democratic living (Kumar 1992/2009), Krishna Kumar's work fires our imagination with his conceptualization of schooling as a force of "counter-socialization," reveals his commitment to the child whom he places at the center of the educational enterprise, and resounds with his critique of the debilitating impact of the market-oriented economy on schooling in India.

## Schooling as "Counter-Socialization"

While schooling has historically been one of the most favored instruments of socialization across cultures, it has been especially so in erstwhile colonies like India. Colonial investment in schooling was inspired not only by the need to produce cheap labor to assist colonial government, but also to garner the support of dominant sections of Indian society to the cause of the British Empire (Kumar 1991). While the British in India exercised their authority primarily through a rule of force (Guha 1989), ascertaining domination purely through violence and coercion was certain to jeopardize the empire's commercial interests. Socialization or "initiating the native into new ways of acting and thinking" (Kumar 1991, 24) made better economic sense. In other words, as advocated by the British intellectual Thomas Babington Macaulay in his infamous *Minute on Education* (1835), colonial funds for public instruction in India were better spent if deployed "to form a class who may be interpreters between us and the millions whom we govern,—a class of persons Indian in blood and color, but English in tastes, in opinions, in morals and in intellect" (para. 34). But even as colonial education helped gain support for the superiority of the colonial regime, it also produced some of the most vociferous critics of colonial rule in India. In fact, the contribution of Western education in producing national activists was viewed by the empire as a failure of colonial education in India (Parsons 2004). Thus we see that, even when intended as an instrument of socialization into the empire, colonial education was also instrumental in exposing the contradictions of colonialism thereby paving the way for resistance movements.

In postcolonial India schools continue to be regarded as ideal spaces for socialization. Socialization via schooling is often perceived as a "closed process...endorsed in the view that the school and community should be complementary to each other in socializing the young" (Kumar 1992/2009, 86–87). At the same time, schooling is touted as an instrument of social change. As a way out of this impasse, wherein schooling is simultaneously viewed as an agent of social preservation *and* social transformation, Kumar (1992/2009, 87) asserts that "we propose counter-socialization as the school's domain." He advances this proposition while dwelling on the worrisome process of "growing up male" in India.

Recollecting his own adolescence, Kumar (1992/2009) notes the separation of boys and girls in Indian society, also reflected in its schools. This separation is not just a literal one, as in the case of all-boys and all-girls schools, or the oppressive treatment of girl students by teachers and male students, but also symbolic, as illustrated by the total silence around sexual behavior and the stereotypical depictions of male and female characters in textbooks. Kumar proposes "counter-socialization" as a way of providing an alternative example of, in this case, the socialization of girls and boys in Indian society. He argues that,

> we need not see the school as an institution working in harmony with the community or the larger society in the matter of sex-role socialization. On the contrary, we need to perceive the school in conflict with the community's code of socialization. (1992/2009, 87)

## Schooling: A Site of Resistance

In *Prejudice and Pride* (2001a), Kumar describes his desire for schooling to be a "site of resistance." The school, Kumar (2010b) points out, is a delicately positioned social institution. On the one hand, school is an agency of the state, rendering schooling a battleground for ideological debates, especially in the face of the political instability and uncertainty suffered by many postcolonial nation-states. The state, however, does not exercise sovereign power within a nation-state, and encounters the limits of its interference into people's lives through, among other things, its interaction in the cultural sphere. This cultural sphere includes the primary sites of a child's socialization, such as the family and community, and in these sites the state's efforts to influence or alter cultural norms are often faced with stiff resistance by the communities. When Kumar calls upon schools to be domains of counter-socialization, he expects them to resist not only nationalistic renditions of society that impose a univocal story of the nation's progress but also those oppressive, culturally sanctioned norms that, as in the case of girls, ensure their subordination and exploitation. But Kumar (2001a) reminds us that any such possibility is dependent upon "the extent to which socialization at school stays aloof from, or even contradicts in certain matters, the primary socialization that takes place at home" (238). In short, schooling as counter-socialization entails resisting *and* compensating for the oppressive and elitist structures of knowledge and societal relations (Kumar 1992/2009).

Kumar's (1983) engagement with the educational experiences of Scheduled Caste (SC) and Scheduled Tribe (ST) students in Indian schools illustrates both the challenges as well as the necessity for schooling as sites of resistance and compensation. SCs include groups who were once regarded as "untouchables" in the Hindu caste system while STs are groups classified as such on the basis of various indicators including "primitive traits," distinctive culture, and geographic isolation (Ministry of Tribal Affairs). Both SCs and STs are on the government list of groups scheduled for protection and positive discrimination. Numerous commentators on the educational experiences of SC and ST students voice the concern that the assimilation of bourgeois values via schooling blunts the "radical consciousness of their oppression" (Kumar 1983, 1572) while also creating fissures between the educated and uneducated among these disadvantaged groups. However, on the basis of his analysis of classroom interaction between teachers and students, Kumar insists that the target of educational inquiry and critique should be the "demeaning educational experiences" (1983, 1572) that compel SC and ST students to drop out while internalizing the backwardness that society ascribes to them rather than the possibility of bourgeoization of a small minority of SC and ST students who might beat the odds to complete their schooling. The latter critique, according to Kumar, amounts to berating "the uselessness of education to bring about change" (1983, 1572), a futile exercise in itself.

The path that Kumar (1983, 1569) inspires us to pursue is to inquire into how curriculum as a microcosm of society succeeds in socializing children into the oppressive structures of society and thereby to find strategies by which schooling might counter them. These strategies, in the case of the above example of SC and ST students, do not entail a separate and "relevant" curriculum for SC and ST students, nor the mere addition of SC and ST characters in textbooks. Rather they should expose students to "the encounters of the oppressed with their existential and social reality" (1983, 1569) and permit the examination of curricular strategies of social control "from the viewpoint of those whose interests are either overlooked or manipulated by the curriculum through distorted presentation" (1983, 1571). In a manner reminiscent of Freire (1970/2008), Kumar suggests that oppressive structures in society dehumanize everyone and hence cease to remain, in this case, an SC/ST "problem." He writes:

> The worst weakness of the prevailing curriculum is not that it is unsuitable to the specific needs of SC or ST children, but rather that it provides a distorted view of social reality to *all* children. The problems of SC and ST children cannot be solved by changing their vision and allowing the vision of the rest of children to remain what it is today. What is needed is a change in the picture of society that education offers to all children. (1983, 1571)

In his notion of schooling as a domain of counter-socialization, Krishna Kumar might be said to be drawing inspiration from Mahatma Gandhi, whose views on the reorganization of society, especially via education, finds a prominent place in Kumar's work. Gandhi proposed his philosophy of basic education or *nai talim* (new education) as an alternative to the colonial model of state-centric education.

Infused with Gandhi's conviction about the desirability of local self-reliance (Kumar 1992/2009), school were envisaged as financially viable institutions by being linked to material production. Kumar's work (1991; 1992/2009; 2005) explores the numerous implications of linking schooling to production. By making a skill involving material production, such as the production of traditional handicrafts, as the motif of educational experience, Gandhi envisioned a pedagogy that would utilize the child's immediate milieu as a resource, thereby ensuring that "classroom activities... resonate and extend the child's life at home and in its surroundings" (Kumar 1992/2009, 113). Such a pedagogic strategy also validates the knowledge of the community as accepted knowledge while guaranteeing that learning entails physical activity.

Apart from reforming schooling to make it child-centered, linking schooling to production also envisaged a sociopolitical transformation of society. First, an economically useful and socially committed school "was supposed to contribute towards the realization of Gandhi's ultimate social ideal of a nation capable of sustaining its population in modest prosperity and governing itself without the help of the state's coercive force" (Kumar 1991, 113). Second, and of great significance to our discussion of education as counter-socialization, by envisaging schooling as centered around a traditional skill, "Gandhi was in effect proposing a radical change in the school's symbolic role vis-à-vis the culture of society" (Kumar 1991, 114). Traditional skills involving material production have been the domain of the lower and untouchable castes, and basic education implied giving those so-called lowly skills the legitimacy of worthwhile knowledge. Gandhi's "social radicalism" (Kumar 1996), however, was not welcome in a newly independent India. Racing to modernize India through rapid industrialization meant that few had patience for "the political economy of the charka [spinning wheel] and its pedagogy... [aiming] at enhancing the stamina and power of the oppressed masses *before* the arrival of advanced tools of production" (Kumar 1992/2009, 92). Instead, the humanist pedagogical agenda of Indian educators like Gandhi, Tagore, Gijubhai, and Krishnamurti was sidelined to make space for the "mechanical devices retailed by American behaviorists" (Kumar 1996, 3). Moreover, Kumar (1983) also suggests that the low social status of the groups associated with these skills ensured the "failure" of basic education.

The fate of basic education in India is ample proof of the fact that deploying education as an agent of social transformation is easier said than done. For one, the success of an educational innovation requires a supportive socioeconomic, political, and ideological environment (Kumar 1992/2009; 2005). That said, having served as the director of NCERT, Krishna Kumar (Srinivasan 2010; Kumar 2012) is acutely cognizant of the fact that political support, which morphs into "political interference," can be a hurdle for academic leadership and reform. Apart from a supportive environment, the call to transform society also necessitates reconceptualizing the internal workings of the educational system, including the process of curricular decision making, teacher training, and teacher autonomy (Kumar 1992/2009). For instance, in the light of Kumar's views that the separation between girls and boys in Indian society is exacerbated by the stereotypical portrayal of female characters in textbooks, it is important to note that one of the various reforms undertaken by the NCERT under Kumar's directorship was to develop a reading series that "marks a departure in the prevailing concept of children's literature, especially in how it handles cultural diversity and gender stereotypes" (Srinivasan 2010, para. 18). And finally, the success of education and especially schooling envisaged as counter-socialization will greatly depend on our views of the young as learners, a central preoccupation of Kumar's work.

## Centering the Child in the Curriculum

The Indian propensity to overlook recommendations for curriculum reform compels Krishna Kumar (2001a) to suggest that education of children is a low priority in India. In *Prejudice and Pride* (2001a), a study inspired by escalating bitterness in Indo-Pak relations, Kumar explores the contribution of schooling, especially of history textbooks, in socializing youth into this unrelenting hostility between the two countries. Examining curriculum policy regarding history textbooks in India and Pakistan, the narrative strategies deployed by the school historians, and the organization of content—both what is present and absent, and the conceptual leaps students are expected to make—Kumar (2001a, 245) argued, they not only underscore the "trivialization of history" but also our "indifference to the child's own intellectual effort, and the manner in which children approach social and historical knowledge" (2001a, 105).

### Learning from Conflict

One of the curricular spaces was this indifference to children, to their everyday realities as well as their anxieties and curiosities, most explicitly evident in the ways in which schools, teachers, and textbooks skirt the discussion of social conflicts raging in society. In *Learning from Conflict* (1996) Kumar narrates a poignant example of this tendency. The assassination of the Indian prime minister Indira Gandhi by her Sikh bodyguards in 1984 unleashed a violent backlash against the Sikh community in northern India, especially Delhi. Sikhs were murdered with impunity, a brutality, which Kumar points out, was witnessed by thousands of children. Yet, when the schools reopened after the riots, principals were asked to ensure that children did not discuss the riots in their classes. The same week Kumar was in a school observing one of his student teachers teaching a sixth-grade English lesson. One of the tasks the trainee gave her students was to form sentences with the verb "arrive," a word in the day's lesson. The students were then called upon to share their sentence and one of them read out the following: "When a Sikh arrived in Delhi, he was killed by Hindus" (quoted in Kumar 1996, 6). In the teacher's stunned silence Kumar (1996, 7) evocatively reads the dilemma of having to choose between "fulfilling the role of a teacher as defined by the institutional norms of the system of education, and fulfilling the expectations woven into the concept of a teacher which underlies the philosophy of education."

Besides a reluctance to "politicize education," institutional norms that suppress the discussion of social conflict presume that children should not be exposed to traumatic events. For Kumar (1996; 2001a), however, all educational activity is always already political and ideological while the reluctance to discuss traumatic events with children reveals the isolation of classrooms from children's everyday life and the education system's lack of understanding regarding the socialization of children. Attending to the world from which children come to school is the first step to recognizing and assessing the school's role as a domain of counter-socialization.

The child in the above example gained his knowledge of Hindu-Sikh riots not from a textbook or a teacher but from the out-of-school environment; by word of mouth from his family and community. When schools deny entry to such knowledge, it not only creates a conflict between school knowledge and the knowledge acquired through socialization at home (Kumar 2001a), but it also increases the possibility of school knowledge being merely associated with knowledge that is required to successfully pass examinations (Kumar 1996). Kumar finds the latter trend especially disturbing in the case of India, where school textbooks, especially history textbooks, are overwhelmingly written from a self-consciously secular perspective; one that is under threat from the increasing popularity of Hindu revivalist organizations. The problem with this self-consciously secular stance into which schools try to socialize the young is that in their commitment to present secularism as a distinguishing feature of the Indian nation-state, this "secular 'received' perspective...ignore[s] the oral lore of Hindu-Muslim [or Hindu-Sikh] relations altogether" (Kumar 1996, 21). The paradox here is that this deliberate denial of the "rival perspective" sharpens its legitimacy as cultural truth (Kumar 1996), while the erasure of the contest of values and ideologies in the received perspective makes it pedagogically barren (Kumar 2001a).

According to Kumar, decades of statist propagation of secularism through education was ineffectual in countering the rise of religious revivalism in India because while education in India is used to propagate secularism through textbooks, "a credible attempt to use education as an agency of socialization and training in secular thought was never made" (1992/2009, 95). Secular training, as envisaged by Kumar (1992/2009; 1996; 2001a) would involve allowing the learner to question the quasi-religious authority of the teacher and the textbook in the classroom, creating opportunities to gain insight into children's views and perspectives about their everyday realities that are "steeped in the consciousness of the other" (Kumar 2001a, 237) and appreciating the role of secularism "as an ideological tool" (Kumar 1992/2009, 98) and a mask used by the bourgeoisie as a symbol of their education and distance from the masses.

Krishna Kumar (2001a) insists that while nation building is a universal aim of educational systems across the world, one of the predicaments of education in newly independent postcolonial nation-states is that nation building and forging a national identity—such as the univocal story of India as a "secular" nation—tend to eclipse the pursuit of the intellectual aims of education, leaving education to become putty for ideological indoctrination. Kumar vehemently champions a curriculum that is sensitive and responsive to the social reality of the young. It is this conviction that makes him suspicious about an overwhelming dependence by states on a "national" framework for curriculum, teacher education, etc. Education in India is the joint responsibility of the central as well as state governments. While Kumar, as the director of NCERT, was actively involved in the design of NCF (2005), he envisaged states to develop their own curriculum frameworks with the NCF as a guideline. Kumar (Srinivasan 2010) viewed this process as imperative in the light of India's diversity, which not only makes the uniform application of a national system of education impossible, but also undesirable. Moreover, Kumar (1983; 1996) also worries that centralizing tendencies in curriculum development such as an unimaginative adherence to a national framework for curriculum design can reduce curriculum decision making to a "mechanical process of bureaucratic imposition" rather than "a matter of community dynamic" (1983, 1571). As long as curricular experiences fail to acknowledge community dynamics and refuse to introspect on the stratified, selective, and elitist nature of education, schooling will lose the ability to help children make sense of the world and instead impart to them a distorted view of society.

## Inhabiting a Divisive School System

One of the attributes of Indian schooling that Kumar holds responsible for social- izing children into a distorted view of society is the very structure of schooling in India. India's highly stratified school system can be broadly divided into govern- ment schools, government-aided schools, and private-unaided schools. Government schools are run by state governments, provide free education, and follow the state syllabus. The aided schools follow the state syllabus and are owned and managed by a nongovernmental or private agency, such as a religious organization, independent trust, etc. They appoint their staff as per government rules and regulations while the government pays for school maintenance and the salary of its teaching and non- teaching staff in return for subsidized education. Private-unaided schools are self- financing institutions free of government involvement.

For Kumar (1992/2009) the children attending school in this divisive system can be divided into two categories: "common" and "exclusive." "Common" refers to children of the poor and marginalized communities in urban and rural India, who depend on the state for their education while "exclusive" refers to children of white- collar middle-class parents who can "buy 'good quality' education for their chil- dren" (Kumar 1992/2009, 44) or are able to send their children to private schools. Despite the apparent expansion of schooling in India, Kumar (1992/2009) argues that this divisive school system is proof enough of India's "backward" and "narrow" educational culture.

Irrespective of the dearth of research on the comparative merits of government and private schools on indicators of quality like infrastructure, teacher performance, and parental involvement (Kumar 2005), scholars (Retnakumar and Arokiasamy 2006; Nambissan 2012) have noted the increasing growth of private schools in India and the abandonment of government schools, primarily by, but not limited to, upper- and lower-urban middle class. This tendency has led to the overrepresentation of students from poor and marginalized communities including SCs, STs, and Muslims, in government schools across India (Nambissan 2012) while states like Kerala are witnessing the proliferation of "uneconomic" government schools or schools where the total strength has fallen below 50 students (Economic Review 2011). The exodus of students from government to private schools is taking place in a discursive context wherein government schools are declared "dysfunctional" while private, fee-demanding schools are associated with "quality" (Kumar 1996; 2005; Nambissan 2012). If there is a consensus among scholars on the reasons for the increasing popularity of private schools in India, it is regarding the provision of English in these schools. Unlike in government and government-aided schools where instruction is carried out in the regional language, with English being introduced as a subject in class/grade five, private schools have English as their medium of instruction and teach English as a subject from grade one. Kumar's assessment of the divisive school system, especially the provision of English, offers a radical and insightful perspective on its pedagogic and sociocultural implications for all young learners.

Competence in English in India, as Kumar (1996, 59) points out, is not only a status symbol but also, unfortunately, a "synecdoche, a socially understood short-hand, for general ability." The siphoning off of middle-class students from government schools by private schools, offering what Kumar (1996) dubs as "immersion programs" in English, means that children attending schools in India are divided along class lines. This overrepresentation of marginalized communities in government schools entails that the parents of children attending these schools do not often have the sociocultural capital to influence the school's functioning. These schools have also been witnessing a decline in their upkeep and standards of state funding and a corresponding demoralization in the teaching staff and principals. As Kumar (1996, 62) reminds us:

> In its worst form, the cynicism of the state school teachers is directed towards children of the most deprived sections of society... [who] get caught in the vicious cycle of the self-fulfilling prophecies... [adding to] the reproductive nature of our divided school system.

Under these circumstances it is natural for someone to wonder, as I did, why government schools in India do not introduce English and thus try to prevent decreases in enrollment. In 2010, I visited a government school in my home state of Kerala, India. It was an upper primary school (grades one to seven) with a large playground and well-ventilated classrooms. According to the principal and the teachers, this school had seen better days. In 2010 it was a school struggling to find students. The previous summer teachers had gone from door to door in low-income households seeking to convince parents to send their children to this free but Malayalam (the regional language of the state) medium school. The teachers told me that even poor families, with parents who worked as daily wage laborers, domestic servants etc, aspired to send their students to English-medium schools even though they were fee-charging. The decision of various state governments to delay the introduction of English to later grades in state-funded schools might be an ideological decision, influenced by India's colonial history and the status of English as the colonizer's tongue, and, especially in the case of states like West Bengal and Kerala, with a long history of leftist rule, intended to make instruction accessible to poor and rural children. Today, however, at a time when English in India has become synonymous with "quality" education and social mobility, this anticolonial and socialist move seems to have become a noose around these schools. In fact, the teachers I spoke to felt that the government was the worst enemy of the government schools, and that it was collaborating in the demise of these schools, a sentiment that Kumar (1996) notes. For Kumar, the solution does not lie in introducing English into government schools because, in his opinion, the qualitative difference attributed to government and private schools is not determined merely by the presence of English alone, but by the particular ethos of these respective schools.

The ethos of private schools that have a formative influence on their students include: an "arduously cultivated" institutional lore and traditions, the selective intake of students on the basis of "merit tests" (Kumar 1992/2009), a "full-blown exposure" to English including "symbolic material that exposes children to the stereotypes of European and American life" (Kumar 1996, 66), access to greater amount and better quality of curricular and other reading material owing to the greater number of publications in English (Kumar 1996), and an emphasis on competition and personal achievement (Kumar 1992/2009). Kumar's work consistently reminds us that the gains of private schools in the Indian context costs the young learner dearly because those very characteristics that make us attribute "quality" to a private school education are the very factors that ensure the "narrowness" of that experience.

The selectiveness of private schools ensures that its students socialize within a restricted environment that does not reflect social reality. For Kumar (1992/2009, 47), "when a school closes its door to the poor, it ceases to be part of the milieu." Moreover, he argues that the conscious attempts made by these schools to create a restrictive universe becomes a "pedagogical drawback" as it robs them of the possibility of using "their milieu as a learning resource" (1992/2009, 47). The dependence on English aggravates this alienation between school knowledge and the child's everyday world (Kumar 1991). This is so not only because English is not this child's mother tongue but also because the competence in English sought by these schools require students to acquire a "negative eligibility" vis-à-vis the regional languages, namely "a disdainful unfamiliarity" about literature and other aspects of the mother-tongue/regional language. An English-medium education gives the private school students the sociocultural capital to compete in a global economy while English reminds the government school child of her/his own "disability and risk of stagnation" (1992/2009, 72). Kumar (1996, 73) fears that, despite these allurements, private schooling condemns the Indian child

to living a kind of half-life…The children's ability to negotiate the knowledge of school subjects, to manipulate it in a cognitive sense, so as to make it a part of their construction of the world, is crippled by the school's monolingual instruction which is in a language with very limited resonance in the wider social milieu.

It is important to note here that Kumar is not advocating for an exorcism of English from Indian schools. Rather what he exhorts us to resist is the temptation to provide a divisive and distorted educational experience to the Indian child from the very beginning of his/her schooling. In other words, he wants children to receive a "common" elementary schooling rooted in their social milieu during the formative years of their socialization, which will help safeguard the quality of education for all children while also preparing them to successfully counter what could otherwise be the alienating influence of an English-dominated educational experience in later years. Kumar (2005, 6) insists that any such plea for educational reform "with its emphasis on equality, dignity of the individual, and room for social justice" can attain fruition only if we find the means to reconceptualize the measures of quality that are currently in vogue in education; ones that are increasingly being determined by the market worthiness of investments in education.

## The "Quality Debate"

For Kumar (Kumar and Sarangapani 2004; 2005; 2010a), one of the most troubling aspects of the dominant discourse about "quality" in education is that, rather than viewing quality as a non-negotiable and essential characteristic of the educational process, educational quality is increasingly being determined by aspects that are not always integral to schooling. The increasing association of quality with privatization of education, as discussed above, is one such example. In the above example, both government and private school students have access to education, but those attending private schools are viewed as having access to a superior "quality" education. Here quality qua privatization is viewed as something that "adds value" to the educational process, paving the way for a hierarchical ordering of that experience.

Kumar and Sarangapani (2004) and Kumar (2005; 2010a) trace the contestation between "quality" as integral to education on the one hand, and as an additive on the other, to an unresolved tension arising from the different meanings of quality when it is applied to education. For quality, as Kumar (2010a, 8) points out, has two meanings, "the first meaning refers to the essential attribute with which something may be identified, and the second meaning refers to the rank or superiority of one thing over another." With globalization and liberalization of economy and the concomitant privatization of social services such as education, the latter meaning of quality is increasingly gaining currency with a distinction made between "education of a certain quality from one which signifies no more than token access to a service provided by the state or non-government agency" (Kumar 2005, 6–7). Moreover, this dichotomy between access and quality exposes yet another tension— that between "equality" and "quality." It suggests that while universalization of educational access might seek equality by countering the ancient and medieval status of education as an elite privilege, "equality can only nurture quantity, while quality would require regulation of equality" (Kumar 2010a, 11). In Kumar's assessment, globalization and the ascendancy of neoliberal policies and practices as well as the influence of international aid agencies on the discourse of educational quality in the developing world has exacerbated these tensions.

## The Access-Quality Dichotomy

For Kumar the dichotomy between access and quality as described above illustrates the degrading effects of aid-driven reform in the Third World. Such reform is not only driven by "the dominance of a 'Western' definition of what constitutes a good education in the rest of the world" (Kumar and Sarangapani 2004, 40) but also by "the popular perception that the time to focus on quality issues has arrived because access goals have been more or less achieved as far as the primary part of the elementary level of education is concerned" (Kumar 2010a, 9). As has been pointed out by others, including the sociologist Andre Beteille (see Kumar 2005), the nature of such aid-driven reform indicates a normalization of the notion that universalization of education need not guarantee quality. Further, these reform efforts are marked by a culture of "haste" whereby institutions like the International Monetary Fund set "dates by when developing countries must reach certain goals" (Kumar 2010a, 9) with dire consequences for any delay that might be incurred. This, in turn, has led to the adoption of short-term goals in education with detrimental effects on the quality of schooling and the professionalization of teachers.

One such short-term goal is the introduction of para-teachers in government schools across India. The unprecedented expanse of the Indian educational system is said to have created an increasing demand for teachers that is to be met by para-teachers. Para-teachers are locally recruited on contract basis, earn less than permanent staff, and undergo only a basic and token teacher training. Kumar (2001b) perceives the phenomenon of para-teachers as a classic site illustrating the shift in public policy and the diminishing role of the state in social services like education, changes influenced by structural adjustment programs seeking accelerated growth in priority areas like education. Besides aggravating the low-status of teachers in India (Kumar 1991; 2005), Kumar (2010a, 14) worries that such short-term, minimalist goals are oblivious to their possible long-term damage, especially considering that "education works in rather long time-horizons, both in the lives of individuals, and more so, in the life of collectives defined by caste, class or gender."

## Looking inside the Black Box

Another troubling feature of the dominant conception of quality in education, according to Kumar and Sarangapani (2004), is the tendency to view schooling as a "blackbox." A blackbox is a device understood in terms of its input and output; its internal operations remain unknown or unspecified. One of the popular indicators of educational quality is pupil achievement on test scores as indicated by the Program for International Student Assessment (PISA), which evaluates school systems in different countries of the world on the basis of their students' performance on assessments in "key subjects"(PISA website), that is, reading, math, and science. In other words, PISA assesses the quality of school systems not only on the sole basis of outcome measures such as test scores but also through a narrow focus on cognitive abilities in select and economically viable subjects. Such assessments of educational quality treat schools like a black box by overlooking the social foundations of education (Kumar and Sarangapani 2004; Kumar 2005) in their fixation with "outcomes," "results," "accountability," and "transparency" (Kumar 2010a).

While Kumar and Sarangapani (2004) admit that this unprecedented focus on educational quality has drawn attention to much neglected aspects of educational planning in countries like India, they worry that rather than looking inside the "black box" of schools and classrooms where the answers to most education dilemmas lie, these "quality" debates have been overwhelmingly influenced by an outcome-based, instrumentalist approach to education. In order to ensure that the conceptions of educational quality are attentive to the intrinsic features of the educational process, Kumar and Sarangapani (2004, 42) insist that the philosophical aims of education, as well as sociological studies like those of Basil Bernstein, Pierre Bourdieu, and Michael Apple, "which opened the black box of the school to look into the classroom, at pedagogic relations, the symbolic character of school knowledge, and the deeper effects of institutional culture," be brought to the table so as to "build on reform ideas that take into account the socio-economic and political context of education, directing policy attention to systematic reconstruction for the improvement of quality." Kumar (2012) argues that in a country like India this can happen only by repairing the alienation between academia and the state and by ensuring that stakeholders in education including university faculty, schoolteachers, students, nongovernmental organizations, and activists play an active role in the educational planning process.

While Kumar emphasizes that equality is integral to educational quality, his characteristic commitment to the young makes him weary of any mechanical treatment of equality and quality. His views on the matter are expressed most cogently in his examination of the pedagogical implications of the differential socialization of girls and boys in Indian society (Kumar 2010b). National reports (Kishore and Gupta 2009) point out that India has achieved "gender equality" in school attendance in urban areas, while the implementation of "child-centered" pedagogy is often viewed as an indicator of educational quality. Kumar (2010b) insists that closing the gender gap in education or implementing child-centered practices in classrooms will not trouble patriarchal gender norms if schools fail to address the cultural forces that differently shape "growing up male" and "growing up female" in India. For instance, how does one implement child-centered pedagogy, which calls for all students to be agentic and exploratory, in a society where girls are brought up to be dependent, self-effacing, restrained, and submissive? Kumar (2010a 16) argues:

> It is necessary to look at equality in the context of each individual's own unique way of growing. Universality cannot mean uniformity, even to a limited degree, if equality is to be treated as an aspect of quality in a characteristically educational way.

Kumar (2010b) admits that troubling patriarchal gender norms that prevail in society by designing schools to be sites that resist oppressive forces of culture and socialize the young to be otherwise won't be easy. This is so not only because it requires schools to take on the forces of culture but also because the school and its curriculum are a microcosm of this patriarchal culture. Added to this is the fact that globalization and the liberalization of economy have aroused fears of unimpeded

Westernization in the cultural realm, which has strengthened the grip of patriarchy over girlhood. On the other hand, neoliberal policies use girlhood as a site for intensifying women's participation in consumer culture. The resultant commodification of girls' bodies and sexuality has, in turn, engendered new forms of patriarchal control. Despite these difficulties, Krishna Kumar is not one to "berate the uselessness of education to bring about change" (1983, 1752). A die-hard believer in the ability of education to reform itself through innovation, Kumar (2010b, 84) finds here, and in other educational dilemmas, the opportunity for social scientists to reassess the "agency of education as a social process."

# Conclusion

I was introduced to Krishna Kumar's work when my friend Ashwani Kumar (no relation) gifted me the *Political Agenda of Education* (1991) in 2010. That book, and every other work by Kumar that I have read since, never fails to grip me with its intimate understanding of the experiences of schoolgoing children, teacher trainees, and schoolteachers in India. As a graduate of Indian schooling and teacher education program as well as a former teacher in an Indian school, I find Kumar's nuanced engagement with the everyday lived experiences of these three stakeholders in education one of the most compelling aspects of his work. Any examination of Krishna Kumar's contribution to curriculum will necessarily be an incomplete project because Kumar is an educationist who has engaged with almost every aspect of schooling in India. One unique aspect of this engagement, and one to which this chapter has not been able to do justice, is the historical consciousness that pervades his work; expressed through the ways in which he traces the historical character of educational aims and dilemmas, such as the role of textbooks and examinations as "instruments of control" and the low esteem and status of teachers, in order to examine schooling and curriculum in the present. Rather than proposing to shed light on all the topical concerns that pervade Kumar's work, the three themes that I have explored in this chapter—schooling as counter-socialization, centering the child, and quality debate—have attempted to attend to the substance and spirit of his remarkable work. In my assessment it is work that engages with education holistically and not in terms of narrow "research interests," making Krishna Kumar a key educational philosopher for our time.

# Acknowledgments

I am deeply indebted to Professor William Pinar for patiently guiding me through this project. I would not have written this chapter but for my friend Ashwani Kumar who introduced me to this book project while also suggesting that I explore the work of Krishna Kumar in my chapter. My friends Shenila Khoja-Moolji, Leya Mathew, and Mosarrap H. Khan set aside their work to read and enrich mine. Also, I owe gratitude to my dad, Mr. P. I. Chacko, who would call me every day from India to inquire into the progress of this chapter.

# Notes

1. Kumar provides us a fascinating glimpse into his schooling and boyhood in his piece *Growing up Male* (1992/2009).
2. That the drafts of these textbooks were reviewed by a National Monitoring Committee was an unprecedented development in the 150 years of textbook publishing in India.

# References

Berliner, David C. 2002. "Comment: Educational Research:The Hardest Science of All." *Educational Researcher* 31 (8): 18–20.

Freire, Paulo. 1970. *Pedagogy of the Oppressed*. New York: Continuum.

Government of Kerala. 2011. *Economic Review 2011*. Trivandrum: State Planning Board.

Guha, Ranajit. 1989. "Domination without Hegemony and Its Historiography." In *Subaltern Studies VI: Writings on South Asian History and Society*, edited by Ranajit Guha, 210–309. Delhi: Oxford University Press.

Kishor, Sunita, and Kamla Gupta. 2009. *Gender Equality and Women's Empowerment in India*. International Institute for Population Sciences.

Kumar, Krishna. 1983. "Educational Experience of Scheduled Castes and Tribes." *Economic and Political Weekly* 18 (36/37): 1566–72.

Kumar, Krishna. 1991. *Political Agenda of Education: A Study of Colonialist and Nationalist Ideas*. New Delhi: Sage Publications.

Kumar, Krishna. 1992a. "Growing up Male." In *What Is Worth Teaching?* by Krishna Kumar, 81–88. New Delhi: Orient BlackSwan.

Kumar, Krishna. 1992b. *What Is Worth Teaching?* New Delhi: Orient BlackSwan.

Kumar, Krishna. 1996. *Learning from Conflict*. New Delhi: Orient Longman.

Kumar, Krishna. 2001a. *Prejudice and Pride: School Histories of the Freedom Struggle in India and Pakistan*. New Delhi: Penguin Books.

Kumar, Krishna. 2001b. "The Trouble with 'Para-Teachers.'" http://www.frontlineonnet .com/fl1822/18220930.htm.

Kumar, Krishna. 2005. "Quality of Education at the Beginning of the 21st Century: Lessons from India." *Indian Educational Review* 40 (1): 3–28.

Kumar, Krishna. 2010a. "Culture, State, and Girls: An Educational Perspective." *Economic and Political Weekly* 45 (17): 75–84.

Kumar, Krishna. 2010b. "Quality in Education: Competing Concepts." *Contemporary Education Dialogue* 7 (1): 7–18.

Kumar, Krishna. 2012. "Quality Constraints in Education: Fallout of the Cartoon Controversy." *Economic and Political Weekly* 47 (22): 12–13.

Kumar, Krishna, and Padma. M. Sarangapani. 2004. "History of the Quality Debate." *Contemporary Education Dialogue* 2 (1): 30–52.

Macaulay, T. B. 1835. "Minute on Education." http://www.columbia.edu/itc/mealac /pritchett/00generallinks/macaulay/txt_minute_education_1835.html.

Ministry of Tribal Affairs. "Definition." http://tribal.gov.in/index3.asp?subsublinkid=303 &langid=1.

Nambissan, Geetha B. 2012. "Private Schools for the Poor: Business as Usual?" *Economic and Political Weekly* 47 (41): 51–58.

National Council for Educational Research and Training (NCERT). 2005. "National Curriculum Framework 2005." New Delhi.

Parsons, Timothy H. 2004. *Race Resistance and the Boy Scout Movement In British Colonial Africa*. 1st ed. Athens: Ohio University Press.

Retnakumar, Janakumaran Nair, and Perianayagam Arokiasamy. 2006. "Explaining School Enrolment Trends in Kerala, India." *Journal of South Asian Development* 1 (2): 231–48.

Srinivasan, Meera. 2010. "It Was a Remarkable Experience Protecting Academic Integrity from Political Attacks: An Interview with Krishna Kumar." *The Hindu*. March 4. http://www.thehindu.com/opinion/interview/article139044.ece.

# Chapter 3

## An Intellectual History and Present Circumstances of Curriculum Studies in India

*Suresh C. Ghosh*

### Introduction

As an academic discipline in education, curriculum studies is a very recent phenomenon. Its marked emergence after 1986 could be attributed to the socioeconomic disorder and political instability in India after the death of our first prime minister, Jawarharlal Nehru, in 1963. His death first led to the splitting of the Indian National Congress party[1] in 1969 when his daughter, Indira Gandhi, was the prime minister of the country and, later, to the declaration of Emergency by her in 1977 when the Allahabad High Court declared her election to the Lok Sabha (Lower House of the Indian Parliament) null and void. A period of non-Congress coalition government followed at the center[2] after the lifting of the Emergency, which ended with the return of Indira Gandhi to power in the general elections of 1980. Four years later, when Indira Gandhi was assassinated by the rebel Khalistan group in the Punjab, the education system was singled out as the "whipping boy" for all the ills of contemporary Indian society.[3] Indira Gandhi's son and successor, Rajiv Gandhi, won the general elections held in 1984. Riding on the sympathy wave after the assassination of his mother, he tried to reform education through the promulgation of the New National Policy on Education in 1986. Prior to that year, curriculum was never seriously studied either by our politicians or by our intellectuals, although most of us agree that our failure to adjust the curriculum inherited from the British Raj (Administration) in 1947 was one of the major factors for the socioeconomic and political disorder of the country.

The curriculum—associated with Western education and the centrality of science had been introduced by the British, between 1835 and 1854, to suit their own imperial needs and requirements—had initially nothing to do with the needs and aspirations of the Indian people who now included those Muslim ruling classes displaced by the former. In fact it bears a strong similarity to the one imported by the Muslim rulers when they set up their own rule in the country from 1206 onward. From then—until recently—we have followed a curriculum imposed on us by our rulers. Yet, for centuries from 1500 B.C.—prior to the coming of Islam—our Aryan sages had developed from our religious scriptures a curriculum taught in the Vedic schools and the Buddhist viharas, which answered all the needs and requirements of our Aryan ancestors and contributed to the development of a civilization which rose to its peak first under the Maurya emperor, Ashok (B.C. 273–232) and, later, under the Gupta emperor, Chandra Gupta II Vikramaditya (A.D. 380–415).

Despite my interest and expertise, I am not going to enter into details about the curriculum in ancient and medieval India (Ghosh 2002).[4] Here I focus on the one introduced by the British in modern India, the one of utmost concern at the moment. For your convenience, I propose to present my account of the intellectual history and present circumstances of curriculum in India in two parts—British India and independent India.

# Part I British India (1757–1947)

During the last days of the decline of the Mughal rule in India under Aurangzeb (1657–1707) in the late seventeenth century, a group of companies from the West—including English, French, Dutch, Danes, and the Portuguese—came to India, not as invaders and conquerors like their Muslim predecessors, but as traders and merchants. They soon found themselves embroiled in quarrels not only among themselves but also with the Indian powers they had to deal with for trading purposes. This converted many of them into conquerors and, then, rulers faced with the problems of administration of the territories they had gradually come to control. The colonists decided to import their own system of education to serve their immediate imperial needs and requirements.[5]

## The East India Company Officials as Patrons of an Oriental Curriculum

Among the companies that came to India the most important one was the East India Company of London (Chaudhuri 1965; Philips 1961).[6] By the end of the seventeenth century, the Company had established its trading posts at Surat, Bombay, and Madras and its headquarters at Calcutta, in 1690. The East India Company initially carried on its trading activities with Persia taking the help of the locals, and it continued to do so even after the grant of the Diwani in 1765 by the Mughal

Emperor Shah Alam II (after the Battle of Plassey in 1757, followed by the Battle of Buxar in 1764) to collect revenues of Bengal, Bihar and Orissa.

A group of Company officials—beginning with Warren Hastings, the first governor-general of the Bengal Presidency,[7] who founded the Calcutta Madrasah, in 1781; Nathaniel Halhed, who wrote *A Code of Gentoo Laws* (1776) and *Bengali Grammar* (1778); Charles Wilkins, who brought out his *Sanskrit Grammar* (1779); and Francis Gladwin who wrote *Institutes of the Emperor Akbar* (1783)—became extremely interested in the existing Oriental curriculum, which received a shot in the arm in 1784 with the foundation of the Royal Asiatic Society at Calcutta under William Jones, a former Persian scholar at Oxford and now a judge of the newly founded Supreme Court at Calcutta. Jones first learned Sanskrit from the local Sanskrit scholars of Nadia[8] in order to translate several important Sanskrit manuscripts. He provided leadership to 30 elite English officials of the East India Company to unearth ancient knowledge in Indian religion and culture, publishing their findings in the journal of the Royal Asiatic Society, *Asiatick Researches*.

Opposed to this group of Orientalists was another group of Englishmen—the Anglicists—who, led by Charles Grant, wanted to rid the Indian society of many of its evils such as Sati, child-marriage, polygamy, and infanticide. They would achieve this through education, for example, through the spread of Western civilization. The Anglicists under Wilberforce in England created a pressure group in the British Parliament. Aided by evangelicals who believed that converting the Indians into Christians would constitute the cure for these evils, the British Parliament passed the Charter Act in 1813, renewing the lease of the Company for another 20 years. The act sanctioned a grant of rupees one lakh (ten thousand pounds at the contemporary rate of exchange) by Clause 43 to further the cause of education in the country (Frijhoff 1983).[9] A committee known as the General Committee on Public Instruction was formed with ten officials interested in Oriental curriculum alone. When funding was made available in 1822, it was mostly spent[10] in setting up Oriental colleges at Delhi and Agra and a Sanskrit College at Calcutta (1824), in recognition of the Calcutta Madrasah founded by Warren Hastings in 1781 and the Sanskrit College at Benares founded by Jonathan Duncan in 1792.

## Resistance to Oriental Curriculum

The activities of the committee created resistance, first, among the local people who, after learning English in the missionary schools, were hopeful of employment in the expanding Company or in the mercantile establishments that were then coming into existence to cater to the needs of the European communities in and around the metropolitan cities. For centuries under the Muslim rule, these non-Muslim people had remained mostly deprived of education and of suitable job opportunities, except for a few among them from the affluent classes who could learn Persian either at home or at the Madrasahs, thrown open to them in the seventeenth century by Akbar (1556–1605).

Leadership was provided by Rammohan Roy, a retired revenue officer of the Company. When he learned of the proposal of the committee to establish a Sanskrit

College at Calcutta, Roy sent a letter to Governor-General Amherst (on December 11, 1823) suggesting that the proposal should be abandoned. Instead, the government should "promote a more liberal and enlightened system of instruction: embracing mathematics, natural philosophy, chemistry, anatomy, with other useful sciences, which may be accomplished with the sum proposed by employing a few gentlemen of talents and learning, educated in Europe and providing a college furnished with accessory, books, instruments and other apparatus."

The Company—whose headquarters in London was now dominated by the utilitarians like James Mill and his son John Stuart Mill who were advocates of English education for modernization of their colonies abroad—also opposed the activities of the Committee in an official letter from the Court of Directors signed on February 18, 1824: "The great end should not have been to teach Hindu learning, but useful learning."

Soon the General Committee on Public Instruction came to be populated with new members who, as students of the Hailebury College in Hertfordshire—established in 1801 to teach the recruits of the Company Oriental languages—had been earlier profoundly indoctrinated with the utilitarian ideas of James Mill and Jeremy Bentham. And they now began to stall the work of the Orientalists in the committee.

## Role of Bentinck in Introducing Western Curriculum

When Bentinck was appointed governor-general of the Company's possession in India in 1828, the fate of the Orientalists was sealed. Bentinck was a disciple of James Mill and from the very beginning of his term, he supported the modernization of India. He added English classes to the existing Oriental colleges, began to replace Persian in the Company's administration, and in 1830 interviewed Alexander Duff. Duff founded the General Assembly's Institution—now known as the Scottish Church College—which soon began to draw a large number of students from the upper classes of Calcutta society. He then appointed Macaulay, the law member of his council, as the president of the General Committee of Public Instruction in 1834. Macaulay was for his known for his erudition.

The ongoing debates over Orientalism versus modernization resulted in a deadlock between the Anglicists and the Orientalists on the General Committee of Public Instruction. The issues were the conversion of the Calcutta Madrasah into an institution of Western learning and the remodeling of the Agra College on the lines of the Calcutta Hindu College, the first institution in the country established by local people to teach Western education and science. Finally the committee referred the matter to Bentinck, who, on February 2, 1835, consulted Macaulay on the matter.

## The Role of Macaulay

Macaulay agreed with the opponents of the English education that it was impossible to train everyone in English education. He advised Bentinck: "We must, at present, do our best to form a class who can act as interpreters between us and the millions whom we govern, a class of persons Indian in blood and color, but English in taste, in opinions, in morals and intellect. To that class we may leave it to refine the vernacular dialects of the country, to enrich their dialects with terms of science borrowed from the Western nomenclature and to render them by degrees fit vehicles for conveying knowledge to the greater mass of the population."

Bentnick acted quickly. On March 7, 1835, without waiting for the necessary approval from his headquarters at London, he passed the necessary governmental order introducing English as the official language, ordering it to be the medium of instruction in the existing Oriental colleges. The act stopped any further grants to Oriental studies as all monies would now go only to the cultivation of English language and culture in the country (Ghosh 1995).[11]

## Western Curriculum Endorsed by Bentick's Successor, Auckland

While Bentinck's landmark decision opened Europe to India and India to Europe, it was Macaulay's advice to Bentinck that provided the necessary framework for the introduction of a Western curriculum. The change of Oriental to Western curriculum brought stiff resistance both from within and outside of the General Committee of Public Instruction. It was left to Bentinck's successor, Auckland, to settle the controversy.

Since his succession to Bentinck through Metcalfe as the governor-general in 1836, Auckland had been watching developments in the field of education. He expressed his views on November 24, 1839, by restoring old grants (sanctioned before March 1835) to Oriental education but maintaining that the improvement of the moral and intellectual condition of the people could occur only through the dissemination of European science and literature, which, he was sure, could only occur through the medium of English. He pointed out that the chief inducement to acquire English education remained the prospect of earning a livelihood.

Influenced by the filtration theory impressed upon the committee that pref-erence be given to "rendering the highest instruction efficient in certain number of Central Colleges, rather than employing funds in the extension of the plan for founding ordinary Zillah schools," Auckland selected Dacca, Patna, Benares or Allahabad, Agra, and Bareilly as the places where the Central Colleges were to be established. He suggested the inclusion of jurisprudence, government, and morals in the curriculum, and he encouraged the use of college libraries. One of the objec-tives of these colleges was to create a class of "inferior school masters." Auckland also proposed to link these colleges with the proposed Zillah schools by a comprehensive system of scholarships, encouraging the ablest students to continue to higher courses of study. Finally, he discussed the question of utility and practicability of using the vernaculars as the medium of instruction in the Zillah schools, but considered such a step premature due to the absence of suitable vernacular textbooks and qualified teachers.

Auckland was unable to put his plan fully into operation due to the outbreak of the Afghan War and his departure from India in 1842. However, he took care to see that his plan was adopted by the government and that the necessary financial provisions were made. Auckland, then, was the first governor-general to establish a comprehensive educational system in India. It continued, with additions and alterations, until 1854.

## Civil Engineering, Introduced by Thomason and Expanded by Dalhousie

In November 1847, James Thomason, the lieutenant governor of the North-Western Provinces, established a new curriculum, civil engineering. The foundation of a civil engineering college at Roorkee—with R. Maclagan as its principal—with a curriculum in civil engineering offered instruction to Europeans, Eurasians, and Indians, with a view to their future employment in the public works of the country.

The demand for civil engineers and other technical personnel grew along with the introduction of the railways, the electric telegraph, and the construction of the roads and irrigation projects started by Dalhousie, the governor-general of India from 1848 to 1856. By 1853 this demand became so great that Dalhousie expanded his initial idea of attaching a civil engineering class to the existing colleges to establishing a civil engineering college in each of the three Presidencies. Since nothing could be done without the approval of the Court of Directors, Dalhousie wrote to them in November 1853 for support. He also requested for the establishment in Calcutta of a school for women (from the upper classes) and for an extension of Thomason's successful scheme of vernacular education (linked to the newly created revenue records in the North-Western Provinces).

## The Education Dispatch of 1854 and the Foundation of a Modern System of Education in India

Dalhousie's proposals reached London in 1853, soon after the British Parliament had renewed the Charter of the East India Company. The Court of Directors had asked Charles Wood, the president of the Board of Control, to draft a dispatch on the introduction of a general system of education in India (Ghosh 1975).[12] Dalhousie's proposals were more or less incorporated in the Education Dispatch of 1854, also popularly and incorrectly known as the Wood's Dispatch. It laid the foundation of a modern system of education in India.

The *Dispatch* emphasized "the general diffusion of useful knowledge," and that such knowledge would not only raise the moral character of its recipients but also supply the Company "with servants to whose probity you may with increased confidence commit offices of trust." Thereby "the material interests" of England would also not remain "altogether unaffected by the advance of European knowledge in India. This knowledge will teach the natives of India the marvelous results of the employment of labor and capital...and gradually, but certainly, confer upon them all the advantages which accompany the healthy increase of wealth and commerce, and at the same time secure to us a large and more certain supply of many articles necessary for our manufacturers and extensively consumed by all classes of our population as well as an almost inexhaustible demand for the produce of British labor."

The *Dispatch* clarified its definition of "useful knowledge" as one of "improved arts, sciences, and literature of Europe" and asserted that "Eastern knowledge abound with grievous errors" (an echo of Macaulay) but that "it should be retained to study the Oriental laws of the Hindus and the Muslims and for the improvement of the vernaculars which could be a fit conveyance at a much later date for the transmission of the European knowledge to the great mass of the people faced with the difficulties of a foreign language." The *Dispatch* thus abandoned the filtration policy propounded by Macaulay in 1835 for the sake of "that general diffusion of European knowledge which is the main object of education in India." Finally the *Dispatch* also appreciated the drawbacks of a purely literary course of instruction as it recommended professional training in Law, Medicine, and Civil Engineering. It stressed the need for establishing vocational colleges and schools of industry. It also emphasized the urgency of educating the women of the country and noted with pleasure "an increased desire on the part of many of the natives of India to give a good education to their daughters."

## The Establishment of Three Universities on the London Model at Calcutta, Bombay, and Madras in 1857

The development of the curriculum as per the guidelines of the *Education Dispatch* was supported by the founding, by the Acts of Incorporation, of the three metropolitan universities at Calcutta, Bombay, and Madras in 1857. Based on the London model, these universities were not teaching centers but examination bodies for courses in Arts and Sciences conducted in their affiliated colleges, which included all the existing ones prior to 1857. There were, however, no geographical limits to the areas of affiliation. Calcutta University, for example, functioned not merely for Bengal, but for Burma, Assam, the Central Provinces, and Ceylon as well; the affiliated colleges were dispersed from Simla and Mussorie to Indore and Jaipur, and from Jaffna and Baticaloa to Sylhet and Chittagong.

As per the rules of affiliation framed by the Calcutta University in February 1857, colleges seeking affiliation had to submit a declaration, countersigned by two members of the University Senate, enumerating staff and courses of study for the previous two years, and describing the institution's ability to impart education up to the standard of the degree of BA. Managed by their own governing bodies, such affiliated colleges came into existence largely through the generosity of governmental and philanthropic societies, missionary bodies, or wealthy Indians committed to the cause. They had no control over their curriculum, which was prescribed by their affiliated universities and merely prepared the students for examinations conducted by them.

## Oriental Curriculum only at the University
## College at Lahore

By 1881–82 the number of such affiliated colleges, mostly managed and staffed by the Europeans with English as the medium of instruction, had risen in number from 27 to 72. But it was only at the University College at Lahore (founded in 1869) that European education was imparted through the medium of the mother tongue and where, in fact, the study of Oriental languages was encouraged. In the other colleges the study of the modern Indian languages was neglected, although in Bombay a modern Indian language could be taken as a subject from the Matriculation to the BA examinations. In 1862, Alexander Grant, director of Public Instruction in Bombay, argued for the abolition of all modern Indian languages from all university examinations except the Matriculation, where its use would be optional, as no standard textbooks were available. There was greater attention to the classical languages. The acceptance of Alexander Grant's views led to the discontinuance of the teaching of Indian languages in colleges. Since their study was optional at the secondary stage, the lower schools also began to neglect them.

## Violation of the *Dispatch's* Directives on Curriculum

Contrary to the suggestion of the *Dispatch* of 1854, English came to be adopted as the medium of instruction at those schools that prepared students for the Matriculation examination of the universities. From 1862 onward, following the example of Calcutta, English became the compulsory medium through which the Matriculation examination in the other two universities could be taken in History, Geography, Arithmetic, and Science. There was no provision for vocational education except in one school in Bombay, where students were awarded a scholarship of Rs.4 (nearly 40 pence at the contemporary rate of exchange) per month for taking training in agriculture. Students were mostly interested in obtaining Matriculation certificates, either to qualify for clerical jobs in government establishments or for entering colleges to earn degrees that would fetch them highly paid jobs.

## Increase in the Number of Students Specializing in
## the Western Curriculum

In 1857 the number of successful students at the first Matriculation examination of the universities was only 219: 162 at Calcutta, 36 at Madras, and 21 at Bombay. But by 1881–82 the number had risen to 2778 out of the 7429 candidates who had appeared at the examination. The standard of examination was very high, and in the first BA degree examination of Calcutta University only 2 out of the 13 who appeared were successful. Those two were Bankim Chandra Chatterjee and Jadunath Bose, both of whom later distinguished themselves as great literary and administrative figures of the time.

## Career Prospects

From 1857 onward, a large number of both successful and unsuccessful English-educated candidates experienced increasing difficulties in obtaining employment in government and mercantile establishments. There were very limited opportunities available for them, and those were mostly for the lower-level positions, such as clerks and assistants. Higher positions in the civil, military, engineering, and education services were reserved for recruits at home. Although the Civil Services became open to Indians in 1853, few could afford to go to London to take the examination. Many became lawyers, journalists, and teachers in private schools; the government and the missionary college staff were Europeans, mostly recruited in England. These unemployed educated Indians soon became hostile critics of an administration that had educated them in European education and science without providing them with any opportunities for employment.

## Formation of the Indian National Congress

In 1885, Allan Octavian Hume, a retired civilian, with support from Governor-General, Dufferin, founded the Indian National Congress to provide a platform where disgruntled educated youth could express their discontent. After a decade during which nothing happened to improve their employment opportunities, many became militant.

## Government Attempts to Control the Spread of Western Curriculum

By then, the government had realized the folly of introducing the Western curriculum because those who received it became critics of the establishment. In his inaugural address at the Conference at Simla in September 1901, Governor-General Curzon (1899–1905) expressed his intention to check the spread of Western curriculum: "When Erasmus was reproached with having laid the egg from which came forth the Reformation, 'Yes,' he replied,' but I laid a hen's egg, and Luther had hatched a fighting cock.' This, I believe, is pretty much the view of a good many critics of English education in the country."

In March 1904 the Indian Universities Act was passed. This legislation provided for the enlargement of the functions of the universities; reduction in the size of the University Senates; introduction of the principle of election; statutory recognition of the Syndicates where university teachers were to be granted adequate representation; stricter conditions for the affiliation of colleges to a university; definition of the territorial limits of the universities; provision of a grant of Rs.5 lakh per year for five years for implementing these changes; and, finally, powers to the government to make additions and alterations to the regulations passed by the Senates before approval by the government. This reform in higher education was camouflaged as an item in the White Paper on Education in India issued by Curzon just a few days before the passing of the Indian Universities Act in order to successfully preempt any resistance from the Western-educated youth (Ghosh 1988).[13]

## Resistance

Curzon's attempt to control the spread of English education through the Indian Universities Act of 1904 was resisted by Western-educated Indians. As Curzon wrote to Hamilton, the then Secretary of State: "The Town Hall and the Senate Hall of the university have been packed with shouting and perspiring graduates, and my name has been loudly hissed as the author of the doom of higher education."

When the Partition of Bengal took place immediately after it, Western-educated Indians organized a boycott movement. They launched a parallel system of education with emphasis on technical education and the use of a modern Indian language as the medium of instruction. However, the basic content of courses—a Western curriculum featuring science—remained almost the same as before. When the Partition was withdrawn in 1911, this parallel education also disappeared (Ghosh 2007).[14]

## The Calcutta University Commission

The demand for European education continued to increase despite the Indian Universities Act of 1904–05. In 1917 the Calcutta University Commission, also known as Sadler Commission, was appointed to design the university education in the country. In its recommendations of 1919, it placed the governance of universities under full-time salaried vice chancellors, decreed universities as teaching centers, and provided them with various statutory bodies: Faculties, Boards of Studies, Academic Councils, and Executive Councils. It recommended appointments to professorships and readerships through various special selection committees, including experts. Thus the commission not only freed the universities from the controls imposed by Curzon but initiated processes of university autonomy and democratization. The commission found many courses of instruction "too predominantly literary in character and too little varied to suit various needs," and it commented on the inadequate provision for "training in technical subjects." It urged the inclusion of applied science and technology in the curriculum and asked universities to make provision for the efficient training of personnel needed for the industrial development of the country.

The commission also recommended the introduction of various courses of instruction toward this end, instituted a three-year degree course after the intermediate stage, Honors courses as distinct from the Pass courses for abler students, and it recommended the inclusion of Indian languages among the subjects for both Pass and Honors degrees. The commission stressed the need for establishing a link between the university and institutes of Oriental learning. It recommended increasing the number of trained teachers, the creation of a Department of Education, and the inclusion of Education as a subject for the intermediate, BA, and MA degree examinations. *It is to the Calcutta University Commission that we can trace the genesis of curriculum of education as a regular course of study in our universities and colleges.*

The commission further recommended the organization of purdah schools for Hindu and Muslim girls whose parents were willing to extend their education up to 15 or 16 years of age, a special board for women's education to look after the courses particularly suited for women, and to organize cooperative arrangements for teaching in women's colleges. It also encouraged the education of Muslims.

## Curriculum Now Seen as an Adjunct to National Movement

While most of the recommendations of the Calcutta University Commission were carried out, the curriculum was not much altered. There continued strong demand for the same literary courses. Without technical training, the number of young Indians who were both educated and unemployed increased. There was growing discontent, including criticism of the British administration. No doubt this discontent—among educated and unemployed Indian youth—fueled the struggle for freedom, which entered a new phase with the appearance—between 1915 and 1918—of Gandhi on the national scene.

In the midst of all these, education was now seen as an adjunct to the national movement, which had brought in its wake the passing of the Government of India Act of 1919 (based on the Montagu-Chelmsford Reforms), which provided for a Council of State and a Legislative Assembly with elected majorities but no control over the ministers at the center and introduced diarchy in the provinces. In November 1927 the British Government appointed the Simon Commission to report on the working of the act. The commission was also asked to submit a report on education, and it appointed for this purpose an auxiliary committee with Philip Hartog, a former member of the Calcutta University Commission as well as a former vice chancellor of the newly founded Dacca University, as its president.

## The Hartog Committee

The 1929 Hartog Committee report condemned the quantitative expansion of education at the cost of its quality and expressed astonishment at a "too large acceptance" in India of the view that "a university exists, mainly, if not solely, to pass students through examinations." The committee tried to reduce the domination of the Matriculation by introducing a more diversified curriculum in the middle vernacular schools and by the admission of a large number of boys intended for rural pursuits. It also recommended the diversion of more pupils to industrial and commercial careers at the end of the middle-school stage, as well as the provision of alternative courses in the high school to prepare students for technical and industrial schools. Following the recommendations of the Hartog Committee, the Central Board of Education was revived to make this radical adjustment, for example, preparing students not only for professional and university courses, but also diverting them to occupations or to separate vocational institutions, and at a presumably appropriate stage: primary, lower secondary, and higher secondary.

The Government of India invited S. H. Wood, director of Intelligence, and A. Abbot, chief inspector of Technical Schools in England, to carry out this reconstruction of education in India. After touring the country in the winter of 1936–37, Wood and Abbot submitted their report in June 1937. The first part of the report concerned itself with the general education and its administration, and the second part, written by Abbot, focused on vocational education.

## Gandhi's Ideas

By the time Wood and Abbot had submitted their report, the Congress Ministries—in the 7 out of 11 provinces that came into existence after the Government of India Act of 1935—were discussing Gandhi's idea[15] of "Basic Education," expressed at the Wardha Conference in October 1937. Asked to submit a report on the idea, Zakir Husain emphasized the educational aspect of the scheme more than its self-supporting aspect. After its acceptance by the Congress Ministries, the non-Congress Ministers in the five provinces as well as the Central Board of Secondary Education became interested in it and appointed B. G. Kher to pursue it.

By the time the Kher Committee submitted its reports—1939—the Second World War had been declared, and the Congress Ministers in the seven provinces, who differed from the British Government in its war-aims, resigned, and the report was shelved. An unique opportunity was thus lost to introduce a vocational curriculum at all levels of schooling thereby provide other opportunities for students who would have had no other alternative but to proceed to the Matriculation and later to the colleges.

## Sargent's Postwar Plan

With the resignation of the Congress Ministers, any hopes of an educational reconstruction under provincial autonomy were lost. However, in 1943, as the victory of the Allied Powers came into sight, the Government of India asked all provincial governments to plan for postwar developments in India. As a part of the general scheme, Sir John Sargent, the then education adviser to the Government of India, was asked to prepare a memorandum on postwar educational development in India for submission to the viceroy's Executive Council for consideration, which he did in the year 1944.

Sargent's report on the postwar educational development in India aimed at attaining the contemporary educational standard of England in 40 years, that is, by 1984. It emphasized the need for preprimary education for children between 3 and 6 years of age, universal free and compulsory education for all children between 6 and 14 years of age, the division of high schools into Academic schools providing instructions in Arts and Sciences, and Technical schools providing instruction in the applied sciences as well as in industrial and commercial subjects. As per the requirements of industry and commerce, Senior Technical Schools with courses in consultation with the employers were established, as were part-time courses for full-time technical employees. The report abolished the intermediate courses by transferring the first year to the high schools and the second year to the universities. The report also emphasized the training of teachers and the introduction of physical education, special education for the physically and mentally disabled, and education for adult illiterates between the ages of 10 and 40.

The report also recommended the creation of an employment bureau for advising students about various recreational activities and the establishment of education departments both at the center and the provinces. All education—except university and higher technical education—should be the responsibility of the states. Sargent's report recommended a comprehensive, indeed realistic, curriculum that deemphasized literary higher education and provided a curricular response to the problem of increasing unemployment in the country.

By 1946 the Central Government had accepted most of the recommendations of John Sargent. As it was trying to implement them, the British left India to face postwar difficulties. A change of government at home as well as with an intensification of the national struggle for freedom—under the leadership of Gandhi, Nehru, and Patel, in India—introduced a very different set of circumstances in which curriculum revision could occur.

# Part II Independent India (1947–2010)

When India became independent, a part of it became Pakistan. India was now faced not only with a depleted civil and military administration after the departure of the British Raj, but also with a constant flow of refugees from both sides of the new border with Pakistan. The government had little time to attend to curriculum change, despite Nehru's call for it (Ghosh 1977; 2008).[16] The immediate needs were to grant India a constitution, draw plans for the development of the country, rehabilitate the refugees, and find ways to fill in the administrative vacuum left by the departure of British officials.

## Expansion of Higher Education

Appointed in 1948, a university commission (under Radhakrishnan) issued recommendations that were almost a repetition of those made by the Calcutta University Commission of 1917–19. The only new subject it proposed to add to the curriculum was a course on ethics, a proposal that did not find much favor with a government bent upon pursuing a secular policy inherited from the British Raj. The commission's recommendations were, then, no answer to the curriculum concerns facing the country. In fact, they only intensified the pressure on the existing science and literary curricula in higher education.

In 1953 a commission on secondary education was appointed (under Mudaliar) to reduce this pressure on higher education—aggravated by the Radhakrisnan Commission—but the most the commission could do was to repeat John Sargent's 1944 ideas on technical and academic high schools. In 1963—in response to the demands of those who were facing increasing difficulties in finding employment—the Kothari Commission was appointed, charged to examine all aspects of education. An educational policy emerged—after five years, in 1968—but its diluted recommendations could hardly be implemented, as the Congress Government faced difficulties at the center (after its split in 1969).

The following years saw a struggle for power among the rising opposition parties. When the Allahabad High Court canceled Indira Gandhi's election to the Indian Parliament, Emergency was declared. In the General Elections that followed, the Janata Party under Morarji Desai came to power. This government had its own ideas about education, certainly not in agreement with those of the preceding government.

## Rise in the Number of the Educated Unemployed

In 1979, the Janata Government tried to divert pressure from higher education by various means, including the introduction of Adult Education (Friedenthial-Haase 1998).[17] It was, however, too late as higher education had expanded explosively, from 19 universities, 277 Arts and Science Colleges, 199 Intermediate, and 140 professional and technical colleges in 1947 to 100 universities and 4000 colleges in 1974. Enrolment in higher education increased by 17 times. Since the Indian economy did not rise in those years sufficiently to absorb the graduates of this unplanned expansion of higher education, most graduates remained unemployed or underemployed. As revealed by the Register of the Directorate General of Employment and Training in 1974, of a total population of nearly 600 million, approximately 4 million remained unemployed.

## Rise of Castes and Tribes

Adding to this army of educated unemployed was the rise of the scheduled castes and tribes, the Dalits and other "backward" classes, who now enjoyed the benefit of a liberal education, thanks to a government policy reserving seats for them in academic institutions. These castes and tribes now clamored for more privileges, including employment. In ancient India—following Persian occupation of the North-West in 519 B.C.—these groups were deprived of any opportunity to attend the Vedic schools by the Sutrakaras (like Manu and Yajnavalka). In medieval India they were joined by the upper classes, as the Vedic schools were shut down, then replaced by Islamic institutions for nearly 650 years. While the fate of the upper classes improved later, thanks to their participation in Western education, the fate of the lower classes remained the same due to their exclusion from education, although some benefited from the missionary schools set up in their locality, often at the cost of their conversion to Christianity.

## The New National Policy on Education in 1986

The educated unemployed among all the castes and classes now became hostile critics of the existing administration, which in itself was mostly monopolized by

Western-educated and well-connected upper and middle classes. While the most disgruntled and the disillusioned among them—including those in the Punjab—resorted to violent protest, the more moderate—in the Uttar Pradesh as well as in Bengal, Bihar, and Orissa—demanded separate states (in the form of Uttaranchal and Jharkhand respectively) to address their problems.

In all these developments wherein the involvement of the educated, both employed and unemployed, had been quite large, there had been no evidence of patriotism, no sense of belonging to one country, and even no recollection of the past sufferings and sacrifices of their ancestors for the freedom of the motherland. India's political and social life was thus passing through a phase that posed the danger of erosion to long-accepted values. The goals of secularism, socialism, democracy, and professional ethics were coming under strain.

The system of education as bequeathed to us by the British Raj was singled out as "the whipping boy." And the government, after the assassination of Indira Gandhi in 1984 by the supporters of the Khalistan Movement in the Punjab, promulgated a New National Educational Policy in 1986 as a panacea for all the evils that were then plaguing the country. The *Program of Action* on the New National Policy on Education announced: "Time is of essence, and unless we act now, we stand in the danger of once again missing the opportunity of educational reform, so critical not only for the development of our nation, but for our very survival."[18]

## A New Curriculum

Without misgivings one can say that, for the first time in the history of education in India since independence, the curriculum contents at the schools came to be scrutinized very carefully. What followed was the formulation of common core in the curriculum program within a common educational structure (like 10 + 2 + 3) dedicated to understanding the diverse socio-cultural systems of India. Also imagined as outcomes were the aspirations of younger generations for international cooperation and peaceful coexistence. A distinct stream within the common educational structure, vocational education was designed to meet the requirements of commerce and industry in rural and urban areas. The task to develop the actual curriculum was left to a national body known as the National Council of Educational Research and Training (NCERT), which had come into existence in 1961, two years before the appointment of the Kothari Commission, and almost five years after the establishment of the University Grants Commission (UGC).

In 1986 it was difficult for the NCERT to visualize the impact on the country of an economic phenomenon known as globalization and develop its curriculum to meet this challenge at the school level. That set of circumstances aside, it also failed in the primary objective of the 1986 Policy to design a core curriculum at the school level to meet the needs and requirements of a multiracial, multicultural, multilingual people who follow diverse religions and faiths and to instill in their hearts a sense of pride in their past heritage, their cultures, and cultivate a sense of mutual understanding and respect for each other to create an environment of peace and harmony. This failure has been regretfully observed in the early years of the present millennium in states like Maharashtra, where parochialism is at its peak now.

## Resistance to the New Curriculum

Meanwhile, the implementation of the curriculum received a severe jolt when the Congress Government that had supported it was replaced by the National Front Government under the Janata Dal leader V. P. Singh in 1989. Many of the constituent political parties of this coalition government had viewed with disfavor aspects of the 1986 Policy. A revision became imperative and with that end in view, a committee was appointed under Acharya Ramamurti in May 1990.

The Ramamurti Committee Report was, however, put into cold storage immediately after its submission on December 26, 1990, as the government that appointed it fell. It was replaced by a minority government under Chandrasekhar for a short time. In the resultant General Election—marked by the tragic assassination of Rajiv Gandhi in 1990—the Congress Party (riding on the sympathy vote for Rajiv) returned to power under P. V. Narasimha Rao in 1991. As expected, the suspended implementation of the recommendations of the 1986 Policy was resumed now.

An event over which the Government of India had no control was soon to change the whole education scenario. Referenced earlier, this was the opening up of India to the world—in trade, commerce, and industry—through the initiative of its finance minister, Manmohan Singh. Singh wanted to save India from impending bankruptcy.

## Implementation of the 1986 Policy

In higher education, implementation brought no drastic changes except the "Indianization" of some programs. Students continued to flock to universities for degrees in Arts and Sciences. Pressure on admission to professional courses in Engineering and Medicine resulted in an increase in the few existing institutions specialized in these fields. Management programs were yet to draw attention from students as they do now. Several of those students who studied Management in the late eighties in India and abroad—including late Prahlad Kakkar, Deepak Jain, Nitin Nohria (dean, Harvard Business School), and Sunil Kumar who was appointed dean of Chicago Business School from January 2011, Vikram Pandit of Citibank—have now achieved remarkable success, either as top management professionals in multinational corporations or as top management teachers in prestigious business schools.

The 1986 Policy was able to draw the attention of many to the study of curriculum. After 1986 the NCERT has taken leadership. While two earlier curriculum surveys conducted at Baroda have reported 69 and 71 studies, surveys conducted by the NCERT first show an increase, then a decline, in the number of such studies. The Third and Fourth Surveys of Research in Education reported 100 and 107 studies. However the Fifth and Sixth Surveys of Research in Education indicate less curriculum research. The number of studies declined from 23 to 10.

A Steering Committee to draft a bill for the establishment of a National Council of Teacher Education (NCTE) was made with the object of establishing a regulatory body.[19] An attempt to make the national literacy mission more visually attractive was also made, while a plan to educate all (including the disabled) was mooted in the *Sarva Shiksha Abhiyan* or the Education for All. The Faculties of Education of several noted central universities have started offering "curriculum studies" as one of the courses at the BEd and MEd levels and also as the subject of investigation at the doctoral level, as shown by the NCERT's *Surveys of Research in Education* for the years between 1983 and 2000.[20]

These studies concentrate on traditional academic subjects; they hardly touch upon the new areas of research that have emerged, among them the Economics of Education, History of Education, Educational Technology, Integrated Education for Disabled Children, Management Education, Environmental Education, Computer Education, Bio-technology, Value Education, and Vocational Curriculum suited to regional needs and aspirations. There are hardly any studies or research on curriculum ideology, innovative enrichment, teachers' roles in the effective translation of curriculum, curriculum models, and comparative methodological studies. Often it seems that issues of passing interest with little prospect of long-term relevance— are those that draw the interest of researchers. The 2005 National Curriculum Framework (prepared by the NCTE) went beyond a traditional classroom curriculum without provision for appropriate changes in the teacher education curriculum that has been followed since the Hunter Commission in 1882–83.

The concept and content of teacher training have remained remarkably stable over a century. The model lessons and the norms of supervision are almost exactly the same as we find them described in nineteenth-century official education reports. Can they then have an impact on the new generation of students? I am reminded of an observation of Rabindranath Tagore, advocating Bengali[21] as the medium of instruction: "A teacher can never truly teach unless he is still learning himself. A lamp can never light another lamp unless it continues to burn its own flame." It is heartening to learn from the Sixth Survey of Education that steps have now been taken to rectify our teacher education programs.

The smooth passage and implementation of reforms of the 1986 Policy was slowed due to the change of the Congress Government, after a coalition of political parties led by the BJP following the election in 1998. The BJP had its own ideas of an "Hindutva" education and appointed a group of experts to reform the curriculum. In 2000, the NCTE submitted a national curriculum framework for teacher and school education. While prepared on the model suggested by the 1986 Policy, the framework was issued at a time when globalization had considerably altered the scenario in the country. Thus it failed to satisfy the national expectations and aspirations.

## Globalization and Its Impact on the Curriculum

The forces of globalization are visible in the country. They have begun to affect almost all walks of our life. The most drastic impact is seen on the curriculum in the higher institutions of learning now poised for a dramatic change. Now students are opting for professional management and engineering courses instead of the venerable Arts and Sciences, as they seek jobs in multinational corporations that have now opened branches in India. New professional courses on management and engineering appear. As existing institutions are unable to meet the increasing demand for such professional courses, a host of private institutions—with or without any standards and adequate staff—has popped up. Thanks to Narayan Murthy's Infosys and Prem Azmi's Wipro in Bangalore and to the outsourcing of Microsoft and other businesses, India is now seen as a great hub for Information Technology. Globalization has opened up opportunities for profitable employment for thousands of previously unemployed graduates.

## Return of the English

But such opportunities in the BPO are only available to those who have a fairly good knowledge of spoken and written English. This gives an advantage to students educated in public schools through the medium of English; only they are able to reap the benefits of globalization. From 1960 onward—due to agitation against English—many schools in some states do not teach the language at all. Now a reverse trend is seen and political leaders like Lalu Prasad Yadav (and many others) who have until very recently spoken against the use of English in schools and colleges have come forward to support it.[22] And so English has now returned to the schools that had shunned it earlier; many centers and institutes outside the formal school system have mushroomed, specializing in spoken and written English.

## Inadequate and Ill-Equipped Curriculum

Yet the curriculum offered in the professional institutes does not prepare students to work for multinational companies and business houses owned and managed by Indians. Often these organizations must provide the necessary skills needed for the job. In this way a sizeable workforce has been built up, which compares favorably with the professionally trained students in some of the prestigious management institutes abroad.

India does have several excellent engineering and management schools in IITs and IIMs, but, as McKinsey estimates, only 25 percent of engineering graduates, 15 percent of finance graduates, and 10 percent of those with other degrees are qualified to work for multinational companies. Multinational companies prefer to recruit graduates from established schools, but Indian companies realize that recruits have to be trained in any case.

Many companies have virtually become universities, employing hundreds of trainers recruited, as do the Infosys and the Tata Consultancy Services (TCS), not from elite engineering colleges but from second- and third-tier colleges, as well as from Arts and Sciences schools. The Infosys Global Education Centre at Mysore trains 13,500 people at a time.[23] For its Arts and Sciences recruits, TCS provides an additional three months of training. In all, many recruits undergo four to seven months of training before starting work. The software industry complains of a high attrition rate—up to 30 percent employees leave every year. This means the companies are training people not just for themselves but for the whole industry. This is another secret of India's successful economic development.

This scenario presents a sad commentary on the ability of our education planners and administrators to prepare a curriculum in our institutions to meet the demands of a rising trade and industry. And as we have just seen, the task has been left largely to privately managed institutions (both at the school and higher level) and to a few government institutions with teachers and administrators who do not often have adequate experience and training. Consequently the old curriculum (with some patching up here and there) continues to be studied; this forces the multinational companies to do what they are doing now—train recruits from the existing institutions for whatever skills are needed for the job.

## Lessons Learned

The main lesson learned is that curriculum should emerge out of the requirements of society and that it should continue to adjust itself to scoiety's changing needs. This is exactly what happened in ancient India when the curriculum in the Vedic schools changed and developed progressively according to the needs and requirements of our civilization. The Muslim rulers imported a curriculum to suit their own needs: the requirements of an Islamic administration and of an Islamic community. The British imported Western curriculum for the same purposes. When their imported curriculum expanded beyond their own imperial requirements, it created a huge problem for their own survival, as it gave birth to the Indian National Congress in 1885, which was composed mostly of unemployed persons trained in the Western curriculum.

After independence we have continued (until recently) studying the same imported curriculum, without thinking about its relevance to the needs and aspirations of an independent developing nation. We have reaped a bitter harvest in socioeconomic and political disorder and social problems. After independence, we established two bodies to look after the curriculum in the country. The NCERT takes care of the school curriculum and the UGC the college and the university curriculum. Often influenced by their political masters, these bodies have occasionally recommended curriculum that has little or no relevance to the real needs of the country and the people. It is a sad commentary on the state of curriculum in the country when it is revealed that a premiere institution of our country, the Delhi School of Economics, has not altered its economics syllabi (at both the graduate and the undergraduate levels) for the last fifty years! The fact of the matter is such national regulatory bodies have little or no control over the curriculum, which is often decided at the higher level by the specialization of the teachers concerned, and at the lower level by the pressure created by the political parties and their leaders who form the government in the various states.

## Why We Have Failed to Develop an Appropriate, Relevant, and Useful Curriculum

Why have we not been able to develop a curriculum at the school and college levels as per the needs and requirements of the society? The most obvious reason is the vastness of the country, inhabited by a huge population of nearly 1.20 billion people, who spread over an ever-increasing number of states and Union Territories (which since independence now stands at 35: 28 states and 7 Union Territories) and who speak varied languages,[24] follow varied religions, cultures, manners, and customs. India's is an extreme case of a plural society and its societal, economic, and political problems, which are always numerous and enormous. It indeed necessitates a Herculean effort to succeed in any kind of reform or innovation, and India certainly does not certainly possess that superhuman power and strength. It is due to size and nature of the country that an appropriate curriculum has not always reached the places and the people where they are most urgently needed.

India is now short of 1.2 million teachers. Some 42 million children (aged between 6 and 14) do not go to school; roughly 16 percent of all village schools do not have primary schooling facilities, and 17 percent schools have just one teacher. Uttar Pradesh does not have a single teacher in more than 1000 primary schools; roughly 15 percent teaching posts lie vacant in schools across Maharashtra. This figure rises to 42 percent in Jharkhand. Only Kerala, with an average of six teachers per school, is the exception in an otherwise bleak picture.[25]

While the vastness of the country and the heterogeneity of the people may be the obvious explanation for our failure to develop and extend appropriate curriculum, I should like to offer my own interpretation for this failure, this thorn in the flesh of the progress in the country. In the first place, many in our country suffer from a kind of inertia and lack of initiative in matters that affect its development. This is indeed a psychological and, more correctly, a colonial, factor, and it has much to do with the prolonged subjugation of our ancestors by foreign powers for nearly thousand years. We were dominated first by Muslim rulers for nearly 650 years, and then by the British for nearly two hundred years. Our ancestors could not play any effective role in the administration of the country as both in the medieval India and in the British India all programs of administration (including education) were decided by the rulers. Now that we enjoy the opportunity to decide on their own affairs, we suffer from indecision and vacillation. Many look to their political masters—holding power at the centrr—for guidance. And this invariably applies to the regulatory bodies like NCERT, NCTE, NUEPA (formerly NIEPA), and the UGC, and they are often chaired by persons who are either recommended or chosen by the HRD minister himself.

This lack of energy and initiative is dominant at the institutional levels to such an extent that despite the sanction and funding of academic posts, nearly 50 percent of them in universities and colleges remain unoccupied. At the school level the percentage is often higher, as vacant teaching posts are not easily filled in the states, except in the left-dominated states like Kerala and West Bengal, where such posts are filled without delay by candidates from their own political parties.

Second, the education system has remained remarkably the same as the one built by the British between 1835 and 1854, and that system did not reach beyond the metropolitan cities and towns in the districts. The Western-educated social elite who dominated the center and the states after independence found this system useful and comfortable. Since there were not many activities on our developmental program in the country until the early 1950s, the elite could remain satisfied with the appointment of two commissions (in 1948 and 1952), which almost repeated, as we have seen, the recommendations of the Sadler Commission in 1919 and of the Sargent Plan in 1944, respectively. It was only after the beginning of the impact of a developmental program in the late 1950s, as envisaged in the Five Year Plans since 1950–51, that policy makers began to feel the need for job-oriented educational programs rather than the existing literary curriculum (which had only increased the number of the educated unemployed in the country). Vigorous reform of the existing education system—demanded by the people—was acceded to by the then Congress education minister, M. C. Chagla, in the appointment of the Kothari Commission in 1964. As we seen, that body provided the basis for the first education policy in 1968, introducing necessary curricular reform in the country after independence.

Third, there has been strong resistance to curriculum change by vested interests (both at the center and the states), and this resistance explains the unusual delay in developing curriculum out of the recommendations of the Kothari Commission in 1966. (Indeed, it was almost abandoned in 1979.) The same fate met the implementation of the curriculum associated with the 1986 education policy, a delay that became acute with frequent changes of government at the center, and that still affects the implementation of the recommendations of the Knowledge Commission that had been appointed by Prime Minister, Manmohan Singh in December 2007, to overhaul our curriculum program to keep pace with the globalization of the country.

The truth is that the annual budget, sanctioned in the budget of the HRD Ministry for the implementation of the recommendations of the Knowledge Commission after the Cabinet approval, has remained largely unspent. As *The Times of India* reported on July 24, 2010, out of an allotment of Rs. 84,000 crore on higher education for establishing new institutes of technologies and management, not quite 30,000 crore has been spent. This has led the Planning Commission to reduce the forthcoming annual allocation for higher education by nearly 50 percent, thereby almost nipping in the bud many of the major recommendations of the Knowledge Commission, among them the establishment of new IITs and IIMs (now been shifted to the Twelfth Five Year Plan). At the level of individual instances, we can cite the very recent case of the Delhi University teachers who resisted a change in their century-old academic calendar year to a semester system usually followed by most universities abroad and by the JNU in India.

Fourth, no reform introduced by a political party forming a government at the center could succeed if it did not remain in power for a considerable period of time, and not only at the center but also in the states. From this point of view, the years before the split of the Indian National Congress in 1969—when the Congress Party dominated both the center and the states—were the "golden period" for curriculum reform or innovation.

After 1969, a coalition government both at the center and in the states became a rule rather than an exception. Each political party has its own agenda for education, which each pursues for the sake of power, determined not only to satisfy the party followers (and thus retain their support) but also to strengthen its own political base at the grassroots level. In a coalition government there are often ideological clashes over various issues, and these too delay the implementation of any program that the majority party in the government endorses. The last decade of the nineteenth century and the first of the present one are characterized by such conflict.

The final and the most important factor that stands in the way of introducing and developing a new curriculum program in education is corruption, which is slowly and silently enveloping the body politic and administrative apparatus of the nation. India ranks 84 among 180 corrupt countries in the world as per the "Corruption Perception Index 2009" compiled by Transparency International. This crisis of corruption is evident not only among the greedy and those avaricious officials in the bureaucracy (both at the center and the states levels) but also among most in charge of key government and autonomous organizations dealing with education. The corrupt not only block new programs but also undermine existing ones, such as *Sarva Shiksha Abhiyan*, especially when implementation involves huge expenditures. Corruption in education has reached such a stage that an ill-equipped medical college or an engineering institution or any other academic organization could easily obtain an affiliation with a central body or the status of a "deemed" university simply by bribing the appropriate authorities. Needless to say, such corruption jeopardizes the quality and standard of education in India.

Who can save our education from corruption? Certainly it will not be those who are at the helm of affairs in our country, either in the executive or in the judiciary. India is a country where the chief minister of a state, say, Jharkhand, Arunachal Pradesh, or Karnataka could easily obtain "slush money" to build a palatial estate with a helipad or divert the center's funds meant for the development of the country, in connivance with bribed officials of the bureaucracy, who also help divert government funds to their own personal accounts in India and abroad! Eight of the sixteen former Chief Justices of the Supreme Court have been recently accused of corruption by a former law minister in the cabinet of Morarji Desai. Cases of corruption proliferate. For example, the media reports at Delhi—on July 28–31, 2010, in *the Times of India*—confirm that six district judges, three of whom later became high court judges at Allahabad, misappropriated government funds for their personal use. More known internationally were the diverting of funds intended for the Commonwealth Games in October 2010 to the off-shore accounts of powerful members of the organizing committee. Corruption occurs even at sacred places, as the case of the Tirumala Tirupati Devasthanam in Andhra Pradesh documents. There, a corrupt managing committee stole the temple jewelry, replacing it with imitations. The then prime minister Manmohan Singh, a person known for his honesty and integrity, had even endorsed the appointment of P. J. Thomas, a corrupt former secretary in the Ministry of Telecommunications, as chief vigilant commissioner of the Central Vigilance Commission (established in 1964), an autonomous body to fight corruption in the country!

## A Silver Lining

Despite present circumstances being gloomy, there is a silver lining to the present educational scenario in the country. One discerns a change in the attitudes of those who matter in the country's education as the demands of globalization have trumped the vested interests of political and social groups who ordinarily undermine curriculum reform.[26] Almost banned from schools and undergraduate colleges in the North from 1960 onward following an agitation against it by the Hindi chauvinists, English has now returned with the blessings of our political leaders, including those who had opposed it earlier. Persuaded by the prospect of the English-language-educated graduates obtaining employment and access to further education in India and abroad, parents have also changed attitudes, now favoring for their children an English education in a private school, often at huge expense. Now parents and their wards want curriculum at all levels that will lead to lucrative and satisfying careers. As reported in *the Times of India*, dated July 22, 2010, "In today's context, good schools do not mean, good academics alone. This means that school has the expertise for their students in psychology, pedagogy, teacher education, leadership development, and *curriculum design*" (italics are mine).

Designing a school-level curriculum is no longer the sole prerogative of teachers, of the government, or of government-controlled educational bodies. As reported in *the Times of India* on August 1, 2010, a Bangalore boy—Shourya Saluja—is developing a curriculum concerning cyber security (with the help of Infosys), which will not only be taught in his school but also in institutions managed by Central Board of Secondary Education at Delhi. Global concerns take local forms. While planning to introduce vocational education at the lower level of the school mostly to meet regional needs and requirements, the HRD Ministry is also thinking of introducing a core curriculum in Science, Mathematics, and Commerce. While it is necessary to align states and regions in education, it is equally important to understand the special needs and requirements, unique strengths, and discrepancies within each region, which now have increased manifold after globalization. An opportunity to enter the workforce needs to be made available to students via the vocational educational route for school dropouts and for the differently abled categories to allow them to find respectable work and individual growth. For students pursuing higher education compulsory skill programs should ensure employability. In a growing economy not everyone can be or should be a doctor or an engineer. Vocational education should not be considered as the last option for school dropouts or underperformers but as a mainstream curriculum providing career opportunities.

As has been recently pointed out by Deepak Jain, former dean of Kellogg Business School of Northwestern University in the United States, teachers should design and develop curriculum not only to answer the needs and requirements of an Indian market but also of the global one. We should design our curriculum at the higher level not only for job seekers but also for *job creators*. In other words, design of a curriculum must develop and involve ideas of innovation and creation at all levels and this can be achieved by putting more emphasis on research, particularly at higher levels.

It seems that the trend nowadays in designing a curriculum (either at the school or at the institutes) is to accent its potentiality to equip a student with a skill for a job. Less emphasized is its capacity to instill in the traditional values of education. It is absolutely necessary to strike a balance between the two objectives, at least at the school level. For, human beings do not live by jobs alone. With a changed, updated, and balanced curriculum in keeping with the forces of globalization, we can always look forward to a brighter and prosperous future of our country.

## A Retrospection

Not only the heart of an education system, curriculum is also an indicator of the nature of the society in which we live. In ancient India it enjoyed a free and spontaneous growth without pressure from above. In medieval India the indigenous curriculum was replaced by an imported one, designed to meet the needs and requirements of an Islamic administration and community. The conquered non-Muslim subjects—including the learned priestly class that created the Vedas and the Upanishads—were excluded. The scenario dramatically changed under British rule when non-Muslims (especially those living in metropolitan cities and towns) could enjoy access to Western education and science. However, Western curriculum was also imported. This curriculum aimed primarily to meet the needs and requirements of the British ruling class, but it soon overreached when it graduated a large number of Western educated persons who could not be absorbed into the colonial administration. Like its medieval counterpart, Western education did not attend to indigenous growth and development. This colonial legacy bequeathed to us by the British went through no significant shift until the fabric of an independent Indian society came under severe stress and strain, portrayed in literary terms by the Nobel Laureate V. S. Naipaul in his book *India: A Million Mutinies Now*.[27]

Only after the assassination of Indira Gandhi in 1984 was serious attention focused on the nature of the curriculum in schools and colleges. Attempts were then made to develop a curriculum in response to the needs and requirements of an independent nation; these were expressed in 1986 in the New National Policy on Education. However, the success achieved was not remarkable due to an unstable central government often in conflict over differences of opinion on the subject. Only recently, in the early years of the present millennium, have we seen shifts as India comes under the full impact of globalization. The forces of globalization have paved the path for the development of a new curriculum in information technology, engineering, management, and the allied sciences, and without any help from our educational planners and leaders. The new curriculum now seems an answer to the needs and aspirations of the young people of this country.

But many remote parts of the country—inhabited mostly by the Dalits and tribal people—have not seen any developmental activities, including educational growth, since independence. The first thing to do in such areas is to spread literacy, backed by a framework of vocational curriculum to suit the local needs and requirements, a curriculum to enable residents to earn their daily living. The failure to provide basic, then vocational, education—a failure of our learned politicians, educational planners, and administrators—has cost India a lot: the loss of human lives first of all and the destruction of national properties by the almost daily violent and disruptive activities of the Naxals,[28] often sympathized with by our disgruntled Maoist intellectuals and political leaders. Laced with colonial legacies, mobilized by economic globalization, and riddled with conflicts among apparently irreconcilable cultural traditions and political movements, the curriculum in India is complicated indeed.

# Notes

1. The break-away group of the Indian National Congress formed a new political party, "the National Congress Party" or the NCP. (Unless otherwise indicated, all notes are Ghosh's.)
2. The use of "center" in these essays means "federal government" in the US sense (editor's note).
3. Scapegoating education is no stranger to the US scenario (see Pinar 2012 xiv; editor's note).
4. For an account of the curriculum in ancient and medieval India, see my book, *Civilisation, Education and School in Ancient and Medieval India, 1500 B.C.-1157 A.D.* based on my lectures delivered at Friedrich Schiller Universitat, Jena, between 2000 and 2001 and published by Peter Lang at Frankfurt in 2002.
5. The major European powers who came to India for trade and commerce were the English, French, Dutch, Danes, and Portuguese. The Portuguese were the first to come by sea-route and established themselves in Goa, Daman, and Diu. The Dutch set up their headquarters in Chinsurah, the Danes in Serampore, and the French in Chandernagore (all in Bengal) and in Pondicherry (Madras now Tamil Nadu). There were frequent hostilities in India among them, which often followed their wars in Europe.
6. The governing body of the East India Company was the Court of Directors, consisting of 24 directors who held office on a rotating basis and who worked from the East India House at London. For details about the East India Company, see C. H. Philips, *The East India Company, 1784–1834*. Manchester, 1961. For an earlier account of the Company, see K. N. Chaudhuri, *The English East India Company, 1600–40*. London, 1965.
7. The other two Presidencies were Bombay and Madras. By Lord North's Regulating Act of 1773, the Bengal Presidency was given a supervisory status over the other two.
8. The Vedic learning at Nadia in Bengal survived the wrath of Islam because of the toleration of the Muslim governors of Bengal who were usually Shias.
9. For an account of how the Education Clause (43) was included in the Charter Act of 1813, see my article based on a paper delivered at the International Conference on History of Education at Paris in 1981 in Willem Frijhoff (ed.), *L'Offre D'Ecole*, Sorbonne (Paris), 1983, 48–52.
10. Some of the funds were spent translating and publishing old Sanskrit manuscripts.
11. It was Bentinck then, and not Macaulay, who introduced English education in India. Yet Macaulay often receives credit for it, partly due his prophetic characterization of Western-educated youth as "Indian in blood and color but English in taste, in opinions, in morals and intellect" and partly due to his contempt for Oriental learning, which stirred anti-British sentiments during the national movement. Another factor was the publicity given by his brother-in-law, Charles Edward Trevelyan, one of Governor-General Bentinck's favorite officials. For details about this interesting episode, see my article "Bentinck, Macaulay and the Introduction of English Education in India," in the *History of Education*, London, 1995, 24 (1): 17–24.
12. The *Dispatch*—based on the materials supplied by Dalhousie—was actually drafted by Wood's Secretary, Northbrook, who later became the governor-general of India before

Dufferin, but Wood, who, as the president of the Board of Control often described himself as "le rois des l'Indes," took credit for it "as the renovator of India," never mentioning the contributions of Dalhousie or his secretary. For an interesting discussion on the subject, see my article, "Dalhousie, Charles Wood and the Education Despatch of 1854," in the summer 1975 issue of *History of Education*, London 4 (2): 37–47.

13. For further details about my discussion on Curzon's university reforms to control the spread of higher education in the country, see my article in Edward Shils's *Minerva*, London, December 1988, 26 (4): 463–92. In the beginning Professor Shils was reluctant to accept my thesis that it was the question of the severity of unemployment among the educated Indians and not a bonafide attempt to put the Indian universities in proper order and functions that had led to this reform of the universities in India. Later he came to agree with me after examining the historical evidence I produced from the microfilm copies of the Private Papers of Curzon and Hamilton (secretary of state) at the National Archives of India, New Delhi.

14. Even an extremist leader like Bipin Chandra Pal was not against Western education and science; indeed he considered India's progress solely depended on it. He totally opposed the idea of reviving Oriental education in the country. What the national leaders like Pal wanted was full control over education. For details, see my chapter on "Bipin Chandra Pal and His Vision of National Education in India" in *India's Freedom Movement,* edited by B.K. Bhattcharya, 76–86. (Delhi, 2007).

15. It is possible that Gandhi borrowed his idea of a self-supporting basic education not only from Tolstoy but also from Tagore, whose educational experiments with the local peasants, artisans, and craftsmen in his "Ashram school" caught Gandhi's attention. Tagore had started this school as a "Brahmacharya Ashram" at Bolpur in 1901. Gandhi was a frequent visitor; he used to address Tagore as "Guru Dev."

16. In the inaugural address at a national conference on education in January 1948, Nehru observed: "Great changes have taken place in the country and the education system must also be in keeping with them. The entire basis of education must be *revolutionised*" (italics are mine). Nehru's observation was quite in keeping with the forces of the time thatsaw emergent nations in Asia, Africa, and Latin America preoccupied with the task of renovating their educational institutions to suit national needs and aspirations. For details, see my book, *Educational Strategies in the Developing Countries* (Delhi, 1977) and *History of Education in Modern India* (Delhi, 2008).

17. The Janata Government—under Morarji Desai—launched the Adult Education program on October 2, the birthday of Mahatma Gandhi. It revived Frank C. Laubach's philosophy of adult education—"Each one, teach one"—and for some time seemed to have caught the imagination of educational planners, leaders, and citizens. For Laubach's contribution to adult education in India, see my article on him in Martha Friedenthial-Haase ( ed.), *Personality and Biography in the History of Aultl Education* (Frankfurt, 1998), Vol. 2, 401–8.

18. I first discussed the genesis of "the 1986 New National Policy on Education" in a lecture delivered at Duke University, in North Carolina, followed by another at the School of Education, Indiana University in September 1988 that was later included in my book *The Education Policy in India since Warren Hastings* published the following year at Calcutta. It is interesting to note here that many of my observations made in 1988 on the future successes and failures of the 1986 Policy have been proved prescient.

19. The author was a member of this steering committee, responsible for drafting a bill on the establishment of the National Council of Teacher Education, which came into existence in 1995.

20. The Sixth Survey—which covers a period of seven years from 1993 to 2000, instead of five as is usual with such surveys—was made in 2007. Since the start of the project at

the NCERT in 1983, surveys of research (usually for a period of five years) are never completed on time.

21. In a Bengali magazine, *Sadhana,* 1892–93 (Ghosh's note).

22. Many politicians as well as academicians in our country do not always practice what they preach in public. While publicly opposing English education, many have always made sure that their children received their education in English medium schools.

23. As reported in *The Times of India,* dated April 25, 2010.

24. The Indian languages are divided into two major groups: Indo-Aryan and Dravidian. The number of officially recognized languages is 22.

25. As reported by the HRD Minister Kapil Sibal in a recent Rajya Sabha debate on education in the last week of August 2010. For details, see *The Sunday Times of India,* New Delhi, September 5, 2010.

26. The case of Uttar Pradesh (ruled by the Samajvadi Party under Mulayam Singh Yadav) is an interesting example. He opposes the introduction of English curriculum in the schools and the use of any modern technology, including computers.

27. I read Naipaul's book immediately after its publication in September 1993 while I was visiting the Faculty of Curriculum Studies at the University of Western Ontario, London, Canada.

28. The Naxal Movement began in the early 1960s. It owes its name to the name of the birthplace of its deceased founder, Charu Majumdar, who was born in Naxalbari in North Bengal.

# References

Bhattacharya, Binay. K., ed. 2007. *India's Freedom Movement: Legacy of Bipin Chandra Pal.* New Delhi: Deep & Deep Publications.

Chaudhuri, K. N. 1965. *English East India Company: Study of the Early Joint-Stock Company, 1600–40.* London: Frank Cass Publishers.

Friedenthal-Haase, Martha, ed. 1998. *Personality and Biography: Proceedings of the Sixth International Conference on the History of Adult Education.* New York: Peter. Lang.

Friejhoff, Willem, ed. 1983. *L'Offre d'école: éléments pour une étude comparée des politiques éducatives au XIXe siècle : actes du troisième colloque international, Sèvres, 27–30 septembre 1981.* Paris: Publications de la Sorbonne.

Ghosh, Suresh Chandra. 1975. "Dalhousie, Charles Wood and the Education Despatch of 1854." *History of Education* 4 (2): 37–47. doi:10.1080/0046760750040204.

Ghosh, Suresh Chandra, ed. 1977. *Educational Strategies in Developing Countries.* New York: Sterling Publishers.

Ghosh, Suresh Chandra. 1988. "The Genesis of Curzon's University Eform: 1899–1905." *Minerva* 26 (4): 463–92. doi:10.1007/BF01096494.

Ghosh, Suresh Chandra. 1989. *Education Policy in India since Warren Hastings.* Calcutta: Pilgrims Publishing.

Ghosh, Suresh Chandra. 1995. "Bentinck, Macaulay and the Introduction of English Education in India." *History of Education* 24 (1): 17–24. doi:10.1080/0046760950240102.

Ghosh, Suresh Chandra. 2001. *Birth of a New India: Fresh Light on the Contributions Made by Bentinck, Dalhousie and Curzon in the Nineteenth Century.* New Delhi: Originals.

Ghosh, Suresh Chandra. 2002. *Civilisation, Education, and School in Ancient and Medieval India, 1550 B.C.-1757 A.D.: Ancient India, 1500 B.C.-1192 A.D., Vedic Schools and Buddhist Viharas and Medieval India, 1192 A.D.-1757 A.D., Maktabs and Madrashas [i.e. Madrasahs], Mosques and Khanqahs.* Frankfurt: Peter Lang Publishing, Incorporated.

Ghosh, Suresh Chandra. 2007. "Bipin Chandra Pal and His Vision of National Education in India." In *India's Freedom Movement*, edited by Binay Bhattcharya, 76–86. Delhi: Deep & Deep Publications.

Ghosh, Suresh Chandra. 2008. *History Of Education In Modern India 1757–2007*. 3rd ed. New Delhi: Orient BlackSwan.

Government of India. 1902. "Report of the Indian Universities Commission." Calcutta: Government Central Print Office.

Government of India. 1917. "Report of the Calcutta University Commission." Calcutta: Government Central Print Office.

Government of India. 1929. "Report of the Hartog Committee." Calcutta: Government Central Print Office.

Kumar, Krishna. 1991. *Political Agenda of Education: A Study of Colonialist and Nationalist Ideas*. New Delhi: Sage Publications.

Majumdar, Ramesh Chandra, ed. 1965. *The History and Culture of the Indian People*. 9 vols. Bombay: G. Allen & Unwin.

Mangan, J. A., ed. 1993. *The Imperial Curriculum: Racial Images and Education in the British Colonial Experience*. London: Routledge.

Ministry of Education and Social Welfare, Government of India. 1949. "Report of the Radhakrishan Commission, 1948–49." New Delhi: Government of India Planning Commission.

Ministry of Education and Social Welfare, Government of India. 1953. "Report of the Mudaliar Commission, 1952–53." New Delhi: Government of India Planning Commission.

Ministry of Education and Social Welfare, Government of India. 1966. "Report of the Kothari Commission, 1964–66." New Delhi: Government of India Planning Commission.

Ministry of Education and Social Welfare, Government of India. 1968. "National Policy on Education." New Delhi: Government of India Planning Commission.

Ministry of Human Resources Development (MHRD), Government of India. 1986a. "Programme of Action." New Delhi: MHRD.

MHRD. 1986b. "The New National Policy on Education." New Delhi: MHRD.

MHRD. 1992. "Programme of Action (Revised)." New Delhi: MHRD.

Naik, J. P., and Syed Nurullah. 1974. *A Students' History of Education in India (1800–1973)*. 6th ed. Delhi: Macmillan.

Naipaul, V. S. 1993. *India: A Million Mutinies Now*. London: Picador.

National Council for Educational Research and Training (NCERT). 1983. "Surveys of Education in India. (Third, Fourth, Fifth and Sixth)." New Delhi: NCERT.

Philips, Cyril Henry. 1961. *The East India Company: 1784–1834*. Manchester: Manchester University Press.

Pinar, William F. 2012. *What Is Curriculum Theory?* 2nd ed. New York ; London: Routledge.

Sargent, John. 1944. *Post-War Plan for Educational Development in India, 1944–84*. Delhi: Government of India.

Sharp, H., and J. A. Richey. 1920. *Selections from Educational Records of the Government of India*. 2 vols. Calcutta: National Archives of India.

# Chapter 4

# Curriculum Studies in India
## Colonial Roots and Postcolonial Trajectories
### Manish Jain

If "the academic field of curriculum studies is embedded in national culture" (Pinar 2005, 26) and our own social, historical, and institutional locations impinge on the questions we ask and the answers we give, then this effort to write about curriculum studies needs to take note of the specificity of India. I attempt to understand meaning and construction of the field of curriculum studies in India along two overlapping axes: (a) colonial experience, trajectory, practices, and tussles of nation building and democracy in India to locate curriculum in relation to larger context and developments, and (b) work in the area of education, curriculum, and textbooks by state and nonstate institutions to understand the ideas that have shaped curriculum studies and debates in India. This survey is used to take an overview of the state of the field of curriculum studies in India, its silences, challenges, and emerging areas of study. But before we undertake this exercise, it may be pertinent to understand the challenges involved in such an engagement.

## Challenges for Curriculum Studies in India

### Syllabus Society and Textbook Culture

The term "curriculum" has a historically specified usage. In the United States and Western Europe, irrespective of the shift from "curriculum development" to "understanding," there has been a tradition of curriculum formulation, implying autonomy for teachers[1] to decide their methods and make choices about the subjects that students would study "to reach a certain educational level" (Dottrens 1962, 82). In India, which following Dottrens may be classified as a "syllabus society," there has been a "textbook culture," implying the low status of teachers with little freedom and little influence over matters of curriculum (Department of Teacher Education 1969; Government of India 1961a; Harap 1959; Lulla 1968).[2] It emphasizes the syllabus and assigns centrality to textbooks and examinations (Kumar 1988, 452–453).[3] Instead of a "child's learning requirement, aims of education and the socio-economic and cultural contexts of learners," examination requirements have led the development of curriculum, syllabi, and textbooks (NCERT 2006, iv). Education psychology has traditionally dominated the teacher training courses (Government of India 1961a; 1961b; Pandey 1969).[4] Such a culture, with its colonial legacy, lays emphasis on memorization, on recitation without meaning, and does not involve cognitive engagement and interaction with the contents of the textbook. This centrality of textbooks in the Indian education system means that concerns, debates, and controversies around textbooks in colonial and postcolonial India must be the focus of our discussion to understand central questions of curriculum, namely, what knowledge is of most worth, what counts as knowledge, whose knowledge it is, and what are the social, political, and ideological underpinnings of the curriculum. Such an attempt has to begin with the recognition that while history textbooks have generated several heated debates[5] (Rudolph and Rudolph 1983; Mukherjee and Mukherjee 2002; Habib, Jaiswal, and Mukherjee 2003), there has been an almost total absence of social histories of curriculum in general, and of controversies and debates about other school subjects.

## Colonial and Postcolonial Trajectories and Diversities

To understand how textbooks have been implicated in the ideological processes and discourses of state in colonial and postcolonial contexts, how and with what effects contestations over formation of citizenship/nationhood and struggles over identity have taken place on the terrain of textbooks, we need to attend to histories of colonialism, trajectories of modernity, state formation, and democracy in India. We also need to understand how the Indian state and education are enmeshed in global relations of political economy, policy prescriptions, and borrowing.

This enquiry becomes increasingly complicated due to regional diversities within India due to linguistic differences, distinct histories of state formation, economic development, provision of education, and institutional capacities. These differences pertain to these regions being part of British India or a princely state, the longevity of colonial contact and colonization, social reform movements, agrarian and industrial relations, workings of democracy, shifts in social power, and the contemporary history of involvement of global networks of funding, research, and advocacy. Understanding of the purposes of education also varies across regions and different caste groups, and different "folk" notions and practices interact with "modern" notions. Further, any attempt to capture the history of concerns about curriculum and textbooks in India needs to move beyond the state system and bring voluntary institutions within its ambit to study epistemological and ideological considerations that have guided ideas and practices of curriculum in India.

## Splits of Language

Formation of metropolitan and regional intellectual class and public spheres in India was/is influenced by the linguistic split created between those educated in the English medium and those in the regional/vernacular languages.[6] English is not just a language; it also encompasses a worldview and denotes power. For researchers like me who did not study in English medium schools and for English is not the first language, the English-vernacular divide constantly shapes and constrains our writings. Irrespective of whether the mediation between these two worlds comes easy or not, one has to mediate, if one needs to enter, survive, and make one's presence felt in academic, intellectual, and civil society circles. A "double check" is constantly required to ensure that while reading and writing in English, metaphoric connections have not been reduced to literal connections and the phenomenon has been dutifully and correctly translated in English.[7]

The complexities of rupture, interaction, and mediation between these two seemingly polar worlds also shape the academic and public debate and anxieties about education and curriculum. In the absence of sufficient number of studies that focus on these regional and linguistic differences and similarities and help us understand the cultural embeddedness of metaphors that describe education, our understanding of meanings and formation of curriculum is bound to remain limited.

## Spheres of Isolation

The discipline of education and the field of curriculum studies was/is largely shaped by its narrow focus on teacher training, on designing curriculum, and on its preoccupation with conceptualizing education as a set of moral aphorisms. Isolation of departments of education, their limited interaction with the larger university community, and the institutional constraints that bear on research in a developing country further impoverish the educational discourse and debates within the discipline of education in India. Absence of a culture of publication and rigorously peer-reviewed journals, small numbers of peer groups who can comment on one's writing, nonexisting or nonfunctional professional associations, a paucity of conferences—although a characteristic of academia in a developing country like India—are far more visible in the field of education. The contexts of production, circulation, and reception of academic knowledge also vary significantly across universities and colleges in the metropolitan centers and provincial areas, public and private educational institutions (including schools), and the heterogeneous population of teachers and students in these institutions.

In such a setting, questions about epistemological authority, how knowledge is produced, represented, and distributed, the nature of curriculum work, what knowledge is of most worth, how do we understand curriculum in the form of policies, culture, economics, identity, and history seem heretical and do not generate interest among the large community of teachers employed in colleges or university departments of education across India.[8] This narrow focus is exacerbated by dearth of books and research journals, scarcity of research grants, and little possibilities of scholarly exchange between colleges/departments of education located in provinces and mofussil towns and those in metropolitan centers of India. The antiacademic micropolitics of institutions mean that even a die-hard researcher finds it difficult to undertake research in such institutional cultures and ethos. We begin our inquiry of curriculum studies in India with an awareness of these challenges.

# Curriculum and Textbooks in Colonial India

Most often, a discussion about the role of education in the nation-building project of countries that were once colonized moves with the assumption that we have left colonialism behind, that colonialism is past, and what is at stake in the present is progress of the national self on the path of/toward modernity. Such a discussion does not take any cognizance of the colonial legacy of education, the ruptures it brought, the ways in which it was appropriated and contested by the colonized, and how ideas and debates about knowledge, national self, and citizenship were shaped by the experience of colonialism. I argue that several concerns about and contests around questions of knowledge and curriculum in independent India, often expressed on the terrain of textbooks, had colonial imprints. The new system of education introduced and developed by colonizers over a long period was based on a distinct understanding of knowledge and education—what should be taught to the young, how should it be organized, what should be the status of teachers, what routines and disciplines and modes of evaluation should be employed—from what was prevalent in India.

This new education never reached the entire population (which also limited the extent of its hegemony), yet its appropriation by the native elite to establish a new pedagogic relationship with the masses and the challenge from below to access it are histories that are yet being played out in contemporary India. Colonial education also introduced idioms of individual rights, equality, and universality, but in the context of the limited availability of mass education, the process of emergence of vernacular public spheres and individuated selves was severely limited. These new spaces and cognitive-political discourses were inhabited, appropriated, mediated, and shaped more by the hierarchies of caste and class, the reified communities, and collectives than individuals (Naregal 2001, 61–62). We can appreciate the significance, import, and echoes of these histories and contests in colonial and independent India, if we look at (a) the ideological frames that guided colonial educational policies, (b) the introduction of new subjects, and (c) the responses of the colonized to colonial policies and their own agency.

## Colonial Frames and Educational Transformations

Colonial educational policies and rhetoric were shaped by the competing and changing perceptions of rulers about Indian society and people, beliefs about the superiority of European civilization, the close relationship between knowledge and power, the needs of the Raj and the responses and demands of the colonized. Enlightenment philosophers had expressed confidence in the capacity of human mind and reason to refashion and improve unjust institutions and a social order based on ignorance, submission to tradition, religious authorities, and absolutist monarchs. They had exhorted human beings to grow out of the stages of immaturity, childhood, and ignorance, and they had associated knowledge with happiness. While in the eighteenth century India was perceived as a developed civilization, the Victorian idea of an Asiatic mind—ignorant, irrational, and emotional—had replaced it by the nineteenth century. Different colonial expositions of educational policies had hoped that by bringing the benefits of European progress and civilization to the colonized, it would break the hold of obscurantist forms of knowledge over ignorant masses and would have a morally uplifting influence on them (Kumar 2005, 28–34).

This new knowledge, which was to be scientific, practical, and useful, was to make new colonial institutions intelligible to the colonized by introducing "new discourses of society and power," bourgeois ideas of private property, order, reason, rights, and individuals and create a new common sense (Kaviraj 1991, 80). A liberal vocabulary of universality, equality, and individual rights was also used to enunciate the differences between the colonizer and the colonized. Controlling these differences that threatened the stability of colonial order was a continuing concern.

## The "New Subjects"

Unlike the precolonial curriculum in ordinary schools, which was not standardized and changed according to ability, and aimed to make one competent in meeting the requirements of the everyday life and agricultural practices of people (Babu 2007), the new colonial curriculum could not draw on the obscurantist forms of knowledge from the native society or not unless these were reformed to serve a new purpose in newer regimes of discipline. Continuing debates on the purposes and character of the school subjects and their textbooks testify to the contestations on the new definitions and criteria of truth introduced in colonial India. While all Englishmen, irrespective of their age, "could enjoy and appreciate exotic tales, romantic narrative, adventure stories and mythological literature for their charm and even derive instruction from them," the colonized subjects were barred from such experiences on two counts—their lack of "prior mental and moral cultivation required for literature" and the "immorality and impurity" assigned to oriental literature. Thus, Kalidasa's *Shakuntala* could delight Europeans but "was disapproved as a text for study in Indian schools and colleges" (Viswanathan 1998/2003, 5–6). On the one hand, English was an aspect of cultural imperialism and on the other, several Indians demanded its introduction.

Geography, for which a school textbook was brought by the School Book Society in Calcutta as early as 1819 (Chatterjee 1996, 17), was introduced to give natives opportunities to look outside their ignorant enclosures by studying the geography of India, Asia, and the world in a scientific and objective manner. This perception about young Hindus being "extraordinarily ignorant of their own country" also guided justification of introducing the first textbook of colonial civics, *The Citizen of India,* in the last decade of nineteenth century as it contained "a great deal of information which it is desirable that they should acquire at school"[9] (*Maharashtra State Achieves MSA* 1902). Colonial rulers had used the binaries of history/myth to bemoan the absence of "objective" historical narratives by natives. In the colonial context, history and a new discourse of historiography acquired a pedagogic character in order to train natives, to rewrite their own history, to legitimize colonial rule, and to establish superiority of Western civilization. It was also used to challenge colonial accounts, express "collective identities of different kinds, and a site of contestation for competing Indian social and political visions" (Deshpande 2007, 79–80). English histories of England, Europe, and India, which were used as school textbooks, introduced the new category of "India" and focused "not on *practicing* history but on knowing it *factually*" (Deshpande 2007, 84–6, emphasis in original). History was to occupy a central place in the textbook controversies in independent India given its significance in narrating the past, envisioning a future nation, and suggesting a political intervention in the present.

Notwithstanding the 1835 decision to privilege European literature and science over Oriental languages and knowledge, science as a distinct subject of study was not introduced in schools till late nineteenth century (Venkateswaran 2007). Western science was seen as "the most problematic in the process of 'engraftment'" by Arnold. Hindu parents were anxious whether introduction of such secular knowledge was part of a larger attack on their religion. Due to these anxieties, Bible classes were not allowed in government schools in Punjab (Allender 2007, 53). Associations of science with colonialism made it a target of xenophobia in certain sections of anticolonial consciousness (Kumar 1992, 9). The place of science in national education was an issue of debate in different proposals in colonial India (Bhattacharya, Sabyasachi 2003). How these anxieties played out in independent India is itself a fascinating story, one I will narrate in the next section.

School curricula and textbooks also became grounds in which to forge standardized versions of vernacular scripts, linguistic and literary *samskara* over those used by more people and other informal channels (Deshpande 2007, 84–91, Orsini 2002, 91–2). They thereby played their role in shaping the "public language and the public sphere" (Orsini, ibid.). Besides school textbooks, another set of printed reading material made available since the early nineteenth century in colonial India was popular old fables and tales focused on morality and ethics. They were adapted and printed by the government to improve morals and provide entertainment (Deshpande 2007, 82–83). Thus, the picture was "more complex than the simple harnessing of new texts as tools of colonial intellectual dominance in the classroom" (Powell 2011, 205).

These new subjects—such as geography and history—caused considerable anxiety among the traditional gurus who were not trained by the new system of teacher training institutions called normal schools. The introduction of these subjects resulted in the decreased enrolment of students from lower-caste backgrounds (Shahidullah 1996). Colonial education had considered indigenous knowledge and practices as deficient and hence not eligible to be part of school curriculum. Students did not engage with the textbooks to interpret them individually and make their own meaning. Concerns about the efficacy, limits, and complexities of using textbooks, about the power of the written word, and of pedagogy to transform the body politic and civilize the natives and native society led to different proposals to reform textbooks. These suggestions included translating textbooks in vernacular languages, writing textbooks in a language comprehensible for students, and replacing European imageries with that from the subcontinent so that they could relate to their own experience (Allender 2006).

The story of modernity in colonial India cannot be complete unless we also note the ambivalence of the colonial state, including shared assumptions of the native elite and the colonial state of its pedagogic relationship with and responsibility vis-a-vis the colonized masses. Nor can we ignore the appropriation of the promises of modernity by the marginalized sectors of Indian society to demand protection and claim rights and dignity.

While colonial state as well as missionaries provided education to lower castes and women, they were ambivalent, at times asserting principles of fairness, equality, and justice, and at others fearing that opening classrooms to lower castes would invite upper-caste opposition and restrict expansion of colonial education. The lower castes themselves challenged upper-caste dominance over education and appealed to colonial rulers to break this monopoly and promote education among them (Constable 2000). Contesting ideas and aspirations of the future station of the lower castes and women led to bitter debates over what these groups should study. Nationalist leaders like Tilak, who considered reforms and loss of caste as loss of nationality, argued that "subjects like History, Geography Mathematics and Natural Philosophy...have no earthly use in practical life." He even considered the teaching of reading, writing, and the rudiments of history, geography, and mathematics to Kunbi (peasant) children harmful. Instead, teaching traditional occupations was advocated as suitable. General education was to be given to those who had a "natural inclination" for it, whereas peasants' children were to receive "the education befitting their rank and station in life" (Rao 2008, 4–6). In contrast, Phule[10] and other anticaste reformers who wanted to form social institutions based on reason and equality argued for a thorough education for lower castes that would teach them to distinguish between right and wrong (O'Hanlon 1985, 118–20).

Questions concerning the suitable curriculum and the extent of education to be provided, fears about educated women with their own desires, voices, choices, and public presence had been part of the discussions about female education among the Indian males from nineteenth century. Men were concerned about the consequences of education of women and their entry into the public sphere on the character of women, their possible neglect of household duties and disrespect for traditional norms, values, and authority and their natural proper domain. At the turn of twentieth century, both government policies and school curriculum were discarding a common curriculum in favor of a separate curriculum for girls that does not "imitate" what is suitable for boys and is "practical" for their future position.[11] Such a curriculum would comprise reading, knowledge of sacred literature, understanding of the myths and legends that spoke of their domestic duties and roles, domestic science (practical skills like cooking and sewing, etc.), and elementary accounts to scientifically manage the refashioned household, perform domestic responsibilities, rear children, and be better mothers, sisters, and companionate wives. In contrast, a woman's magazine *Bamabodhini*, defended education for girls to develop their faculty and open their inner eye, "give confidence to women to use their own judgement and thereby reduce their dependence on men" and "generate self-respect" (Sarkar 1999, 103–5).

Irrespective of its loud expressions of concern about the condition of women, the colonial state spent far less on education of girls than the native private initiatives. This was in consonance with its larger strategy to minimize conflict with the self-proclaimed native leaders attempting to protect Indian culture from the interventions of the colonial state. This duality allowed the patriarchal colonial state to project itself as a progressive force constrained by the backward Indian society that it was trying to improve and reform. And it also signaled its patience to wait for an appropriate moment and not force change (Kumar 2010, 76). These moves of high moral aspirations to protect women and move with caution were in reality a series of expressions over the "women question" by the patriarchal state in independent India as well.

It is quite evident that a historical lens may be quite enriching, but the field is marked by paucity of studies of colonial textbooks and curriculum with reference to these social struggles around caste and gender to establish and legitimize social dominance of the native elite through use of colonial categories of civilizational hierarchy (Basu 2010) or to counter and accommodate the challenges posed to existing social relations (Jain 2009). Transfer of education to the hands of the Indians after the First World War did bring some changes in civics textbooks. My historical study of the colonial civics curriculum since late nineteenth century shows that in the period after the First World War, the nationalist elite strongly emerges as the new speaking voice of the nation. It used different strategies to challenge the colonial state in these textbooks, which were also a site of contestations over constructing "the idea of India." Character as a major theme in the discourse of civics and citizenship in this period expressed a range of concerns that had colonial and national roots. Concerns of commentators and educationists about the future state of the nation and the role of citizen in the colonial context/freedom struggle and independent India also shaped textbooks (Jain 2009).

## Textbooks, Controversies, and the Voice of the Colonized

Given the centrality of textbooks as a pedagogic device in the colonial education system, it is disconcerting that very little research exists on the content, debates, and controversies over textbooks in colonial India. Thus, our knowledge about shifts in ideological agendas of textbooks and composition of textbook committees at particular phases of colonial rule and how they reflected political concerns and anxieties over the stability of the Raj is quite modest. The complexity of the processes of textbook production and use, space for precolonial Indian books in the curriculum, perspectives guiding textbooks, the degrees of congruence between colonial textbooks and "approved" British texts, the selection of textbook authors and their anticipation of readers' influence over texts (including the provincial setting where the textbook was read), and from where criticism emerged: these are important issues that have received scant attention (Powell 2002, 2011). We need more studies that locate a colonial textbook with reference to other cultural texts where politics and discourse of colonial dominance were being played out, that examine the reasons for the selection or rejection of a textbook, including the precise government orders issued to promote a textbook in order to advance ideological and pedagogical objectives (Jain 2009). In the context of amnesia about the colonial legacy of education, significance of such work for curriculum studies in India need not be overemphasized.[12]

On the basis of the existing evidence, we can say that at least from late nineteenth century, textbooks were receiving significant attention in the emerging but restricted public sphere in India. Textbook policies (practiced and proposed), writings, petitions, and newspaper reports show that colonial officials, missionaries, and representatives of religious communities were no homogenous group. There were different voices within each group and they differed from each other and changed positions over a period of time. These differences pertained to the use, role, and purpose of education to question or promote certain religious beliefs and identity, to introduce religious and moral instruction in government schools, and to identify the role of state in enabling or restricting aggressive religious agendas. Whether education should present colonial ideals of manliness and promote imitation of English manners and history did not evoke a common answer (Allender 2007; Bellenoit 2007; Seth 2007). Different religious communities in India kept a close eye on how textbooks represented their religious beliefs and history and submitted petitions to correct the objectionable passages, words, and addresses (Jain 2012).

The first textbook of civics in colonial India (1897), *The Citizen of India*, authored by William Lee-Warner, and the controversy over its introduction, content, and language, is a significant instance to understand these contests, its participants, the concerns of the incipient national community, and the legacy that continued to shape the subject until very recently. Lee-Warner profiled the citizen by pointing out the shortcomings of the native personality, society, and its institutions. In this textbook one can find a simultaneous articulation of the idea of the modern liberal citizen unmarked by any traditional/parochial identity except that of the "nationhood" and state and a reference to the lack of a sense of citizenship and "national" community in India. The vocabulary employed to discuss the desirable virtues of the citizens and the role of state had its ideological roots in the social philosophy of liberalism and was related to the colonial task of creating civil society and maintaining colonial rule in India. Reason and loyalty to colonial state became the marker of a citizen's identity as opposed to that of the native, who, governed by uncontrolled emotions and passions, could rebel against the colonial state. Lee-Warner's textbook projected state as an agent of change within the "native" society and the creator of a civil society according to universal values of progress. This affirmation of an ideal citizen and an ideal political state through the civics textbook was in essence an affirmation of the colonial state (Jain 2009). These frames of civics—projections of state and discourses of lack among citizens—were to continue after independence until 2005 when the National Curriculum Framework (NCF) replaced civics with politics at the elementary level classes.

The series of objections to Lee-Warner's textbook can be classified into two categories—pedagogic and political-ideological—and can be quite instructive to understand contestations over textbooks. *The Citizen of India* was also criticized for ove-emphasizing the superiority of British to native rule, for its propensity to give rise to "very undesirable controversies and recriminations," its assessment of Indian society, and its assigning of weakness to natives. Students pointed to the ill-effects of colonial policies and raised doubts about colonial claims. Pedagogic concerns pertained to its difficult language, which was seen as far above the level of even students of English schools. Its length and heavy use of statistics were criticized for adding burden "to an already somewhat overcrowded course of studies." It was alleged that the author did not have "an intimate knowledge" of the standard of attainment of Indian school boys and dealt with questions that were above their considerations (Jain 2011). These concerns continue to reverberate in discussions over textbooks and curriculum in independent India.

## Curriculum and Textbooks in Independent India

### Challenges of Nation Building

Of the several paradoxes of the history of modernity, modern democracy and nation-state, one is that the autonomous, rational, thinking, political individual who is to exercise democratic choice is simultaneously the subject in whose name modernity, democracy, and nation-state exists and is the pedagogical object that is to be transformed and made an acting subject for self and these modern formations. For the newly independent India, challenges involved in accomplishing these pedagogic and political tasks were further compounded by the enormity of nation building in the context of colonial legacy. Given the recent history of partition, the new Indian state was anxious about nation building in the face of its plurality. These anxieties and a monolithic conception of nation were to become a staple concern of the educational discourse in independent India. In school textbooks, the citizen of this nation was to remain an abstract unmarked individual without any cultural and community markers that gave a hint to his/her identity.

In Western countries, tasks of modernity, industrialization, democracy, and mass education had not been taken up quite so simultaneously. In contrast, the postcolonial state in India undertook a historically challenging task to institutionalize democracy in conditions of mass illiteracy, poverty, and absence of massive industrialization (Kaviraj 2000). Stepping into the footprints of its predecessor—the "colonial state"—the postcolonial state in India had to accomplish the historical task of transforming a "backward-looking" colony into a dynamic "modern nation." In the enunciation of the role of education in this national task, the battles for self and agency were/are waged through the intersecting corridors of patriarchy, class, and caste; they left their stamp on the debates over identity, community, difference, and similarity conducted in the deliberations over curriculum and textbooks.

The debates over curriculum and textbooks in independent India also reflect challenges of developing institutions and mechanisms through which curriculum and textbooks are framed, the frameworks that guide them, the struggles over participation of civil society, its fractures, and the relationship between civil society and state in these areas.

## Curriculum in the Age of National Reconstruction and Modernization

The key concerns about curriculum and textbooks in the first commission after Indian independence that focused on school education, namely Secondary Education Commission (SES), revolved around "isolation" of the existing education system from life, its failure to provide "insight into the every-day world" in which students lived, for overcrowding of subjects and their watertight compartmentalization (GoI 1953, 21–23). It recommended enriching the curriculum by including material that will "give joy and insight to students." It also underlined the need to promote the "habit of independent thinking" and not limit students to prescribed textbooks (ibid.). The central government was expected to assume "greater responsibility" in the area of "the production and selection of better textbooks" (ibid.).

These recommendations of SEC to enrich the curriculum stand in contrast to the concern and obsession of the report of the Education Commission (EC, 1964–66), popularly known as Kothari Commission, submitted a decade later. EC was moving with urgency to meet the "great explosion of knowledge" (NCERT 1970, 10, para 1.70). Such an emphasis led to an increase in the curricular load on the child and contravened the significance attached to the child in the construction of knowledge (Arora and Goyal 1984).[13] Conferring importance to the child had to wait for another four decades (GoI 1993).[14]

Modernization, social and national integration, and political development were the key frames that guided the Kothari Commission in its conceptualization of the key concerns of its time. It then suggested the role of education in addressing them. It envisaged both economic and cultural role for science by linking education to productivity, "better use of material and human resources," and by strengthening the "commitment to free enquiry" along with the removal of superstition and fatalism. The discourse of the EC in many ways is reminiscent of nineteenth-century "nationalist" attempts to invent (exclusionary) traditions based on brahminic texts, and an effort to manage *artha* with *dharma*. The recurring uneasiness—since the latter half of the nineteenth century—over the diversity of India, the place of religious minorities, and an ongoing concern to accommodate religion with modernity were also present in this report. Given the limited attention of the EC to the social, economic, and political transformations necessary to create a society visualized in the Constitution, the pedagogic opportunities for a child to understand the social reality were also obviously restricted. These frames were subsequently challenged by the emerging critique of "development" by social movements and the new paradigmatic shifts in the social science discourse.

## Concerns about Textbooks and Curriculum Research

A series of other concerns about the quality and content of curriculum and text-books also influenced discussion and initiatives in the field. A 1959 report (Harap 1959, 7–8) noted with concern that the textbook was "a subject of common criticism in the daily press as well as by the teachers and administrators" and these pertained to their accuracy, obsolete character, grammar, literary style, and about their being based on life in Britain, etc. In an early evaluation of curriculum research, Desai and Roy (1974, 264–69) have faulted curriculum development in India for being "rigid," not being "based on empirical research findings," and for exhibiting a "time lag in developing and implementing a new curriculum." Curriculum research was cri-tiqued for lack of "sound methodology," the "limited scope" of sampling, with only few studies using experimental designs with rigorous statistical analysis, for failing to delve "deep into the problems of curriculum development" (Desai and Roy 1974, 264–69), and for "over-dependence on the use of questionnaires and test" with a majority of them being "descriptive surveys"[15] (Dave and Dave 1991, 576). A large number of these studies focused on techniques of teaching in general or in a particu-lar subject; many compared different teaching methods but few focused on concept attainment. Although a later evaluation reported curriculum to be fourth among seventeen areas of research (Dave and Dave 1991, 569), the number of research studies was considered inadequate given the large number of school systems at work in different provinces of India (Buch and Govind, cited in ibid., 570). Paucity of studies in this area in the early years (Roy 1979)[16] was also attributed to the fact that fewer national agencies sponsored curriculum research (Desai and Roy 1974)[17] and to an absence of their counterparts in the states. With the establishment of the NCERT[18] and its Department of Curriculum, Methods and Textbooks, studies were undertaken "about allocation of time to various subjects at school stage, improv-ing the methods of teaching and developing new textbooks" (Desai and Roy 1974, 264). Among the "different components of curriculum," 21.9 percent studies were classified as related to objectives and syllabus and 29.3 percent on learning experi-ences (Dave and Dave 1991, 574). The focus in the official discourse was always on making and improving curriculum and not on problematizing and reflecting on the meaning and significance of "what is worth teaching" from a social perspective.[19]

## Influence of the Bloom School

This absence of sociological perspectives on curriculum and curriculum develop-ment being shaped more by a psychological orientation followed the emergence of the technocratized educational discourse that arose in the United States with the rise of the Bloom School (Kumar 1986, 1682). Nine young teacher educators from India were selected "to study the new ideas on curriculum and evaluation, especially with Bloom in Chicago" through a US assistance program in the 1970s (Sarangapani 2006, 124–25). The "behavioral objectives" of education schematized in a "Taxonomy of Educational Objectives" developed by Bloom and his concept of "mastery learning" exerted considerable influence on the NCERT[20] (Malik 1962), state departments, and on the university departments of education[21] (Kumar 1986, Sarangapani 2006, 119, 124–25). With the promise of providing technical ways "to transcend the milieu" and legitimize "such transcendence in the name of effective instruction," this model found appeal among Indian educationists, who, like colonial masters, perceived "socio-cultural milieu as an obstruction rather than an asset for education" (Kumar 1992, 15–16).[22] That this perspective continued to guide ideas and practices about curriculum formation, teaching, learning, and assessment was evident by the concept of "Minimum Levels of Learning" (MLL), first spelt out by the NCERT in 1991, promoted by the Education for All (EFA) since 1993, and emphasized in the DPEP programs. It was developed under direction of "one of Bloom's most influential students," R. H. Dave, who served as the head of the Department of Curriculum and Evaluation at NCERT (Sarangapani 2006, 124–25).

## Emergence of Sociological and Critical Perspectives

The field of sociology of education (SOE) began to emerge in India in the late 1960s when the Kothari Commission brought together sociologists to discuss education. It received impetus with the publication of a seminal volume, *Papers in Sociology of Education in India* (Gore et al. 1967) and with the establishment of the Research Unit in the Sociology of Education (RUSE) at the Tata Institute of Social Sciences in 1970 and Zakir Husain Centre for Educational Studies (ZHCES) at the Jawahar Lal Nehru University. But the questions of curriculum, interactionist studies of classrooms and schools, remained outside its ambit for a long time (Nambissan and Rao 2013, 3–14). The publication of *Sociological Perspective in Education: A Reader,* jointly edited by Sureshchandra Shukla[23] and Krishna Kumar,[24] was a milestone in India, as it introduced an understanding of curriculum rooted in the new sociology of education developing in the Western academia. This collection brought together critical writings from Western and Indian scholars including Pierre Bourdieu, Basil Bernstein, and Michael Apple, and had a separate section on the sociology of teaching and curriculum. Since the late 1970s, Poromesh Acharya, a widely respected scholar in the areas of history and sociology of education, used his involvement with the literacy movement to analyze how Bengali *bhadralok*[25] in colonial and postcolonial Bengal with its emphasis on English, developed and included such primers and literary texts in the school curriculum that were devoid of the language of the laboring rural poor and reflected the world of the urban *bhadralok*. Like Krishna Kumar, Acharya brought the history and sociology of education together to reflect on questions of power, politics, identities, social structure, and aims of curriculum.[26]

These institutions and scholars inspired a large number of studies in the area of textbooks and curriculum that used the critical framework on politics of curriculum and knowledge to argue that these texts represent legitimate, "official knowledge" (Apple 2000) to the young; exclude, denigrate, and misrepresent marginalized groups and their culture;[27] legitimize cultural capital of the dominant groups;[28] work as instruments of social control; aim at the production of a homogenized, normalized, and socially functional citizen; and involve contestations over the formation of cultural community/citizenship/nationhood[29] and struggles over identity. Studies on the gendered character of textbooks have pointed to a lower representation of women in them: their portrayal as inactive, and located within homes in contrast to males, characterized in positions of power and prestige[30] (GoI 1992; Kumar 1989), their use of sexist language (Kalia 1986), and the binaries of "active-passive, emotional-rational, nature-culture and dependent and autonomous" (Bhog 2002, 1642) to represent masculine and feminine.

Using power as the central concept, studies undertaken by the feminist group Nirantar[31] examined how women are marked as biological reproducers and cultural signifiers of the traditions of the nation that bestows rights on men and obligations on women. Through an analysis of the language, disciplining of the student body, narration of the nation, description of its space and institutions in the textbooks, they point out how the nation is imagined in the textbooks in interaction with the fashioning of the regional identity and culture through interlocked operations of gender, class, caste structures, and hierarchies and cultural differentiation (Bhog et al. 2009).

## Contested Terrain of Subjects

Concerns about the content and quality of textbooks were far more expressed in the domain of history than any other school subject. Reminiscing her own engagement with the writing of history textbooks in the 1960s and 1970s, one of the foremost historians of India Romila Thapar (2009) discusses how the invitation to write a textbook that presented secular and national history was seen as a national duty in the wake of concerns about national integration and the existence of poor quality history textbooks that used communal, religious, and colonial stereotypes and were oblivious to the developments in the field. Later these secular textbooks were to be embroiled in a controversy over the two attempts by Hindutva[32] forces in 1977 and 2000 to replace them. The response of historians to the Hindutva attempts to rewrite history textbooks and to earmark a space for histories of communities and localities along with the nationalist account of history in school curriculum shows that in comparison to other social scientists, historians as an academic community have been more vigilant with regard to their discipline, have had fierce debates about different perspectives on history and nation and how do/should they inform school curriculum.[33]

This long engagement stands in contrast to the involvement of political scientists with civics as a subject that offered sanitized versions of the political institutions of state without any of the messiness of politics and democracy or the instability of the trope of unity in the wake of daily experience and without an awareness of the diversity, cultural differences, politics, and power in their local contexts among teachers and children (Balagopalan 2009; Yadav 2007). What this distinct engagement may suggest is the centrality of certain disciplines in the narration of the nation and the possibility of a hegemonic consensus about the purposes and functions of other school subjects and hence the need to also understand the field of curriculum studies in a disaggregated manner.

In independent India, science had come to express the promise of modernity to free people of superstitious beliefs. India's first prime minister Jawaharlal Nehru called for cultivating "scientific temper." Several rationalist associations have attempted to expose the magic and miracles claimed by religious "gods" and many People's Science movements and organizations have also worked in the area of education. On the other hand, postcolonial critics of modernity have questioned the "marriage" between the "valorized narrative of science to the world of capital" (Srivastava 1998, 52) as the legitimizing ideology of the developmentalist nation-state to deny democratic rights of citizens, enrich multinational companies (Menon 2010, 184), and create a pedagogic other. This faith in the power of scientific method and the profile of the ideal citizen "who reasoned clearly, thought independently, made judgements on the basis of facts, reason and tested data and thereby supported democracy and progress" is seen as the profile of the "civil servant of the postcolonial state who stood outside the class relations and structures of society and under a progressive leadership had to fulfill the historic task of changing the backwardness expressed in lack of education, poverty and inequity, caste and hold of superstitions" (Jain 2009, 235). Amid these raging debates is the solemnity of science, which, like other school subjects, is also being taught as a body of facts to be memorized by young schoolchildren. There is, in general, little possibility for a majority of students to experiment and observe on their own the very premises and procedures of science. I shall recall this context when we discuss about Kishore Bharati, Eklavya, and the *Hoshangabad Science Teaching Program* (HSTP)[34] in the next section.

## Curriculum Innovations

Developments in the academic field of curriculum studies in India since the 1970s cannot be summarized without reference to the innovative work in the field of education of various voluntary organizations started by highly committed and motivated scholars and activists in mostly nonmetropolitan, semiurban, and rural contexts with children from the marginalized sections. Some of these initiatives tried to bring working children into regular schools or worked with children who hadn't been reached, while others aimed at improving school education either through intervention within the government school system or by establishing their own schools to try out, develop, and showcase new ideas, materials, and practices (Ramachandran 2003). Initiatives of both these kinds involved interaction with scientists, historians, linguists, educationists, and other academics working in respected national institutions and local colleges. Mechanisms of support were negotiated and established with state institutions and the bureaucracy of education departments.[35] To understand the contribution of these efforts to the practices and discourse of curriculum in India, we may focus our attention on two seminal organizations, Eklavya and Digantar.

From 1972 onward Kishore Bharati and its later avatar, Eklavya, started several programs, namely Hoshangabad Science Teaching Program (HSTP), Social Science Teaching Program (SSTP) and Prathamik Shiksha Karyakram(Primary Education Program, PRASHIKA) in the government schools in Madhya Pradesh[36]. These programs addressed the existing conditions of the schools, the milieu and the context of children, the nature of knowledge in different subjects and their method (e.g., scientific/historical), as well as questions of appropriate science in a rural context with paucity of resources. They also attempted to engage with children's sense of history and power centers in a society undergoing multiple transitions and continuities. They explored "radical possibility in the curriculum through dialogue between the lived experiences and textbook narratives" and involved shifts from "the framework of 'popularisation of history' to 'democratization of production of historical knowledge'" (Saxena 1998, Subramaniam and Paliwal 2003).

Some of the members of Kishore Bharati themselves critically reflected on these programs, their political nature, and on the impact of these initiatives. They argued that although Total Education Program of Kishore Bharati used production-process-based pedagogy and agricultural projects for certain subjects, with its focus on modern agriculture, "education remained a one-way process" and the "dichotomy between the demands and the requirements of intense political struggle and the education program" created practical and program-related tensions that remained unresolved (Saxena 1998, 269–70, 275). The experience of the HSTP and discussions among people's science groups raised questions about the need to acknowledge or discuss social and political hierarchies in the society in an innovative curriculum program, on neutrality of science, "the relevance of disseminating scientific information in a feudal society," and the need to suggest ways of collective effort to change the situation (ibid., 279–80). The concept of pupils as scientists was questioned because it made science difficult. Questions were also raised concerning the inability of children to use these processes outside school, espousing "the classical inductive-empiricist approach towards knowledge," "ignoring the role of informed speculation and constructive imagination in processes of discovery" and emphasizing on taking note of "children's constructions of experience" (Rampal 1992, 57–59).

Reviewers of Social Science textbooks developed by Eklavya (Batra 2010) have appreciated these textbooks for presentation of concepts and contexts concretely using case studies, examples, and narratives in a lucid language; for a shift from state centeredness to assigning agency to people in civics textbooks; and for a greater understanding of human geography. They also point to their limits with retention of human-physical duality in geography textbooks, absence of discussion about the principles that underlie different institutions, and possibility of discussion remaining confined to concrete experience and not leading to abstraction.

Digantar brought the question of aims of education to centrality in discussions on curriculum or practice. By bringing the rigor of the philosophy of education to these discussions, it asked probing questions about the theoretical assumptions that guided their own and others' work with children. It insisted on training its own staff, teachers, and other practitioners to be self-aware of the assumptions and perspectives that guided their ideas and practices. This rigorous collective discussion demanded a professional seriousness to educational work that was not limited to the spirit of voluntarism and idealism to work for the disadvantaged. It thereby opened possibilities for self-reflection on practices and theories and gave a premium to a professional identity based on rigor of both ideas and practice (Digantar 2013).

Besides the richness, innovativeness, and criticality of these initiatives and reflections, they become significant for several reasons. First, the field of education in India in 1970s was in a much more formative stage and the field of sociology of education revolved around scholars trained in the discipline of sociology. These initiatives strengthened the reflective and critical trends in the area of curriculum studies that received momentum from the late 1970s onward. Second, NCERT, the national body officially responsible for leading research and curriculum reform including textbook preparation in the country, had argued that given the state of middle schools in India, the country could not afford the luxury of science teaching through experiments (Saxena 1998, 277). HSTP provided counterevidence to this view. Third, these innovations scrutinized curriculum in relation to children and their context, pedagogy, epistemology, understanding of discipline, and social structure. These issues also reverberate in the debates on the National Curriculum Framework for School Education (NCFSE) 2000 and the National Curriculum Framework (NCF) 2005 (Akhtar 2005; Bhattacharya 2009; Bhog 2002; Dhankar 2000; Habib 2005; Sarangapani 2009; Saxena 2006).[37] Fourth, these initiatives offered a possibility to integrate these experiences into a knowledge of the discipline, to theorize, and to renew formulations of systemic reforms. Fifth, members of these organizations made significant contributions to the critical discourse on curriculum through their writings in different books and journals, both national and local (Dhankar 1995; 2000; 2003; Paliwal and Subramanian 2006; Saxena 2006; Subramanian and Paliwal 1989; Sunny 2006).[38] Till NCF 2005, this discourse had a marginal status in the mainstream and official discourse on curriculum and these initiatives were seen as local and not suitable for the entire country.[39] The magazines published by Eklavya and Digantar in the last one-and-a-half decade, namely *Shaikshik Sandarbh* (Educational Contexts) and *Shiksha Vimarsh* (Educational Discourse), had original articles and translations of writings of Indian and Western researchers on issues of curriculum and textbooks in Hindi. Thus, they provided both a platform and resources for developing the field and the discourse of curriculum studies in an indigenous language.

# The Contemporary Scene: Absences, Challenges, and Promises

This overview shows that a variety of methodologies (content analysis, symbolic interactionism, hermeneutics, discourse analysis, ethnography, pedagogic interaction, perceptions of children) and perspectives (Piagetian, social-cultural reproduction, resistance, feminist, dalit, historical, disciplinary, Foucauldian, and postcolonial) has been used to examine curriculum and textbooks. While the various textbook studies employing critical perspectives showcase the promise of curriculum studies in India, they also point to the limitations of the field.[40] There is an absence of research that analyzes the enactment of textbooks in the classroom, for example, the pedagogic interaction between the teacher and the student. There is a dearth of studies that looks at the relationship among curriculum policies, research, and school practices or the development of curriculum in school or the strategies used by teachers and students to negotiate with the official curriculum. Studies of schools and learning by Thapan (1991), Srivastava (1998), Sarangapani (2003), and Sriprakash (2010)[41] remain an exception, as we know little about the daily enactment of the school curriculum and the daily life of school experience either with reference to the different axes of social marginalization like gender,[42] caste, poverty, and ethnicity, or in relation to teachers' work or various spaces and time schedules within the school, such as morning assembly, playgrounds, library, canteen, lobby, club spaces, teachers' staff room, and staff meetings.

Given the existence of diverse trajectories of educational development and different systems of education in various states in India, there is a need to research the regional dimensions, histories, and settings of the curriculum in India comparing the various states. Curriculum studies in India can also be enriched by researches about state examination bodies, SCERT's historical analysis of CABE, teachers' institutes, normal school curriculums, and institutional histories. Attempts to address paucity of research in this area face challenges of absence of preservation, maintenance, and accessibility to official reports, archival sources, and records.

At present "curriculum" has emerged as a significant concern in the mainstream educational discourse. The idea of curriculum, aims of education, the process of formation of curriculum and textbooks, social, political, and ideological underpinnings of the curriculum and pedagogy are key concerns in the contemporary debates on curriculum. Studies in the area of curriculum are increasingly engaging with the significance/relevance of constructivism in the Indian context, in the ability of children to make meaning and construct knowledge, place of disciplinary knowledge, and boundaries, "local" knowledge and formation of nation in the school curriculum.

Terms like child-centeredness and critical pedagogy have become part of the vocabulary without an understanding of their epistemic and political basis and meanings or the institutional preparation of translating them into textbooks and classroom practices. One partial explanation of this gap may relate to absence of individuation in Indian society, an unfinished project of modernity but this still raises a question as to whether it is possible to imagine the postcolonial space without the referent of "lack." And this discourse of "lack" can imagine people only as irrational, superstitious, communal, casteist, and patriarchal, who are to be reformed through a modern, progressive, and secular education. In this very process it reproduces the colonial binaries, the only difference being that this time the pedagogic authority has been assigned to the postcolonial state and its partners in the civil society who remain oblivious to or may be have too much confidence derived from their own dominant location. What is being questioned here is not the need to question the above beliefs but the denial of agency to people. Here a political project of transformation led by state with people as followers is to be accomplished without the messiness of politics and conflicts in the society. And this peculiarity of the postcolonial state is a question that rarely gets discussed in discussions on curriculum by those who are located in the academic discipline of education.

This modernity question resurfaces when we ponder over the frames of debates on history and the architecture of civics. If the claim of secular history is only with reference to its objectivity and scientific character, then how should a school history curriculum engage with the subterranean alternative historical knowledge and narratives of the past that are produced and circulated "through practices of cultural production and modes of socialization" (Bhattacharya 2003, 17) and continue to shape popular historical sense? Similarly, why the vibrancy and contestations that mark democracy in India find no space in civics, a subject entrusted to develop citizens, is a question that needs to be probed beyond the welcome shifts introduced through *Social and Political Life*, which has replaced civics at the elementary school level. These concerns about the absence of debates and the distance of the faculties of education from existing practices and initiatives of curriculum reforms such as HSTP also raise questions about the nature and status of education as a discipline and whether it can be self-reflexive (Sarangapani 2011, 77). These are concerns with consequences for the emergence of curriculum studies as a distinct field.

With more scholars from disciplines other than education reflecting on questions of curriculum[43] (Aporvanad 2007; Bhattacharya 2009; Yadav 2007), growth of new journals in English and Hindi that give significant space to different issues related with curriculum, use of different critical perspectives and engagement of organizations of different marginalized groups with questions of knowledge, representation, and pedagogy, we can expect that the conventional ideas of what is to be problematized may get increasingly challenged within the academic field and practices of curriculum and textbooks. Increasing interest in curriculum issues has created a larger community of scholars and scholarship than in the 1970s and 1980s who may be addressed and drawn upon for support and criticism of one's work. New MA Education programs at three universities Tata Institute of Social Sciences (TISS), Azim Premji University (APU), and Ambedkar University, Delhi (AUD), offer excellent opportunities to both teachers and students to reflect in curriculum studies way. This interdisciplinary reflection on and engagement with curriculum may lead to the emergence of a distinct field of curriculum studies but unless the universities and colleges outside metropolitan centers receive critical human and financial support for their revival, this field may remain restricted to fewer participants, thereby limiting its possibilities.

A new policy discourse—operating with categories of "choice," "management," "accountability"—has gained ground, with consequences for curriculum, teachers' work, their work conditions, and the school experience for diverse groups of students in the hierarchically stratified school system in India. Another significant development that may have serious repercussions on the possibilities and opportunities for curriculum research is the growing privatization of higher education, which is likely to gather greater momentum with proposals for public-private partnerships and permission granted to foreign universities to establish campuses in India. How these new regimes of discipline and management instituted at these private and foreign universities interested in making quick profit determine the work conditions of teachers and researchers, the agendas of research, and relevance of researches in the area of curriculum that do not address the administrative and technical focus on designing of curriculum or contemporary concerns of "school improvement" is a moot point.

# Notes

1. At present this autonomy is under attack by school reform movements, discourses, and practices of testing, "accountability," and "efficiency."
2. Concern about absence of representation of school teachers in the textbook and syllabus committees populated by the officials of the state education department was present in several official reports as well. See Harap (1959, 8, 86); Government of India (1961a, 134–136); Department of Teacher Education (1969, 1–2); Lulla, B. P. (1968, 4).
3. This dominance of textbooks had invited criticism from Mahatma Gandhi as well. It has been expressed as a concern in different reports but its hold continues. See, Lulla (1968: 8–9), ibid.
4. Several reports noted that Education Psychology was a common paper in the teacher training courses across different stages. But the list of compulsory courses did not include a paper on curriculum. See, Government of India 1961a: 179; Government of India (1961b 58); Pandey, B. N. (1969 49).
5. See, Lloyd I Rudolph and Susanne Hoeber Rudolph (1983, 15–37); Thapar (2009); *Seminar* (2003). Rewriting History, No. 522, February; Mridula Mukherjee and Aditya Mukherjee (eds.) (2002); Irfan Habib, Suvira Jaiswal, and Aditya Mukherjee (2003).
6. Recently, concerns have been expressed about the decline in the number of bilingual intellectuals who were proficient in both English and another Indian language and wrote in both the languages.
7. Here, I have drawn upon my discussions with Padma Sarangapani. She may share some of these concerns but not necessarily their articulation.
8. This articulation about key concerns of curriculum has benefited from discussion with Nandini Manjrekar.
9. Maharashtra State Archives (MSA), 1902.
10. Phule was an eminent figure in the anticaste movement. He along with his wife opened several educational institutions for lower castes and girls and established *Satyashodhak Samaj* (Society in/for Pursuit of Truth). For a biographical introduction to his life, work, and ideas, see, O'Hanlon (1985).
11. See Government Resolution on Education Policy 1913.
12. Basu (1974) stands out for its rich historical analysis of raging controversy over the colonial state's attempt to acquire greater control of the textbook committees at the turn of nineteenth century. For another notable exception and an excellent study in this area, see Sudipa Topdar (2010). Incidentally, both these studies are by trained historians. Several works referred in the course of discussion on the new school subjects are also by historians who only underline lower importance assigned to such examination by researchers located in the departments of education.
13. For another expression of these anxieties about "updating the curriculum" with the pace of change in "social, economic and political order," see G. L. Arora, and B. R. Goyal, (1984, 32–33).
14. Yashpal Committee Report (1993) titled *Learning without Burden* critiqued this obsession and was to later become the guiding framework for the *National Curriculum Framework* (NCF) 2005. Government of India (1993).
15. Buch and Govind, An Overview, in *Third Survey of Research in Education*, "Methodological Shortcomings" cited in Dave and Dave 1991: 576.
16. "The Third Indian Year Book of Education (1968) published by the NCERT gave a review of thirty one studies on curriculum and eighty five studies on methods of

teaching school subjects, the studies being mostly M.Ed. dissertations, and very few at doctoral level" (Roy 1979: 276).

17. After independence in 1947, the following agencies were involved in research in this area: the National Institute of Basic Education, the All India Council for Secondary Education, and the Central Bureau of Textbook Research; but these institutions did not develop any "programme of sustained and long term research in curriculum" (Desai and Roy 1974: 264).

18. National Council for Educational Research and Training (NCERT) was established as an apex national level body in the early 1960s and since then has been involved in school curriculum, textbooks, teacher training, and research. The curriculum and textbooks produced by NCERT bear a certain legitimacy and authority and have a far greater influence than the number of actual users of its textbooks.

19. I have borrowed the phrase "what is worth teaching" from Krishna Kumar's book (1992) with this title. World Bank sponsored District Primary Education Programme (DPEP) introduced in 1990s in the deliberations on curriculum in its teacher training restricted it to "difficulty levels for the child" and the problems faced by teachers without any "serious or substantiated discussion on concepts of education, school, desirable society or the aims of education" (Dhankar 2003: 18–19). The National Curriculum Framework (NCF) 2005 and the position paper of the national focus group on curriculum, syllabus, and textbooks address these questions.

20. A monograph published by the NCERT in 1962 reviewed several books in the area of curriculum, all of which had been published in the United States in the 1950s. The author of this monograph was President's scholar at Columbia University Teachers College, New York, during 1954 and 1955.See, Anand Malik (1962). Many monographs and essays in the area of curriculum published by or authored by Ministry of Education, NCERT, and Faculty of Education and Psychology, M. S. University of Baroda were titled "curriculum improvement" and "objective-based conceptual analysis." Some others focused on curriculum planning, curriculum implementation, curriculum evaluation, and curriculum administration. Prof. J. K.Shukla, head, Department of Teacher Education, NCERT, called for discarding "scissor and paste method" and "develop a curriculum in a scientific manner." See, Department of Teacher Education (1969: 6)..

21. Hilda Taba's work in the Bloomian tradition of learning objectives was a standard book in courses on curriculum in masters of Education courses in India. For example, Department of Education at the University of Baroda for long engaged with questions of curriculum in this mode. Bloom's taxonomy was considered significant for doctoral research as late as 1991. A PhD research by R. S. Sachan (1991) from Agra University, titled *Validity Study of Bloom's Taxonomy of Educational Objectives in the Cognitive Domain*, examined his six-tier and three-tier taxonomies, the relationship between process responses and product responses and the impact of objective-based teaching on development of category systems of the cognitive domain (Sabharwal 2000: 1097). Critical review of curriculum was to emerge as a distinct area in India in 1980s and is discussed later.

22. For an example, see Dave and Dave (1991). P. N. Dave who worked with NCERT in his evaluation of "Research in Curriculum" in India with his coauthor Jyotsna P. Dave defined curriculum having four "major components, namely, (a) objectives defined in terms of expected learning outcomes, (b) content, (c) learning experiences (learning and teaching strategies), and (d) tools and techniques of evaluation." According to them the "guiding principles of curriculum construction" are: "Flexibility, Relevance, Functionality and Productivity" (1991: 568). They felt that it was an "uphill task but also is strewn with insurmountable impediments, sociocultural as well as pedagogic

ones." Efforts needed to continue to meet "the needs and aspirations of diverse groups of learners," especially those who were denied education with the "question of equity in a democratic set-up" being of "paramount importance in curriculum construction."

23. Sureshchandra Shukla had opened the chapter of Comparative Education Society in India, was reading new sociology of education, and was instrumental in bringing Basil Bernstein to India. He served as president of The Comparative Education Society of India (CESI) for six years since its establishment in 1979. Some of his writings are: Sureshchandra Shukla (1983; 1998; 2002).

24. 1985, Delhi: Chanakya Publications.

25. The term *Bhadralok* refers to status, class, cultural attitudes, and values of a certain social group among caste Hindus who emerged in colonial Bengal in the nineteenth and twentieth centuries. This group though internally differentiated and occupying contradictory class positions was located in urban Bengal, had property in rural Bengal and earned income from it, availed Western education and used it to monopolize new professions, like lawyers and teachers, along with positions in different rungs of colonial bureaucracy, adopted liberal values with it, and a certain section within it formed a distinct civil society in colonial period.

26. His writings include Acharya (1978; 1981; 1982; 1986; 1995; 1997).

27. Studies on textbooks and class interaction have pointed out (Kumar 1983; Nambissan 2009; Ritubala 1997; 2001) that scheduled castes and scheduled tribes are portrayed as exotic, ignorant, or backward; their culture, struggles, and perspectives are absent from the, curriculum; the aims and efforts of heroes from these communities are belittled; their silence in class and nonparticipation in cocurricular activities are remarked upon; teachers perceive their lack of ability, intelligence, and thus feel they do not deserve to study; class interaction informed by the discourse of modernity and of history as factual and being independent of any perspective paints them as backward, with little understanding, respect, or space for their epistemology, history, culture, social background, and self-identity, and contributes to these students being pushed out of the school system. Textbooks also construct a demonology of uneducated and illiterates and identify the literates with "legitimate qualities" (Kumar 1993; Jain 2004).

28. Talib (1998; 2003) has argued that the textbooks naturalize inequality and reinforce superiority of mind and intellectual labor over manual labor. While teachers remain unaware of the distance between the reality of textbooks and of children's lives, children use different "removal strategies" to reject and resist such education, and in the process are declared unsuitable for education and themselves internalize such demeaning evaluations about themselves. Scrase (1993) in his study of English textbooks in Bengal has noted that middle-class occupations predominate in comparison to those of peasant labor. The former are located in the present and they represent the middle class as helping and assisting whereas village life is either idealized or stereotyped and peasant labor is identified with the past or has indeterminate status to indicate its technological backwardness and/or social irrelevance. NCERT (2005: 25–31) has noted that emphasis on "pure" language, "literature and other 'knowledge' of society . . . produced by higher castes," absence of "women's specialised knowledge and skills," and of the knowledge and language of lower castes, which is rooted in productive processes, devaluation of "lesser" dialects, cultures, traditions, and folklore of dalits and adivasis as also of peasantry," reflect brahmanization of curriculum and it being depicted as "urban elite male-centric and bereft of the country's rich cultural diversity."

29. In a significant study on the formation of nation, Advani (2009) tried to understand the shifting definitions and relationship of tradition and modernity in the construction of the national identity on the terrain of English, which is simultaneously a symbol of

global power, represents the entrenched status of the postcolonial elite, and the aspirations of the marginalized for social mobility.

30. See Government of India (1992); Krishna Kumar (1989).
31. These studies examined the textbooks of regional language, English, and Social Sciences (History, Civics and Geography) in four states and those published by NCERT.
32. *Hindutva* as a political ideology and project based on ideas of religious nationalism with the aim of constructing a *Hindu Rashtra* (a Hindu nation-state) needs to be differentiated from *Hinduism*, the religion.
33. NCERT also paid attention to history textbooks and developed guidelines. See NCERT (1972).
34. The HSTP program drew its inspiration from the Nuffield Science Project in the United Kingdom, and it was scientists rather than educationists who played a key role in this program. It had started with 16 government schools in 1972 and at the time of its abrupt end by the Government of Madhya Pradesh (MP) in 2002, it was working with 1000 schools and 2000 teachers in MP (Balagopalan 2003: 97).
35. The history of their relationship with state institutions has also been a story of several hiccups, set-backs, arbitrary and abrupt closure notices. See, Balagopalan (2003) for an insight into the experience of Eklavya.
36. For insider narratives and review of these different programs, see Kishore Bharati (1991); Joshi, Sushil (2008); Batra, (ed.) (2010); Agnihotri et al. (1994: 33, 45–54); Anil (2000); Saxena (1998:: 265–98); and Balagopalan (2003).
37. See Bhog (2002), Dhankar (2000), Sarangapani (2009), Bhattacharya (2009), Habib (2005), Akhtar (2005), and Saxena (2006).
38. Some of these writings include, Subramanianand Paliwal (1989); Paliwal and Subramanian (2006); Dhankar (1995); Dhankar (2000); Dhankar (2003); Saxena (2006); Sunny (2006); and George (2004).
39. Members of these organizations served on different committees during the formulation of NCF 2005 and the subsequent textbooks produced by NCERT. They have also played an important part in the formulation of the *National Curriculum Framework for Teacher Education* (NCFTE 2009) brought out recently by the National Council for Teacher Education, New Delhi. In the last one decade in particular, these organizations have also been invited by different state governments and for different programs for revision of textbooks, teacher education curriculum, and in-service teacher trainings.
40. I am grateful to Nandini Manjrekar and Padma Sarangapani for discussions on this aspect.
41. Thapan (1991) in her ethnographic study of the Rishi Valley school notices the tension between the educational vision of Krishnamurti and the pressures of operating as a school where students achieve "academic success" as testified by the results in board examinations. Srivastava (1998) uses a cultural studies perspective to examine how Doon School, an elite school established in colonial India, constructs the nation, ideal citizen, and its *other* through its emphasis on rationality, secularism, modernity, and science. Sarangapani (2003) employs ethnographic methods to unravel the beliefs, ethos, (folk) understandings, attitudes of teachers, parents/community, and children about education, school, worthwhile knowledge, and learning as distinct from daily life, educability, success, failure, childhood, and discipline. Sriprakash (2010) observes how messages of social boundaries and hierarchies were communicated to children in an innovative program *Nalli Kalli*.
42. Manjrekar (1999) has discussed how children from largely migrant families learn gender norms through different practices and interactions at school.
43. See Aporvanad (2007), Bhattacharya (2009), and Yadav (2007).

# References

Acharya, Poromesh. 1978. "Indigenous Vernacular Education in Pre-British Era: Traditions and Problems." *Economic and Political Weekly* 13 (48): 1981–88.

Acharya, Poromesh. 1981. "Politics of Primary Education in West Bengal: The Case of Sahaj Path." *Economic and Political Weekly* 16 (24): 1069–75.

Acharya, Poromesh. 1982. "Abolition of English at Primary Level in West Bengal." *Economic and Political Weekly* 17 (4): 124–28.

Acharya, Poromesh. 1986. "Development of Modern Language Text-Books and the Social Context in 19th Century Bengal." *Economic and Political Weekly* 21 (17): 745–51.

Acharya, Poromesh. 1995. "Bengali 'Bhadralok' and Educational Development in 19th Century Bengal." *Economic and Political Weekly* 30 (13): 670–73.

Acharya, Poromesh. 1996. "Indigenous Education and Brahminical Hegemony in Bengal." In *The Transmission of Knowledge in South Asia: Essays on Education, Religion, History and Politics*, edited by Nigel Crook, 98–118. New Delhi: Oxford University Press.

Acharya, Poromesh. 1997. "Educational Ideals of Tagore and Gandhi: A Comparative Study." *Economic and Political Weekly* 32 (12): 601–6.

Advani, Shalini. 2009. *Schooling the National Imagination: Education, English and the Indian Modern*. New Delhi: Oxford University Press.

Agnihotri, R. K. et al., 1994. *Prashika: Eklavya's Innovative Experiment in Primary Education*. New Delhi: Ratna Sagar.

Akhtar, S. 2005. "A Critical Note." *Social Scientist* 33 (9–10): 37–40.

Allender, Tim. 2006. *Ruling through Education: The Politics of Schooling in the Colonial*. New Delhi: Sterling Publishers Pvt. Ltd.

Allender, Tim. 2007. "Surrendering a Colonial Domain: Educating North India, 1854–1890." *History of Education* 36 (1): 45–63.

Aporvanad. 2007. "Kaun Si Pustaken Pathya Hain?" *Shiksha Vimarsh* Jan-Feb: 7–20.

Apple, Michael W. 2000. *Official Knowledge: Democratic Education in a Conservative Age*. London: Routledge.

Arora, G. L. and Goyal, B. R. 1984. "Growing Expectations from Curriculum in India." In *Reflections on Curriculum*, edited by G. L. Arora, New Delhi: NCERT.

Babu, Senthil. 2007. "Memory and Mathematics in the Tamil Tinnai Schools of South India in the Eighteenth and Nineteenth Century." *The International Journal for the History of Mathematics Education* 2 (1): 15–37.

Balagopalan, Sarada. 2003. "Understanding Educational Innovation in India: The Case of Eklavya, Interviews with Staff and Children." *Education Dialogue* 1 (1): 97–121.

Balagopalan, Sarada. 2009. "'Unity in Diversity': Social Cohesion and the Peadgogical Project of the Indian State." In *Thinking Diversity, Building Cohesion: A Transnational Dialogue*, edited by Mokubung Nkomo and Saloshna Vandeyar, 133–50. Amsterdam: Rozenberg Publishers.

Basu, Aparna. 1974. *The Growth of Education and Political Development in India 1898–1920*. Delhi: Oxford University Press.

Basu, Subho. 2010. "The Dialectics of Resistance: Colonial Geography, Bengali Literati and the Racial Mapping of Indian Identity." *Modern Asian Studies* 44 (1): 53–79.

Batra, Poonam, ed. 2010. *Social Science Learning in Schools: Perspective and Challenges*. New Delhi: Sage.

Bellenoit, Hayden J. A. 2007. *Missionary Education and Empire in Late Colonial India, 1860–1920*. London: Pickering & Chatto.

Bhattacharya, Neeladri. 2003. "The Problem." *Seminar* Rewriting History (February): 12–18.

Bhattacharya, Neeladri. 2009. "Teaching History in Schools: The Politics of Textbooks in India." *History Workshop Journal* 67: 99–110.

Bhattacharya, Sabyasachi. 2003. "Introduction." In *Educating the Nation: Documents on the Discourse of National Education in India 1880–1920*, edited by Sabyasachi Bhattacharya and Chinna Rao Yagati, ix–xxvii. New Delhi: Kanishka Publishers in association with Educational Records Research Unit, Jawaharlal Nehru University.

Bhog, Dipta. 2002. "Gender and Curriculum." *Economic and Political Weekly* 37 (17): 1638–42.

Bhog, Dipta, Disha Mullick, Purwa Bharadwaj, and Jaya Sharma. 2009. *Textbook Regimes: A Feminist Critique of Nation and Identity*. New Delhi: Nirantar.

Chatterjee, Partha. 1996. "The Disciplines in Colonial Bengal." In *Texts of Power: Emerging Disciplines in Colonial Bengal*, edited by Partha Chatterjee, 1–29. Calcutta: Samya and Centre for the Studies in Social Sciences, Calcutta.

Chitnis, Suma. 1967. *Papers in the Sociology of Education in India*, edited by M. S. Gore and Ishwarlal Pragji Desai. New Delhi: NCERT.

Constable, Philip. 2000. "Sitting on the School Verandah: The Ideology and Practice of 'Untouchable' Educational Protest in Late Nineteenth-Century Western India." *The Indian Economic and Social History Review* 37 (4): 383–422.

Dave, P. N., and Jyotsna. P. Dave. 1991. "Research in Curriculum: A Trend Report." In *Fourth Survey of Research in Education*, edited by M. B. Buch, 565–85. New Delhi: NCERT.

Department of Teacher Education. 1969. *Primary Teacher Education Curriculum: Report of the National Work-Shop of Teacher Educators Organised by the Department of Teacher Education, National Institute of Education, NCERT*. New Delhi: NCERT

Desai, D. B., and Sunirmal Roy. 1974. "Curriculum, Methods and Textbooks: A Trend Report." In *A Survey of Research in Education*, edited by M. B. Buch, 264–69. Baroda: Centre of Advanced Study in Education, Faculty of Education and Psychology, M. S. University of Baroda.

Deshpande, Prachi. 2007. *Creative Pasts: Historical Memory and Identity in Western India, 1700–1960*. New York: Columbia University Press.

Dhankar, Rohit. 1995. Lessons to Learn, *Seminar* 436: 32–34.

Dhankar, Rohit. 2000. "On Curriculum Framework." *Seminar* 493.

Dhankar, Rohit. 2003. "The Notion of Quality in DPEP Pedagogical Interventions." *Contemporary Education Dialogue* 1 (1): 5–34.

Digantar. 2013. "Drafts of Internal Evaluation Reports of Digantar's Impact."

Dottrens, Robert. 1962. *The Primary School Curriculum*. Paris: UNESCO.

George, Alex M. 2004. "Children's Perceptions of Sarkar: The Fallacies of Civics Teaching." *Contemporary Education Dialogue* 1 (2 Spring): 228–57.

Government of India. 1953. *Report of the Secondary Education Commission*. Delhi: Ministry of Education, Government of India.

Government of India. 1961a. "Report of the First National Seminar on the Education of Primary Teachers in India". Vigyan Bhavan, New Delhi: Ministry of Education, Government of India, Publication No. 530.

Government of India 1961b. *Report on Teacher Training*. Delhi: Government of India, Committee on Plan Projects.

Government of India. 1992. *Towards an Enlightened and Human Society: An Analysis of NPE 1986* (Acharya Ramamurthi Committee Report), New Delhi.

Government of India. 1993. *Learning without Burden*, Report of the National Advisory Committee (Yashpal Committee Report). New Delhi: MHRD, Department of Education.

Habib, Irfan. 2005. "How to Evade Real Issues and Make Room for Obscurantism." *Social Scientist* 33 (9–10): 3–12.

Habib, Irfan, Jaiswal, Suvira and Mukherjee, Aditya. 2003. *History in the New NCERT Textbooks: A Report and an Index of Errors.* Kolkata: Indian History Congress.

Harap, Henry. 1959. *Improvement of Curriculum in Indian Schools.* New Delhi: Ministry of Education, Government of India.

Jain, Manish. 2004. "Civics, Citizens and Human Rights: Civics Discourse in India." *Contemporary Education Dialogue* 1 (2): 165–98.

Jain, Manish. 2009. "Civics Curriculum and the Idea of Citizen since Late Nineteenth Century." PhD Thesis, Delhi: Department of Education, University of Delhi.

Jain, Manish. 2011. "Introducing a Textbook: Policies and Contestations in Nineteenth Century Colonial India." In Hyderabad: University of Hyderabad.

Jain, Manish. 2012. "Textbook and Identity in Colonial Bombay and United Provinces."

Joshi, Sushil. 2008. *Jashn-E-Talim: Hoshangabad Vigyan ka Shaikshik Safarnama* (Celebration of Learning: Educational Travelogue of Hoshangabad Vigyan). Bhopal: Eklavya.

Kalia, Narendra Nath. 1980. "Images of Men and Women in Indian Textbooks." *Comparative Education Review* 24 (2): Part 2: 209–223.

Kaviraj, Sudipta. 1991. "On State, Society and Discourse in India." In *Rethinking Third World Politics* edited by *James Manor*, 72–99. London: Longman.

Kaviraj, Sudipta. 2000. "Modernity and Politics in India." *Daedalus* 129 (1, Multiple Modernities): 137–62.

Kishore, Bharati. 1991. *Ek Samajik Prayog Ke Sametne Par* (One End of a Social Experiment), A Report, Hoshangabad.

Kumar, Krishna. 1983. "Educational Experience of Scheduled Castes and Tribes." *Economic and Political Weekly* September 3–10: 1566–72.

Kumar, Krishna. 1986. "'NCERT's Silver Jubilee." *Economic and Political Weekly* 21 (38/39): 1682.

Kumar, Krishna. 1988. "Origins of India's 'Textbook Culture.'" *Comparative Education Review* 32 (4): 452–64.

Kumar, Krishna 1989. *Social Character of Learning.* Delhi: Sage Publications.

Kumar, Krishna. 1992. *What Is Worth Teaching?* Hyderabad: Orient Longman.

Kumar, Krishna. 1993. "Market Economy and Mass Literacy: Revisiting Innis's Economics of Communication." *Economic and Political Weekly* 28 (50): 2727–34.

Kumar, Krishna. 2005. *Political Agenda of Education: A Study of Colonialist and Nationalist Ideas.* 2nd ed. New Delhi: Sage.

Kumar, Krishna. 2010. "Culture, State and Girls: An Educational Perspective." *Economic and Political Weekly* 45 (17): 75–84.

Lulla, B. P. 1968. *Problems of Curriculum Administration and Text-Book Selection in India.* Baroda: Centre of Advanced Study in Education, Faculty of Education and Psychology, M. S. University of Baroda.

Maharashtra State Archives (MSA). 1902. *The Citizen of India by Sir W Lee Warner Information required by the Govt of India as regards suitability and use of—in schools and colleges Bombay, Presidency.* Education Department Publications, Vol. 49.

Malik, Anand (1962). *Curriculum Development: Suggestions for the Consideration of Teachers and District Education Officers.* Chandigarh: NCERT, Department of Extension Services, Govt. Post-Graduate Basic Training College.

Manjrekar, Nandini. 1999. "Through the Looking Glass: Gender Socialization in a Primary School." In *Culture, Socialization and Human Development: Theory, Research and Applications in India*, edited by T. S. Saraswathi, 336–55. Delhi: Sage Publications.

Menon, Nivedita. 2010. "History, Truth and Nation: Contemporary Debates on Education in India." In *Understanding Contemporary India: Critical Perspectives*, edited by Achin Vanaik and Rajeev Bhragava, 179–99. Hyderabad: Orient BlackSwan.

Mukherjee, Mridula and Mukherjee, Aditya. eds. 2002. *Communalisation of Education: The History Textbook Controversy.* Delhi: Delhi Historians' Group.

Nambissan, Geetha B. 2009. *Exclusion and Discrimination in Schools: Experiences of Dalit Children.* Working Paper Series. Delhi: Indian Institute of Dalit Studies and UNICEF.

Nambissan, Geetha B., and S. Srinivasa Rao, eds. 2013. *Sociology of Education in India: Changing Contours and Emerging Concerns.* New Delhi: Oxford University Press.

National Council of Educational Research and Training NCERT. 1970. "Education and National Development: Report of the Education Commission 1964–66." New Delhi: NCERT.

NCERT. 1972. *Preparation and Evaluation of Textbooks in History: Principles and Procedures.* New Delhi: NCERT.

NCERT. 2005. *Report of the National Focus Group on Problems of Scheduled Caste and Scheduled Tribe Children.* New Delhi: NCERT.

NCERT. 2006. *Position Paper National Focus Group on Curriculum, Syllabus and Textbooks.* New Delhi: NCERT.

O'Hanlon, Rosalind. 1985. *Caste, Conflict and Ideology: Mahatma Jatirao Phule and Low Caste Protest in Nineteenth Century Western India.* Cambridge: Cambridge University Press.

Orsini, Francesca. 2002. *The Hindi Public Sphere 1920–40: Language and Literature in the Age of Nationalism.* New Delhi: Oxford University Press.

Paliwal, R. and Subramanian, C. N. 2006. "Contextualising the Curriculum." *Contemporary Education Dialogue* 4 (1): 25–51

Pandey, B. N. 1969. *Second National Survey of Secondary Teacher Education in India.* New Delhi: NCERT.

Pinar, William F. 2005. "Curriculum Studies and the Politics of Educational Reform." In *Discourses of Education in the Age of New Imperialism*, edited by Jerome Satterthwaite and Elizabeth Atkinson, 25–45. Staffordshire: Trentham Books.

Powell, Avril A. 2002. "History Textbooks and the Transmission of Pre-Colonial Past in North-Western India in the 1860s and 1870s." In *Invoking the Past: The Use of History in South Asia*, edited by Daud Ali, 91–133. New Delhi: Oxford University Press.

Powell, Avril A. 2011. "Old Books in New Bindings: Ethics and Education in Colonial India." In *Knowledge Production, Pedagogy, and Institutions in Colonial India*, edited by Indra Sengupta and Daud Ali, 199–225. New York: Palgrave Macmillan.

Ramachandran, Vimala. 2003. *Getting Children Back to School: Case Studies in Primary Education.* New Delhi: Sage Publications.

Rampal, Anita. 1992. "School Science in Search of a Democratic Order?" *Social Scientist* 20 (7/8 July/ August): 50–74.

Rao, Parimala V. 2008. *Educating Women and Non-Brahmins as "Loss of Nationality": Bal Gangadhar Tilak and the Nationalist Agenda in Maharashtra.* Delhi: Centre for Women's Development Studies.

Ritubala. 1997. "Madhyamik Star Par Pustakon Mein Vanchiton Ki Chhavi: Ek Vishleshnatmak Adhyayan." MPhil Dissertation, Delhi: Department of Education, University of Delhi.

Ritubala. 2001. "Pathyapustakon Ki Rajniti." *Shiksha Vimarsh* March-April: 19–25.

Roy, Sunirmal. 1979. "Curriculum, Methods and Textbooks: A Trend Report." In *Second Survey of Research in Education (1972–1978)*, edited by M. B. Buch, 276–84. Baroda: Society for Educational Research and Development, M. S. University of Baroda.

Rudolph, Lloyd I., and Rudolph, Susanne Hoeber. 1983. "Rethinking Secularism: Genesis and Implications of the Textbook Controversy, 1977–79." *Pacific Affairs* 56 (1) Spring: 15–37.

Sabharwal, Virinder K. 2000. "Curriculum Development." In *Fifth Survey of Educational Research 1988–92*, edited by M. B. Buch, 2:1090–1101. New Delhi: NCERT.

Sadgopal, Anil. 2000. *Shiksha Mein Badlav Ka Sawaal.* Delhi: Granth Shilpi.

Sarangapani, Padma M. 2003. *Constructing School Knowledge: An Ethnography of Learning in an Indian Village.* Delhi: Sage Publications.

Sarangapani, Padma M. 2006. "The Tyler Paradox." *Contemporary Education Dialogue* 4 (1) Monsoon: 119–41.

Sarangapani, Padma M. 2011. "Soft Disciplines and Hard Battles." *Contemporary Education Dialogue* 8 (1): 67–84.

Sarkar, Tanika. 1999. "Strishiksha, or Education for Women." In *Words to Win: The Making of Amar Jiban: A Modern Autobiography,* edited by T. Sakar, 67–112. New Delhi: Kali for Women.

Saxena, Sadhna. 1998. "Education of the Poor—A Pedagogy of Resistance." In *Education, Development and Underdevelopment,* edited by Sureshchandra Shukla and Rekha Kaul, 265–98. New Delhi: Sage.

Saxena, Sadhna. 2006. "Questions of Epistemology: Re-Evaluating Constructivism and the NCF 2005." *Contemporary Education Dialogue* 4 (1): 52–71.

Scrase, Timothy J. 1993. *Image, Ideology and Inequality: Cultural Domination, Hegemony and Schooling in India.* New Delhi: Sage Publications.

Seth, Sanjay. 2007. "Changing the Subject: Western Knowledge and the Question of Difference." *Comparative Studies in Society and History* 49 (3): 666–88.

Shahidullah, Kazi. 1996. "The Purpose and Impact of Government Policy on Pathshala Gurumohashays in Nineteenth Century Bengal." In *The Transmission of Knowledge in South Asia: Essays on Education, Religion, History and Politics,* edited by Nigel Crook, 119–34. New Delhi: Oxford University Press.

Shukla, Sureshchandra. 1983. "Comparative Education: An Indian View." *Comparative Education Review* 27 (2): 246–58.

Shukla, Sureshchandra. 1998. "Nationalist Educational Thought: Continuity and Change." In *The Contested Terrain: Perspectives on Education in India,* edited by Sabyasachi Bhattacharya. Hyderabad: Orient Longman Private Limited.

Shukla, Sureshchandra. 2002. "Caste, Class and Education: Reformulating the Classic Positions." In *Education and the Disprivileged: Nineteenth and Twentieth Century India,* edited by Sabyasachi Bhattacharya. Hyderabad: Orient Longman Private Limited.

Sriprakash, Arathi. 2010. "Child-Centred Education and the Promise of Democratic Learning: Pedagogic Messages in Rural Indian Primary Schools." *International Journal of Educational Development* 30: 297–304.

Srivasatva, Sanjay. 1998. *Constructing Post-Colonial India: National Character and the Doon School.* London: Routledge.

Subramanian, C. N. and Paliwal, R. 1989. "The New Dispensation and School Education: The Limits of Development without Democratisation." *Social Scientist* 17 (9/10): 74–85.

Subramaniam, C.N., and Rashmi Paliwal. 2003. "Teaching History: Exploring Alternatives." *Seminar* 522: 63–66.

Sunny, Y. 2006. "Analysing Current Practices in Geography Education." *Economic and Political Weekly* 42 (3): 270–78.

Talib, Mohammad. 1998. "Educating the Oppressed: Observations from a School in a Working Class Settlement in Delhi." In *Education, Development and Underdevelopment,* edited by Sureshchandra Shukla and Rekha Kaul, 199–209. New Delhi: Sage.

Talib, Mohammad. 2003. "Modes of Learning-Labour Relations: Educational Strategies and Child Labour." In *Child Labour and the Right to Education in South Asia,* edited by Naila Kabeer and Geetha B. Nambissan, 143–63. New Delhi: Sage.

Thapan, Meenakshi. 1991. *Life at School: An Ethnographic Study.* New Delhi: Oxford University Press.

Thapar, Romila. 2009. "The History Debate and School Textbooks in India: A Personal Memoir." *History Workshop Journal* 67: 87–98.

Topdar, Sudipa. 2010. *Knowledge and Governance: Political Socialization of the Indian Child within Colonial Schooling and Nationalist Contestations in India (1870–1925)*. University of Michigan: Dissertation submitted in partial fulfilment of the requirements for the degree of Doctor of Philosophy (History).

Venkateswaran, T. V. 2007. "Science and Colonialism: Content and Character of Natural Sciences in the Vernacular School Education in the Madras Presidency (1820–1900)." *Science & Education* 16 (1): 87–114.

Viswanathan, Gauri. 1998. *Masks of Conquest: Literary Study and British Rule in India*. New Delhi: Oxford University Press.

Yadav, Yogendra. 2007. "Loktantra Aur Schoolee Shiksha." *Shiksha Vimarsh* July-August: 5–14.

# Chapter 5

# Curriculum and Its Possibilities
## Schooling in India
### Meenakshi Thapan

## Introduction

This chapter seeks to examine the "curricular" in the context of schooling in India. It is an effort to make sense of the "curricular" where the curriculum is confined largely within a framework that allows very little flexibility or modification, in contrast to one which emphasizes the significance of children's perspectives and their everyday lives. Curriculum in India appears as an "open" subject to the extent that we may all discuss it, write about it, and have very articulate views about its content. By convention, however, school curriculum in India is a state-produced entity, removed from debate and discussion, good practice, and importantly, from children's and teachers' lives. How else do we explain the arbitrary closure of one of the first innovative curricular interventions by concerned citizens and scholars in Madhya Pradesh, a state in central India?[1]

Through various bodies and agencies, the state controls the framing, organization, content, and transaction of school curriculum through a central body and a variety of state and district level bodies. There is one overarching public body, the National Council of Educational Research and Training (NCERT) in New Delhi, and there are several state-level State Councils of Educational Research and Training. Governance is a matter of political will; at one time a political party, ruling the center, may decide to appoint a particular educator to the central body who frames the curriculum following a particular stance. Another educator may come to power at another time, who then may bring in a completely different perspective concerning school curriculum. Ashwani Kumar (2012) has succinctly described the political scenario, governed by party politics, that governs selection to this very important post and the ramifications this may have on the framing of the school curriculum.[2]

The influence of the state includes not only the classification of knowledge into categories governed by criteria such as legitimacy and authenticity but also the transaction of such knowledge by practitioners who are deemed to be "fit" (adequately "trained") to transmit it. It is therefore essential for all schools to be affiliated to one or to the other recognized school boards in the country, so that all curricular content emanates from the central body, all textbooks to follow central or state level directives, and all teachers to have teacher training from recognized institutions for this purpose. In 2005, NCERT brought out the National Curriculum Framework, a kind of umbrella document that provides the framework for the goals of the school curriculum, delineates the content, as well as provides guidelines for teacher education. While this particular version of the document (NCF 2005) has moved away from earlier frameworks and establishes a more innovative approach to the education of schoolchildren, including the use of newly prepared textbooks, it is nonetheless an instrument that is effected by the state, which can be used or misused depending on the ideological goals espoused by the agents of the state. It is this aspect of the role of the state in the education of schoolchildren that gives power to the textbook as the most effective tool of state policy on education and the goals it seeks to achieve.[3]

The textbook in India is considered a sacred tool in the hands of teachers in the public education system across the country. Krishna Kumar (1989) has underscored the "influence" of the text in terms of both content as well as form. Kumar (1989, 129) suggested that textbooks are linked to the "value-system entrenched in the school time-table" as "aspects of an industrial culture" that seeks to orient students to a culture of punctuality, specialization, and obedience that characterizes the precision and rigidity of industrial societies. However, unlike other scholars who stress the sacredness of textbooks in schools, I have sought to emphasize, like Marjorie Sykes, that "books have played only a minor part in the nurture of the young" (Sykes 1993, xxv). An overemphasis on the influence of textbooks on children's learning at school serves to understate other important influencing characteristics in learning processes. It also tends to ignore the role children themselves play in the reception of knowledge, even in authoritarian and controlled settings. Textbooks are not always sacrosanct to students in school; they do appreciate that they have to be mastered for purposes of evaluation, but they are only one aspect of a life at school that encompasses more than official knowledge.

The fact remains however that it is the state and its functionaries that control the school curriculum in India, as perhaps in other parts of the world. This hegemonic control however leaves very little space for schools, teachers, and students to be flexible with even the modes of transaction, as all schools are also affiliated to one or to the other school boards for examination and certification purposes. It is therefore a significant movement *against* this regulation when nongovernmental organizations, schools, and individuals seek to construct alternative curricular frameworks and content. Their efforts reflect a concern for change and innovation that lie outside the control of the state and therefore open up the possibilities to be focused on the participants in the educational process: children and their teachers. Where does all this leave students and teachers? Are they active and engaged participants in the process, or are they mute spectators going through the motions, with neither commitment nor passion? How are they empowered to act as engaged citizens, and what are the processes in schools that enable them to do so? These are some of the questions addressed by this essay.

# Schooling in India

Schooling in India occurs in vastly different contexts that are dependent on a particular school's history and setting, institutional goals, location, available infrastructure, linguistic medium of instruction, the relevant school board to which the school is affiliated, the social class of students and the teachers, caste identities, and a host of other influencing factors. There are three types of schools in India: government, aided, and private (recognized and unrecognized). Those that are run by central, state, or local governments are referred to as government schools; aided schools are those that are run by private managements but funded by government grant-in-aid; and private schools that receive no aid are referred to as private schools although there is an important subdivision among those that are recognized by the government (i.e., they fulfill certain criteria) or are unrecognized (Kingdon 2005). The most significant distinction between schools is that between the government and private schools. There has been a substantial increase in private schools in recent years as well as a massive growth in the government school system (De et. al. 2011). This has resulted in a huge heterogeneity in the schooling system in the country as there are vast differences among private schools and government schools depending on location, fees charged, availability of resources and infrastructure, teacher qualifications, and several other factors.

A recent study has found that in rural India, enrolment in school is at high levels but that this is in no way indicative of the fact that learning levels are equally high. Over 96 percent of all children in the age group 6 to 14 years are now enrolled in school, with the largest numbers enrolled in private schools. In fact, since 2009, private school enrolment in rural areas has been increasing at an annual rate of about 10 percent. If this continues, by 2018 some 50 percent children in rural areas would be enrolled in private schools (ASER 2013, 47). Being enrolled in private schools does not mean children have access to improved infrastructure, more committed and conscientious teachers, a more creatively designed curriculum with innovative content and teaching methods, and, as a result, enhanced learning levels. In fact, according to ASER (2013), learning levels are abysmal in rural India: for example, 67.7 percent of the children enrolled in Class III in government schools cannot read Class I textbooks and arithmetic learning levels have dropped across schools except in some states in southern India. The survey shows that students who have access to private tuition outside schools achieve superior learning levels than those who do not have such access (ibid., 48).

These facts document the alarming state of primary school education in rural India. With an overt emphasis in government policy to enrol more and more children in school, increasingly higher figures are reported for enrolment across India (NCERT 2012). This does in itself prove that more and more children are being educated, as the drop-out rate remains very high, especially among girls between the age of 11 and14 years (ASER 2013). This scenario is further complicated by the prevalence of a curricular framework that has over the years evolved from being a largely colonialist enterprise to one that, though embedded in a colonialist model, seeks to provide quality education for all.[4]

It has been suggested that structures and practice in educational settings in India are dominated in part by the history of the educational ideal of the colonial citizen (Kumar 1991). The colonial citizen has been produced and reproduced through the advent of "modern" education in the late eighteenth and nineteenth centuries. That education sought to perfect the individual through moral education (provided by the missionaries) and civic education (exalted, prescribed, and perpetuated by the colonizers).[5]

The aim itself was suspect: to civilize the native, to replace indigenous knowledge with "modern" forms of knowledge and ways of accessing it, and to produce a bevy of mindless beings who would acquiesce into submission to the colonizers and their methods of knowing and evaluation of this knowledge. Such a view was undoubtedly instrumental in its aim to further colonial ideals at the cost of indigenous perspectives. It resulted in producing a citizen who defined himself in terms of the education he received, as first and foremost, a representative of "another" culture and civilization. It has also been argued that the British were really after a "cultural conquest": "the primary purpose was to build a cultural dependency among the educated and the ruling classes so that revolutionary overthrow would never be a likely alternative" (Carnoy 1974, 100). This "Anglicist policy" resulted among the native population, who had access to such education, quite clearly in a "respect and awe for the aristocratic virtue of the majestic English language" and concomitantly, in "contempt and disdain" for their own culture and people (ibid., 101).[6]

This form of education engendered a form of inequality that persists today: the elite constituted by the English-speaking, educated "modern" human subject, and the large mass of Indians educated in the vernacular in subjects that often do not connect to their everyday existence, for example, an abysmal quality of educational tools and pedagogic practices and almost no infrastructure. To put it simply, colonialism and its legacy ensured the establishment of particular kinds of schools for the upper classes and the privileged elite. The rest of the population languished in government schools to which no serious attention has been paid over the years.[7] The Doon School, an elite boarding school for boys in northern India, is a premier example of a form of distinction that was established as a marker of the social class the students inhabited. At the time when colonialism was on its way out, a new middle class, driven by a changing form of modernity, was seeking to gain a foothold in parts of northern India.[8] The setting up of the "Indian Public *Schools* Society,"[9] Sanjay Srivastava tells us, "was charged precisely with the duty the plural in its name implies," that is, the establishment of a large number of "public" schools in India: "hundreds of little beacons strategically located in a sea of cultural and political darkness, and beaming out into that darkness messages of democracy, equality and secularism" (Srivastava 1998, 41). These schools were to take India into a new modernity, born of colonialism, but located within a secular fabric of democracy, apparent equality, and freedom.

Even those private organizations and institutions that seek to organize and transact different curricular practices are almost always affiliated to a state or national school boards for examination and certification purposes. There are 36 school boards to which all secondary schools in India are affiliated and great variation in the curricula offered by them.[10] The Central Board for Secondary Education (CBSE) conducts final examinations annually for the All India Senior School Certificate Examination (AISSCE) for Class 10 and Class 12. The board also annually conducts the AIEEE exam for admission to undergraduate courses in engineering and architecture in numerous colleges across India. It also conducts the AIPMT (All India Pre-medical Test) for admission to the major medical colleges in India. The CBSE has a high success rate: 80 percent of the students who took the Class 12 examination passed it in 2012. A vast number of schools consider it the most suitable, and its affiliation to the CBSE assures acceptance among the parent body and a certain legitimacy in the wider educational environment.[11]

There are other school boards as well. The Council for the Indian School Certificate Examinations (CSISC) is an autonomous educational body to which several private schools are affiliated. It conducts two examinations in India: the Indian Certificate of Secondary Education (ICSE) and the Indian School Certificate (ISC). The CISCE was established in 1956 to administer the University of Cambridge Local Examinations Syndicate's Examinations in India. It is an all-India, but not a government-sponsored, board (unlike the CBSE and the National Institute for Open Schooling [NIOS]). A large number of private schools are affiliated with this board. It has a reputation for providing greater flexibility in the curriculum, allowing schools, and thereby students, more selection of courses across disciplines for the Class 12 school leaving examination. This flexibility has an enormous impact on students' learning as they are not locked into disciplinary frameworks, such as Science, the Arts or Humanities, and Commerce. This allows them to have a broader learning base that ensures that their career choices will be based on a wider spectrum of knowledge, not limited to specific careers that are seen as a result of choosing a Science, Commerce, or Arts stream of subjects in high school. The CBSE curriculum is in this sense more rigidly organized and structured. However, these boards rely on the central government body, the National Council of Educational Research and training (NCERT), for the development of a curricular framework as well as the textbooks to complement curricular demands.[12]

The most recent framework for schools across India, the National Curricular Framework (NCF 2005), was path-breaking in many ways. It sought to be more inclusive, child friendly, and oriented toward nurturing aware and engaged citizens through an emphasis on treating the student as a partner on the path of learning. The NCF 2005 resulted in the writing of new and well-written textbooks for use in schools across India. Both the framing of disciplinary frameworks as well as the preparation of new textbooks was very well received in the media and by scholars and academics who also pointed out several drawbacks.[13] This curricular framework has been in place since then in schools across India, with some private institutions making their own choice with respect to the transaction of the curriculum, using pedagogic tools and methods that fit with their objectives, constructing their own curricular content, and writing textbooks that seem to be most appropriate and relevant from their point of view, doing away with rigidity in the organization, content, and transaction of knowledge.

## Schooling for the "Model" Citizen

As a sociologist of education, one of my abiding concerns has been understanding the role of schooling in the construction of the student as a "good citizen." What is meant by this term? It suggests a "model" citizen, in the Durkheimian sense, well versed in the norms and values of society, geared to their reproduction without much contestation or rebellion, focused on building harmony and consensus for the well-being and growth of society. Society in writing itself through its socialization practices, beginning in the family and through educational processes, emphasizes conformity, similarity, homogeneity. This is evident in our curriculum and evaluation practices, all of which have a benchmark against which a child's performance is measured.

The academic conformity expected of children is only one aspect of the problem that plagues education in the severely competitive Indian secondary school system. The greater predicament is the normative expectation of the student's commitment to society and its goals and the perception that the task of schools is to ensure that students learn how to "adjust" and "fit into" society. In my view, the good citizen is one who *engages with* social issues, norms, and values, practices and policies, and is concerned with the meaning and intent of all action. In India, however, the terms and contexts in which schools have sought to create good citizens have varied. Many of these have modeled themselves on what have been socially considered appropriate values for the inculcation of appropriate ideals for society's development.

The idea of the good citizen established itself in northern India in the late nineteenth century as part of a Hindu revivalism exemplified by the Arya Samaj,[14] which espoused an education that was grounded in both the Vedas and in the Western sciences. A dissenting branch of the Arya Samaj set up a "*Gurukul*" in Kangri where "pure Vedic instruction" took place. *Gurukuls* in the heartland of *Jat* society[15] in the Punjab (a state in northwest India) took root as oppositional forces to Western models of education. They were examples of a mix of Hindu religiosity, character education based on Vedic rituals and tradition, and a slew of disciplinary practices with the avowed aim of instilling virtue (Dutta 1998).[16]

Relationships were built between *gurus* (teachers) and *brahmacharis* (celibate young Hindu men) that surpassed those between fathers and sons, and set examples for the reproduction of a unique identity, the *Arya*, that gave rise to an exclusive *Jat* identity that enabled the contestation of upper-caste Hindu and Muslim identities, the colonial state, and the lower castes. At the same time, such an education represented an antiwoman bias, a focus on the control of male sexuality and an idealization of virtues associated with individual control and social uplifting. The Gurukul was an outcome of a reform movement that took religion as its *leit motif* and education as the medium through which to attain the twin goals of religious education and controlled manhood, both of which were viewed as being of paramount significance for social transformation in a society that was increasingly been overtaken by Western ideas and practices.

This has not necessarily been the trajectory followed by all *Gurukuls* in India. The International Society for Krishna Consciousness (ISKCON) has set up *gurukuls* in different parts of the country and abroad.[17] The Bhaktivedanta Gurukula and International School, founded in 1977, is one such *gurukul* run as a boarding school for boys only in Vrindavan in northern India. The Bhaktivedanta Gurukula and International School (BGIS) in its own words, "offers a unique balance of the best of both worlds—the traditional and the modern, the Vedic and the contemporary, the spiritual and the temporal" (school website).[18] The BGIS offers modern-day schooling with an academic program, options in sport and physical activity, as well as what the school no doubt considers essential to its existence: "the students imbibe in their hearts and devotion to Lord Krishna based on the teachings of the *Bhagvad-Gita*.[19] Teachings that are delivered not sentimentally or dogmatically but in a philosophical and cultural way, using both contemporary and traditional educational methods."[20] In order to promote itself as a "modern" institution, the school also advertises the fact that there are several graduates from the premier engineering institutions in the country on its faculty. In addition, modern day gurukuls are affiliated with recognized school boards that grant them a certain legitimacy in the education market and make them attractive to parents who seek a modern education grounded in traditional values for their children. Being a "good" citizen is in the language of these gurukuls is clearly linked to a religious worldview that emphasizes qualities that embody a sanctified humanity based on particular kinds of religious discourse. This is further accentuated in institutions associated with the RSS.[21]

Schools run by the *Rashtriya Swayamsevak Sangh* (RSS) are distinct from the gurukuls established by the Arya Samaj, which inspired the establishment of the Dayanand Anglo-Vedic (D.A.V.) institutions. The latter were formed primarily as a reaction to Christianity and missionary education for the teaching of Vedic Hinduism, its forms of worship, and also later, included the Western sciences and the English language. They did not, however, propagate hatred for another culture, religion, or people. In contrast, the *Saraswati Shishu Mandirs*, a group of schools run by the RSS, seek to indoctrinate Hindu children with an ideology that laments the decline of morals and values in Indian society, propagates pride in being Hindu, and in the Hindu *rashtra* (nation), as well as, consequently, an intolerance for other communities and people.[22]

In this entire exercise, it is assumed by scholars who are looking at the problem of indoctrination from the point of view of the school and a particular ideology alone, that children are mindlessly accepting the ideological prescriptions that are being provided through pedagogic practices and other school activities. While adhering to school norms and practices, students do not necessarily subscribe to the values espoused by different kinds of schools. They are attending school to obtain an education with a view to upward mobility, to help them learn a language, preferably English, gain knowledge that will ostensibly help them find employment. Peggy Froerer's work (2007) on the Saraswati Shishu Mandir Primary School in Chattisgarh is focused on precisely this unexplored dimension of school life.

Froerer examined the relationship between Hindu nationalist ideology and the disciplinary practices of the Saraswati Shishu Mandir Primary School in Chhattisgarh in central India, suggesting that students very well understand their goals and seek to fulfill them. Moral education or moral improvement (*sadachar*) is the principle underlying the ideological emphases on the preservation of Hindu culture and a sense of nationalism and moral values in such schools. The idea of discipline is central to the enterprise of building the nation through a well-trained body and a strong sense of personal restraint. Froerer's work, rich in ethnographic detail, shows that a link is slowly established between corporeal discipline, which is slowly accepted as a "moral good," and educational success. In fact, this connection between discipline and a moral "goodness" is clearly tied to the idea of discipline as "a vehicle for educational attainment" (Froerer 2007, 1066). Froerer shows that the effort to attain a higher sense of morality results in the opposite, that is, the overriding aspirations of children who value educational success and a career *over* creating a Hindu nation. Students, even young children, are not silent or passive participants in the process of being molded into model citizens. Froerer's work points to the ways in which children perceive their being disciplined into "good," obedient students as essential to their schooling for educational attainment and success. In the end, this is what counts for them: to be schooled is to be good and thereby capable of attracting the right kind of attention for educational accomplishment and upward mobility. This is the aim of young people, boys and girls, in school who seek education as a route to achievement and attainment of goals that include social and, above all, economic mobility.[23]

Education for all is thus imparted in very different kinds of educational institutions, and what goes on in these institutions therefore also varies depending on the kind of institution it is.[24] While such complexities prevail and characterize educational practices across schools in India, curriculum in India is further shaped by the characteristics of "secular" schools, or those that are identified with a particular religious or cultural identity. All these factors influence what goes on in schools and shape schooling processes in different ways. Simultaneously, it is important to reiterate that students in schools are not passive subjects and willingly express their perspectives, goals, and aspirations, if we listen to them. The student as "good" or "model" citizen is not created by schooling processes alone, and he/she has agency, voice, and perspective. Efforts in school to nurture the ability of students to articulate their views without fear or intimidation are the hallmarks of practices within schools that engender an atmosphere of equality, shared understandings, and mutual trust. This is not the case in all schools, and there are great variations among schools that seek to "discipline" students in one way or another; such schools also usually have strict norms for teacher conduct and for the methods followed in transacting the curriculum.

In India, it would not be an overstatement to say that almost all government or state schools have this kind of practice embedded in their cultures that seek to inculcate obedience, deference, and conformity.[25] A questioning spirit, an aspect of critical inquiry, is not seriously encouraged. Nor is independence, autonomy, and freedom for teachers or students. The kind of teaching that takes place is therefore stilted and circumscribed, lacking creativity and passion, limited by an overbearing syllabus that needs to be "completed" well ahead of the annual examinations. Students learn to accept this as the norm and view the education process as something they must endure as an inherent necessity of life's transitions.[26]

There is thus very little scope in general for innovative curricula to be in place in different kinds of schools. There is a plethora of privately funded "alternatives" that have flooded the Indian educational marketplace professing a "global outlook" or an "excellence" in academic skills, even promising to develop "sensitive" human beings. Such developments are products of the market and ultimately submit to the demands of the market in which they are located and due to which they exist. Their existence depends upon developing a vocabulary of change, by creating a sense of difference and distinction from the huge mass of existing schools that claim no special status for themselves. In fact, many of these institutions do not go beyond their entrepreneurial objectives of promoting educational innovation with their gaze set clearly on the generation of income through the very high fees they charge.

There are other schools in India that have a genuine commitment to innovative school curricula indicating a commitment to the student as an engaged participant in the learning process. There is an awareness among these that the student—as child or young adult—is an equal participant in the learning process. The student is not inferior to the teacher in any way as both grapple with learning new skills, new ideas, and reinventing traditional or conventional knowledge in different ways. This comes out clearly in the inventive methods that are used by the proponents of such approaches in the very different educational terrains they inhabit. The work of private schools run by the Krishnamurti Foundation, India (KFI), the schools in Auroville, the Centre for Learning (CFL) in Bangalore, and other mainstream private schools like Aditi International School, the Vasant Valley School, some international schools in the metropolitan cities, and others stand out for offering quality education.[27] Such institutions set about their task of enriching students' learning through more innovative conceptual frameworks and relevant texts and material with a view to enhancing their potential for critical and independent thought.

The Hoshangabad Science Teaching Program (HSTP) set up in 1972 was a pioneer of sorts in the reinvention of school curricular practice, especially in the teaching of science in government schools in Madhya Pradesh. They later expanded their work to encompass social science teaching as well as making interventions in primary school education. At present, the NGO works with schools and the community through publication and research initiatives.[28]

There are other "alternative" approaches to curricular organization that have been initiated by private organizations such as the Krishnamurti Foundation (India), Auroville, the Aurobindo Ashram Trust, Pratham, Nirantar, and a host of other nongovernment organizations that seek to provide meaningful and holistic education, using innovative tools and techniques to thousands of children across rural and urban India. There is a recognition that, in general, government and private schools sorely lack the potential to enable children to grow to their full potential as a result of stunted and irrelevant curricular practices, limited teaching skills or commitment, lack of good quality textbooks and learning material, and several other problems such as student dropouts, teacher absenteeism, parental apathy, and so on. While it is not possible to provide an assessment or even an introduction to all alternative forms of educational processes present in India,[29] it might be useful to consider one such intervention that has not only provided an alternative to mainstream private schooling but more recently has had an enormous impact on rural and urban public education through its pioneering pedagogic tools and classroom practices. This is the work in education of the Krishnamurti Foundation in India and their Rishi Valley Institute for Educational Resources (RIVER) program.[30]

## J. Krishnamurti and the Schooling of Society

The KFI runs five schools in India based on the educational thought of J. Krishnamurti (1895–1986). The KFI is increasingly engaged with rural educational initiatives in almost all its schools and runs one after-school program for young children as well. Its educational activities include the annual publication of a *Journal of the Krishnamurti Schools* with essays by schoolteachers and educators. Krishnamurti was an extraordinary philosopher who sought to change people through the process of self-discovery, not as a narcissistic fantasy about oneself and one's relationships with others, but through facing the truth of the present, "what is," and immediately acting upon it. He advocated complete honesty in facing the reality of one's behavior and actions, not succumbing to illusions about oneself. Krishnamurti's philosophical thought has undoubtedly shaped his perspective on education as a process that allows for the possibility of change through interaction with the unconditioned and free minds of young children.

Krishnamurti spent his entire life speaking about education as being the agent not only of inner renewal but also of social change. At the heart of Krishnamurti's work was the understanding that society can change only if there is transformation in an individual's consciousness, and this can come about through "right education." For Krishnamurti, with his emphasis on "daily" existence in all its perplexing psychological complexity, "living" was far more important than grappling with an obscure search for "truth" or the "meaning of life" that was disconnected from everyday reality. Goodness for him therefore did not emerge from a search or striving for transformation but from understanding and "right" actions.[31]

Krishnamurti always asserted the individual's responsibility to the social order: "You are the world." One individual's action therefore affects another, since "to be is to be related" (Krishnamurti 1970, 22), and in this sense there is no individual consciousness, only a collective human consciousness. Krishnamurti points to the harmonious development of the inner and outer worlds of an individual: "what one is inwardly will eventually bring about a good society or the gradual deterioration of human relationship." This harmony, however, "cannot possibly come about if our eyes are fixed only on the outer." The inner world is the "source and continuation of the disorder," and for Krishnamurti education should be concerned with changing the source, which is the individual, since it is "human beings who create society, not some gods in heaven" (Krishnamurti 1981, 93–94).[32] In his pursuit of the good society, Krishnamurti therefore emphasizes the individual's relationship to society as well as his/her responsibility for establishing such a society: "You are the repository of all humanity. You are the world and the world is you. And if there is a radical transformation in the very structure of the individual's psyche, it will affect the whole consciousness of man" (Krishnamurti 1993, 133–34).

There is no doubt that Krishnamurti's stress on "goodness" as the foundation of a new society underlies his plea for a society devoid of any kinds of contradictions or dichotomies. A society without "national economic divisions" underscores his obvious concern for the ending of economic and social inequalities. However, none of this could come about without an inner renewal or change, and education is therefore the foundation on which the good society will build itself.

At his annual talks to teachers and students at two KFI schools in India—Rishi Valley School in Andhra Pradesh and Rajghat Education Centre at Varanasi—Krishnamurti often asked the students questions about the meaning of education, the quality of education they received, the teachers' roles and attitudes, and their own contribution to the learning process. He discussed with them the purpose of education—not merely to pass examinations after learning a few facts and acquiring some skills, but to understand the complexity of life. He urged the students to appreciate their role in the creation of a "new" world without fear, conflict, or contradiction. This could only be done if there was "right education" in an atmosphere of freedom, without fear or authority, where intelligence and goodness could be nurtured.

In Krishnamurti's view, a child is not an instrument for the fulfilment of either parental or social expectations. The first step in understanding the child is therefore unconditional love, that is, the complete acceptance of the child as she is, without any expectations, motivations, or desires. This involves responsibility on the part of both the family and the educator, and it also implies a different kind of revolution ("not in a reactionary sense," as he used to say) that is about living in a totally different dimension. Conformity, imitation, or fitting in with social norms and expectations had no place in Krishnamurti's vision. The child should grow up to be a completely different human being who has the courage to question authority, challenge tradition and convention, and the fearlessness to live life on his or her own terms. It is therefore essential to ensure that learning includes an understanding and deep cultivation of psychological processes as much as academic excellence.

The KFI schools have different ways through which they seek to help children understand their psychological processes, including "talking" with them about everyday situations, their psychological fears, and problems. There is also an effort to nurture a quiet mind, to engender stillness, to suspend the chattering of thought for some time so as to experience silence. The silence that fosters the meditative mind, creativity, and intelligence goes together with the intense activity of a rich and diverse academic program. In the Rishi Valley School in rural Andhra Pradesh, for example, children from the senior school quietly gather atop a ridge to sit silently for 15 minutes evening to watch the sun set behind three hills in the distance. This is not a contradiction that engenders conflict, as some educationists may argue, between the challenging and demanding structures of school life and the stillness of a quiet mind. Rather, by maintaining a balance between the inner and the outer worlds, the psychological and technical, the mind and the heart, it is a strategy to develop the best talent and the most sensitive humanism essential for a sane and just society. In the KFI schools, this approach is simultaneously linked to the development of learning processes that seek to awaken curiosity, creativity, and intelligence.

These schools are different from other "alternative" schools not only in their intent and purpose but also in the remarkable expanse of physical and natural beauty in which they are located. For Krishnamurti, a large, natural environment combined with a sense of space is essential to learning, and students from these schools remember the natural beauty of the environment in which they received their learning. One outgoing student wrote about her experience of learning:

> The unique milieu of Rishi Valley School, in which I have been located for the past seven years, has made me realize my relationship with nature. My interaction with the environment around me has instilled a deep stillness and sense of calm in me... I have come to understand myself as an entity within the web of life that comprises nature... I feel that once one establishes a unique link with the environment, caring for it comes as a natural aftermath. (George 2008)

Rishi Valley is a unique institution, a part of the larger Rishi Valley Education Centre (RVEC), and is the oldest KFI school, established in 1926. It has a large sprawling campus, with 360 boarders from different parts of India, aged 8–18 years, and 60 faculty members.[33] The main difference between Rishi Valley and other boarding schools is that there is an absence of the authoritarianism, rigidity, and control that are characteristic features of other private schools in the country. The curriculum is flexible and is transacted in an open and nonauthoritarian manner. The students reside in an atmosphere of freedom and absence of fear in relationships although there are rules no doubt that are essential for the functioning of the school as an institution.[34]

## Rishi Valley School

The intention of the schools run by KFI is to awaken the intelligence of the student so that he or she may "flower in goodness." The cultivation of a global outlook and a concern for our fellow human beings are all part of this scheme of education. Some further goals of the educational philosophy of Rishi Valley Education Centre are:

- to educate students so that they are able to explore both the natural world and the world of feeling;
- to inculcate a love for nature and respect for all forms of life;
- to create an atmosphere of affection, order, and freedom without either fear or licence; and
- to not condition students into any particular belief, either religious, political, or social, so that their minds may remain free to ask fundamental questions, enquire, and learn (school website).

Affiliated to the ICSE and ISC school boards for its senior school examinations, Rishi Valley offers subjects in the conventional disciplinary frames of Science, Arts, and Business. In addition, there is a specially designed General Studies Program "broadly focusing on environmental crisis, and its impact on human societies on food security and issues of poverty" (school website). The school is well known in the country as one offering excellent academic education in addition to a large array of cocurricular activities. In their own words, "The academic curriculum is balanced by arts and crafts, dramatics, sports and participation in a variety of clubs ranging from journalism, to astronomy and chess. Participation in other work of the centre such as afforestation, rural health, and rural education is also encouraged and organized. Students are also encouraged to research topics of their interest and present these at morning assemblies. Assemblies, student-council meetings and specially convened staff-student meetings are forums where discussion and debate over issues of concern in the school community or in the world are encouraged. Culture classes—intended to extend intellectual and emotional horizons of the students—remain an integral part of the timetable, right until class 12" (http://www.rishivalley.org).

Schools like Rishi Valley are few and far between in the vast educational landscape of India. The mix of academic excellence, cocurricular development, and the presence of a culture that is oriented toward students' psychological needs and processes, a concern for nature and the environment, the presence of a rural health and education program that involves students, and other activities that make it an alternative school lends it a unique quality. It is remembered by students for that special quality or experience that is taken with them when they leave school. Students leaving school in 2005 told me that they were taking with them the quality of "innate goodness" that is "out there—intangible, inexpressible," but an undeniable part of their experience of everyday life. They said, "You feel it. It's in the air and it enters you" (Thapan 2006a). A teacher of philosophy at an undergraduate college at the University of Delhi summarized: "Students from Rishi Valley have a different take. I don't know what it is, but they are different" (Thapan 2006b). Perhaps, these students lack artifice, driving ambition, and are content in being themselves.[35]

These schools, and others like them, cater to the middle class and to elite sections of urban Indian society who have the resources to send their children to these institutions that offer private school education through the medium of the English language. Although the recent RTE Act ensures education for all through reservation of 25 percent in all such schools for children for the economically weaker sections, the educational outcomes of this legislation are not yet fully known. Schooling in contemporary India remains sharply divided into the government school system all over the country, which is perhaps rapidly declining in quality, in part due to the availability of private schooling open to all, at a cost.

The KFI has addressed this lacuna in its own work by taking on board village schools and has come up with a Multi-Grade Multi-Level (MGML) approach to primary education that has been implemented in a vast array of rural and urban schools across the country. Rather than viewing the school as an isolated institution, RIVER views schools "as resource centres for the community they are located in" (RIVER website). They therefore seek to decentralize educational processes and work at a local level, addressing the needs of a vast diversity of children and their families. This enables them to work with "the multiple learning needs of children viewed as members of a community—having fathers and mothers with cultural traditions and diverse livelihoods; children who were otherwise alienated and eventually lost in abstract, information-based learning" (RIVER website). The focus therefore has been on developing an appropriate tool kit for use by both teachers and students (known as School in a Box prepared in the Telugu language and translated into different Indian languages) and a focus on classroom interaction with multigrade teaching simultaneously taking place, an emphasis on teaching training, development, and providing support to teachers. RIVER has thus engaged in capacity-building partnerships with several national and international institutions conducting teacher training programs for the implementation of this method. The results have been very encouraging and not only has RIVER won accolades both nationally and at a global level for this pioneering intervention, but the method, popularly known as the Rishi Valley method, has also been implemented in government-run primary schools across the country.[36]

As have other nongovernmental agencies and institutions, the Krishnamurti Foundation (India) has changed the landscape of private education in partnership with government initiatives. This is viewed as one way in which to consider the future of schooling in India: bringing together private initiatives and government schooling in ways that seek to maximize gains for the stakeholders: students, teachers, and the community. This is not to say that all private schooling is of better quality than government school education. There is a need to be open to private initiatives in the field of education without their outright dismissal by those who rightly seek to fix the responsibility of the state for the schooling of its children at affordable costs.

Small-time players in private education cannot offer good quality education for the low fee that is charged, Nambissan (2012) has argued, noting that there are larger business interests that press for low-cost private schooling as one of the many answers to India's schooling problems. At the same time, the recent ASER (2013) clearly points to the lack of appropriate learning levels among children in school as one outcome of the recently enacted RTE that enables teachers to promote children without examinations. Parents want their children to learn and do not seek easy options like these and argue for stringent evaluation practices. They also seek out private education, which, they think, ensures better learning than government schools.

ASER (2013) provides a nuanced understanding of the benefits and disadvantages of private schooling in the regions it has researched. Clearly, private education is not the most appropriate solution to the vast problems that beset education in India, but schooling for all under government auspices alone is unable to deliver quality education, for example, with trained teachers and adequate infrastructure. The enormity and complexity of the problems that beset education in India therefore need further research without harming the interests of the stakeholders. We must also endeavor to stay free of ideological commitments of one kind or another in our search for the best answers to India's problem of *quality* education for all.

# Conclusion

This essay has sought an understanding of the curriculum in India, taking into account initiatives at both the state and private levels. The pursuit of educational ideals has undoubtedly been influenced by the legacies of colonialism; but there have been other approaches to education, private or state initiated, that must be also be contextualized within an overall concern for the education of all. The production of the educated person remains a distant reality for the large mass of schools in spite of government allocation of resources and initiatives. This conundrum deserves our attention as scholars seek to recognize curricular reform and change in a rapidly growing and changing India.

At the same time, it is the understanding of human agency in institutional contexts that has somehow eluded those scholars who seek to establish the significance of the structural and ideological frameworks within which schooling processes are embedded. Once we understand that students are keen and active participants in the processes in which they are embedded our views about schooling, curriculum, and its possible outcomes should change. Young people in schools are driven by perspectives that increasingly idolize or even celebrate a culture of violence in one way or another, inside school or in the streets, alleys, and corners where large numbers of young people make sense of their social worlds. The media manufactures images of extreme violence that add up to an ongoing emphasis on the macabre and intense physical violence. This violence may in fact constitute the everyday world of students in India who have access to such resources in their social universe. At the same time, there is no doubt that an excessive concern with building a spirit of nationalism and patriotism through curricular practices prevails in most government and private schools where the ritual of morning assembly requires singing patriotic songs and building a culture of deference to an idealized nation and the moral superiority of a particular religion or community over others.[37]

If we accept the view that students at school are not mute subjects, but thinking, acting, feeling actors, it is possible for schools to also consciously engage students in other practices that move away from inculcating and reproducing intolerance, violence, and difference. This engagement would result in very different kinds of activities and practices, and these do take place in some of the private schools described above. The effort to inculcate a culture of questioning, skepticism, and criticism is no doubt a laudable aim, replacing those schooling processes that have numbed the minds of children through decades of rote memorization and recitation. Such methods are insufficient to encourage understanding difference, heterogeneity, and complexity in social and cultural life.

Obeyesekere, quoting the Buddha, cautions us: "Hatred that burns on the fuel of justifications must be quenched with the water of compassion, not fed with the firewood of reasons and causes" (1991, 232). This idea implies working differently with teachers and young people through formulating feelings and devising compassionate "imaginative action." Writing in the context of education in South Africa, Yusuf Waghid (2005) argues for a policy of citizenship education that advocates "compassionate action." Compassionate action suggests an understanding and experience of compassion that is not necessarily derived from rational choice and explanation. Compassion, Waghid appreciates, is prerequisite to understanding the suffering of others and consequently "pushes the boundaries of the self" outward (Nussbaum, as quoted by Waghid, ibid., 334).

The important point is to make such processes a part of all schooling practices without labeling such efforts as meaningless exercises that "soften" students and do not allow them to become part of a process of critical inquiry and radical change. All change need not reflect a dramatic moment in the life of an institution. Allowing minds to develop and grow in subtle ways enables the giving of space without indoctrination of any kind. To begin with, children, youth, and teachers must understand that suffering is unacceptable. The cultivation of compassion depends on the elimination of difference and the ability to acknowledge some sort of community among ourselves. This understanding of education needs to prevail if schools are to inculcate a cosmopolitan curriculum of compassion and justice in the complex times in which we now live.

# Notes

1. I am referring to the work of the Eklavya Foundation and the government-school interventions by the Hoshangabad Science Teaching Program (HSTP) that were closed down by the government of Madhya Pradesh in 2002. See Balagopalan (2003) for an understanding of different perspectives concerning the closure.
2. Ashwani Kumar (2012) describes how the document produced by NCERT that defines school curriculum, pedagogy, and evaluation, that is, the National Curriculum Framework (NCF) was very different in 2000 (governed by the right-wing ideology of the ruling government) from the one produced in 2005 (governed by a more liberal and left-wing ideology). Two very different individuals, influenced by these prevailing ideologies, headed the institution at the different times the NCF was produced.
3. See Krishna Kumar (2001) for an analysis of history textbooks in India and Pakistan; see also Scrase (1993) for an early study of textbooks in West Bengal. In an excellent essay, Philip Wexler (1982) discounts the overall influence of textbooks on children in schools.
4. The colonial influence on the curricular framework rests in the organization of the school day according to a British perspective prevalent at the time schooling became Westernized in India. Missionary run schools and other schools established a particular way of conducting the school day that continues to the present: by allocating time to different activities in the curriculum, privileging some subject disciplinary areas over others, an overt emphasis on the English language, the mode of evaluation, and the examination and certification system. See Viswanathan (1989) for an understanding of how the English language became a tool for colonial domination. See also Advani (2009). Above all, it is in the impact on the framing of educational objectives for school education in India that a colonialist framework is most obvious; see Krishna Kumar (1991) for an analysis of the "homonymy" between colonialist and nationalist objectives for education in India.
5. It is to be noted that Catholic missionaries were the first who established schools in southern India. It is remarkable that they learned and used the vernacular languages, established schools for people, and taught students practical knowledge, the three Rs as well as the Christian doctrine (Myrdal 1968: 1637). Myrdal further notes that the missionaries were the ones who introduced printing in the vernacular languages (ibid., 1638) and who played a significant role in furthering the cause of popular education in India. This does not mean that they did not teach the English language and followed a particular mode of teaching, establishing the supremacy of the teacher and the text, thereby set the frame for what was to be followed in later years.

6. For an account of the tussle between the use of English and the vernacular, including regional languages, as a medium of instruction postcolonialism, see Naik (1997, 74ff). For an understanding of the use of the English language in contemporary schooling in India, see Advani (2009).

7. There has been a vast improvement in the government schools with several initiatives to bring children into school and to keep them there, but there is still an overwhelming lack of commitment on the part of the state for school education. The recent Union of India Budget presented (on February 28, 2013) by the then finance minister indicates a budget outlay of Rs. 52,701 crores, an increase of 8.0 percent over the previous year's figures of Rs. 48,781 crores, for school education and literacy programs (Budget Document: indiabudget.nic.in/ub2013–14/eb/sbe59.pdf). This apparently enormous outlay portends well but delivery is a significant problem as the difficulties that beset Indian school education range from poor quality, teacher absenteeism, lack of infrastructure, student dropouts, inequalities of gender and caste, to name a few.

8. Sanjay Srivastava lays bare the canvas of a post-British modernity and its necessary corollary, a middle-class masculinity, that was the hallmark of the Doon School (1998). See also MacDougall (2005) for a more nuanced understanding of being a student in the Doon School.

9. The Indian Public Schools Society was formed in 1929 (under the Indian Companies Act) and was registered as a nonprofit making body. It owns the Doon School and runs the school through a board of governors. Source: http://www.doonschool.com/the-school-and-campus/origins-a-history.

10. The Central Board for Secondary Education (CBSE) affiliates all *Kendriya Vidyalayas*, all *Jawahar Navodaya Vidyalayas*, private schools, and most of the schools approved by the central government of India. http://en.wikipedia.org/wiki/Boards_of_Education_in_India, accessed on March 8, 2013.

11. For further details, see the CBSE website: http://www.cbse.nic.in.

12. http://www.ncert.nic.in provides further details on the organization and functioning of this governmental body.

13. See Roy (2005), Panda (2006), Batra (2005), among others.

14. The Arya Samaj was a Hindu reform movement started by Swami Dayanand Saraswati in 1875. He believed in the infallibility of the *Vedas* (a large body of Sanskrit texts originating in ancient India). The Arya Samaj set up a large number of educational institutions in Punjab and in northern India.

15. The *Jats* are a dominant landowning caste in Punjab in northern India and not only have control over the agricultural land, but have political power at the local village level as well as at the state level (Jodhka 2003, 12).

16. Dutta (1998) provides a historical review of the Gurukuls set up in rural southeast Punjab.

17. Source: http://en.wikipedia.org/wiki/Gurukul.

18. Source: http://www.bgis.org/who_we_are/ accessed on March 12, 2013.

19. Krishna is the eighth incarnation. http://en.wikipedia.org/wiki/. Avatarof the "*Vedic* Supreme God Vishnu in Hinduism." Source: http://en.wikipedia.org/wiki/Krishna The *Bhagvad Gita*, known as the *Gita*, is a "700-verse scripture that is part of the Hindu epic Mahabharata." Source: http://en.wikipedia.org/wiki/Bhagavad_Gita.

20. Source: http://www.bgis.org/who_we_are/ accessed on March 12, 2013.

21. The RSS—*Rashtriya Swayamsevak Sangh* (literally National Volunteer Organization) —is a right-wing, Hindu nationalist party established in 1925 essentially to counter British colonialism and Muslim separatism. The RSS regularly conducts *shakhas* (literally, branches, or camps) on a large open ground with the hoisting of a saffron flag, singing patriotic songs, performing yoga and martial arts, marching to a beat, and meeting people in the community.

22. *Saraswati* denotes the Goddess of Learning in Hinduism, *shishu* is a child, *mandir* is a temple: essentitally, *Saraswati Shishu Mandirs* denote temples of learning for children.

23. See the work of Jeffrey, Jeffery, and Jeffery (2008), Sarangpani (2003), and Froerer (2012) for examples of the different ways in which students' aspirations are linked to upward mobility through the route of educational certification and success.

24. For discussions of different forms of inequality that prevail in a variety of educational institutions, see, for example, Chanana (1988), Karlekar (1988), Wazir (2000), Vaugier-Chatterjee (2004), Deshkal Society (2010), Miles and Singal (2010), Velaskar (2010), Nambissan (2011), Majumdar and Mooij (2011).

25. See Thapan (2014) for ethnographies of some government schools in Delhi.

26. It is not necessary that students have access to greater upward mobility as a result of the educational certification they receive. See for example Swaminathan (2007), Jeffrey (2010) and Thapan (2013) who point to the fraught relationship between education, the decline in livelihood opportunities, and the tenuous links between student aspirations and educational outcomes.

27. Auroville is a community that runs private schools based on the philosophy of Sri Aurobindo Ghose (1872–1950), an Indian nationalist and philosopher who lived in Puducherry. See http://www.edu.aurovilleportal.org/integral-education for details of the Auroville curriculum and education project. The CFL is a school, based on the philosophy of J. Krishnamurti, but independent of the KFI. Located in Bangalore, it is a private school with a rich and varied curriculum. See http://cfl.in/ for further details. The Vasant Valley school is also a private school run by the India Today group, a media conglomerate, in New Delhi, and the Aditi Mallya International School is another private school in Bangalore. Both cater to the elite but are well known for their progressive pedagogies inspite of being bound to the tightly controlled Central Board of Secondary Education. See http://www.vasantvalley.org and http://www.aditi.edu.in/ for further details.

28. For further details, see www.eklavya.in, the official website of the nongovernment organization.

29. See Mehrotra (2007) for an overview of schooling alternatives in India.

30. See Thapan (1991, 2006); the websites of the KFI and the RIVER projects provide some insights into their work: www.kfionline.org http://www.river-rv.org/. See also http://www.rishivalley.org/rural_education/RIVER.htm; for the KFI *Journal of the Krishnamurti Schools*, see http://journal.kfionline.org/

31. See Krishnamurti (1973, 1974, 1981, 1989, 1993) for understanding his perspective on education. See also Thapan (2004, 2007) and Ashwani Kumar (2012/2013).

32. Herzberger has argued that Krishnamurti's view that human beings are in relationship and are therefore connected and constitute the world suggests a loss of individual identity as the individual would always find himself or herself in another (Herzberger 2007).

33. For further details, see http://www.rishivalley.org. See also Thapan (1991, 2006) for a sociological analysis of the school.

34. These rules are often questioned by students on the Democracy Board in the senior school where students are allowed to question rules, make suggestions, propose alternatives, as long as they take responsibility by attaching their names to the notice. See Thapan (1991, 2006) for a commentary on this practice.

35. It is not as if students from Rishi Valley do not experience difficulties of different sorts, in settling down in life outside its protected boundaries, of having to deal with authoritarian teachers and regulations in University life, of having to find their way in the very different world that exists outside school walls, of being harassed because they dare to be different, independent, and questioning in their attitude. These are considered

by students as hazards of having been products of Rishi Valley and although students lament about these issues in private conversations, they do not regret their time in Rishi Valley.
36. For a recent review of this program, see Ram Mohan (2012/2013). See also http://elibrary.worldbank.org/content/workingpaper/10.1596/1813-9450-2530.
37. The work of Sarkar (1993), Benei (2009), and Sundar (2005) describe this process in particular kinds of schools.

# References

Advani, Shalini. 2009. *Schooling the National Imagination: Education, English and the Indian Modern*. Oxford, Delhi: Oxford University Press.

ASER. 2013. *Annual Status of Education Report (Rural) for 2012*. New Delhi: Pratham.

Balagopalan, Sarada. 2003. "Understanding Educational Innovation in India: The Case of Eklavya. Interviews with Staff and Teachers." *Contemporary Education Dialogue*.1: 97–121.

Batra, Poonam. 2005. "Voice and Agency of Teachers. Missing Link in National Curriculum Framework 2005." *Economic and Political Weekly of India* 40: 4347–56.

Benei, Veronique. 2009. *Schooling India: Hindus, Muslims and the Forging of Citizens*. New Delhi: Permanent Black.

Carnoy, Martin. 1974. *Education as Cultural Imperialism*. New York: Longman, Inc.

Chanana, Karuna. 1988. *Socialisation, Education and Women: Explorations in Gender Identity*. New Delhi: Orient Longman Ltd.

Deshkal Society. 2010. *National Report on Inclusive Classrooms, Social Inclusion/Exclusion and Diversity*. Delhi: Deshkal Publications with support from UNICEF.

George, Jyotsna Sarah. 2008. "Essay on the 'Most Significant Learning Experience at School.'" Author's personal collection.

Herzberger, Radhika. 2007. Introduction. J. Krishnamurti: The Path and the Pathless, *KFI Gathering Booklet, Rishi Valley*: 3–19.

Jodhka, Surinder Singh. 2003. "Contemporary Punjab. A Brief Introduction." In *Punjab Society: Perspectives and Challenges*, edited by M. S. Gill, 3–25. New Delhi: Concept.

Froerer, Peggy. 2007. "Disciplining the Saffron Way: Moral Education and the Hindu Rashtra." In *Modern Asian Studies*, 1033–71. Cambridge: Cambridge University Press.

Froerer, Peggy. 2012. "Learning, Livelihoods, and Social Mobility: Valuing Girls' Education in Central India." *Anthropology & Education Quarterly* 43 (4): 344–57.

Jeffrey, Craig. 2010. *Timepass: Youth, Class and the Politics of Waiting in India*. Stanford: Stanford University Press.

Jeffrey, Craig, Roger Jeffery, and Patricia Jeffery. 2008. "School and Madrasah Education: Gender and the Strategies of Muslim Young Men in Rural North India." *Compare* 38 (5): 581–89.

Karlekar, Malavika. 1988. "Women's Nature and the Access to Education." In *Socialisation, Education and Women. Explorations in Gender Identity*, edited by Karuna Chanana. New Delhi, Orient Longman Ltd.

Krishnamurti, J. 1973. *Education and the Significance of Life*. New Delhi: B. I. Publications.

Krishnamurti, J. 1974. *On Education*. Chennai: KFI.

Krishnamurti, J. 1981. *Letters to the Schools*. Madras: KFI.

Krishnamurti, J. 1989. *The Last Talks*. Chennai: KFI.

Krishnamurti, J. 1993. *A Timeless Spring: Krishnamurti at Rajghat*. Chennai: KFI.

Kumar, Krishna.1989. *Social Character of Learning.* New Delhi: Sage Publications Ltd.

Kumar, Krishna. 1991. *Political Agenda of Education: A Study of Colonialist and Nationalist Ideas.* New Delhi, Newbury Park, London: Sage.

Kumar, Krishna. 2001. *Prejudice and Pride: School Histories of the Freedom Struggle in India and France.* New Delhi: Penguin Books.

Kumar, Ashwani. 2012. "Indian Social Studies Curriculum in Transition: Effects of a Paradigm Shift in Curriculum Discourse." *Transnational Curriculum Inquiry.* 9 (1) http:// nitinat.library.ubc.ca/ojs/index.php/tci Accessed on March 15, 2013.

Kumar, Ashwani. 2012/2013. Fundamentals of a Meditative Education. *D. S. Kothari Centre for Science, Ethics and Education (University of Delhi) Working Paper Series,* I: 1–22.

Majumdar, Manabi and Jos Mooij. 2011. *Education and Inequality in India: A Classroom View.* Abingdon, New York: Routledge.

Mehrotra, Deepti Priya. 2007. "Origins of an Alternative Education in India: A Continuing Journey." In *Alternative Schooling in India,* edited by Sarojini Vittachi and Neerja Raghavan, 25–43 New Delhi, London, Thousand Oaks: Sage.

Miles, Susie and Nidhi Singal. 2010. "The Education for All and Inclusive Education Debate: Conflict, Contradiction or Opportunity?" *International Journal of Inclusive Education* 14 (1):1–15.

Naik, J. P. 1997. *The Education Commission and After.* New Delhi: A. P. H. Publishing Corporation.

Nambissan, Geetha. 2011. Education of Tribal Children in India: Sociological Perspectives in *Schooling Stratification and Inclusion, Some Reflections on the Sociology of Education in India,* edited by Yoginder Singh. Delhi: NCERT.

Nambissan, Geetha. 2012. October 13. "Private Schools for the Poor. Business as Usual?" *Economic and Political Weekly.* 47: 41–58.

Obeyesekere, Gananath. 1991. "Buddhism and Conscience: An Exploratory Essay." *Daedalus.* 120 (Summer).

Panda, Minati. 2006. "Mathematics and Tribal Children." *Economic and Political Weekly of India.* January 14: 117–20.

Ram Mohan, Rohini. 2012/2013. "Child-Centred Learning in Praxis: Issues and Challenges in Context of Rural Schools of Rishi Valley." *D. S. Kothari Centre for Science, Ethics and Education (University of Delhi) Working Paper Series,* IV: 1–27.

Roy, Kumkum. 2005. "Looking Ahead: History Syllabus in NCF 2005." *Economic and Political Weekly.* October 5: 4303–04.

Sarangpani, Padma. 2003. *Constructing School Knowledge: An Ethnography of Learning in an Indian Village.* New Delhi: Sage.

Sarkar, Tanika. 1996. "Educating the Children of the Hindu Rashtra: Notes on RSS Schools." in *Religion, Religiosity and Communalism,* edited by P. Bidwai, H. Mukhia, and A Vanaik. New Delhi: Manohar Publishers.

Scrase, Timothy. 1993. *Image, Ideology and Inequality: Cultural Domination, Hegemony and Schooling in India.* New Delhi: Sage.

Srivastava, Sanjay. 1998. *Constructing Post-Colonial India: National Character and the Doon School.* London and New York: Routledge.

Sundar, Nandini. 2005. "Teaching to Hate. The Hindu Right's Pedagogical Program." In *Revolution and Pedagogy,* edited by Tom Ewing, 195–218. New York: Palgrave Macmillan.

Swaminathan, Padmini. 2007. "The Interface between Employment and Education in India: The Need for a Discourse." In *Education and Social Change in South Asia,* edited by Krishna Kumar and Joachim Oesterheld, 325–58. New Delhi: Orient Longman.

Sykes, Marjorie. 1993. "Keynote address." In *Democracy and Education in India,* edited by Krishna Kumar. New Delhi: Nehru Memorial Museum and Library.

Thapan, Meenakshi. 1991 (2006, 2nd ed.). *Life at School: An Ethnographic Study*. Delhi: Oxford University Press.

Thapan, Meenakshi. 2006a. "Introduction." In *Life at School. An Ethnographic Study*. 2nd ed. New Delhi: Oxford, Oxford University Press.

Thapan, Meenakshi. 2006b. "Learning to Be Yourself." *The Hindu*. 23 July.

Thapan, Meenakshi. 2007. "Education and the Purpose of Living: The Legacy of J. Krishnamurti." *Contemporary Education Dialogue* 5 (1): 64–77.

Thapan, Meenakshi. 2013. "Waiting for Change: Enduring Educational Outcomes." *Nordic Studies in Education*. Special issue: Educational Research on Everyday Life. 32: 140–51.

Thapan, Meenakshi. 2014 (ed.) *Ethnographies of Schooling in Contemporary India*. New Delhi, Washington DC, Singapore, London: Sage Publications.

Vaugier-Chatterjee, Anne (ed.) 2004. *Education and Democracy in India*. New Delhi: Manohar and *Centre des Sciences Humaines*.

Velaskar, Padma. 2010. "Quality and Inequality in Indian Education: Some Critical Policy Concerns." *Contemporary Education Dialogue* 7 (1): 58–93.

Viswanathan, Gauri. 1989. *Masks of Conquest: Literary Study and British Rule in India*. London: Faber and Faber.

Vittachi, Sarojini and Neerja Raghavan. 2007.(eds.) *Alternative Schooling in India*. New Delhi, London, Thousand Oaks: Sage.

Waghid, Yusuf. 2005. "Action as an Educational Virtue: Toward a Different Understanding of Democratic Citizenship Education." *Educational Theory* 55 (3): 323–42.

Wazir, Rekha. 2000. (ed.) *The Gender Gap in Basic Education: NGOs as Change Agents*. New Delhi, Thousand Oaks, London: Sage.

Wexler, Philip. 1982. Structure, Text and Subject: A Crtitical Sociology of School Knowledge. In *Cutural and Economic Reproduction in Education,* edited by Michael Apple, 275–303. London: Routledge.

# Chapter 6

---

# The Exchanges
*William F. Pinar*

Internationalization is a conversation complicated by one's insulation within the intellectual histories that inevitably imprints our work as well as the present circumstances that press upon us, demanding our attention and threatening to submerge us in the moment at hand. While increasingly influenced globally, these present circumstances are indelibly local, as they encode specific histories the materialization of which creates the world we inhabit now. The history of the present tends to be opaque to the uninformed outsider. Only by serious study—focused here by questions—can one glimpse the present as a melting moment in time and decode the dynamism of what appears as unchanging. In the quest for understanding, the outsider cannot suspend all of his or her assumptions—no questions can be asked unless they originate in what one knows or thinks one knows—but can seek clarification. That is, if those with whom we are in conversation are willing to teach us what we do not know. Poonam Batra, Mary Ann Chacko, Suresh Ghosh, and Meenakshi Thapan kindly consented to teach.[1] Lesley Le Grange and Hongyu Wang kindly consented to study, first through reading the essays (now chapters 1–5) and then seeking clarification of specific concepts and circumstances from the scholar-participants themselves.

To preserve the exchanges as they occurred I have kept my editor's touch light. Organizing the exchanges by topic may seem more "reader-friendly," but it risks obscuring the actual sequencing of questions and answers. Immediacy is already sacrificed in the absence of face-to-face meetings: when I first formulated an extended study of "internationalization" I was committed to the conference—with the physical presence of the scholar-participants and the International Panel members.[2] These exchanges occurred online and over an extended duration. To compensate the dissolution of immediacy that extended online exchanges encourage, I organized questions and answers not by topic but by person. In addition to underscoring the individual character of the exchanges, by organizing this chapter by person readers can more easily reference the relevant chapters and an extensive index—the importance of which I suggested in the introduction—that can help readers pinpoint specific issues and their recurrence in both chapters and exchanges.

In chapter 7, I will shift from "editor" to "author," although still positioning myself in fidelity to the essays and exchanges by quoting them extensively. But I will organize the chapter by topics, clear that in so doing their original exchanges become reconstructed by my own agenda. Given my lifelong interest in life history, my embeddedness in the West and, specifically, my cultural inheritance, I will emphasize the particular and distinctive within those topics. The topics that structure chapter 7 emerge here: colonialism and its aftermath, including globalization; Kumar's concepts of counter-socialization and deliberation; the 2005 curriculum reform; the controversial curricular status of English and ongoing questions of gender, the state of schools in India, the counter-traditions of education associated with Tagore, Gandhi, and Krishnamurti; the political dissensus that both invigorates and threatens to destroy parliamentary democracy, cultural complexity, and conflict; and the steadfast efforts of the scholar-participants to educate within such present circumstances, informed by multiple, not always welcome, intellectual histories.

# Exchanges with Poonam Batra

Crucial questions of colonialism, culture, and postcolonialism structured the exchange between Poonam Batra and Lesley Le Grange. There is an intriguing exchange over the uncritical importation of Western concepts, including "child-centeredness," here associated with neoliberalism. This is followed by an even more interesting exchange concerning "reflectivity" in teacher education, as Le Grange and Batra contrast the concept's contrasting meanings in America and India. Hongyu Wang focused first on issues of disciplinarity, asking: Is there a specialized, formalized field of curriculum studies in India? Batra provides an explanation of why there is not, including a succinct history of the present, culminating in the National Curriculum Framework, 2005. This revealing exchange concludes with post-NCF, 2005, developments and ends with Poonam Batra's sage reminder regarding the very *raison d'être* of education.

## Lesley Le Grange with Poonam Batra

"Thank you for your informative paper, Professor Batra!" began Lesley Le Grange. He found Batra's depiction of the relationship between colonial education and indigenous education "quite interesting." At the outset of her chapter, Le Grange noted, Batra referenced Holmes's argument that "despite tensions between the colonial view of education and the nationalist postcolonial aims of education, British essentialism grew unassailable roots in India partly because 'colonial values coincided with those of indigenous traditions.'" Le Grange then asked: "According to your own view, what are those values that both seem to share?"

"Both shared values rooted in hierarchical structures of society," Batra replied, values concerning "who can be educated; by whom and which knowledge is worthwhile." Macaulay's[3] views regarding native culture and knowledge as "inferior" to Western knowledge are well known," a view that also translated, she added, into "who should have the right to vote." In India, Batra continued, "we had strong brahamanical (upper caste) hegemony of knowledge, specifying who could be taught and by whom. We have come a long way from the time when Dalits (lower caste) were not allowed to read sacred texts and were treated as complete outcastes by the upper caste brahamans.[4] There are "remarkable examples of resistance in Indian history," Batra continued, referencing the lives of Pandita Ramabai and Jyotiba Phule. They "defied the social order and initiated movements that led to the education of masses including girls, women and lower castes. But these were exceptions."

Referencing Michael Nagler's argument that the nonviolence movements leading to independence of India left less bitterness and resentment between India and Britain than war would have, translating into less acrimonious postindependence relations between the two countries. "I don't know if he is presenting the situation in a romantic way," Le Grange admits, "but do you think this might be a factor in education too?"

"This could be one way of looking at it," Batra agrees, "even if a bit romantic!"

"Two hundred years isn't a short time," she continued. Contemporary India, she acknowledged, is "built" upon the "legacies" of British rule. "Our systems of bureaucracy, federal institutional structures, and university arrangements including nomenclatures continue the way we adopted them during the British regime." The nonviolent movement was "the result" of a "plural, diverse and therefore more resilient and liberal society," and that movement "further strengthened our conviction that maintaining harmonious relationships is the way forward." The nonviolence of Gandhi "emerged triumphant" because "we were convinced of the many messages he conveyed through the example of his own life." Although everyone could not be conscious of the "nuances of Gandhian ideals," as "his concept of 'swaraj' (self-rule) was as much an individual endeavor as a political and social endeavor." It was one, she added, that resonated deeply in a country that had "awaited freedom for almost a hundred years after the first war of independence, infamously known as the mutiny of 1857."

"Regarding the relationship between colonial knowledge and indigenous knowledge," Le Grange wrote, "there is a general recognition that indigenous knowledge is excluded in school curriculum." Referencing her essay, Le Grange noted that Batra cited several educational efforts—Tagore, Gandhi, Sri Aurobindo—who focused on educating the whole person. He asked: Are these embedded in "Indian indigenous traditions" that are "different from the colonial approach?"

"Yes," Batra replied, "there needs to be a distinction made between dominant values of the indigenous traditions of education and the several indigenous traditions that were articulated and even practiced by well-known thinkers." Both Tagore and Gandhi's ideas of education constituted "a critical response to the colonial system of education." Batra drew the following contrast: "while the colonial system was a system of education which draws from the outside inwards (emerging out of the renaissance and the positivistic school of thought that became pervasive—and still is), indigenous ideas spoke of education as a process of drawing out from within." In fact, "the key indigenous principle" is "forging a link between the outer material reality with the inner capacity to reflect and develop insight." Batra referenced Sri Aurobindo's "integral education" as an example, based as it is "on integrating various aspects of a being—the physical, vital, mental, psychic and spiritual." For "many thinkers" in India, she continued, "reflecting on the material reality including one-self is a process that draws from within. In this sense, there are no dualities, only processes that co-exist but are seen as dichotomies in the circumscribed view of the logical 'mind,' which several scholars of the West have also challenged, including John Dewey and G H Mead."

"But in the mainstream school curriculum," Le Grange asserted, "this is not reflected." In fact, he continued, "it seems parents from various backgrounds welcome education in English in order to make their children competitive. Do you think good a relationship between the two—indigenous and imported language and knowledge—can exist in the Indian school curriculum?" In her essay, Batra reminded, the examples she provided were the Krishnamurti schools "where education is imparted in the English medium; skills of reading, writing, numeracy, computer literacy are developed through a curriculum and pedagogy focused on the teachings of Jiddu Krishnamurti while also negotiating the curriculum of the CBSE Board public examination. Schools patterned on Sri Aurobindo's integral education do the same." There are, she reported, "several such examples but these have yet to become part of mainstream schooling."

"The tension between the two," Le Grange continued, "seems to contribute to the tension between school and culture, yet in the latter part [of the essay] when you discuss cultural nationalism, it seems to be more related to religions." "Is culture 'broader' than religion in India?" he asked. "Oh yes," Batra replied, "most certainly." Religion is "but one aspect of culture" but "unfortunately" it is "projected as synonymous with culture." Separating the two[5] is "the most significant challenge—the challenge of bringing culture meaningfully into school curriculum and pedagogic practice, so that it can be interrogated while being built on to derive meaning and develop insight." Batra then referenced "cultural nationalism," an "ideologically motivated" project to 'homogenize' the plural fabric of Indian society" through the "imposition of 'Hindu' religious values and hues, even when 'Hindu' itself is neither a monolithic religion nor a monolithic way of life." India's "plurality," she continued, "lies in a myriad of societal aspects, including religion, language, communities, food, clothing, folk traditions and these are often complex mixtures rather than classifiable into neat categories—culture lies here."

Le Grange then asked: "Is it possible to integrate Indian cultural elements into school curriculum without igniting religious disputes? Is it possible to heal the divide between school and culture in the new century?" "Yes," Batra replied, "I do think it is possible." Culture can become, she suggested, "an educational pursuit as much as a context for educating." As "we have always done," she continued, "religion (understood as organized religion) needs to be kept out of formal school education. This was the insight developed by Gandhi over the years." Keeping religion out of the school curriculum represents a "challenge." "We will need to foreground capacities to reflect, to contemplate, to witness, and to become compassionate," she declared.

These are the "significant aims and the processes of education." These become possible "only when we (re)design educational experiences in a manner that engage[s] learners and educators with the inner as much as with the outer."

"In the post-colonial modernization project," Le Grange continued, referencing Batra's essay, "the focus was on higher education and particularly in science and technology (this volume), but the mainstream school curriculum was not really influenced." He asked, "What has led to such a gap between school and higher education?" Can college students become better off due to the higher education curriculum alone? Must not its "foundations at school level" also be taken into account? Batra confirmed Le Grange's reading of her essay, acknowledging that "the nation prioritized higher technical and scientific education given the thrust on modernization and the need to industrialize in the early post-independence years. As a result, school education, or shall we say mass education, got neglected. We are paying the price for this neglect." "Why is school curriculum so slow to change?" Le Grange asked. Batra replied: "Curriculum at all levels has been slow to change. It was not so much a matter of preference between two curricula, but of choosing to invest in higher technical education as it was seen as the route to modernity and scientific development."

"I am a bit unclear," Le Grange continued, "about what 'child-centered' education means in the context of Indian education." Referencing a phrase in Batra's essay—"this narrow interpretation of child-centered education" (this volume)—Le Grange asked: "What is that interpretation?" Many teachers, Batra began, "carry very rudimentary ideas and concepts related to 'child-centered education' that have emerged from contexts other than ours." As an example Batra cited Piaget's stage theory of development. While the basic vocabulary of Piaget's schema is in circulation, there is little appreciation of "the theoretical frames in which they are located and developed," Batra reported.[6] Due to their uncritical importation, Batra suggested, "cultural notions of children and childhood are not adequately engaged with, conceptions of child-centered learning remain narrow and do not provide any meaningful frames to draw upon. This narrow conception of child-centered education contains the risk of marginalizing 'knowledge' and 'subject-matter' in the process of education."

Le Grange wondered, "How do child-centered education and outcome-oriented, behaviorist go together?" Batra agreed: "They don't go together. Much classroom practice is behaviourist in orientation." Batra blames those "narrow" conceptions of child-centered education too many teachers been bequeathed. Accompanying the domination of classroom practice by "behavorism," she continued, "is the ascendancy of neoliberalism in India, with its emphasis on outcomes." The "neo-liberal agenda," she notes, "fits better with the behaviourist frames of teaching and learning."

Next Le Grange asked about "the relationship between the child as a citizen—*social and cultural*"—and (quoting Batra's essay)—"*psychological* underpinnings of curriculum design with the child at the centre" (this volume). This phrase, Batra explained, "means that curriculum developers recognized in principle that curriculum needs to be developmentally appropriate; however, the conception of the child as indicated by text materials and classroom practice was predominantly that of a

'social and cultural' citizen. Universalistic notions of a child embedded in psychological theory seem to provide a framework for the education of 'ideal' citizens." Le
Grange followed: "And what is the relationship between child-centered education
and indigenousness of school curricula?" The former, Batra replied, designates "a
focus on children and their development sans subject content," with the accompanying "tendency to marginalize 'knowledge' in curriculum and foreground 'method'
(activity-based, discovery method)," both of which were supposed to "draw children
towards self-discovery and learning by doing." The latter—the "indigenousness of
school curricula"—translated into an emphasis on cultural values that were "narrowly focused on religious values. These are largely defined in behavioural terms—
hence, here too 'knowledge' tends to get marginalized."

Le Grange then expressed appreciation for Batra's "insights" about teacher education and development, "important for any curriculum change or improvement."
Especially, he appreciated that Batra devoted a section of her essay to teacher education curriculum. "Indian philosophy and Indian (alternative) education have had
a tradition of educating the whole person," he continued, "and I wonder to what
degree that orientation has been introduced into teacher preparation. Without
teachers themselves attending to wholeness, how can we educate students to be the
whole person? Could you discuss a bit more on such initiatives—if there are—in
Indian teacher education today?"

"A focused study of self and identity, human relationships, adult-child gaps,
assumptions, beliefs and attitudes," Batra responded, are "integrated through theory
and practicum courses in the BElEd program."[7] Various "dimensions of self are
explored through drama, art, music and craft activities," she added, "which often
provide non-judgmental and non-threatening learning environments. This enables
examining of stereotypes; going beyond prejudices, leading to greater social sensitivity. This focus on the self leads to processes of inner reflection; through activities
of the intellect, the heart and hands teachers get opportunities to experience themselves as 'integrated' beings and to relate to others as such. Several alternatives based
on Krishnamurti's and Aurobindo's philosophy that integrate the mental, the vital
and the spiritual have been deployed to train teachers as well."

Le Grange then alluded to the centrality of "reflection" in American teacher
education. Despite rhetorical allegiance to the concept, in the United States, he
continued, often "reflection stays at the level of reflecting what happens in teaching
and seldom goes into depth of subjectivity and personhood. Does Indian teacher
education also privilege knowledge/skill/competencies over in-depth understanding of teacher's (or teacher-to-be's) own personal growth?" Yes, Batra replied, this is
indeed the case with the currently dominant models of teachers preparation. Person
growth "forms a very significant part of the BElEd programme which I have referenced in the essay." She cited "compulsory theory and practicum courses," specifically "Human Relations and Communication (HRC)" and "Self-Development
Workshops (SDWs)." She then quoted a BElEd graduate, a former elementary
schoolteacher and now teacher educator: "The HRC and SDW demanded that I
reflect on myself and my experiences with the help of theoretical constructs of identity. They first made me aware of various stereotypes and then conscious about how
I had internalized them. These workshops made a deep impact on my personality,

helping me to evolve as a more secular and tolerant person. Above all, I learnt to aspire as a teacher, to take pride in myself after overcoming the grip of my own socialization."

The BElEd, Batra emphasized, is "designed to provide opportunities for reflection," and "not only over matters outside oneself but along with and in the context of the inner aspects of the person." "In fact," she continued, "these inner aspects become the core engagement of some of the courses which, when interfaced with other (particularly) social science courses, create a unique chemistry of experiences and processes of engaging with social reality, questioning oneself and the social milieu, reflecting on oneself and one's position in society and developing a sense of agency. Slowly, but surely we are in the process of developing strategies and mechanisms to scale up these ideas after having achieved an articulation of them in the form of a national curriculum framework for teacher education."

## Hongyu Wang with Poonam Batra

"I benefitted greatly from the insights you shared on schooling and curriculum in India over time," Hongyu Wang began her exchange with Poonam Batra. "In your essay you take the reader through different moments in the development of the school curriculum in India. Changes in the school curriculum appear to be marked by pendulum swings from a dominance of universal knowledge and values to an emphasis on local content and values." Wang then asked: "Does Curriculum Studies exist as a field/discipline in India?"

Replying to that question, Batra explained that while "individual scholars across different social science disciplines have worked on curriculum and have written on the subject, we do not have an institutional platform for concerted work or research in the area of curriculum studies." Replying to Wang's request to date the present interest in curriculum, Batra wrote that "curriculum became an area of interest for a diverse set of scholars around the time when there were systematic ideological attempts to capture the 'space'—in the late 1990s." Then Wang wondered if "the field had influenced the development of school curricula in India, and/or has the field been influenced by the different moments in the development of the school curriculum in India that you describe?" "The latter," Batra replied. "One reason why curriculum studies has not really developed as a field of research and enquiry is because typically university departments of education in India have engaged more with programs of teacher training/education and less with the pursuit of educational studies/research in education—issues of curriculum, knowledge and practice."

"Who are the key curriculum scholars," Wang continued. There is no specific stable set of curriculum scholars, Batra explained, as in India "institutional engagement in education has focused on the training of teachers. Educational—including curriculum—research has therefore been "more of an individual interest and activity of scholars within education and in the social sciences. Individual scholarly writing spans a range of critical areas of education rather than specialized writing in curriculum studies or any other field." That fact acknowledged, Batra proceeded to name several scholars associated with curriculum research. Krishna Kumar[8] came first.

Kumar has written on several subjects, Batra explained, "on teachers in the colonial period, on the political agenda of education, and on curriculum and culture, including a comparative study of school histories in Pakistan and India." Other scholars who have written on curriculum have focused on "specific domains." On the teaching of history Neeladari Bhattacharya, Kumkum Roy, and Narayani Gupta are prominent. On mathematics education Ravi Subramanium is well known; on science education Batra listed Amitabha Mukherjee and Arvind Kumar; on language education she listed Ramakant Agnihotri and Shobha Sinha. Wang pursued the issue of disciplinarity,[9] asking "are there academic conferences with a specific focus on curriculum held in India and are there academic journals with a dedicated focus on curriculum? About what do Indian curriculum scholars mainly write?" There is "not yet," Batra repeated, "a specialized discourse." Those who write on issues of curriculum reside in "specific disciplinary areas, even in NGOs who have engaged with the school system by way of intervention, research and documentation." As an example Batra referenced "major research" undertaken by Nirantar, a NGO based in Delhi that "analyzed school textbooks in four states of India, focusing on the construct of 'nation' and 'national identity' through the gender lens." Conferences on education, she continued, typically "look at several issues in education such as curriculum, pedagogy, policy and practice simultaneously. Attempts to put together contextualized research in disciplinary areas of sociology, philosophy and history of education are more recent."

"I found the role of the NGO sector, particularly Eklavya interesting," Wang offered. She asked: "What were the social, political and education conditions in India that made it possible for Eklavya to influence the school curriculum reform in Madhya Pradesh and other states?" Batra started her reply historically, citing the 1966 National Education Commission—popularly known as the Kothari Commission—and its call for "a modern and scientific outlook through school education." During the early nation-building years, Batra explained, the Indian government invested primarily in higher and technical education than in school education. When, in early 1972, a group of scientists, engineers, educationists, and social activists expressed a "vision of school science teaching close to the ideal envisaged in various policy directives, they received political and social support." Two NGOs—Friends Rural Centre (FRC), Rasulia, and Kishore Bharati (KB)— undertook a pilot project on science teaching in 16 middle schools spread over two blocks of the Hoshangabad district of Madhya Pradesh[10] with permission from the state government in May 1972. This project, Batra continued, led to "the birth" of the Hoshangabad Science Teaching Program (HSTP). "Taking inspiration" from the Harvard and Nuffield Science Programs,[11] "the aim of HSTP was to improve the quality of science teaching in government schools." The "political regime at the centre" was the Congress Party.[12] Party officials, she continued," "admired the HSTP interventions in government schools, viewing it as 'Nehruvian thought in action.' It also supported efforts of a non-governmental organization, as policy and government resources were not yet directed towards school[13] education sector as a matter of priority."

The program received support from the All-India Science Teachers Association (Physics Study Group) and from the Tata Institute of Fundamental Research

(TIFR), Mumbai. A group of young scientists from the University of Delhi joined the effort in 1973, "leading" to the formation of Eklavya a decade later. In order to create an "autonomous agency" for science education, curriculum, pedagogy, and teacher training, Batra explained, Eklavya was established in 1982, supported by the Planning Commission and the Department of Science and Technology in the Ministry of Education. The University Grants Commission (UGC) granted fellowships to faculty members from Delhi University and other academic institutions so they might participate in the program in the villages, and, Batra noted, the government of Madhya Pradesh permitted its undergraduate science teachers to interact with Eklavya "on a regular basis." The All India People's Science Network, she continued, "took the initiative to translate the science textbooks (Bal-Vaigyanik) developed by Eklavya into fourteen Indian languages, and many states started using the material in a variety of ways."[14]

"Am I correct," Wang asked, "that you were suggesting in your essay that the demise of Eklavya's programmes after 30 years was due to a second phase of neoliberalism in India? What was the first phase of neoliberalism, and what was significant about the second phase of neoliberalism that saw a decline in donor-aided education reform?" "Yes," Batra confirmed, "Eklavya was forced to close down its program during the second phase of neoliberalism, unsurprisingly when the Congress party was in power, the party that had provided it patronage to begin with." The first phase of neoliberalism had begun in the "early 1990s, with economic reforms." In the mid-1990s, Batra explained, "India took aid from the World Bank to initiate a nation-wide program of school education, called the District Primary Education Program (DPEP)." The DPEP "brought into convergence" several programs undertaken by individual states (with permission from the central government) with foreign aid (DFID, Sida)."[15] Eklavya was "called upon to participate in the DPEP in a major way, leading to the spread of its science, social science and primary education curriculum across different states." Then circumstances changed. "Interestingly," Batra continued, "a different political regime—the Bharatiya Janata Party (BJP), the Hindu right wing, had come to power—in the state of MP between 1990 and 1992, just before the DPEP. "Eklavya faced the threat of closure even then but for reasons embedded in cultural nationalism."

The "second wave" of neoliberalism, Batra reported, occurred a decade later. It "meant high economic growth and a decline in donor-aided reform." States'[16] fiscal deficits declined; in some instances there were surpluses. It was during this time that the state of Delhi[17] sponsored the writing of school textbooks for elementary education after being denied permission of copyright to use the NCERT[18] textbooks of the pre-NCFSE, 2000 (referred to as the "saffronized" curriculum). With improved economic health, individual states were exercising their autonomy not only in matters of curriculum development, but also in matters of education policy more generally.

"If neoliberalism was in ascendancy in India," Wang asked, "what made it possible for NCERT to develop the new National Curriculum Framework, 2005, that involved a deliberative process (national consultation) with all role-players and the incorporation of ideas from among other organizations such as Eklavya?" Batra began her reply by recalling that the National Democratic Alliance (NDA) was in power "at the centre" during the period 1999–2004. The NDA was a coalition government led by the BJP, the largest party in the NDA. This Hindu right-wing party attempted to institutionalize cultural nationalism through school curriculum. This move led to a "huge controversy" over history textbooks, including numerous "public debates and a court case." When another political coalition, the United Progressive Alliance (UPA) came to power at the center (with Congress as the lead party), the agenda of the new political regime was to "detoxify" or "desaffronize" the school curriculum that had been developed during the NDA regime. The NCF, 2005 was, then, an exercise of reviewing the NCFSE 2000 of the NDA government. The academics who conducted this review, Batra explained, "took the opportunity to develop a curriculum that addressed some of the key questions related to the purpose of education, including its link with society, pedagogic approaches, and bringing the child, the teacher and curriculum onto centre-stage—hence a deliberative agenda!"

"We could say," Batra continued, that "this opportunity was seized by the Director of NCERT—Krishna Kumar—as well as by those who had been associated with the writing of NCF and the school textbooks." It was "in fact," Batra empha-sized, the "first time" that "significant position papers" had been composed on each of the themes critical to schooling, including "the aims of education, questions of gender, education for the marginalized and for work." In all, twenty-one (21) position papers were produced, articulating for the "first time," she continued, a "progressive discourse on issues of curriculum, teachers and educational practice." This occurred, she reminded, during a period of strong economic growth, permitting academics from different universities, others from civil society, from NGOs (including Eklavya) to participate in this "mammoth exercise." As neoliberal policies gained traction, Batra added, "we can see the prominence of the curriculum discourse declining and the discourse of efficiency, accountability and learning outcomes gaining currency, with concerted efforts at institutionalizing mechanisms towards this end."

Then Wang turned to "post-NCF, 2005," when "debates pivoted on ideas of local knowledge, child-centered constructs and the pedagogic frame of constructiv-ism." She asked: "Who were the key role-players in these debates?" These debates, Batra began, "emerged from the ideologically left" who regarded local knowledge as "retrograde." In their view local knowledges "threatened the idea of rationality and objectivity that formal education represented." Local knowledge, they worried, has the potential of privileging cultural practices that "maintain hierarchies and divisiveness in society." To address this issue, the NCF, 2005 preamble was "revised" so that the Indian Constitution became the "litmus test for deciding which local knowledge is worthy of including in school curriculum and why."

Regarding the debates concerning "constructivism" and "constructs" of child-centeredness, Batra explained that these were debated on "ideological" and on "educational" grounds. There were, she continued, "genuine questions" concerning "how" child-centered ideas can be enacted in the diverse and hierarchical settings of Indian society, including what constructivism "really means when we teach the chil-dren of the poor, the marginalized, and first generation learners within constraints of infrastructure and other resources."

"How," Wang concluded her questioning, "in your view should an emphasis on local knowledge be balanced with knowledge that is perceived to be more powerful in a globalized world?" As an example, Wang again invoked Batra's essay. There Batra had referenced the insistence of the Gondi tribal parents that their children be taught in English and Hindi (and not in the Gondi language) because they perceived these to be "more powerful" languages for the "social mobility" and future "employment" of their children. "I think this balance," Batra replied, concerns "not only about knowledge selection and legitimacy. It is also about the purpose of education and the intimate relationship between education and society. If the education project is about creating and sustaining a socially just, democratic and humane society (which is what I think it is), then the educational discourse will need to be freed from dichotomies and dualities so we longer remain trapped in forced choices."

"Dichotomies" and "dualities" trap us in "forced" choices, Batra concludes, now the false choice between education for economic growth or for human development and enlightenment. To assume that the latter is a 'natural' outcome of the former is in serious question. The intertwined demands of education for economic growth; democracy, and humanity, Batra makes clear, require "balance." Balance—that state in which various elements form a satisfying and harmonious whole, in which nothing is out of proportion or unduly emphasized, especially at the expense of any other—is forever fragile. Its fragility—inflected by history, politics, and culture—becomes an ongoing emergency, one today we summarize as neoliberalism. In India, it is clear from these exchanges, the eternal verities of our calling have not disappeared despite the disproportionate power of the economistic present.

## Exchanges with Mary Ann Chacko

In their exchanges with Mary Ann Chacko, Lesley Le Grange, and Hongyu Wang sought clarification concerning key concepts associated with the work of Krishna Kumar. Both Le Grange and Wang, for instance, noted that Kumar's conception of curriculum development as "acts of deliberation" rather than "social engineering" resonates with curriculum research conducted elsewhere, for example, with Joseph Schwab's promulgation of the "practical." Le Grange found other resonances as well, among them Kumar's notion of schooling as "counter- socialization," which he linked "with the work of radical curriculum scholars in the USA and elsewhere (such as Paulo Freire)." He and Wang pressed Chacko to specify the distinctiveness of Kumar's conception. Dealing with a similar dynamic,[19] Wang wanted to know if Chacko could describe the "relationship" between indigenous and "modern" knowledge, especially as it is structured in curricular controversies over English, a topic that also interested Le Grange. Chacko replied at length and in essay form.

### Hongyu Wang with Mary Ann Chacko

The characterization of schooling as "counter-socialization" Hongyu Wang found "provoking." Since school is only one of several institutions that "mediates" socialization, Wang wondered to what extent schools can be said to serve the function of counter-socialization. She asked: "Can teachers and principals and staffs simply go against what they have been socialized into to educate their students with new expectations?" Given that India is a "religiously, socially, and culturally diverse society," Wang wondered, "which or whose socialization is at stake here?" She appreciates that Kumar is referencing not only the legacies of colonial education but the oppressive norms of communities, these perhaps mediated by the child's home and community as positive resources.[20] Given this complexity, Wang asked, "Where are the resources for counter-socialization? I would like to hear more about how Kumar envisions what makes schools capable of counter-socialization."

Chacko began her reply by acknowledging that "Kumar himself seems to be grappling with these issues in his own work." She suggests that he acknowledges those complexities of counter-socialization that Wang identified. "Yet," Chacko continued, "like Freire (1970/2008) and Giroux (1981), Kumar resists pessimism concerning the possibilities of schooling. Just as Freire highlights the necessity of shifting from 'banking education' to a 'problem-posing' one, and Giroux asserts a 'radical pedagogy,' Kumar too places his faith in school's ability to counter-socialize." The school in which Kumar places his faith is not one narrowly conceived, as in 'outcome based' models or one dependent on "teacher education as it is currently practiced in India." Kumar places his faith in the school "that seeks to transform the students' quality of life itself."

Kumar's conception of schooling as a counter-socializing force, Chacko continues, "is found with particular force and detail" in his discussions of schooling for students belonging to "disadvantaged communities, such as religious minorities, scheduled castes (SC), scheduled tribes (ST), those living below the poverty line, and particularly the schooling of girls belonging to these communities." While "a relentless critic of the unequal treatment meted out to these students," and not only in schools but also in educational planning, policy, and implementation; curriculum design; and textbooks[21] as well, Kumar (1983, 1572) believes that berating "the uselessness of education to bring about change" in their lives would be "unproductive."[22]

To illustrate, Chacko points out that in Kumar's response to critics who suggest that the schooling of SC and ST students is only a means to socialize them into bourgeois values, Kumar counters that, given schooling in India today, "there is far less danger of an assimilation of bourgeois values by these students than the possibility of these students dropping out while internalizing the backwardness that society ascribes to them."[23] Chacko points out that when Kumar (1992/2009, 87) proposes "counter-socialization as the school's domain," he, "like other radical curriculum scholars, is asserting that schools should not be conceived merely as a mirror of society."

While affirming the necessity of being vigilant about the ways in which schooling and curriculum socializes students into the oppressive structures of society, Chacko points out that Kumar also affirms the necessity of finding strategies and resources to counter this socialization. What Kumar is "proposing," Chacko continued, "is to look for tools and spaces for social transformation within the institution of schooling and in its engagement with the community, and thus to deploy schooling as a subversive force." Chacko is confident that Kumar is "cognizant of the enormity of the task that he sets before schools, particularly for the adults working there in different capacities." She quotes Kumar's (2010b, 75) recognition that "customary devices [that govern gender relations] wield an extraordinary power over the behavior of both men and women in their various roles. The power is extraordinary because it has the capacity to adjust to changing circumstances and milieu."

"Under such circumstances," Chacko asks, reiterating Wang's question, "where *does* one find the resources for counter-socialization?" Again she quotes Kumar. Here, Chacko notes, he is explicating "his vision of the ways in which a school can serve as a 'counter-socializer' in sex-role learning":

> If the community believes in segregating the sexes during adolescence, the school must set an alternative example by mixing the sexes. Similarly, while the larger social ethos offers stereotyped models of the roles of men and women, the school must insist that the adults working in it will not act in stereotyped and stereotyping ways. In the world outside the school, knowledge about sex is taboo; in the school such knowledge must be accessible. Cinema and television cash in on conservative images of women and men; the school's media—that is, textbooks and other materials—should offer images and symbols that motivate the reader to look at human beings in terms of their own struggle for an identity, rather than as reciting prefabricated conversations. And finally, if acceptance of the prevailing order and its norms is what society demands, then the school should demand the spirit of inquiry and offer opportunities to practice it. If all this sounds an idealistic, tall order, then one must remember that the agenda of changing women's place and role in society is no different. (Kumar (1992/2009, 87)

Chacko points out that Kumar is also suggesting here (in Chacko's words) that "no concept in education, whether it be childhood, globalization, universalization, quality, equality, or counter-socialization, should be conceived in a uniform manner for all concerned. Rather, they should be addressed in ways that are relevant and responsive to the nature of oppression and inequality faced by these students; hence the significance of a gendered perspective." It is not only in India that there is "an unfortunate overlap between the societal perception of girls and women and the educational goals set for them."[24] Chacko notes that Kumar (1992/2009) is responding to such circumstances when he argues that "we need not see the school as an institution working in harmony with the community or the larger society in the matter of sex-role socialization. On the contrary, we need to perceive the school in conflict with the community's code of socialization" (1992/2009, 87).

While discussing the functioning of the Kasturba Gandhi Balika Vidyalaya (Kasturba Gandhi Girls' School: KSBV) scheme, Chacko explained, launched by the Government of India in 2004 to provide residential schooling for rural girls belonging to disadvantaged communities, Kumar and Gupta (2008, 19) remind us—Chacko pointed out—that gender disparity in society cannot be addressed merely by ensuring the "physical presence of girls inside school boundary walls" (see also Kumar, 2010a). In the current "ideological climate" of "haste" wherein developing countries are goaded by international aid agencies to pursue short-term goals, Chacko suggested (referencing Kumar 2010b) that addressing gender disparity through the universalization of education is recoded as ensuring the enrolment and attendance of girls in schools. Opposed to such a "minimalist program of education" (Kumar, 2010b, p.11), Kumar and Gupta (2008, 19) argue that,

> what matters is the range and rigor of learning experiences and forms of knowledge made available to girls in the process of schooling, so that they develop the confidence and the skills to shape their destiny and participate in the governance of society. This is the toughest challenge in the context of girls' education.

Chacko notes that Kumar (2010a; 2010b; see also Kumar and Gupta, 2008) identifies "the contamination of educational goals and pedagogical relations by the different societal aspirations from educated girls and educated boys as being responsible for their disparate schooling in Indian society."[25] For instance, Chacko continued, "while an educated girl is viewed as an ideal candidate for 'matrimony in accordance with the community's values,' a boy is educated so that he might acquire 'the skills and knowledge necessary to participate in the modern economy'" (Kumar and Gupta, 2008, 19)." Such sexist instrumental rationality shows up in those academic discourses wherein, Chacko explains, "female literacy is encouraged on the basis of a statistically significant link between female literacy and reduced fertility" (Kumar, 2010a). While Indian educational policies emphasize the "empowerment of girls," Chacko allowed, "it is often operationalized as one-shot empowerment programs such as distribution of bicycles or computers to girls." Kumar and Gupta (2008) characterize these tokenistic measures as "symbolic minimalism," which, while possibly prompted by laudable intentions, do little to address the enormity of the problem of "cultural oppression" of girls.

While Kumar appreciated the "empowerment strategies" undertaken by some KGBVs—such as "personal development, enhanced "communication capacities," and "health-related awareness"—Chacko notes that Kumar points out that these goals acquire more visibility than girls' scholastic achievements. Kumar and Gupta (2008, 23), she continues, "argue that, in the case of girls from disadvantaged communities who not only have to 'face the community's general deprivation [but] also have to fight the negative and suppressive forces' faced by all girls in society, providing them access to schools, empowerment programs, and opportunities for critical reflection of discriminatory practices will need to be accompanied by 'substantial learning designed to cover the full spectrum of curricular choices.'"

The resources a school requires to serve as a site of counter-socialization, Chacko explained, derive from an "ethos where children can draw upon 'designed curricula'" (Kumar 2006, 4033) taught by "competent" and "sensitive" teachers (Kumar and Gupta 2008) trained to help the students "make sense of experience by constructing knowledge" (Kumar 2006, 4033). A gender-sensitive curriculum "will not limit girls to the traditional roles" ascribed to them by society. It will instead "provide them opportunities to acquire the skills and dispositions necessary for participation in the modern economy." A gender-sensitive curriculum, Chacko summarizes, "not only requires textbooks that critically examine the gendered experiences of girls and boys in society but also demands teachers who refuse to perpetuate in girls the sense of inferiority, self-denial, lack of autonomy, and subordination that society engenders in them." When Kumar and Gupta (2008, 22) refer to "competent teachers" they imply teachers who know their subject matter, while "sensitivity" implies "teacher's awareness, stance, and ability in the context of rural deprivation and gender issues, especially as they pertain to teenage girls."

In the primacy that Kumar places on providing girls access to schooling experiences characterized by academic rigor and gender sensitivity, "one can detect one difference between Giroux and Kumar." While for Giroux (1981) acquiring proficiency in academic disciplines is important, Chacko suggested, "he places greater emphasis on the potential of schooling and a radical pedagogy to awaken 'political consciousness' in students which might in turn lead to social transformation." In Chacko's judgment Kumar's position is "more reminiscent" of that of the African American educator Lisa Delpit (1997). Referencing black educators' resistance to the "holistic" writing process approach to literacy, Delpit affirmed that "educational movements should take into account and accommodate the concerns, experiences, and voices of minority educators and students." Educational institutions, Delpit insisted (and Chacko paraphrases), have the responsibility to prepare students, especially minorities, to be successful, that is acquire financial and social status, in mainstream society by teaching them, in this case "oral and written forms demanded by the mainstream" (1997, 18). Here, Chacko points out, "it becomes clear that for scholars like Kumar and Delpit, a rigorous curriculum that prepares students from disadvantaged communities for employment and upward mobility are essential resources for transforming not only their personal lives and the deprivation faced by their communities but also for altering societal attitudes about these students and their communities in the long term." Here is "counter-socialization" on a vast scale.

In 1991, in the *Political Agenda of Education*, Chacko continued, Kumar elaborated "the historical character of this particular narrative of modernity and progress." India's struggle for independence was not only a fight for freedom from British rule but "contained within it," Chacko explained, "the struggle of non-Brahminical castes for liberation from Brahminical domination." As Kumar acknowledged, education constituted "a critical site for the expression of the aspirations and value-orientations that undergird these various struggles." Contesting "idealistic" claims concerning the potential role of colonial education in the political awakening of lower-castes in India, Kumar advanced, Chacko tells us, "a more modest assessment of the role of education" (1991, 98). Again Chacko quoted Kumar:

> The lower-caste elite found in the British presence an audience and an agency for fighting against Brahmin domination. This struggle was many centuries old; it certainly predated colonial education and its supposedly enlightening influence. If this is true, then we need to recognize that it could not be so much the intellectual aspect of education as its relationship with employment and status which contributed to the ongoing egalitarian struggle of the non-Brahmin castes by crystallizing it. (1991, 98–99)

This observation, Chacko continues, underscores "the pertinence of the question raised by Professor Hongyu Wang, namely that (quoting Wang) "India is a religiously, socially, and culturally diverse society, so which or whose socialization is at stake here?" Kumar's insight, Chacko explained, illustrates that "any examination of the concepts of socialization and counter-socialization should be historically sensitive and context-specific."

And so one reads, Chacko is suggesting, Kumar's (1992/2009) advocacy of education as a "long term" investment in human capital (see also Kumar, 2010a). He invokes these concepts, she explains, in response "to anti-reservation or anti-affirmative action advocates who insist on recognizing merit irrespective of differences on the basis of gender, class, caste, or region," presumably in the interests of making India "globally competitive." Reminding readers of the history of inequality in India, Kumar (1992/2009, 136) suggested that "education works in rather long time-horizons, both in the lives of individuals, and more so, in the life of collectivities defined by caste, class, or gender." Affirmative action, Chacko continued, "becomes crucial in enabling historically disadvantaged individuals and groups to surmount, over time, those factors that prevent them from competing with others on the basis of educational merit or brilliance."

"As evident from his perspective on affirmative action," Chacko points out, "Kumar is a staunch supporter of state intervention in education," although, she adds, "he recognizes the limits of the state in intervening and transforming the cultural oppression of girls via education." Chacko notes that "while Kumar and Gupta (2008, 23) are extremely critical of the poor quality of the residential life of teachers and students at many of the KGBV schools, they appreciate these residential schools for enabling the girls to 'distance themselves from societal practices which are not only morally reprehensible but also illegal' such as early marriage." Moreover, Chacko points out, Kumar and Gupta "view these hostels as providing these students the opportunity to travel outside their homes, to interact with individuals from other communities, and to be independent."

Recognizing the contextualized character of education is crucial in appreciating an apparent paradox in Kumar's thinking. True, Chacko acknowledges, "the idea of residential schools as counter-socializing strategy—distancing and thereby 'protecting' these students from the 'morally reprehensible' and 'illegal' cultural practices of their communities—seems to fly in the face of Kumar's appreciation of the Gandhian philosophy of basic education." But, she points out, it becomes reasonable when contextualized in the historical evidence concerning "the role of the modern state in the cultural sphere" (Kumar 2010b, 75). Chacko quotes Kumar (2010b, 76): "The manner in which the modern state conceptualizes and deals with culture carries the imprint of colonialism, both as an ideology and as the historical experience of colonial rule of the modern state." The moral agenda of the colonial rulers to establish civil society in India was a complex one, Chacko reminded, and it contained elements of "liberal political and economic doctrine, paternalism, and evangelism" (Kumar 1991, 26). Efforts, for instance, "to abolish the Hindu custom of *sati* or the burning of the widow on her husband's funeral pyre brought the colonial state in bitter confrontation with the elite custodians of culture, a segment of society whose consent was imperative for maintaining the legitimacy of colonial rule in India." These complexities underline the limits of the state's "functional capacities [in] matters pertaining to girls and women" (Kumar 2010b, 77).

So contextualized, Chacko continued, Kumar and Gupta "seem to view residential schools (in the specific case of KGBVs) as a way in which the state might attempt to 'protect' the girls from oppressive cultural norms while at the same time aspiring to transform these norms in the long run by educating the girls in these communities." However laudable its intentions might be, she continued, "state intervention for the 'uplifting' of 'disadvantaged communities through residential schools will remain a sensitive issue as evidenced by the unabated controversy around residential schooling experiences of First Nations/Native Americans in North America."

One "paradoxical" issue, Hongyu Wang suggested, is the "relationship" between indigenous and "modern" knowledge. "I find it interesting," Wang wrote, "that the language of English is associated with quality education for many Indian parents, including those who are socially economically disadvantaged." She wondered if instruction in private schools could include native languages as well as English? Should it be taught earlier in government-sponsored schools? Is bilingual education possible? To what degree, Wang continued, can indigenous and colonial knowledge be kept completely distinct in contemporary India? Should they be integrated, or critically reconstructed? "Do you think," she asked Chacko, "this relationship (indigenous vs. colonial knowledge) can be potentially worked out constructively in Indian education?"

## Lesley Le Grange with Mary Ann Chacko

Lesley Le Grange also asked about language, specifically its curricular role in bridging difference, specifically between the local and the global. He wondered if Chacko thought that "a strong focus on the local" would not "limit the becoming of Indian children in a globalized world (with its negative and positive effects)?" "Your discussion of English as the language of teaching and learning in Indian schools," Le Grange continued, "raises a similar concern. You seem to hold a different view on the role of English in Indian schools to that of Kumar. Is this so?"

"Post-independence India," Chacko began her reply, previously divided into the provinces of British India and princely states, "was re-organized into linguistic states." Language became "a crucial marker of regional identity as well as of exclusion and inclusion." The national language "strategy" proposes "a three language formula," which, Chacko explained, "has been implemented with considerable intra-state and inter-state variations" (NCERT 2006). As an example she referenced the south Indian state of Kerala where Malayalam is the regional language. Middle and high school students there are taught the regional language or "mother tongue" as the "First Language," Hindi or English as the "Second Language," and English or any other Indian language not selected as the second language as the "Third Language." The "mother tongue" is the medium of instruction at the primary school level (Grades 1–4).

Schools affiliated with private or nonstate school boards, Chacko continued, where the medium of instruction is English from K-12, do offer the "native language" or the regional language/mother tongue as an "option." In government or government-aided schools or schools affiliated with state boards, she added, the medium of instruction is the regional language, unless it is specified as an "English medium school." In the case of regional "medium" schools English is offered only from Grade 5. Thus, Chacko notes, those students attending "government schools fail to get a 'head start' in English," in contrast to those students attending English "medium," government-aided, and private schools, where students are taught English from kindergarten or the lower primary grades, and then is used both as a medium of instruction and as a subject of study.

Because government schools are regional schools, Chacko continued, even when English is offered as a second or third language from the upper primary grades onward, the medium of instruction, and the textbooks in subjects other than English, continue to be in the regional language. Three state boards in India—that of Kerala, Goa, and Tamil Nadu—have a dual medium policy. That is, she explained, one school can house two sections—one where the medium of instruction is in the regional language and the other, in English. Government schools in Kerala, however, are permitted to open an English-medium section only if they fulfill certain conditions:

> Schools managements can claim a parallel [English] division only if they have at least 51 students [in one grade], the minimum number to have two divisions as per the existing rules, out of which the parents of at least 30 students should agree to English as their children's medium of instruction. But the catch lies elsewhere; the grant of parallel division neither entails allocation of qualified additional faculty nor extra means. That means, these schools will have to run the new division with existing faculty who need not necessarily be well versed in English. (Praveen 2013, paragraphs 4 and 5; quoted by Chacko)

The "bigger catch," Chacko continued, "in my opinion, and one that is increasingly closing off any possibility for government schools of having an English medium section, is the condition that they need to have 51 students per grade." At a time when Malayalam "medium" government schools are "struggling to find students—for instance, one of the government upper primary schools (Grades 1–7) I visited only had a total of 81 students in the whole school—a scenario where they will have 50 students per grade and *then* open an English medium section seems unlikely."

Government schooling throughout India is, Chacko allowed, "in a state of crisis." Even so, "it would be unfair to suggest," Chacko cautioned, "all government schools view their future as equally bleak." Chacko visited a second government school in Kerala, an upper primary Malayalam "medium" school. Enrolled were 263 students in total (137 boys and 126 girls) and enrolment was on the rise. "I attributed the differences in the two schools," she tells us, "primarily to the nature of leadership in these schools. In the 'failing' school, within 3 minutes of the last bell almost all the teachers left the school premises." Chacko spent "considerable time" in the staff room and learned that "serious and engaged discussions about the school, its activities or students were rare." The principal was "approachable" but he did not seem to exert a "significant influence on the staff."

In contrast, in the "successful" school Chacko discovered that staff room conversations "revolved around school or work related issues." The principal was "often" in the staff room and "impromptu staff meetings were a common." The principal ate his lunch with the teachers in the staff room. The staff respected him and even "looked up to him." A "common refrain" was that "he had changed the face of this school." He was a "hard worker" and a "role model." "One morning," Chacko reports, "I saw him preparing soil in the garden with a spade alongside the Parent Teacher Association (PTA) president." "Quite a few" of the parents were "actively involved" in the school, which was very "well-maintained" and furnished, "including computers with broad band connection, TV, tape recorder, LCD projector, an overhead projector, a herbal garden, vegetable garden (from which they often get vegetables for the mid-day meal), rain water harvesting facility, and a mothers' library from which parents could borrow books." It was "indeed heartening to visit a school where the staff, administrative leadership, and parents, along with funds provided by government-initiated programs such *Sarva Shiksha Abhiyan* (a program for universalizing elementary education), were working in tandem to strengthen the school." It "remains to be seen," Chacko concludes, "if the intensive efforts of individual schools as well as private-public partnership initiatives such as the Promoting Regional Schools to International Standards through Multiple Interventions (PRISM) project in Kerala, will be able to check the declining enrollments in government schools across India."

Returning to the curricular role of English in the current crisis in Indian schooling, Chacko believes that the dichotomization between "indigenous knowledge" and "colonial knowledge"—in this case between regional language and English—is "an unproductive one, especially at a time when even politicians would hesitate to berate English in India today as a colonial tongue." Hindi may be the official language of India, but, Chacko reports, "English is recognized as an "additional" official language. "Moreover," she continued, relationships among regional languages are "complex." As an example, Chacko alluded to non-Hindi-speaking states, such as Tamil Nadu in southern India, where there has been "stiff resistance at what is seen as the 'imposition' of Hindi."

"Taking a cue from Kumar," Chacko admits that "it is difficult to isolate the absence of English alone as the sole reason for the plight of government schools in India." She recalled that while teachers at the "failing" school she visited cited the absence of English as "one of the primary reasons for the decline of their school," she heard no similar complaints from the teachers of the second, more successful, government school. The "widely recognized" fact is, Chacko allowed, "that English is a necessity in India today." It is this "status" that makes its absence or presence in schools of such "great significance."

Chacko cited Kumar's suggestion—admittedly "idealistic" in current circumstances but one that "touched a chord in me owing to my own experiences of private schooling"—that "common" elementary schooling be provided for all children in India wherein the medium of instruction will be the regional language of a particular state. Such schools, Kumar believes, will enable the students to be rooted in their local social milieu during their "formative years" and help "safeguard the quality of education for *all* children." Such counter-socialization could protect them from "what could otherwise be the alienating influence of an English dominated educational experience in later years." When Kumar refers to the alienating influence of an English-dominated educational experience, Chacko explains, "it is important to recognize that he is not referring to the 'alien' nature of English per se but to the arduous cultivation of an ethos that entails a deliberate distancing from the regional language and its other socio-cultural aspects."

Transposing Kumar's explication of counter-socialization to gender roles, Chacko argued that "we also need to counter-socialize our distorted perception of the relationship between English and the regional languages of India." Chacko herself studied in an English "medium" school established by the central government where three languages were offered: English, Hindi, and Sanskrit. Malayalam, the regional language of the state of Kerala, was not an option. Chacko tells us: "I took 'pride' in not knowing to write Malayalam even as I wore my English language skills as a badge of superiority." She comments: "counter-socialization in this case, as in all cases, is made complex by the layers of unequal relationships that undergird our distorted perception of the inter-relationship between these languages."

As Kumar (1996) points out, Chacko continued, "the differential status of these languages is 'intricately tied' to the differential status attributed to the schools where these languages are the medium of instruction—government schools in the case of regional languages and private schools in the case of English—as well as the differential socio-economic status of those who attend these respective schools." The intricate relationships among "language, quality, and socio-economic status" are evident in "yet another example from my school days." When "any of their three children misbehaved my upper-middle class parents would often threaten to remove us from the private English medium school we were attending and enroll us in a Malayalam medium government school. Needless to say, the threat had its intended effects, for even at that young age we had been well-schooled in a deficit view of Malayalam, Malayalam medium schools, and the students attending those schools."

In a second set of questions, Lesley Le Grange wondered about those "social and political conditions in India which made it possible for a radical curriculum scholar (who criticized early state curricula in India) to be appointed as Director of NCERT and overseeing the development of a National Curriculum for India?" Relatedly, Le Grange wondered about the political and social conditions in India that made it possible for the National Curriculum development process to be an "act of deliberation?" Despite efforts to make the curriculum development process "deliberative" and inclusive of local content, Le Grange continued, "is the very idea of a National Curriculum not antithetical to Kumar's idea of 'schooling as counter-socialization'?"

Hongyu Wang also referenced the canonical conception of "deliberation," noting that "curriculum as deliberation has a tradition in both the United States and the United Kingdom." She asked: "Do you see if there is any connection or/and dissimilarity between these traditions and Krishna Kumar's notion of curriculum as a deliberative act?"

The next question concerned the originality of Kumar's work, as Le Grange asked if it comprised "his individual ideas" or were these "already shared by a community of curriculum scholars in India? Are they shared now?" To what extent, Le Grange asked, has Kumar's ideas contributed to the development of curriculum as a field/discipline in India? Le Grange also asked about the tension between local and the global: "Will a strong focus on the local (including linking schooling with production) not limit the becoming of Indian children in a globalized world (with its negative and positive effects)?" More specifically, he added, "your discussion of English as language of teaching and learning in Indian schools raises a similar concern. You seem to hold a different view on the role of English in Indian schools to that of Kumar. Is this so?"

Le Grange referenced Kumar's argument that the notion of quality has become distorted by agencies such as the World Bank, the United Nations, and others, and that equality has become reduced to access. A South African philosopher of education, he noted, has made the distinction between two types of access: formal access and epistemological access. Epistemological access is giving students access to the goods of education—knowledge from the academic disciplines and from local communities. He asked: "Do you concur that this expanded notion of access resonates with Kumar's notion of (e)quality education rather than the limited notion of equality associated with formal access only?"

Chacko replied: "I definitely think that Kumar is proposing an 'expanded notion of access' as well as a re-conception of quality." Kumar has found it "troubling," she reported, that the notion of "access" is often decoded as the "bare provision of schooling," or simply enrolling children in schools. And rather than regarding "quality" as an "integral" element of education, it is often perceived as an "add-on." Acknowledging Kumar's arguments around girls' schooling in India, Chacko feels certain that "epistemological access" is a crucial concern for Kumar as well. As Kumar and Gupta (2008, 19) point out, she reminds, "providing girls access to a school building is not enough: 'what matters is the range and rigor of learning experiences and forms of knowledge made available to girls in the process of schooling.'"

Hongyu Wang asked: "Is there an existing literature discussing Krishna Kumar's curriculum ideas and contributions in India? I am interested in knowing how others examine or study his thought. Is he perceived more as a philosopher of education or as a curriculum scholar in India?"

"In my searches conducted in relation to writing this chapter," Mary Ann Chacko began her replies to the questions posed by LeGrange and Wang, "I did not come across a single work which focused on Krishna Kumar's contributions to the field of curriculum in India." While many essays and articles as well as book-length studies on schooling in India reference his work (especially his 1991 *Political Agenda of Education: A Study of Colonialist and Nationalist Ideas*), Chacko could not locate articles or books solely dedicated to discussing Kumar's contributions.

That said, she continued, Krishna Kumar is regarded as a curriculum scholar of "high repute" in India, although Chacko regards the designation "philosopher of education" as more appropriate, given his broader set of concerns.[26] His work, Chacko argues, is "nuanced," and it discloses an "in-depth understanding of the problem of education—conceived both as an academic discipline and as schooling—in colonial and postcolonial India." From the history of education to more specialized topics—the benefits of storytelling, especially "traditional stories" that are native to a region, in elementary schools (Kumar, 1992/2009)—Kumar treats the question comprehensively. Moreover, Chacko pointed out, he writes in both English and Hindi, making his ideas accessible to a wide vernacular audience.

As a "liberal secular humanist," Chacko continues, Kumar's work reflects his "angst both over efforts of right-wing groups to use school curriculum to shrink the secular, democratic fabric of India as well as that of pseudo-secularists who propagate secularism through textbooks but make no effort to train children in secular thought." His commitment to the democratization of schooling is also reflected in his "vehement critique" of the Indian state's "increasing propensity" to permit "private capital" to provide schooling. This move, Chacko points out, "not only allows the state to withdraw from fulfilling its primary responsibilities but also transforms it into a mere 'facilitating institution in the enhancement of private interests' (Kumar 2012, 18)." In her chapter Chacko underscored Kumar's commitment to "deliberation" in educational decision making because it enacts his "commitment to secular practices" through his "efforts as NCERT Director to enhance 'public' engagement in schooling."

Kumar, Chacko continues, emphasizes a philosophical engagement with education. In his critique of the National Curriculum Framework, 2000 (NCF, 2000), Kumar critiques the National Council of Educational Research and Training's (NCERT) neglect of the philosophy of education and the work of Indian "teacher-philosophers" like Gandhi, Rabindranath Tagore, Sri Aurobindo, and J. Krishnamurti. Such neglect is evident in the "behaviorism" that informed NCERT's educational decisions, including the Minimum Levels of Learning (MIL) approach NCERT promulgated during the 1990s. For Kumar, Chacko underscores, "intellectual or reflexive activity" is imperative to "put a break on the obsessive urge to dip every aspect of education in behaviorist solutions."

Chacko finds Pinar's (2007) history of the US field "useful to think of Kumar's contribution in terms of understanding Indian curriculum." Kumar's exhortations to conceive of curriculum as a "problem" rather than "received knowledge" reflects his conception of curriculum, in Pinar's phraseology, as historical and political text. As intimated by his description of curriculum as "a series of choices made under the demands placed by the social milieu on education and the constraints placed upon pedagogy by children's psychology and the conditions prevailing at school" (1996, 18), Kumar's work was influenced by sociological approaches to knowledge such as the work of Karl Mannheim, Basil Bernstein, and Andre Beteille (e.g., see Kumar 1991; 1992/2009; 2005) as well as the work of psychologists, especially Jean Piaget and Lev Vygotsky (e.g., see Kumar 1992/2009), both of whom placed the child at the center[27] of the learning experience.

Chacko also referenced Schwab—as well as William Reid and J. Wesley Null— but pointed out (referencing Sen 2005) that "the argumentative tradition based on deliberation, public debate, and reasoning, has had a rich history within the Indian subcontinent." She also cited Gandhi's emphasis on the decentralization of political rule by devolving power and responsibilities from the state to local institutions, evident in the idea of *grama swaraj* (village self-rule: Mukundan and Bray 2004). Such notions may well, Chacko suggests, have influenced "Kumar's commitment to involve those directly impacted by educational policies such as teachers and parents in the deliberative process." Chacko also pointed out that, while heavily critiqued for tokenism, "decentralization" and "community-participation," expressed organizationally through a tiered system of governance in urban and rural areas (Jain, 2001; Mukundan and Bray, 2004), have been institutionalized in postindependent India.

Chacko notes that in his discussion of curriculum as "an act of deliberation," Kumar (1992/2009) does not make any references to Schwab or, for that matter, to any other curricular theorists. That does not, however, rule out the possibility that Kumar might be drawing upon the work of Schwab, among others. This is not an uncommon practice. As Null (2006) tells us, Chacko notes, although Schwab himself did not list a single reference in his *Practical 1* (1969) essay, it was clear that he was influenced by and drawing upon a rich, moral, and philosophical tradition, including the work of Aristotle.

Schwab formulates this conception of deliberation, Chacko reminds, while elaborating the nature of curriculum. Writing in 1969 Schwab famously declared the US field of curriculum as "moribund" and in a state of "crisis." He blamed the field's crisis on an overdependence on theory and an apparent unwillingness to engage the "practical." Importantly Chacko points out: "while Schwab does not dismiss theoretic problems, he argues that an inquiry into theoretic problems entails the formulation of sweeping generalizations. Such generalizations, however, are inadequate for the tasks in the field of curriculum because it is a practical rather than a theoretic discipline." She continues: "By practical Schwab (1969, 1–2) does not mean that it is 'easy' or 'familiar' but rather that it is 'the discipline concerned with choice and action, in contrast with the theoretic, which is concerned with knowledge.'" Writing, as Eisner (1984, 201–202) reminds us—Chacko continues—at a time when the field of curriculum was in the grip of "teacher proof curriculum and instructional objective banks for those who would not or could not write them," Schwab (1969) diagnosed the crisis in the field of curriculum as a "crisis of principle." Concluding her succinct summary, Chacko explained that this "crisis... was a state where principles had proven to be exhausted and inadequate for the problems and tasks posed by the field. Rather these theoretically formulated principles appeared to simplify and sanitize the messy complexity of the problems of curriculum."

With Schwab, Chacko juxtaposes Kumar, noting that "one can locate a similar suspicion of generalizable and fixed knowledge" about curriculum. She cites a passage from Kumar (1992/2009, 1–2) that could appear in Schwab:

> There are no principles for developing a curriculum, nor can there be any. By challenging the well-established notion that there are certain time-honored, proven rules capable of guiding us when we want to prepare a curriculum for the education of children, I wish to emphasize that there is no escape from reflecting on the condition prevalent in society and culture, if we want to design defensible curriculum.

Schwab (1969) expressed concern, Chacko continued, over the fragmented nature of curriculum planning—those based on social and behavioral theories, theories on different subject matters, on the individual, or on societal needs and changes. While acknowledging the difficulty of building bridges between these different theories as well as the impossibility of formulating one unifying theory for the practice of curriculum—I am here paraphrasing Mary Ann Chacko—Schwab (1969) famously asserted that a "defensible curriculum" will be one that pursues an "eclectic" approach and draws contributions from diverse theories in ways that are relevant to the "real," specific, and local curricular problem or task at hand. "In a comparable vein," Chacko explains, Kumar identified a "fracture between the discourse of those who are involved in the everyday life of schools—the teacher, teacher

trainer, and parents—and those of the educational planners and administrators."
She concluded: "Both Kumar and Schwab insist that choice and action in the field
of curriculum should be driven not only by theories but by an intimate knowledge
of the curriculum as lived in a particular time and place. However their vision for
the field of curriculum is not satisfied with theoretical eclecticism and an intimate
knowledge of classrooms but calls for 'deliberation' as a necessary *method* for the
practice of curriculum."

The explication of the method of deliberation, in both Schwab and Kumar,
Chacko continued, "gestures to their commitment to the creation of a democratic
public for purposes of decision making and problem solving in the field of curriculum.[28] She quotes Schwab, who explains that deliberation "will require the formation of a new public...a representative variety of all those who must live with the
consequences of the chosen action" (1969, 21). For Kumar (1992/2009, 13), Chacko
continued, "even reaching an agreement to 'perceive curriculum design as an act
and product of deliberation' is an important step in the process of creating such a
public as it disrupts the perception of curriculum as 'a given, rational construct'—a
strategy which has hitherto enabled certain groups to perpetuate their dominance
through the curriculum." For both Schwab and Kumar, Chacko concludes, "deliberation is a method that can serve as an antidote to the culture of isolation, hegemonies and privileges, and silencing that has permeated the field of curriculum."
While Schwab was "particularly concerned about the hegemony of particular subject matter specialists and theories," she added, "for Kumar (1992/2009, 2) it is the
acute awareness of the silencing of oppressed groups by economically and culturally
dominant groups who have exerted a monopoly over the fundamental question of
'what is worth teaching'?"

Next, Chacko cited Null (2006), who pointed out that, by espousing the deliberative tradition, Schwab positioned deliberation, rather than the subject matter
or the child, at the center of curriculum. This move is evident, Chacko notes, in
Kumar's (1992/2009, 2) chapter titled "What Is Worth Teaching?" To address the
key questions: (1) "What is worth teaching? (2) "How should it be taught?" and
(3) "How are the opportunities for education distributed?" Kumar suggested two
routes. One, Chacko suggests, requires addressing these questions "from a learner's
point view" while the second addresses them according to the "intrinsic value of a
particular content." She points out that Kumar explored "both these routes," judg-
ing them "incapable of solving the problem of curriculum because for a child what is
important is *how* we teach something rather than *what* we teach and what is worth
teaching is determined not by the intrinsic worth of that knowledge but by the
relationship between that knowledge and power relations in society." Consequently
Kumar concluded that "...the problem of curriculum cannot be dealt with as an act
of social engineering. It is an act of deliberation" (1992/2009, 13).

Then Chacko referenced Schwab (1969) who, reflecting on the deliberative process, wrote that "the education of educators to participate in this deliberative process
will be neither easy nor quickly achieved." Why? The "present generation of specialist researchers" will have to learn to "speak to the schools and to one another," and
that, Schwab worried, "will doubtless be [the] hardest of all, and on this hardest
problem I have no suggestion to make" (1969, 22). Chacko pointed out that, due

to Schwab's assessment of these difficulties, it is "noteworthy" that Kumar "implemented the 'arduous and complex'" (Schwab 1969, 20) method of deliberation during his tenure as NCERT director.

Responding to Le Grange's concern that the very idea of a National Curriculum could be "antithetical to Kumar's idea of schooling as counter-socialization," Chacko replied that the National Curriculum Framework, 2005 (NCF 2005)—"the product of the deliberative effort I elaborate in the chapter"—represented a revision of a "preexistent framework." It is not a "National Curriculum" but instead a "framework" that proposes "broad aims of education" (NCF 2005, vii) in relation to the syllabus, the examination system, and teacher training. These "broad aims" are in accord with the "Constitutional vision of India as a secular, egalitarian, and pluralistic society" (2005, vii). Professor Le Grange's concern, Chacko continued, is that a national or state-directed curriculum framework is "a recipe to preserve the legitimacy of the state and its normative discourses via schooling qua socialization." If that were the case, "what are its counter-socializing possibilities?" Here, Chacko suggests, "it is pertinent to ask—What is being countered?"

Chacko reminded that Kumar was appointed director of National Council of Educational Research and Training (NCERT) immediately following the exit of the coalition government, the National Democratic Alliance (NDA), led by the Hindu right-wing Bharatiya Janata Party (BJP). This coalition had led the national government from 1998 to 2004. This period was marked by what critics of the right-wing government—including Kumar himself—characterized as a process of "saffronization." Saffron, Chacko explained, is the color of the robes worn by Hindu monks and priests and is thus associated with Hindu religion in India. "Saffronization," and in this context, the "saffronization of education," Chacko continued, references to "the ways in which the educational domain— policy, textbooks, especially history textbooks, and national institutions, including the NCERT—'came under strong pressure to accommodate the ideology of religious revivalism'" (Kumar 2001, 34; see also Gohain 2002; Kumar 2002; Thapar 2009). Numerous decisions taken by the NCERT during this time, Chacko explained, "including the contents of NCF (2000)," were regarded as "controversial" across India. Among the controversial measures was a new NCERT policy to "seek the approval of the selection and representation of historical facts from religious and caste leaders" (Kumar 2002, 822). Another measure was NCF's (2000) emphasis upon "value education," for many a euphemism for "the propagation of a 'Hindu heritage' (Gohain 2002), and the speedy release of new history textbooks whose contents boost Hindu right-wing ideology" (Kumar 2002; Thapar 2009). While not the first time in India's history that Hindu nationalists at the center had attempted to intervene in the question of what is worth teaching? (Kumar 2002; Thapar 2009), Chacko acknowledged, "this was certainly the first time that such efforts were successful in penetrating institutions of national importance."

As documented in the personal memoir of the renowned Indian historian Romila Thapar (2009)—who had authored history textbooks for the NCERT—"anyone who is appointed by the government to any position of significance," Chacko emphasized, "tends to be dubbed as 'statist.'" Appointed director of the NCERT by the United Progressive Alliance (UPA)—another coalition government led by the center-left Indian National Congress Party, which replaced the NDA in the 2004 general elections—Kumar, Chacko asserted, "will also undoubtedly face a similar accusation." In contrast to what the term implies, Chacko tells us that, as the director of NCERT Kumar labored "to transform the centralized character of this organization" precisely because "he believed it was responsible for its vulnerability to political interference" (see Kumar, 2002; Srinivasan, 2010). Moreover, she adds, Kumar believed that "freedom from political interference enabled us [at the NCERT] to commit ourselves to the task of providing academic leadership for the challenge of radical reforms in school education" (Srinivasan 2010, para 1). "Thus," Chacko concludes, returning to Le Grange's concern, "the counter-socialization that was sought in this case by the secularists was the reversal of the attempts that had been made by the NDA government to appropriate the state apparatus of education so as to project India as a Hindu state."

Kumar's views and concerns about Indian schooling, its institutions, policies, curricula, and practices, are "certainly" shared by a community of scholars. For instance, following the publication of NCF (2000)—this at a time when the right-wing Bharatiya Janata Party (BJP)-led government was at the center—Kumar and a group of "concerned" scholars presented a special issue of the *Seminar* magazine titled "Redesigning Curricula: A Symposium on Working a Framework for School Education." Introducing the issue, Kumar (2000, para 10) wrote, "We may be stung and pained by such an unabashed national display of callousness towards children, but we have no choice in taking the occasion of this document's appearance seriously. Hence this issue of *Seminar*." The launch of the journal *Contemporary Education Dialogue* in 2003 can also be regarded as an expression of this "community" of curriculum scholars. Kumar served on the advisory editorial board of this journal. He has also contributed to the formation of well-known educationists in India, including Padma Sarangapani, one of the managing editors of *Contemporary Education Dialogue*.

The work of Krishna Kumar, Chacko concludes, has not only contributed to the field of curriculum studies in India, but to increased public understanding of the staggering significance of curriculum to the life of the nation. His "prolific publications," she pointed out, signaling "his engagement with topical issues of deep relevance to education" have appeared in national newspapers like *The Hindu* as well as the widely read social science journal *Economic and Political Weekly* (EPW). His "consistent participation," Chacko emphasized, "in pressing debates in Indian society over secularism, privatization of education, and questions of gender socialization have been influential in securing for the academic discipline of education greater visibility and respectability in India."

## The Exchanges with Suresh Chandra Ghosh

Here the questions were historical, as Le Grange and Wang asked Ghosh for clarification concerning the state of curriculum studies, including its genesis. Ghosh cites 1986 but his sweeping historical perspective does not allow him to stay there, as he quickly situates that year and those events in a much broader historical understanding, for example 650 years of Islamic rule during the Middle Ages, 190 years of British rule ending in 1947, and today's globalization. Detail punctuates the panorama, as it does Ghosh's charges of corruption in contemporary India, a problem also in the United States, as I referenced in the introduction. Near the end of a distinguished career, Ghosh minces no words in his replies.

## Lesley Le Grange with Suresh Ghosh

Thanking Professor Ghosh for "the opportunity to engage with your chapter"—Lesley Le Grange referenced the recency of curriculum studies as an academic discipline in India. "You mention that Curriculum Studies emerged as a discipline after 1986," Le Grange wrote, and "I assume that its emergence is associated with the development of a New National Educational Policy in 1986. What were the particular circumstances then that gave rise to curriculum studies as a discipline?"

In his reply Ghosh emphasized one "particular circumstance," namely "growing unemployment among the educated Indians." Unemployment "cuts across the social barriers and includes Dalits, Scheduled Castes/Tribes, Other Backward Classes as well as the scions from the Middle and Upper Classes." The unemployed are "lured" by the multiple political parties with their "sometimes new, sometimes old, always *instant* solutions" to problems. It was also during this period, he continued, that the "Naxals, who have now become a terrible menace for our government, appeared on the scene." It was in the midst of this economic and political turmoil, Ghosh replied, "that the Government of India came to realize, just as the British rulers had realized prior to the formation of the Indian National Congress in 1985, that the real trouble lay in the existing colonial courses of studies which are not job oriented."

Le Grange then asked: "Who is involved in conversations about curriculum studies in India and in which forums do they take place? Are there conferences dedicated to curriculum studies? Is there a journal with a dedicated focus on Curriculum Studies?" Ghosh replied: "There were no journals or conferences prior to the formulation of the 1986 Policy. Only the close advisers of the Prime Minister and a Government-run institution now known as the National University of Educational Planning and Administration were then involved." After the new curriculum policy was announced, however, "a series of conferences was held at the universities throughout the country." Despite differences of opinion among the political parties, the curriculum was "heavily influenced by the ideology of the ruling Congress Party." As a consequence, its implementation faced roadblocks whenever there was a change of government.

"You mentioned the influence of globalization on curriculum development and curriculum policy in contemporary India," Le Grange wrote, and "you refer to an imported curriculum. What policy borrowing (if any) has taken place in contemporary India?" Referencing curriculum history in his own country, Le Grange added: "In South Africa outcomes-based education was imported from the global North after 1994 to legitimate the new South African state struggling to survive in a global economy. Has there been a similar development(s) in India after independence and what might have given rise such a development(s)?"

In his reply Ghosh focused on the phrase "imported curriculum," which he suspects "was not clear." The phrase references, he explained, "more than 650 years of Islamic rule during the Middle Ages and 190 years of British rule until 1947." During the Middle Ages, Ghosh continued, "as well as during modern times, the curriculum was imported into India, always to suit the interests of the rulers, not those of the subjects." After independence (1947) the Indian National Congress—consisting "mostly" of Western-educated Indians—"ruled" the country without interruption until 1969 when it split under the leadership of Indira Gandhi. The Indian National Congress continued the "past colonial curriculum," as that "suited the interests of the ruling classes." That scenario shifted "after globalization," Ghosh noted. With multinational companies opening branches in India; a "demand" was created for a new class of professionals. And it has been "not our government, but private institutions and business corporations that have come forward to meet the challenge." As a consequence, curriculum is now created presumably "tailored" to meet global demands, and that curriculum is "often heavily influenced" by curriculum in Europe, America, and Asia—"Except in Information Technology and the mathematical sciences," Ghosh allowed, as in these India has "taken the lead." He cited India's engineering curricula—exported, as they are "global now"—that include a required study of one or two foreign languages. In 2005, Ghosh reminded, the government appointed a Knowledge Commission designed "to sustain a knowledge-based economy. Its report was submitted in 2007. However, Ghosh added, "a series of scandals involving ministers of government precipitated general resistance in Parliament (and outside it)." The effect has been to "paralyze governance and consequently the Knowledge Commission's recommendations still await implementation, leaving our higher education in the doldrums."

Le Grange asked: "What is the current state of curriculum studies as a discipline in India?" In his reply Ghosh focused on the school curriculum, noting that the National Council of Educational Research and Training is "now preoccupied with the problem of curriculum." Its current contribution is an "imperfect" National Curriculum Framework (2005). Regarding the academic field of curriculum, Ghosh added, "as yet there is no particular journal on curriculum studies in India." There are several universities—he referenced Delhi University—that are planning to establish Curriculum Studies Centres "soon." Ghosh added that Delhi University is also planning to start a "Meta College" where courses will be "open to students belonging to any discipline."

"From your response," Le Grange began his second round of questions, "I gather that an interest in curriculum studies developed due to unemployment amongst educated Indians." In addition to "how school curricula might be developed/designed to respond to growing unemployment, post 1986 new courses were developed to replace existing colonial ones." "My inquiry," he emphasized, "is about curriculum studies as an academic discipline/scholarly enterprise—curriculum as an object of study. Am I correct in assuming that the changes to the school curriculum in India in the middle 1980s was the consequence of a study of the colonial school curriculum and its failure to address the needs of Indian society as the time? And in this sense, we might claim that this marks the first point at which curriculum becomes the object of study in India?"

Le Grange continued: "You state that after the new curriculum policy was announced in the middle 1980s that several conferences were held at university level. I gather that the impetus of these conferences mainly focused on the introduction of a new curriculum policy. But this was not sustained—right?—that is, annual or biennial conferences were not held to help develop an academic discipline called curriculum studies, even a journal dedicated to curriculum studies. It appears that the new National Curriculum Framework (2005) again sparked an interest in Curriculum Studies in India. Unlike countries such as the USA—where curriculum studies is an established field/discipline (regular conferences are held, there are dedicated journals, professorships in the field and volumes of books produced over decades)—in countries such as India and South Africa academic interest in matters curriculum tend to be centered on changes in national education (curriculum) policies. And, that one cannot really talk about an established field called curriculum studies in these countries."

"I did understand your use of the term 'imported curriculum,'" Le Grange replied. "I am interested in *what* India has imported in an era of globalization, in an era where we are witnessing the ascendancy of neoliberalism. The importing I am referring to has become commonly known as 'policy borrowing.' This is different to the wholesale importing of a curriculum that occurred in colonial India, for example." Le Grange then referenced Poonam Batra, who pointed out that India has borrowed ideas from US scholars such as Tyler, Bloom, and Dewey. "But also—interestingly—she claims that India (like South Africa) also introduced an outcomes-based orientation to child-centered education. In India the reference is to the District Primary Education Program (DPEP) of the 1990s."

Hongyu Wang would raise several of these same questions; Ghosh would reply to them all at once and at length.

## Hongyu Wang with Suresh Ghosh

"Your historical analysis of Indian education and curriculum is," Hongyu Wang wrote to Suresh Ghosh, "highly informative." She requested more information regarding "curriculum studies" as a term or as a field in India. Referencing his chapter, Wang noted that Ghosh mentioned that after 1986, "the Faculties of Education of some of the noted central universities started offering 'curriculum studies' as one of the courses at the B. Ed. and M. Ed. levels as well as subjects of investigation at the doctoral level." Wang asked Ghosh: "When curriculum studies was offered as one of courses, what topics did the course cover? How did it define the concept of 'curriculum'?" Wang wondered if the term referenced "general issues, or was it only related to academic subjects? If it was defined in subject terms as you seem to imply in your essay, then was there also a part that addresses the general issues related to curriculum across different subjects, such as the relationship between the knower and the known? Or those relationships between and among curriculum, society, individual student, and teacher? How about now, almost three decades after 1986? Have any new tendencies emerged?"

Wang then located these questions within her own academic history. "I came to the United States from China in 1996," she explained. "Chinese curriculum studies did not emerge until the late 1980s when reform intended to change national curriculum system and diversify curriculum structure, content, and delivery, so it did address broad and general issues. But subject experts have had much longer history and have had direct influences on Chinese curriculum several decades before curriculum reform in the 1980s and 1990s emerged. As an academic field, U.S. curriculum studies has had a much longer history—a century-long—with its own definition and re-definitions, quite different from Chinese curriculum traditions." She asked: "What do you think about curriculum studies in the Indian context in the near future?"

Wang found it "interesting" that education, as Ghosh reported in his essay, was made the scapegoat whenever social, political, and cultural crises erupted. "As much as I can tell from your essay," she continued, the "effects of colonization" and efforts to manage "political instability" were—after Independence—among the "major" factors affecting Indian education. Educators enjoyed little autonomy. "Even when you credit globalization for diversifying educational institutions and providing professional training in the past decade," she continued, "it was not educators but employers who played a crucial role." She asked Ghosh: "Do you think educators in India may have a chance to become more independent in the future, or will they remain as the victims of politics and the economy?" Wang alluded to the situation, wherein, she noted, "educators have lost much of their influence over curriculum and even teaching," events associated with a series of "crises," however "manufactured." "Do you think there might be alternative pathways for educators to deal with such a sense of crisis and find room for their own educational work in India?"

Wang then asked Ghosh if he thought India's "multilingual, multicultural, and multi-religious" society constituted an "obstacle" to the implementation of national curriculum policy. "Due to such diversity," Wang asked, "do you think a unified national platform is necessary or desirable?" She asked if the different states have had their own curriculum initiatives? Or have they been following faithfully the national policy? "You also mentioned that despite all the proposals, there have been hardly any substantial changes in school curriculum or teacher education at the level of practice, at least not until the recent decade." Wang wondered: "If the policy from the center has not substantially influenced what happened at the state, school, or university level, then perhaps initiatives can start from the local? I also found it difficult to imagine that educational fund was not even used in half in that first term: If it was made available to the local efforts in education, how could it not even be used?"

From the local Wang moved to the global. "You seem to be quite optimistic about the positive influence of globalization, especially its ability to absorb unemployed graduates from higher education." She asked: "If corporations are better at training potential employees, then what is the role of educational institutions?" She noted that in his essay Ghosh "credited" the curriculum in the Vedic schools as "adaptive to the needs of society and also argue for the balance between value education and skills for job" (this volume). She asked: "In a broader context, do you think Western learning and Indian traditional learning can be integrated in productive ways?"

Finally, Wang noted that Ghosh had mentioned Mahatma Gandhi "briefly." She asked: "to what degree did his leadership of and work on nonviolence influenc

Indian education? Is the principle of nonviolence reflected in Indian curriculum or in curriculum studies in any way? Here I am thinking about his broader philosophy, not his specific suggestions for basic education."

Starting with Wang's—and Le Grange's—question concerning the genesis of curriculum studies in India, Suresh Ghosh returned to 1986. It was then, he said, that curriculum studies began to be "emphasized," and that was due to the New National Education Policy. "But," he underscored, the new curriculum program could "not be implemented" due to "roadblocks, partly due to the instability of the central government, and partly due the opposition of various political parties." There were exceptions, Ghosh noted, like the curricula on the "Freedom Movement," which escaped opposition because they were thought to teach patriotism. The "old curriculum largely continues," Ghosh observed, and not only in public schools but also at the "research level," where relatively few universities seem to be "enthusiastic" about curriculum studies as an academic specialization. "Would you believe," Ghosh continued, "that in 1966 I appeared in the final examination of my BA (Hons. in History) addressing the same courses which were determined by the first standing committee of the Calcutta University set up in 1857?" The Indian government—here Ghosh called it an "elephant"—moves "rarely" in education and "when it moves, it moves very slowly!" Ghosh cited the Knowledge Commission "appointed under the pressure of globalization in 2005." After many "squabbles," it issued its recommendations in January 2007. "Five years have elapsed," he noted, and "these are yet to be debated for implementation!"

The future of curriculum studies in India, Gosh continued, "largely depends on the kind of push given by the unforeseen socio-economic and political developments as well as on the kind of drive given by an education-friendly government at the centre." It would not seem likely, given present circumstances, for example, "bitter political rivalry and a slugfest among the numerous political parties to capture power to loot the country." The government at the time of this writing (2013)—Ghosh called it a "Petticoat Government"—under a learned prime minister showed "some enthusiasm in updating our education system," but he "soon found that he was presiding over a Cabinet with ministers involved in huge scams everywhere and that he is actually an obliging puppet. I don't think this is the case in China, America or Canada."

Ghosh is unaware of any new curricula, except those ongoing efforts to align existing curricula "with the demands of globalization." Adjusting old programs is also a feature of higher education, he suggested; only a few institutions—like Delhi University—are experimenting with new programs within the guidelines of the national regulatory bodies. Industrial and corporate entities are now allowed to establish their own institutions. Despite the demands, funds are "always available," and "at all levels including local!" But these, Ghosh lamented, are either "misused, misappropriated or left unused through inertia." Inertia aggravates "all-round corruption," evident in the awarding of degrees and certificates and the admission of unqualified students.

Education, Ghosh continued, is largely controlled by governmental organizations like the NCERT. While the demands of globalization have encouraged a few corporate and industrial houses as well as other private organizations to offer innovative courses and programs, he noted, these must still be approved by the central regulatory bodies referenced above. Due this control, Ghosh charged that "educators in our country have no initiative to develop new programs." Nothing substantial happens as everything must be left to government for approval and for implementation." In earlier periods, when such centralized control was not in place, "private organizations could make experiments, as Tagore did on vocational education in his Ashram School at Santiniketan in the late 1920s onwards." It was from Tagore, Ghosh continued, that Gandhi formulated his idea of Basic Education. Basic Education was adopted by the short-lived Congress governments in seven provinces in 1938–39 and also after independence, but failed after several years due to lack of support from the central government, which, Ghosh continued, "seemed to be more interested in stereotyped higher education—by its appointment of the Radhakrishnan Commission in 1948—than job-oriented educational programs" in the schools. "The people who controlled education at the government level," he explained, "were all Westernized educated classes who hardly bothered about the people of the country at large and its development." It was only after recent rounds of globalization, he insisted, that the central government's attention has turned to the vast potentialities of skill-oriented programs. Only recently is the government "taking necessary steps to meet the demands of students and parents."

Recently a few universities have "become sensitive to social issues," Ghosh continued, referencing intentions by Delhi University to introduce a curriculum of gender studies and, more specifically, a program in the martial arts for women, that following a recent (December 2012) gang-rape on a Delhi bus, an event, he added, "which has stirred the Indian nation." But, Ghosh concluded, "education in our country can never become independent as it was earlier in the United States or is now in Canada perhaps. It will largely remain a respondent to changing economic, political and social conditions in the country." When conditions favor the educational development, Ghosh explained, infrastructure is absent, and corruption and incompetence inhibit what could occur. He offered the 2010 "Right to Education" policy (for children aged 6–14) as "one of many" examples. This policy did increase school enrolment in rural areas but at the cost of deteriorating standards, already aggravated by the government's existing 50 percent reservation policy for specific groups. Deteriorating standards have, Ghosh reports, "driven the most brilliant among the general category of students (50 per cent) to look for greener pastures abroad." He cited a recent survey by a NGO that documented that fifth-grade students cannot read at the second-grade level or complete second-grade arithmetic problems.

Ghosh also cited a scandal involving primary teacher recruitment; the chief minister of that state is now imprisoned. "No surprise," he commented, "that 99 per cent of primary school teachers failed the eligibility exam." The deterioration of standards is hardly limited to K-12 Education, Ghosh continued, pointing to the fact that "not a single institution of higher learning (except one or two business schools) could be found among the first four hundred at the world level and among the first thirty at the Asian level." Ghosh blames the government's reservation policy for "driving out our brilliant students." Once abroad, "most students do not return."

What can be done? "I always think," Ghosh wrote, "it is desirable to have a uniform national education policy and program in our diverse country." He acknowledged that the present government (at the time of this writing this) is trying to achieve such uniformity through the institution of the Knowledge Commission. As noted earlier, the commission's recommendations (submitted in January 2007) are yet to be implemented. While the central government "largely controls the higher education scenario," the states control the local schools. Ghosh knows of no innovation at this local level, as education in the states is "largely regulated by the NCERT which, under pressure of globalization has prepared an imperfect National Curriculum Framework in 2005." The central government, he noted, "is trying to extend its control" by decreeing a uniform/common maths and science curriculum as well as a common/uniform entrance test for admission to some select professional programs, such as Management and Technology.

Ghosh then turned to "our religion, known," he pointed out, "for tolerance from the days of the Vedas and the Upanishads since 1500 BCE." Vedic sages—Ghosh cited Yagnavalkya and Manu—"have taught us about the identification of human soul with the universal soul as the gateway to liberation from the cycle of birth and death (i.e. human suffering)." Ancient India was the home of the Buddha and the Mahavira, Ghosh reminded. Medieval India was the home of Nanak and Kabir, and modern India was where Tagore and Gandhi preached nonviolence. "Our courses in educational institutions are always non-violent," he asserts. "These do not reflect any violence at all and so there can be no question of Gandhi having an impact on them. Tagore and Gandhi's non-violence were inspired by the teachings of our sages in ancient and medieval India. For violence, you will perhaps have to look for a Jehadi Institution in a neighboring Indian country, say, Pakistan!"

In reply to a question from Wang concerning his use of the term "Westernized Indians," Ghosh replied that he was referencing "those Indians who were educated in English medium either at home or abroad." Beginning in 1960 or, he continued, the leadership of education shifted from "Westernized groups of Indians" to "another group of Indians who belonged to the lower castes in the society and had the benefits of a liberal education such as the Scheduled Castes/Tribes/Dalits and Other Backward Classes." In many states various coalitions comprising these groups formed governments and thereby they "broke the monopoly" of the Congress Party.

Schooling is controlled by the states, Ghosh reminded, and in several of them, particularly in West Bengal and Kerala, where Leftist Parties dominate, they infuse the curriculum "with Communist or Marxist ideas." In West Bengal the Leftist Parties have substituted Bengali for English as the medium of instruction in schools and colleges. Even so, he added, "the first grade metropolitan colleges continue to stick to English as the medium of instruction." The same linguistic politics occurred in other states, before the advent of globalization, he emphasized, "when political leaders in the Uttar Pradesh, Bihar and Madhya Pradesh began to understand the importance of English." Still, "only a few" among the 28 States and 7 Union Territories have adopted English as the medium of instruction, while the majority follow regional languages or the mother tongue as the medium of instruction. "Needless to say," Ghosh added, "the standard of education, under the circumstances, cannot be uniform or up to the mark of those schools which teach through the medium of English." Students from schools with regional languages are, Ghosh tells us, often "outsmarted" by students from English and missionary schools. "It is for the sake of justice to all students, Ghosh asserts, "that I have suggested uniformity in some basic courses like mathematics, politics, economics, commerce and sciences and medium of instructions for all the schools."

Next Ghosh turned his attention to higher education, controlled by the central government through the University Grants Commission, the All India Council of Medical Education, Council of Scientific and Industrial Research, and the All India Council of Technical Education, all located in New Delhi, the capital. Even though the state governments regulate the public schools, the central government exercises a control over them "indirectly, in two ways, through Central educational organizations and through occasional issue of national educational schemes."

First, Ghosh continued, the central government can offer "advise"—through the National Council of Educational Research and Training—on the preparation of textbooks for state schools. The central government controls the appointment of the chairman and the members of the Central Advisory Board of Education and of the Central Board of Secondary Education (CBSE), which administers the annual School Leaving Examinations of the students of its member schools. Not all secondary schools are members of the CBSE, Ghosh notes, and they have their own State Boards of Examination. Second, the central government exerts control over state schools by issuing curriculum guidelines and offering financial support. State governments are expected implement the former. "However," Ghosh adds, "such schemes, though very rare in our history of education, are often introduced with great fanfare, but without adequate infrastructures." So they often end up with "a dismal performance, as seen in the cases of *Sarva Shiksha Abhiyan* (Education For All) introduced in 2000 and the recently introduced Right to Education (2010) which aims at the liquidation of illiteracy in the country."

Wang had also asked about violence and its representation in textbooks. "As far as violence in textbooks is concerned," Ghosh replied, "we do not have violence" evident in, say, the United States. "Such textbooks are obviously a reflection of the American society," which, he notes, "came into existence through Wars of Independence (1776) and the Civil War later." Ghosh agreed with Wang that any "forceful imposition of political or religious ideas through school textbooks is a kind of intellectual violence." In fact, he continued, "we have this kind of violence in the school textbooks in the States ruled/dominated by the Left Parties."

Ghosh does not disapprove of the representation of violence in textbooks if, he emphasized, it conveys accurate knowledge of India's history and cultures. "Many of the ills of our society," Ghosh asserted, "can be traced to...curricula which do not reflect our past heritage and cultures, marked by mutual respect and toleration." India's past heritage and culture of two thousand and a half years were, Ghosh continued, "eclipsed by Islamic rule of 650 years in the Middle Ages and ultimately restored by the British Orientalists and the European Indologists in the late eighteenth and early nineteenth centuries." Ghosh regrets that "very few" of the young know this history, due to an imperfect curriculum.

"As a matter of fact," Ghosh wrote, continuing his candor, "our government's concern with education is limited to its capability to help the ruling party to retain its power and position and to help it survive the next General Election." The government's exploitation of education as a political issue reminds him of the Right to Food

Security Act. Inaugurated on Rajiv Gandhi's birthday—August 20, 2013—this act promised to feed 820 million people (67 percent of the total population) while "tons of food-grains rot outside for lack of storage." Food was imagined as "a game changer," Ghosh notes, designed to victory at the next General Election. "Reforms in education are never planned well," Ghosh judges, "and sometimes schemes are announced but hardly implemented. When a new party takes power, he adds, the scheme is "scrapped."

As an example Ghosh cited the 2005 Knowledge Commission to reform higher education. Its recommendations were issued in 2007 "but," Ghosh reports, "six years and a half have elapsed and these remain unimplemented and if the present government does not return to power in the next year (2014) General Elections its successor is unlikely to go forward with the reform." Promises by the same government to guarantee schooling to all children aged between 6 and 14 years within three years are now "broken," as the deadline has passed. After a study of 71 districts in 13 States, CRY (Child Rights and You) reported in June 2013 a continuing inadequacy of infrastructures. For example, 11 percent of schools are without toilets, 20 percent don't have safe drinking water, and 74 percent are without a library. Only 18 percent schools have separate toilets for girls and the absence of this facility often pushes girls out of school.

Responding to a second round of questions from Hongyu Wang, Suresh Ghosh stated simply: "Education in our country is in a mess now." He allowed that "various schemes like *Sarva Shiksha Abhiyan* and the RTE have increased the number of children going to schools but not to any advancement either in literacy or in knowledge." He was critical as well of the government's reservation policy, which makes available only 50 percent of the seats in the existing institutions of learning, thus "debarring many brilliant students with more than 90 percent marks obtained in School Leaving Examinations." Many of these, he reports, now go abroad, the numbers increasing by 256 percent according to a recent report in the September 9, 2012, issue of the *Times of India*. Those in the "reserved category" are often, he says, "not so brilliant," and unlikely to "contribute to our existing knowledge." It is, he adds, "no wonder that not a single university [in India] could find a place in the first 100 Asian institutions of higher learning." According to a report published in the October 1, 2012, issue of the *Times of India*, India contributes only 3.5 percent to the world's research.

Moreover, Ghosh continued, "the government's policy towards elementary education is disastrous." The Annual Status of Education Report (ASER) reported in the January 8, 2013, issue of the *Times of India* has found that the number of grade 5 students who could not read grade 2 level text or solve a simple arithmetic problem has increased. In 2010, some 46.3 percent were unable to read at grade level, but the percentage has increased to 51.8 percent in 2011 and 53.2 percent in 2012.

Reminding me of the problems with "for-profit" education in the United States, Ghosh then pointed to the existence of "fake institutions, fake teachers, fake degrees, fake certificates" circulating in India, and often obtaining approval from government and other accrediting bodies through "graft and bribery." (In the United States these are termed "lobbying.") "The education scenario in the country," he summarized, "is aggravated by all-round corruption." India, Ghosh complained, is now among "the most corrupt country in the world." He referenced a survey of 1.14 people in 107 countries by the Global Corruption Barometer 2013—reported in the *Times of India* on July 10, 2013—that reports that India suffers "corruption" at "double the global average." It is "corruption," Ghosh concluded, "that is killing the Indian Elephant!"

# The Exchanges with Meenakshi Thapan

Questions of relationship seemed to structure the exchanges among Lesley Le Grange, Hongyu Wang, and Meenakshi Thapan. The constituent core of society, *relationship* was also theorized as a central insight into the nature of the world. More modestly, relationship was also acknowledged as the "stitching" upon which curricular organization depends; it structures public debates over curriculum reform. Referencing J. Krishnamurti, Krishna Kumar, Padma Sarangpani, and Paulo Freire, Le Grange, Thapan, and Wang then discussed a series of significant subjects, among them upward mobility and career opportunities, Hindu nationalism, and race-caste-gender, concluding with a brief but reverberating exchange over "difference." I start with Professor Thapan's exchanges with Lesley Le Grange.

## Lesley Le Grange with Meenakshi Thapan

Curriculum in India, Lesley Le Grange, began, appears to be an "open" subject, in that almost anyone seems entitled to express his or her view. He asked: "Why do Indian scholars write about the curriculum? Where do they share their views about curriculum matters, and where are their works published?" While anyone is free "to discuss, write and critique curriculum," Meenakshi Thapan replied, "in the end there are formal bodies that determine what curriculum is all about." Thapan then cited the *Economic and Political Weekly of India*, published in Mumbai, a "very lively forum for articles on the subject, and many scholars write about curriculum in this journal." They also write about curriculum issues in *Contemporary Education Dialogue*, published in Bengaluru.

   In asking his next question Le Grange referenced her essay, noting that Thapan had stated that the "school curriculum in India is a state produced entity, removed from debate and discussion, good practice and importantly, from children's and teachers' lives" (this volume). When Krishna Kumar was director of NCERT, he initiated a deliberative process of developing a national curriculum framework (2005) that involved consultation with all stakeholders/role players, for example, communities, teachers, etc. "So it does seem," Le Grange asked, "that there has been a state initiated process that involved participation on the part of local communities and that their inputs were included in a National Curriculum Framework. Do you agree?" Le Grange then referenced Thapan's prediction that in the near future more than 50 percent of rural schools will be private. "Do these developments not suggest that the school curriculum in India is becoming less of a 'state produced entity'?" he asked.

"It is state produced," Thapan explained, "to the extent that even private schools are obligated to adhere to the National Curriculum Framework." The framework was "an enormous effort," and "pathbreaking in many ways." Thapan is not quick to judge it without "careful study and understanding." There are exemptions, she allowed, among them private schools that seek to adhere to the International Baccalaureate (IB) or the Cambridge Board. But such schools, she continued, are "very few" in number, and rural private schools "would certainly adhere to state produced and developed curricula."

Again Le Grange quoted Thapan's chapter: "At the heart of Krishnamurti's work was the understanding that society can only change if there is transformation in individual's consciousness and this can come about through 'right education.'" Then Le Grange asked: "Does Krishnamurti's work have any similarities to those espoused by proponents of 'critical pedagogy' informed by Critical Theory? Is Krishnamurti's idea similar or very different to Paulo Freire's notion of 'conscientization'?"

Krishnamurti is "very different" from Freire," Thapan replied, as Freire was concerned specifically with freedom from oppression, in cultivating a "critical consciousness that would enable this freedom." Thapan noted that Freire is also different from Krishnamurti in the methods he proposed to attain such freedom. Krishnamurti is concerned with "change at all levels of society's development," she explained, with "change that concerns human relationships that in a sense lie at the crux of society," he would argue. Change in these relationships, she summarized, would result in freedom from different forms of oppression.

Le Grange then quoted Krishnamurti's insight that "to be is to be related." In South Africa, he noted, there is a word—*ubuntu*—that derives from indigenous languages. It means "humanness," and "importantly," that "humanness is developed in relation with others (both other human beings and the biophysical world)." In contrast to the Cartesian equation (I think therefore I am), *ubuntu* suggests, "because we are, therefore I am." Do you think that Krishnamurti's idea resonates with that of *ubuntu*?" Le Grange asked. "I think I agree with this comparison," Thapan replied, and with the idea that "without relationship I cannot exist." Relationship—"or interdependence"— is "the basis" of society, Thapan emphasized, and "we must endeavor to understand *ubuntu* (humanness) and the possibilities it creates for endurance, peace, and change from the violence and terror we appear to accept as the norm."

## Hongyu Wang with Meenakshi Thapan

Hongyu Wang began by referencing her own coming-of-age in China, where the state-controlled system of education is also hierarchical. Despite those circumstances, Wang continued, "I witnessed wonderful teachers who negotiated with the system to provide the best and most caring education for their students. The same was also true with students who navigated through the system successfully without sacrificing their independent minds." In India, she asked, "what resources do you think have these teachers and students been able to rely on to claim their own agency in a highly constrained system?" Wang referenced a study Thapan cited suggesting that "it was students' determination to be successful that helped them, and [that] students did not buy into Hindu nationalism." Wang asked: What "value orientations"—in addition to "the appeal of upward mobility and career opportunities"—do teachers and students hold? Are there other "non-religion cultural orientations that were available for teachers and students to draw upon in order to respond to the imposition of Hindu nationalism or the general tendency of seeking to 'inculcate obedience, deference and conformity'?"

Thapan affirmed that "for many Indians, a job, career and upward mobility are very important reasons for being educated." Education is not often pursued for "its own sake." Rather, it is being pursued, often in "very difficult and constraining contexts," for the sake of a "better life," especially "moving up the social and economic ladder," including "moving out of caste-based inequalities." Thapan referenced the work of Padma Sarangpani (2003), who asked children attending a school (not far from Delhi) about their goals for the future. Their reply: "to become a big man (bada aadmi)!" This phrase, Thapan explained, connotes a man who is "enormously successful, not only in monetary terms but one who has influence and power." Especially among the "marginalized, the poor, and the vulnerable," Thapan continued, the idea of success through education is "very important." Among the "elite," she added, "education may well be pursued for other goals."

There are "wonderful teachers," Thapan affirmed, in many private, fee-paying schools—and also in some state schools—across India. Given the scale of the educational landscape, these, she noted, comprise a "minority." In other another essay (2013), "I have examined how education "puts young people into a period of waiting, what Craig Jeffrey calls 'timepass.' Often this is a period of 'dejection,' as students face a job market that does not necessarily align with the education they have achieved." But the appeal of upward socioeconomic mobility is not the only dynamic in play, Thapan added, as there are "other forms of non-culture" upon which students and their families rely as "resources." They can "open up other worlds of learning" and "provide students experiences they then can bring to their educational settings." Students and teachers can draw upon these often extra-institutional resources in becoming "independent minds."

While the caste system has been abolished in India, Wang recalled that Thapan mentioned "caste identities" in her essay. Because "race" is no longer a former or institutional marker of legal discrimination in the United States, Wang noted, it does not mean "race" is not in play across the "multiple terrains of social and political life." Wang asked: Is "caste" likewise still in play in India? Has caste, for instance, "been translated into social stratification? If so, in what ways? Do Indian textbooks address issues related to caste system in any substantial way? If caste identities still play a role, how do educators identify themselves?"

Thapan affirmed that "there are no formal structures supporting caste-based discriminatory and exclusionary practices." But, she added, "caste is still an important issue in Indian education." To address inequality today, Thapan continues, "we need to emphasize the position of children of particular groups—tribes—who suffer other disadvantages in the educational system (see Nambissan 2011). "Gender adds another dimension to caste and tribe-based inequalities," Thapan pointed out. In some school teachers may have "dismissive attitudes" toward children from lower castes. "Textbooks do not address caste as far as I know," she added, "but I may be wrong. I know this was not the case some years ago when textbooks were anti-minority in different ways."

The 2005 National Curricular Framework, Wang continued, has been greeted with both "enthusiasm" and "critique." Since it is "the newest initiative," perhaps it is "too early" to judge its (long-term) consequences. "According to your viewpoint," Wang asked, "is there any progress in fulfilling its promise of inclusion, child-centeredness, and engaged citizenship? What are the major issues in promoting its implementation?" Are there "traditions" in India—"not necessarily school traditions as I recognize that schools are sometimes less progressive than many countries"— that "support and encourage such initiatives?" "Perhaps," Thapan replied, "there has been some progress, but recent newspaper reports suggest that NCF 2005 has still not been implemented in several schools in states that continue to rely on old textbooks and curricular frameworks."

"Thank you," Wang tells Thapan, "for the discussions of KFI schools as a viable alternative. I appreciate the combination of 'demanding structures of school life and the stillness of a quiet mind.' To locate a school in a place where students can have 15 minutes of quiet time to watch the sunset is simply wonderful!" Wang then referenced the premodern Chinese academy wherein "open discussions and debates could be held." These academes were often located in mountain areas, Wang reported, where the landscape was "beneficial for the cultivation of mind." "I am particularly impressed," she continued, "that those schools do well not only in terms of personal growth but also in science and in other state-prescribed subjects. If both can be achieved, why are there not many more such kinds of schools?" Is it the problem of numbers, Wang wondered, noting that 360 boarding students with 60 faculty members at the Rishi Valley Education Center "does not sound like a model that can be adopted in any massive scale." Wang then recalled Thapan's acknowledgment of "a sharp distinction" between private/elite education and public/mass education. "Is Rishi Valley school mostly for upper class or upper middle class?" she asked. If so, "would it not seem to be contradictory to Krishnamurti's 'concern for the ending of economic and social inequalities'" (this volume)? Besides financial issues, are there other "major obstacles for such kinds of school to become more accepted in the mainstream in India?"

The Rishi Valley School has a "long tradition," Thapan began, "of including working-class children on its rolls." Due to socioeconomic differences as well as differential access to English, this "integration" has, Thapan acknowledged, "not always worked." Still, efforts to integrate and innovate continue. Those children whose parents cannot afford the fees benefit from scholarships. The school has been "engaged in rural education," including undertaking "innovative rural education programs based on new methodological tools," and these programs have received "national and international attention." Thapan cited this work as "directly geared" toward "Krishnamurti's insights concerning the ending of economic and social inequality." Efforts at the Rishi Valley Education Center to cultivate "humane values, a global outlook, concern for the earth and the local physical and social environment—everything Rishi Valley seeks to do"—constitutes a "contribution to creating different kinds of values that nurture Krishnamurti's ideals."

Rishi Valley School is no "elite" school, Thapan emphasized, although there are parents who worry that schools "like Rishi Valley" are "utopian," and, as such, "make children unfit for society." They express concern that graduates may struggle to "adjust" to "social norms and values." Many parents want their children to become "engineers, doctors and computer whiz kids" who make "oodles of money in global settings!" *That* expectation is the main obstacle to schools like Rishi Valley, schools that teach "very different values," among them that "small is beautiful," that "working in natural habitats is as fulfilling as living in big cities," that "earning huge amounts of money is not the only ideal in life." These values, Thapan acknowledged, are not always accepted as appropriate by parents who demand "a different lifestyle for their children."

Wang turned to the concept of compassion, which, she agreed with Thapan, is related to being "able to experience the suffering of another," and "committed to alleviating the suffering." She quotes from Thapan's essay: "the cultivation of compassion therefore depends on *the elimination of difference* and the ability to acknowledge some sort of community between oneself and the other" (italics added). "What do you mean, Wang asks, "by 'difference' and 'the elimination of difference'?" In the United States, Wang continued, "under the influence of postcolonial theories and post-structuralism, social and cultural differences have become recognized as something positive rather than negative, and the difference between self and other is seen as the site for mutual learning. I wonder what would be your response to such different approaches to difference."

Thapan replied by expressing her concern that in overemphasizing "difference"—which she agreed "may the site for mutual learning"—"we may not see ourselves as a common humanity." Unless we see ourselves so, she continued, "there can never be a cessation of the violence we witness in the world today." No one advocates "dissolving one culture into another," Thapan suggested, and that "difference" must be construed as "part of our being human together."

That eloquent answer to Wang's crucial question concluded the exchanges between these erudite scholars. The acknowledgment of difference as "site" for "mutual learning underlines its educational instability. True, it can—on occasion, in certain places, under the guidance of professional prepared educators—enable educational experience. But it can as well, as Thapan appreciates, blind us to the actuality of our "common humanity," no universal set of homogenizing elements but an ethical embrace of "our being human together."

# Notes

1. Due to time constraints Manish Jain did not participate in the exchanges.
2. See Pinar 2006, 169. Alas, funding for the conferences—separate from the research project itself (or so the Social Science and Humanities Research Council decreed)—was denied.
3. The adoption of Macaulay's minute in 1835 led to the legitimization of the colonial construction of Indian society, which in turn shaped the official nineteenth-century school curriculum in India.
4. "Indian society is not rid of the caste system," Batra acknowledged, "we are still fighting its more subtle and in many instances blatant forms." Le Grange followed by observing

"it seems that school curriculum has not changed much in the post-colonial period despite nationalistic efforts. Did those shared values contribute to the stability of school curriculum?" "Perhaps yes," Batra replied, "but there would be other reasons as well."

5. Scholars have provided empirical evidence of how various organizations bring in religious symbols and texts into the school curriculum in the name of culture and tradition.

6. Evidently, dereferentialization (see Pinar 2013, 53) is a problem not only in the United States.

7. As discussed in Batra's chapter.

8. Kumar is the subject of chapter 4.

9. I focus on issues of disciplinarity—including organizational and intellectual infrastructure—in the intellectual advancement of the field (2007).

10. A state in central India (Batra's note).

11. "Begun in the late sixties in the U.S. and Great Britain respectively," Batra reminded.

12. "The origins of the Congress Party," Batra explained, "are in India's freedom struggle."

13. K-12 education in North American terms.

14. The brief history of HSTP is retrieved from "Closure of Hoshangabad Vigyan" by Vinod Raina, July 13, 2002 (Batra's note).

15. Two donor agencies: Department for International Development (DFID-UK) and Swedish International Development Cooperation Agency (Sida-Sweden).

16. Education in the Indian Constitution is primarily a state responsibility (Batra's note).

17. Also the capital city (Batra's note).

18. National Council of Educational Research and Training.

19. That dynamic is the circulation of ideas and material goods arcoss national borders, influenced by History, specifically colonialism and imperialism. Le Grange is asking if Kumar incorporated the concepts of Americans (North and South), and Wang wonders how efforts to affirm indigenous languages and cultures play out in the curriculum.

20. Wang acknowledged Gandhi's emphasis upon home and community as affirmative, a fact Chacko notes in the chapter.

21. See Kumar 1983; 1992/2009; 2008, 2010a; 2010b, Chacko advises.

22. This is Chacko's word.

23. These are Chacko's words.

24. These are Chacko's words; she is addressing the situation in India. I added that the situation is, unfortunately, hardly unique to India.

25. These words are Chacko's.

26. Certainly curriculum concerns can be "broad." I would accord the status of "philosopher of education" to a scholar whose concepts are philosophical and who consciously works within the intellectual traditions of that specific specialization. As an outsider, I must say that Kumar seems more a curriculum theorist than a philosopher of education as several disciplines—including philosophy but also sociology, history, politics, psychology, and gender analysis—inform his interdisciplinary opus.

27. In a second round of questions, Wang asked Chacko about Kumar's positioning of the child as central given Batra's comments concerning simplistic conceptions of child-centeredness being uncritically imported from the West. "The best way to judge the worth of knowledge from a child's perspective," Chacko replied, "'seems to be to make that decision on behalf of children'" (Kumar 1992/2009, 4). "And one of the ways of determining the worth of knowledge on behalf of children can be to say: 'it is worth teaching something only if it can be learnt'" (5). But, she added, Kumar allows that "our understandings of child psychology and pedagogy cannot help us decide what knowledge is worth teaching." It is, Chacko suggests, only after we answer the curriculum question—what knowledge is of most worth?—that pedagogical knowledge comes into

play (see Kumar 1992/2009, 6–7). Its position in this sequence does amount to devalued importance, Chacko points out, as Kumar still concludes (in Chacko's words) "that what is more important is how we teach rather than what we teach, what he means is for a *child* how we teach is more important than what we teach."

28. At this point Chacko referenced Reid, 2006. Based on the recent—2012—ASER report.

# References

Berliner, David C. 2002. "Educational Research: The Hardest Science of All." *Educational Researcher* 31 (8): 18–20.

Broudy, Harry S. 1955. "How Philosophical Can Philosophy of Education Be?" *The Journal of Philosophy* 52 (22): 612–22.

Delpit, Lisa. 1997. *Other People's Children: Cultural Conflict in the Classroom*. New York: The New Press.

Eisner, Eliot. 1984. "No Easy Answers: Joseph Schwab's Contributions to Curriculum." *Curriculum Inquiry* 14 (2): 201–10.

Freire, Paulo. 1970. *Pedagogy of the Oppressed*. New York: Continuum.

Giroux, Henry A. 1981. "Hegemony, Resistance, and the Paradox of Educational Reform." *Interchange* 12 (2–3): 3–26.

Gohain, H. 2002. "On Saffronisation of Education." *Economic and Political Weekly* 37 (46): 4597–99.

Jain, Shilpa. 2001. "Rethinking Decentralization for Nurturing Learning Societies." http://www.swaraj.org/shikshantar/resources_jain_2.html.

Jeffrey, Craig. 2010. *Timepass. Youth, Class and the Politics of Waiting in India*. Stanford: Stanford University Press.

Jeffrey, Craig, Patricia Jeffery, and Roger Jeffery. 2008. *Degrees without Freedom? Education, Masculinities, and Unemployment in North India*. Stanford: Stanford University Press.

Kumar, Krishna. 1983. "Educational Experience of Scheduled Castes and Tribes." *Economic and Political Weekly* 18 (36/37): 1566–72.

Kumar, Krishna. 1991. *Political Agenda of Education: A Study of Colonialist and Nationalist Ideas*. New Delhi: Sage Publications.

Kumar, Krishna. 1992. "Growing up Male." In *What Is Worth Teaching?* edited by Krishna Kumar, 81–88. New Delhi: Orient BlackSwan.

Kumar, Krishna. 2000. "The Problem." *Seminar* 493 (September 2000).

Kumar, Krishna. 2001. *Prejudice and Pride: School Histories of the Freedom Struggle in India and Pakistan*. New Delhi: Penguin Books.

Kumar, Krishna. 2002. "Education Reforms: Inspired Incompetence." *Economic and Political Weekly* 37 (9): 822–23.

Kumar, Krishna. 2005. "Quality of Education at the Beginning of the 21st Century: Lessons from India." *Indian Educational Review* 40 (1): 3–28.

Kumar, Krishna. 2006. "Childhood in a Globalizing World." *Economic and Political Weekly* 41 (38): 4030–34.

Kumar, Krishna. 2010a. "Culture, State, and Girls: An Educational Perspective." *Economic and Political Weekly* 45 (17): 75–84.

Kumar, Krishna. 2010b. "Quality in Education: Competing Concepts." *Contemporary Education Dialogue* 7 (1): 7–18.

Kumar, Krishna. "Pedagogy Market: The CBSE-Pearson Tie-Up." *Economic and Political Weekly* 48 (47and 48): 18–20.

Kumar, Krishna, and L. Gupta. 2008. "What Is Missing in Girls' Empowerment?" *Economic and Political Weekly* 43 (26/27): 19–24.

Mukundan, Mullikottu-Veettil, and Mark Bray. 2004. "The Decentralization of Education in Kerala State, India: Rhetoric and Reality." *International Review of Education* 50 (3/4): 223–43.

Nagler, Michael. 2004. *The Search for a Nonviolent Future.* Novato, CA: New World Library.

Nambissan, Geetha B. 2011. "Education of Tribal Children in India: Sociological Perspectives." In *Schooling Stratification and Inclusion, Some Reflections on the Sociology of Education in India*, edited by Yoginder Singh. Delhi: NCERT.

NCERT. 2005. *National Curriculum Framework 2005.* New Delhi: NCERT.

NCERT. 2006. "Position Paper: National Focus Group on Teaching of Indian Languages." http://www.ncert.nic.in/new_ncert/ncert/rightside/links/pdf/focus_group/Indian _Languages.pdf.

Null, J.Wesley. 2006. "Introduction: Teaching Deliberation: Curriculum Workers as Public Educators." In *The Pursuit of Curriculum: Schooling and the Public Interest*, edited by William Arbuckle Reid, xiii–xxi. Greenwich, CT: Information Age Publishing Inc.

Pinar, William F. 2006. *The Synoptic Text Today and Other Essays: Curriculum Development after the Reconceptualization.* New York: Peter Lang.

Pinar, William F. 2007a. "Crisis, Reconceptualization, Internationalization: U.S. Curriculum Theory since 1950. Paper Presented at East China Normal University, Shanghai." In *The International Handbook of Curriculum Research*, edited by William F. Pinar, 2nd ed., 521–32. New York: Routledge.

Pinar, William F. 2007b. *Intellectual Advancement through Disciplinarity: Verticality and Horizontality in Curriculum Studies.* Rotterdam and Tapei: Sense Publishers.

Pinar, William F. 2013. *Curriculum Studies in the United States. Present Circumstances, Intellectual Histories.* New York: Palgrave Macmillan.

Praveen, M. P. 2013. "Sorry State of Government, Aided Schools in Ernakulam." *The Hindu*, February 15. http://www.thehindu.com/news/national/kerala/sorry-state-of-government -aided-schools-in-ernakulam/article4416330.ece.

Ram Mohan, Rohini. 2012. "Child-Centred Learning in Praxis: Issues and Challenges in Context of Rural Schools of Rishi Valley." *D. S. Kothari Centre for Science, Ethics and Education (University of Delhi) Working Paper Series* IV: 1–27.

Reid, William Arbuckle. 2006. *The Pursuit of Curriculum: Schooling and the Public Interest.* Greenwich, CT: Information Age Publishing Inc.

Sarangapani, Padma. 2003. *Constructing School Knowledge: An Ethnography of Learning in an Indian Village.* New Delhi: Sage.

Schwab, Joseph J. 1969. "The Practical: A Language for Curriculum." *The School Review* 78 (1): 1–23.

Sen, Amartya. 2005. *The Argumentative Indian: Writings on Indian History, Culture and Identity.* New York: Picador.

Srinivasan, Meera. 2010. "It Was a Remarkable Experience Protecting Academic Integrity from Political Attacks: An Interview with Krishna Kumar." *The Hindu*. March 4. http:// www.thehindu.com/opinion/interview/article139044.ece.

Thapan, Meenakshi. 2013. "Waiting for Change: Enduring Educational Outcomes." *Nordic Studies in Education.* Special issue: Educational Research on Everyday Life 32: 140–51.

Thapar, Romila. 2009. "The History Debate and School Textbooks in India: A Personal Memoir." *History Workshop Journal* 67 (1): 87–98. doi:10.1093/hwj/dbn054.

Wang, Hongyu. 2014. "A Nonviolent Perspective on Internationalizing Curriculum Studies." In *The International Handbook of Curriculum Research*, edited by William F. Pinar, 2nd ed. 67–76. New York: Routledge.

# Chapter 7

# Curriculum Studies in India
*William F. Pinar*

Historical (dis)continuities, cultural conflict, economic globalization, and political tension characterize the present circumstances of curriculum studies in India. Each of these abstractions becomes concrete in preceding chapters and exchanges.

The persistence of the past—for Manish Jain as "echoes"—seems paramount, and I devote a section to summarizing what the scholar-participants and panel members have said about colonialism. The rapidity and scale of economic growth today in itself creates conflict, dislocation, inequality, "echoes" of a colonial past now present in "globalization." Cultural clashes, ancient and contemporary, and the political tension they aggravate also contribute to a present that sometimes seems too complex to grasp. Despite this fact the scholar-participants are clear about what is at stake: the present and future lives of actually existing children. Indeed, the gap between the official curriculum and the actual lives of children, Poonam Batra suggested, creates underachievement, and an ongoing failure to universalize equally the opportunities education offers.[1]

The materiality of the present—in curricular terms in textbooks, so central that India has been characterized as a "syllabus society"[2]—cannot be grasped without situating the present moment historically[3] and globally, including within ancient and recent animosities, aspirations, and achievements. Suresh C. Ghosh returns to the thirteenth century to help us to understand the antagonism created by curriculum "imported" from elsewhere. Ghosh recounts pivotal points of the British colonial past. Among the remains, in curricular terms, is a "textbook culture" wherein too many teachers enjoy little freedom and, specifically, insufficient influence over the curriculum. For many—not Meenakshi Thapan (see note 2)—the syllabus "rules," positioning not children or teachers as central, but textbooks and examinations.

Despite dehumanizing hierarchies associated with colonization, there have been, all along, courageous individuals who have insisted on a different idea of India.[4] Rabindranath Tagore, Mahatma Gandhi, and Jiddu Krishnamurti are among those who established schools with curricula that addressed the gaps between intellectual ideas and everyday life, between children and adults, between the past and the present, itself compressed also by the weight of the future. The curricula they—and the crucial contemporary figure, Krishna Kumar—influenced warrant worldwide attention. These curricula are distinctive in their attentiveness to society through subjectivity, attempting nothing less than *counter-socialization*, occurring, in part, through *deliberation*.[5] These key concepts of Kumar's testify to the potential of children—through education—to inhabit and reconstruct the present.[6]

More specific curricular questions surfaced in the chapters and exchanges. The curricular status of English—complicated by its colonial legacies, propelled its present utility within globalization—remains vexed. Gender—specifically controversies concerning the education of girls—is implicated in contentious cultural, historical, and economic currents, in "modernity" itself. Modernity and its unruly stepchild, neoliberalism, cut at least two ways in India.[7] While neoliberalism undergirds, indeed, compels privatization (as Jain and Batra discuss) and its concomitants, including inequality, it also combats familiar forms of corruption (as Ghosh notes), while introducing new ones.

Are the aspirations associated with *counter-socialization* (countering, in part, gender inequality) and *deliberation* (with its endorsement of rationality and democratization) also "progressive" legacies—Indian reconstructions—of colonialism and its neoliberal version, globalization? Do these progressive concepts replace the historical centrality of textbooks and examinations with another rather different but nonetheless dominating "syllabus," this "new" one denoting reparation rather than recitation, meaning rather than memorization? Can history be turned on its head within one institution: the school? Americans used to think so; many still do. Unlike in America, the faith in education expressed in these pages does not seem a secular form of religious faith (Tröhler 2011).[8] Or is it?

# The Persistence of the Past

Poonam Batra suggests that "British essentialism"[9] took root in India partly because "colonial values coincided with those of indigenous traditions." Lesley Le Grange asked Batra what the two traditions shared; Batra replied: "Both shared values rooted in hierarchical structures of society." Mary Ann Chacko also referenced these historical sedimented "hierarchical structures." India's struggle for independence was not only a fight for freedom from British rule, she explained, but "contained within it the struggle of non-Brahminical castes for liberation from Brahminical domination." Education, Chacko pointed out (referencing Krishna Kumar) constitutes "a critical site for the expression of the aspirations and value-orientations that undergird these various struggles." While focused politically, the struggle for independence was, evidently, multidimensional and is, in an important sense, ongoing.

Such historical continuity—accompanied and restructured by cultural tension and political conflict—was perforated by the educational efforts of Tagore, Gandhi, Sri Aurobindo. Their educational ideas constituted "a critical response to the colonial system of education," Batra explained. "While the colonial system was a system of education which drew from the outside inwards (emerging out of the Renaissance and the positivistic school of thought that became pervasive—and still is)," she continued, "indigenous ideas spoke of education as a process of drawing out from within."[10] The split between the social and the subjective, between formal education and the everyday reality of children, in Batra's view, "lies at the root of India's poor performance in universalizing critical education."

"In the mainstream school curriculum," Le Grange pointed out, "this [inner contemplation] does not seem reflected." True enough, Batra allowed, reminding him of Tagore's Shantiniketan, of Gandhi's "Nai Talim," conceived as "a national system" of education, "an alternative to colonial education," and an integral part of the nationalist struggle for freedom; it was a response "to both the elite system of colonial education perceived to be culturally and economically irrelevant as well as to the upper caste hegemonic control over who can be educated."[11] Despite that success, Batra continued, "Gandhi's proposal to replace colonial education was tried only in small pockets of India and never really became part of mainstream education." The focus on the subjective—"drawing out from within," rooted in Indian philosophical orientations—occurred, it seems, within colonialism.

After independence, Jain reported, science came to present "the promise of modernity," presumably freeing people from superstitious beliefs. India's first prime minister, Jawaharlal Nehru, called for the cultivation of "scientific temper." People's science movements and organizations worked toward this end. Jain cited postcolonial critics of modernity who have questioned the intimacy between scientific and economic, specifically capitalist, development, a reciprocity that places at the forefront "development" as a crucial concept in the national narrative. Such an ideology, Jain complains, enriches multinational corporations as it denies the democratic rights of its own citizens. This postindependence faith in the power of scientific method wedded to capital—and the concomitant profile of the ideal citizen who "reasons" and thus makes judgments on the basis of "evidence"[12]—reiterates, Jain argues, the colonial state's commitment to eradicating "backwardness expressed in lack of education, poverty and inequity, caste and hold of superstitions." Jain is not opposed to the scientific method per se; he is drawing attention to its political appropriation in legitimizing the "developmental" model of the postcolonial state. Jain also draws attention to how the teaching of science in India lacks a spirit of questioning and examining evidence on one's own. "This double whammy of coupling of scientific *knowledge* with the imperatives and *power* of 'postcolonial development' where both produce and legitimize each other and absence of promoting a culture of questioning in schools," Jain explains, "poses a distinct set of challenges for education and curriculum studies in India. These challenges cannot be simply understood with reference to only 'science' or 'postcolonial state' and its 'development.'"[13]

Also after independence, the Secondary Education Commission acknowledged the "isolation" of the existing education system from everyday life, its failure to provide "insight into the every-day world" in which students lived, for the overcrowding of school subjects, and their compartmentalization. The commission recommended enriching the curriculum by including material that might "give joy and insight to students." It also endorsed the promotion of "independent thinking," not limiting students to prescribed textbooks. These recommendations, Jain points out, stand in contrast to the Education Commission (EC, 1964–1966), popularly known as Kothari Commission.[14] The EC focused on the "great explosion of knowledge," a fact certain to increase "the curricular load on the child." Specifically, it asserted both cultural and economic roles for science—affirming the analyses of both its proponents and its critics—and an association between education and productivity.

Indira Gandhi's son and successor, Rajiv Gandhi, undertook reform of education through a New National Policy on Education in 1986. "Prior to that year," Suresh Ghosh tells us, "curriculum was never seriously studied, either by our politicians or by our intellectuals, although most of us agree that our failure to adjust the curriculum inherited from the British Raj (Administration) in 1947 was one of the major factors in the socio-economic and political disorder of our country." Long before British rule, Ghosh reminds, India had "imported" curriculum. "From 1206 onwards," Ghosh recounted—when Muslims began ruling India—"we have followed a curriculum imposed on us by our rulers which has often very little to do with our interests and aspirations."

This scale of the consequences of curriculum—as "one of the major factors in the socio-economic and political disorder of our country"—is reiterated when Ghosh depicts the "New National Educational Policy in 1986" as posing to be "a panacea for all the evils that were then plaguing the country." The *Program of Action* announced: "Time is of essence, and unless we act now, we stand in the danger of once again missing the opportunity of educational reform, so critical not only for the development of our nation, but for our very survival" (quoted in Gosh, this volume). This is the same rhetoric politicians have employed in the United States, where national survival apparently depends not upon military prowess or social vitality—never mind political integrity—but on curricular credibility.[15]

Even in 1986 there were public officials, Ghosh complained, largely unaware of globalization. By 2000 no one could ignore the phenomenon—and the proliferation of privatization[16]—but, Ghosh continued, that framework "failed to satisfy the national expectations and aspirations." Critical of market-driven private schools, especially those promising success in the global marketplace, Meenakshi Thapan appreciates the "work of private schools run by the Krishnamurti Foundation, India (KFI),"[17] including their "Rishi Valley Institute for Educational Resources (RIVER) program," the "schools in Auroville," the "Centre for Learning (CFL) in Bangalore, and other mainstream private schools like Aditi International School, the Vasant Valley School, some international schools in the metropolitan cities, and others." These, she tells us, "stand out for offering good quality."[18]

The KFI is engaged in several rural educational initiatives, Thapan explains, and it operates one after-school program for young children as well. Its activities include the annual publication of the *Journal of the Krishnamurti Schools* that features essays by schoolteachers. "Krishnamurti was an extraordinary philosopher," Thapan testifies, "who sought to change people through the process of self-discovery, not as a narcissistic fantasy about oneself and one's relationships with others, but through facing the truth of the present." In the Rishi Valley School in rural Andhra Pradesh, Thapan reports, "children from the senior school quietly gather atop a ridge to sit silently for 15 minutes evening to watch the sun set behind three hills in the distance." Rishi Valley is a "unique institution," part of the larger Rishi Valley Education

Centre (RVEC); it is the oldest KFI school, established in 1926. Its curriculum is "flexible," Thapan tells us, "and is transacted in an open and non-authoritarian manner."

Poonam Batra also referenced contemporary Krishnamurti schools as well as schools "patterned on Sri Aurobindo's integral education," noting that the educational philosophy of these schools has "yet to become part of mainstream schooling." Schools that follow Krishnamurti[19] or Vivekananda are "distinct," different from schools that follow Sri Aurobindo's approach of integral education, which are themselves "distinctly different" from Gandhi's Nai Talim or Tagore's Shantiniketan. Given this complexity, it is, Batra advises, "a fallacy to talk of school curriculum in India as a homogenous entity. We could perhaps talk of a wide set of curricula that operate across different parts of the country." That acknowledged, Batra does posit an "essential aim of education in each of these traditions." That is "to develop the inner self along with the ability to reason, acquire other mental faculties and skills— the focus being the whole person."

Batra explains that the curriculum of mainstream schooling[20] in India can be studied in two ways, through "a detailed study of national curriculum documents" and "through the close examination of prevalent school practices."[21] Batra focused on national curricula documents prepared postindependence India by the "apex institution of education," the National Council of Educational Research and Training (NCERT), of which she provided a history. In the 1950s, "the aim of education was perceived to prepare youth to participate in industrialization and technological advancement." Alongside "national development" and the "need" to "replace the old with the new," Batra continued, the "central role of India's states in addressing diversity along language, culture, and tradition was also recognized." The "emphasis," Batra noted, was on "the national, and not the local." In fact, the specific guidelines for history outlined in the 1975 curriculum document cautioned against the introduction of "local history" because it "runs the risk of promoting 'parochialism and regional cultural chauvinism.'" But in 1988 indigeneity was endorsed, this time in service of encouraging "productive Indian citizens." Batra characterizes both the 1975 and 1988 curricular emphases as narratives of "secular nationalism."

When the Bhartiya Janata Party (BJP)-led coalition government came to power in 1999, indigeneity became "cultural nationalism," what Batra described as an "ideologically motivated" project to 'homogenize' the plural fabric of Indian society" through the "imposition of 'Hindu' religious values and hues, even when 'Hindu' itself is neither a monolithic religion nor a monolithic way of life." Efforts were made, Batra reports, "to thwart scientific inquiry within the social sciences, undermine the study of history, and introduce Vedic astrology as a subject of higher studies."[22] As "we have always done," she continued, "religion needs to be kept out of formal school education. This was the insight developed by Gandhi over the years."[23] A change of national government in 2004 led to the NCERT curriculum review in 2005, an effort by the ministry, Batra suggests, to "detoxify" school curriculum.

In recent years, discourses of "modernization" and "globalization" have coincided with the reemergence of the Hindu right wing.[24] This has led left leaning secular political groups to raise objections against the idea of multiple textbooks and local knowledge. In their view, Batra explained, local knowledges "threatened the ideas of rationality and objectivity that formal education represented." Local knowledge has the potential of privileging cultural practices that "maintain hierarchies and divisiveness in society." To address this issue," Batra explained, the NCF, 2005 preamble was "revised" so that the Indian Constitution became the "litmus test for deciding which local knowledge is worthy of including in school curriculum and why." What was "missing" in these debates, Batra pointed out, was "the voice of the teacher."[25] Since NCF, 2005, the potential of social science to support development of a "just and peaceful society" has been emphasized. "For the first time in India," Batra reports, "the curriculum debate is linked to the professional and pedagogical concerns of the child and the teacher." Meenaksi Thapan acknowledged this point as well, asserting that the framework positioned "the student as a partner on the path of learning."

# Reform

The five "guiding principles" of the 2005 reform included: "connecting knowledge to life outside the school, ensuring that learning is shifted away from rote methods, enriching the curriculum to provide for overall development of children rather than remain textbook-centric, making examinations more flexible and integrated with classroom life, and nurturing an overriding identity informed by caring concerns within the democratic polity of the country" (quoted by Batra, this volume). In this reform, Batra pointed out, the curriculum became a "deliberative act" that "subsumes" classroom discourse and processes.

"Never before in India," Batra emphasized, had a national curriculum document "engaged deeply with questions of learning, knowledge, the socio-cultural context of learners and pedagogic approach." It addressed the deep divide between home and school knowledge, deemphasizing "textbook culture" while affirming "knowledge creation" as processes of "social construction." Central to democracy, it was acknowledged, were "dialogue, meaning-making and developing rational thought." Reform of the curricular treatments of citizenship, gender, and diversity was also introduced. No longer an abstract concept ("learner"), the student was now assumed to have an "identity" that is associated with a particular "socio-cultural context." Batra summarized: "The significant strength of the new NCERT texts is the manner in which knowledge is presented and connected to the lived realities of children's socio-cultural milieu. The real problem was one of engaging teachers with the nuanced debates on issues of child-centered and constructivist approaches as well as the politics of knowledge selection and presentation." That "problem" Batra associates with teacher education, programs, she suggests, that have been "frozen in the colonial frame."

The significant revision of teacher education required for curriculum reform in India has been undertaken at the University of Delhi. Batra described a four-year integrated program of elementary teacher education developed there, a program including practicum courses of theatre, craft and self-development. Drama, Batra pointed out, creates the "possibility of catharsis, which when complemented with personal growth workshops, carries immense therapeutic and educative value." Not only are "deeply personal" issues addressed, these courses provide "non-threatening spaces for addressing social issues of gender, identity, exclusion and injustice." These issues "emerge within the processes of dramatic improvisations, text readings, poetry sessions and personal sharing that enable student teachers to reflect on their own positions and develop deep feelings of empathy and social sensitivity."

The program at the University of Delhi—as Batra describes it—would seem to require more nuanced and complex subjective engagement than the concept "reflection" requests in many US teacher education programs, especially when "reflection" represents a prompt to align teaching with so-called best practices or increases student scores on standardized exams. Lesley Le Grange worried that in the United States "reflection stays at the level of reflecting on what happens in teaching and seldom goes into depth of subjectivity and personhood." He asked Batra: "Does Indian teacher education also privilege knowledge-skill-competencies over in-depth understanding of teacher's own personal growth?" Yes, Batra replied, but not at the University of Delhi where personal growth "forms a very significant part of the BElEd program which I have referenced in the essay." The BElEd, Batra emphasized, is "designed to provide opportunities for reflection," and "not only over matters outside oneself but along with and in the context of the inner aspects of the person.... Slowly, but surely we are in the process of developing strategies and mechanisms to scale up these ideas after having achieved an articulation of them in the form of a national curriculum framework for teacher education." Scholars worldwide will want to keep abreast of such important developments in teacher education; they represent a significant challenge to Western efforts to restrict certification to skill development—so-called best practices—focused solely on raising student test scores.

# Recontextualization

While this term was not invoked, the phenomenon of "recontextualization" (Pinar 2011a)[26] was discernible when Batra described the uncritical importation of the Western concept of "child-centeredness," first from the United Kingdom (from the Plowden Report) and then from the United States, through the work of John Dewey. "Terms like 'child-centeredness' and 'critical pedagogy' have become part of the vocabulary, Manish Jain also observed, "without an understanding of their epistemic and political basis and meanings or the institutional preparation of translating them into textbooks and classroom practices." Such problems of recontextualization are simultaneously political, cultural, and gendered. "How does one implement child-centered pedagogy," Mary Ann Chacko asked, "which calls for all students to be agentic and exploratory, in a society where girls are brought up to be dependent, self-effacing, restrained, and submissive?" After its arrival, Batra explains, the concept of "child-centeredness" remained "largely rhetoric...reduced...[and] oversimplified." In India, recontextualization of this concept has risked the centrality of "knowledge" and "subject-matter" in the "process of education" (Pinar 2010).[27]

In a question concerning Kumar's conception of "centering the child," Hongyu Wang asked Mary Ann Chacko if Kumar thought "how we teach is more important than what we teach." Also alluding to Batra's concern about the curricular consequences of "child-centeredness," Wang wondered how Kumar might respond. Context is key, Chacko affirmed, referencing Kumar's acknowledgment of child-centeredness as arising in early twentieth-century America, amid industrialization and the rise of the US bourgeoisie. The concept cannot be transferred to contemporary India without recontextualization. "The best way to judge the worth of knowledge from a child's perspective," Chacko tells us, quoting Kumar, "seems to be to make that decision 'on behalf of children' (Kumar, 1992/2009, 4). And one of the ways of determining the worth of knowledge on behalf of children is to say: 'it is worth teaching something only if it can be learnt'" (1992/2009, 5). From the child's perspective, Kumar reasons, how we teach—how we make academic knowledge accessible—is more important than what we teach.[28]

Not only decontextualized Western concepts are to blame for the marginalization of academic knowledge in the curriculum, so is an emphasis on "Indian" cultural values projected by certain groups that have been, in Batra's words, "narrowly focused on religious values. These are largely defined in behavioral terms (Huebner 1999)[29]—hence, here too 'knowledge' tends to get marginalized." Historical knowledge, it seems to me, constitutes "knowledge of most worth" in an era when "faith" substitutes for "fact," however blurred the boundaries between the two concepts can be. When the past persists, can the study of the past become the curricular medium of its surpassing? Consider the question of gender.

# Gender

The 1854 *Education Dispatch*, Suresh Ghosh reminded us, anticipated the education of girls. Ghosh also cited the 1917 Calcutta University Commission,[30] which "recommended the organization of purdah schools for Hindu and Muslim girls whose parents were willing to extend their education up to 15 or 16 years of age, a special board for women's education to look after the courses particularly suited for women, and the organization of co-operative arrangements for teaching in women's colleges."[31] Jain expressed cynicism concerning the intentions of the state, suggesting that attention to the condition of women "allowed the patriarchal colonial state to project itself as a progressive force constrained by the backward Indian society that it was trying to improve and reform."

The moral agenda of the colonial rulers in India was complex, Chacko emphasized, and, referencing Kumar, contained liberalism, paternalism, and evangelism, a mix evident in efforts to abolish the Hindu custom of *sati* or widow burning. These outraged the elite whose consent was useful to the British colonists. Attempting to address the problem of gender—specifically the status of girls and women—requires contextualization, Chacko emphasized, referencing Kumar. The school is, Kumar had noted, a microcosm of patriarchal culture.[32] As globalization and liberalization of the economy have stimulated fears of Westernization, patriarchy has intensified.

The consequent commodification of female bodies and sexuality has produced a patriarchal political reaction. Despite the odds, Kumar affirms the power of education to support change. In fact, Chacko characterized him as a "die-hard believer" in the "agency" of education.

The gendering of educational experience was also evident in Thapan's discussion of the "relationships between *gurus* (teachers) and *brahmacharis* (celibate young Hindu men)." These, she tells us, "surpassed those between fathers and sons." The intimacy of such pedagogical relationships enabled the "reproduction of a unique identity, the *Arya* that gave rise to an exclusive *Jat* identity that enabled the contestation of upper caste Hindu and Muslim identities, the colonial state and lower castes." Such an education, Thapan points out, also "represented an anti-woman bias, a focus on the control of male sexuality and an idealization of virtues associated with individual control and social uplifting."

From the nineteenth century on, Manish Jain reminded, questions concerning a "suitable curriculum" accompanied—perhaps sometimes stimulated—male fears of educated women, "with their own desires, voices, choices, and public presence." As in the United States, men worried over women's "possible neglect of household duties and disrespect for traditional norms, values and authority and their natural proper domain." In the early twentieth century, a gender-distinctive curriculum replaced the common one. The girls' curriculum included attention to "domestic duties and roles," to what in North America was termed "home economics," for example, the "scientific" management of the home: cooking, cleaning, childrearing, and attending to the needs of the husband. There were dissenting voices: Jain reports that in a woman's magazine *Bamabodhini* there were calls for the education of girls to "develop their faculties" and "open their inner eye." The NCF, Batra notes, addresses the question of "gender asymmetry," but more importantly, underscores "the need to break away from patriarchal frames of knowledge" in redesigning curriculum.

# English

Previously divided into the provinces of British India and princely states, Mary Ann Chacko reminded, "post-independent India was re-organized into linguistic states." Language became "a crucial marker of regional identity as well as of exclusion and inclusion." "Almost banned from schools and undergraduate colleges in the North from 1960 onwards following an agitation against it by the Hindi chauvinists," Suresh Ghosh reminded, "English has now returned with the blessings of our political leaders, including those who had opposed it earlier." For Jain:

> English is not just a language but also encompasses a worldview and denotes power. For researchers like me who did not study in English medium schools and English is not the first language, English-vernacular divide constantly shapes and constrains our writings.... The complexities of rupture, interaction and mediation between these seemingly two polar worlds also shape the academic and public debate and anxieties about education and curriculum.

Its curricular status points to its symbolic significance. The national language "strategy" proposes "a three language formula," which, Chacko explained, "has been implemented with considerable intra-state and inter-state variations (NCERT 2006)." Hindi may be the official language of India, but Chacko reports that English is recognized as an "additional" official language. The "widely recognized" fact is, Chacko allowed, "that English is a necessity in India today." It is this "status" that makes the matter of its absence or presence in schools of such "great significance."

One reason for the "increasing popularity of private schools in India," Chacko reports, is the teaching of English. Until recently, in government and government-aided schools (where instruction is conducted in the regional language) English was not introduced until grade five.[33] From grade one, however, private schools used English as their medium of instruction and teach English as a separate subject. English is linked to a "global outlook" and the rhetoric of "excellence," Thapan emphasized, with some schools going so far as to promise not only linguistic competence but "to develop 'sensitive' human beings" as well.[34]

Kumar proposed the establishment of a "common" elementary schooling for all children. The medium of instruction would be the regional language of the state. Such schools, Kumar believes, will help students become rooted in their local social milieu during their "formative years" and "safeguard the quality of education for *all* children." Such "counter-socialization"—a key concept for Kumar, to be discussed later—could protect children from "what could otherwise be the alienating influence of an English-dominated educational experience in later years." When Kumar refers to the alienating influence of an English-dominated educational experience, Chacko explains, "it is important to recognize that he is not referring to the 'alien' nature of English per se but to the arduous cultivation of an ethos that entails a deliberate distancing from the regional language and its other socio-cultural aspects."

Does affirming the specificity of regions and locales—by learning their languages, being taught in local language, in studying the "local"—risk, Lesley Le Grange asked, "socialization" into the local? Isn't a generative tension among the local, state, national, and global required to encourage noncoincidence with each? Le Grange also asked about tensions between local and the global: "Will a strong focus on the local (including linking schooling with production) not limit the becoming of Indian children in a globalized world (with its negative and positive effects)?" To what degree, Hongyu Wang asked, can indigenous and colonial knowledge be kept completely distinct in contemporary India? Should they be integrated, or critically reconstructed? "Do you think," Wang asked Chacko, "this relationship (indigenous and colonial knowledge) can be potentially worked out constructively in Indian education?"

What Kumar is advocating, Chacko replied, is the provision of educational experience that is not "divisive" and "distorted." A "common" curriculum, Kumar argues, contributes to children's socialization so that when they encounter English later it will not be an alienating experience. For Kumar there can be a social justice agenda, Chacko explained, "only if we reconceptualize the measures of quality that are currently in vogue in education; ones that are increasingly being determined by the market worthiness of investments in education."

Wang asked about government schools, about the vexed curricular position of English, and about Kumar's suggestion about common elementary schooling: "Does he refer to government schools or all schools?" Chacko began by reminding that her own comments on government schools are associated with "my understanding of government schooling in one state in India, Kerala. Making this explicit is crucial because there are considerable inter-state variations," she added. Government policy toward teaching English, she continued "could be understood in a few different ways." The "opposition" of certain governments to the introduction of English, Chacko explained, "could be viewed as an attempt to reiterate state sovereignty and legitimacy, especially considering the fact that India is divided into linguistic states.

The curricular question of English in regional medium schools can also be viewed, Chacko suggested, "as following from particular theories of the link between cognitive development and linguistic ability," here referencing the 2005 National Curriculum Framework. That framework, Chacko continued, was "endorsed" in the Kerala Curriculum Framework (KCF 2007) published by the Kerala State Council of Educational Research and Training (SCERT). The KCF 2007, Chacko notes, quotes Mahatma Gandhi: "The baby takes its first lesson from its mother. I, therefore, regard it as a sin against the motherland to inflict upon her children a tongue other than their mother's for their mental development."

Regardless of what the curriculum frameworks declare, Chacko continued, teachers in Malayalam-medium[35] primary schools have introduced English as a subject from grade one on. "This was the case in the Malayalam medium primary schools that I visited in 2010," Chacko recounted. "These teachers believed that it was imperative to introduce English if they wanted to retain their students." But, she added, "the absence of English alone cannot be held responsible for the crisis of government schooling and the steady rise of enrollment in private unaided schools in India." Chacko referenced the neoliberalism underway even in Kerala State. "Even after government made interventions to improve the quality of government schooling through efforts such as the World Bank funded District Primary Education Program (DPEP) and the initiative called the *Sarva Shiksha Abhiyan* (SSA)," she noted, "they have not been successful in turning the tide of declining enrollment," adding that Kumar is "highly critical" of both the DPEP and the SSA.

## Alternative Curricular Frameworks

Given state control of the school curriculum, "it is therefore a significant movement *against* [state] regulation," Meenakshi Thapan points out, "when non-governmental organizations, schools, and individuals seek to construct alternative curricular frameworks and content." Such efforts, she suggests, communicate a "concern for change and innovation outside the control of the state." They are often, Thapan argues, open to a greater participation by children and their teachers in the educational process.[36]

The NGO sector[37] is noteworthy, Hongyu Wang observed, citing Batra's revealing historical discussion of Eklavya. Curriculum for Eklavya meant not only "presenting subject-matter in a coherent manner," Batra reported, but also "framing critical questions" and "generating dialogue." The Eklavya curriculum, Batra continued, was dedicated to "individual freedom" and, specifically, "human agency." As an illustration, Batra pointed to the civics curriculum[38] that invited teachers' engagement with subject matter, including the questioning of social issues: "gender, caste, social hierarchies, development, religion, tribal culture and national identities."

After receiving overwhelming support and patronage from the central government for over two decades, "a change of power equations between the state government and Eklavya led to its closure in 2003.[39] The influence of neoliberalism grew stronger, evident in the renaming of the Ministry of Education to the Ministry of Human Resource Development. Curricular standardization and an emphasis on outcomes followed. This meant that behaviorism—first introduced in the 1960s by Western planners, confident it would solve the problems of education in India—persists. It is supported, Batra pointed out (referencing Kumar), by incorporating the old colonial assumption that the sociocultural milieu is a problem rather than an asset. The system of mass examinations and the accompanying inculcation of a textbook culture[40] complete this system of curricular constraints.

Despite these circumstances, the NCF, 2005, drew upon the "curriculum discourse" associated with the Eklavya experiments, especially in science and social science curricula. Middle school "civics" textbooks, Batra reports, were replaced with interdisciplinary textbooks focused on "social and political life," patterned after the Eklavya texts. "The NCF 2005," Thapan agrees, "resulted in the writing of new and well-written textbooks for use in schools across India."

Digantar brought the question of the aims of education to the center of discussions of curriculum and practice. It insisted on training its own staff, teachers, and other practitioners to be self-aware of the assumptions and perspectives that guided their ideas and practices. These rigorous collective discussions demanded, Jain reported, a professional seriousness that was not limited to spirit of voluntarism and idealism on behalf of the disadvantaged. Digantar opened possibilities of self-reflection on practices and theories, he concludes, and gave a premium to a professional identity based on rigor of both ideas and practice.

Besides the richness, innovativeness, and criticality of Eklavaya, Digantar, and other initiatives, they were significant for other reasons as well, as Jain explained in his chapter. First, these alternatives supported "critical" and "reflective" trends in the academic field of education, trends that were influenced also by studies in the sociology of education.[41] NCERT had argued that the country could not afford the luxury of science teaching through experiments, but experiments like the Hoshangabad Science Teaching Program (HSTP) provided counterevidence. Because these innovations scrutinized curriculum in relation to children and their contexts, Jain argued, and in relation to pedagogy, epistemology, discipline, and social structure, they influenced debates on the National Curriculum Framework for School Education (NCFSE) 2000 and the National Curriculum Framework (NCF) 2005. Jain also judges that participants and students of these innovations "made significant contributions to the critical discourse on curriculum through their writings in different books and journals, both national and local." He cited magazines published by Eklavya and Digantar—specifically *Shaikshik Sandarbh* (Educational Contexts) and *Shiksha Vimarsh* (Educational Discourse)—that featured "original articles and translations of writings of Indian and Western researchers on issues of curriculum and textbooks in Hindi."

# Krishna Kumar

For Krishna Kumar curriculum development is no simple act of engineering. It is, instead, a complex undertaking of ongoing *deliberation*. His commitment to this concept was clear throughout his five-year term as director of NCERT, during which time he undertook the formulation of the National Curriculum Framework (NCF). Chacko points out that NCF, 2005, was formulated through "intensive deliberations" structured by 21 National Focus Groups comprising scholars from different disciplines, NCERT faculty, schoolteachers, and nongovernmental organizations. Conferences were organized to obtain the views of rural teachers while public opinion was solicited through advertisements in national and regional newspapers.

Like Batra, Chacko underscores the unprecedented character of the National Curriculum Framework (NCF, 2005), "unique for the processes of nation-wide deliberation through which this document was developed." A "progressive discourse on issues of curriculum, teachers and educational practice," NCF, 2005 faced several challenges, Batra added, and "we can see the prominence of the curriculum discourse declining and the discourse of efficiency, accountability and learning outcomes gaining currency, with concerted efforts at institutionalizing mechanisms towards this end."[42]

Importantly, the concept of *deliberation*—along with *counter-socialization*, the key conceptual contributions of Kumar to curriculum research in India—Batra associates as originating with Gandhi.[43] Perhaps Krishna Kumar does as well, as Chacko points out that in his critique of the National Curriculum Framework, 2000, Kumar cites the National Council of Educational Research and Training's (NCERT) neglect of the work of Indian "teacher-philosophers" like Gandhi, Rabindranath Tagore, Sri Aurobindo, and J. Krishnamurti. "Historical consciousness pervades his work," Chacko observes, as is evident in Kumar's tracings of "the historical character of educational aims and dilemmas, such as the role of textbooks and examinations as 'instruments of control' and the low esteem and status of teachers, in order to examine schooling and curriculum in the present."

In reply to a question from Hongyu Wang, Chacko provided an intellectual life history of this "titan" in the field. A PhD graduate from the University of Toronto's Ontario Institute for Studies in Education, Kumar was influenced by the work of Basil Bernstein, Pierre Bourdieu, and the Frankfurt School. Kumar's doctoral dissertation, Chacko tells us, was "an interactionist analysis of Canadian and Indian school textbooks wherein he examined the nature of social relations depicted in the textbooks" (Kumar 1989). Replying to Wang's question concerning "Kumar's location in India's intellectual and educational landscape," Chacko concluded "that while the field of sociology of education is India is plagued by various institutional, methodological, and theoretical concerns, it would not be erroneous to say that sociology of education and the work of sociologists like Krishna Kumar...continues to be the major force in educational research in India. And Krishna Kumar is a titan not only in this field but also in the discipline of education in India." We shall consider the concept of deliberation next.

# Deliberation

Hongyu Wang located the concept of "deliberation" in the West, noting that "curriculum as deliberation has a tradition in both the United States and the United Kingdom." She asked: "Do you see if there is any connection or/and dissimilarity between these traditions and Krishna Kumar's notion of curriculum as a deliberative act?" Chacko concurred that Kumar (1992/2009) made no references to Schwab or, for that matter, to any other curriculum theorists. That does not rule out the possibility that Kumar might have been drawing upon the work of Schwab, Chacko allows. She noted that Schwab himself did not list a single reference in his *Practical 1* (1969) essay, but it was clear that "he was influenced by many others."[44] Both Kumar and Schwab "shared similar suspicions of generalizable and fixed knowledge" about curriculum, Chacko pointed out. For both men, "deliberation is a method that can serve as an antidote to the culture of isolation, hegemonies and privileges, and the silencing that has permeated the field of curriculum." While Schwab was "particularly concerned about the hegemony of particular subject matter specialists and theories," Chacko added, "for Kumar it is the acute awareness of the silencing of oppressed groups by economically and culturally dominant groups who have exerted a monopoly over the fundamental question of 'what is worth teaching'?"

Despite efforts to make the curriculum development process "deliberative" and inclusive of local content, Lesley Le Grange asked: "Is the very idea of a National Curriculum not antithetical to Kumar's idea of 'schooling as counter-socialization'?" Chacko replied with a question: "it is pertinent to ask—What is being countered?" She continued: "the counter-socialization that was sought in this case by the secularists was the reversal of the attempts that had been made by the NDA government to appropriate the state apparatus of education so as to project India as a Hindu state." It is not only contemporary events that provide context here; Chacko also invokes colonial rule, when "socialization" was central to British hegemony. Despite these historical and political antecedents, "counter-socialization and his critique of neoliberalism" reveal, Chacko argues, Kumar's "commitment to the child whom he places at the center of the educational enterprise, and [it] resounds with his critique of the debilitating impact of market-oriented economy on schooling in India." The concept of "counter-socialization," Chacko concludes, "entails resisting *and* compensating for the oppressive and elitist structures of knowledge and societal relations." To enable this, Batra argues, "it is necessary to break the false neutrality and apolitical posture within which teachers are usually prepared."

# Counter-Socialization

Like his conception of *deliberation*, Kumar's concept of *counter-socialization* may also have been inspired by Gandhi. Gandhi's aspirations for the reorganization of society via education, Chacko suggests, find "a prominent place in Kumar's work." Constructing "an economically useful and socially committed school" is key for both men. Yet the failure of basic education to provide for either economic prosperity or political democracy underlines the scale of Gandhi and Kumar's aspirations.

The school in which Kumar places his faith, Chacko underlines, is not one narrowly conceived, as in "outcome based" models, but one "that seeks to transform the students' quality of life itself." For Kumar, she emphasizes, schooling should be a "counter-socializing force." That concept—like others[45]—is not "applied" insensitive to context. "Rather," Chacko noted, "they [these concepts] should be addressed in ways that are relevant and responsive to the nature of oppression and inequality faced by these students." Kumar's engagement with Scheduled Caste and Scheduled Tribe students underscores both the challenge and necessity of schooling as counter-socialization. Kumar asserts that because the prevailing curriculum fails to address the specific challenges faced by SC or ST children, it provides a distorted view of reality, thereby failing all children.

Wang expressed appreciation for Kumar's commitment to counter both colonization and the caste system, as well as "counteract the traditional gender system which oppresses girls and women." It is the "choice of language," Wang continues, that "makes me pause." She questions the implication that socialization is "necessarily negative," as well as the "dualism between school and society" that that implies. Wang references nineteenth-century American Indian residential schools (Pinar 2009)[46] that also attempted to counter-socialize students. Rather than "setting school above society," Wang asked if "the resources in Indian traditions or hybrid traditions... can be recuperated to generate new possibilities for today's education?"

Kumar's conceptualization does not construe socialization as only "negative," Chacko replied. The truth is, she reminded, that "schools have also, and very often unintentionally, created a milieu for resistance movements and conceptions of an alternative social reality to take shape." As employed by Kumar, Chacko continued, "counter-socialization" is a concept that "attempts to integrate the two apparently contradictory perceptions of schools: schools as agents of socialization and schools as agents of social transformation."[47] On one occasion, politics and historical moment converged with culture to accord "counter-socialization" a very specific calling, illustrating the concept's incorporation of both "socialization" and "transformation."

This occasion was the assassination of Prime Minister Indira Gandhi by her Sikh bodyguards in 1984. Riots ensued, aimed against the Sikh community in northern India, especially in Delhi. Despite the fact that murder of Sikhs was witnessed by thousands of children, school principals were directed to prevent children from discussing the riots in their classes after schools reopened. "Attending to the world from which children come to school," Chacko pointed out, "is the first step to recognizing and assessing the school's role as a domain of counter-socialization."

"Counter-socialization," Chacko emphasized, positions "social dialogue" as central to curriculum that bridges academic knowledge and everyday life. She continued: "A curriculum should reflect these issues and concerns so that they are made the focus of inquiry and deliberation within schools."[48] The "resources for counter-socialization," Chacko summarized, "can be found within the contemporary issues and problems that we seek to transform."

The everyday world of "contemporary issues" is one, as Poonam Batra has pointed out, in which culture can conflate with both religion and politics. Despite decades of teaching secularism, schools have failed to counter religious "revivalism" because they have failed as agencies of counter-socialization, Chacko argued, in part due to the distorted view of society communicated by "India's highly stratified school system...divided into government schools, government aided schools, and private-unaided schools."[49] Government schools have, Thapan tells us, been "abandoned" by middle and upper classes' private schools that have proliferated. Thapan also reported "a substantial increase" in private schooling in recent years as well as "massive growth" in the government school system, resulting in a "huge heterogeneity in the schooling system in the country."

It is "also important to note," Batra wrote (when reading an earlier draft of this chapter), "that there is a deep hierarchy within the government schools (in terms of quality and resources)." Curriculum, she added, has a part to play. "Reflective engagement (via curriculum) with the 'cultural self,'" Batra argues, "impels a discerning shift from the passive acceptance of social inequity to a syncretic response within a diverse and locally rooted society."

## Globalization as Neocolonialism

Associated with British rule, colonialism both preceded and followed it, now as "globalization." The former is familiar but bears repetition, as the present cannot be understood—or lived through—if severed from the past. In the late seventeenth century, a group of companies from the West—including English, French, Dutch, Danes, and the Portuguese—came to India, "not as invaders and conquerors like their Muslim predecessors," Suresh Ghosh pointed out, "but as traders and merchants." In his chapter Ghosh provides details; suffice to say here that colonization was characterized by commercialization.

But not only commercialization, he notes. The *Education Dispatch* of 1854, Ghosh suggested, laid the foundation for the modern system of education in India. European knowledge, the British believed, "will teach the natives of India the marvelous results of the employment of labor and capital...and gradually, but certainly, confer upon them all the advantages which accompany the healthy increase of wealth and commerce, and at the same time secure to us a large and more certain supply of many articles necessary for our manufacturers and extensively consumed by all classes of our population." With updated language, this 1854 rationale could serve as a contemporary justification for globalization.

Geography, Manish Jain pointed out, was taught so that "natives" could "look outside their ignorant enclosures by studying...the world in a scientific and objective manner." The colonial construction of young Hindus[50] as being "extraordinarily ignorant of their own country" also informed the first civics textbook, *The Citizen of India*, published in the last decade of nineteenth century. Other subjects served the colonial cause as well. "Given its significance in narrating the past, envisioning a future nation and suggesting a political intervention in the present," Jain explains, the school subject History would also occupy "a central place" in the textbook controversies in independent India. Science was not introduced until the late nineteenth century.

The story of modernity in colonial India, Jain argues, cannot be complete unless we also note the ambivalence of the colonial state, including assumptions shared by the native elite and the colonial state regarding their pedagogic responsibility vis-à-vis the colonized masses. Nor can one ignore, Jain notes, the appropriation of the promises of modernity by the marginalized sectors of Indian society to demand protection and claim rights and dignity.

"The aim," Thapan recounts, was "to civilize the native, to replace indigenous knowledge with 'modern' forms of knowledge and ways of accessing it, to produce a bevy of mindless beings who would acquiesce into submission to the colonizers and their methods of knowing and evaluation of this knowledge." The outcome was the citizen, defined "as first and foremost, a representative of 'another' culture and civilization," Thapan emphasizes, was not only a cultural but a political "conquest" as well, as colonialism begets cultural dependency.[51] This inculcation of cultural dependency went beyond the encouragement of professional training in Law, Medicine, and Civil Engineering. The 1854 *Dispatch* had also noted, Ghosh reminds, the urgency of educating the women of India; it noted appreciatively that "an increased desire on the part of many of the natives of India to give a good education to their daughters."

As we have seen, colonialism cut two ways, incurring cultural dependency and political subjugation *and* encouraging modernization with its rhetoric of rights and reparation. Gender remains a key if contentious concern.[52] Here, however, let us return to the colonialism-commercialization nexus and note its contemporary occurrence: "globalization." In her study of Kumar, Mary Ann Chacko referenced his critiques of contemporary market-driven reform as characterized by a culture of haste. Institutions like the International Monetary Fund set dates by when "developing countries" are told they must achieve their objectives. Delays threatened dire consequences. Neocolonialism, Chacko concludes, has led to the adoption of short-term goals with "detrimental effects on the quality of schooling and the professionalization of teachers."

One such effect of "short-termism" has been the introduction of "para-teachers" in government schools across India. Para-teachers are locally recruited on contract basis, earn less than permanent staff, and undergo only a basic and token teacher training, justified, Chacko points out, given the unprecedented expansion of schooling in India. Never mind underinvestment: PISA assesses the quality of school systems, Chacko reminds, solely on outcomes, narrowly focused on so-called cognitive abilities in selected vocational subjects. Once an advance over colonially imposed liberal arts—as Ghosh describes in his chapter—now such reductionistic assessments of educational quality convert schools into black boxes, decontextualized and split off from locale, history, and actually existing children.

# Conclusion

In India, Meenakshi Thapan tells us, curriculum is an "open" subject, in that anyone can "discuss it, write about it, and have very articulate views about its content."

Open it may be, but school curriculum in India, Thapan underscores, is "a state-produced entity, removed from debate and discussion, good practice and, importantly, from children's and teachers' lives." Despite qualified praise for NCF 2005, Thapan reminds us that "it is nonetheless an instrument that is effected by the state which can be used or misused depending on the ideological goals espoused by the agents of the state."[53]

This insight was evident when the Bhartiya Janata Party (BJP) led coalition government came to power in 1999, and for Suresh Ghosh it is the case today, although the "ideology" in question would seem to be an ancient one we might term "moral failing." "The final and the most important factor that stands in the way of introducing and developing a new curriculum program," Ghosh concluded, "is the corruption which is slowly and silently enveloping our body politic and administrative apparatus." With a former computer company executive appointed director of educational technology in the US Department of Education, the same must be said of the United States.[54]

For Ghosh, globalization[55]—with its emphasis upon technology—represents "a silver-lining to the present educational scenario in the country." It is the power of globalization, he suggests, that has "trumped the vested interests of political and social groups who ordinarily undermine curriculum reform." Against the curricular legacies of colonialism—always including, as Jain points out, the rhetoric of "lack"—Ghosh affirms curriculum with the "potentiality to equip a student with a skill for a job." But, Ghosh cautions, "human beings do not live by jobs alone." Ghosh embraces a curriculum of "balance," writing that "with a changed, updated and balanced curriculum in keeping with the forces of globalization, we can always look forward to a brighter and more prosperous future of our country."

Such curricular "balance" remains a remote possibility in certain sections of the country, Ghosh acknowledges. Inhabited mostly by the Dalits and tribal people, Ghosh tells us, these areas have seen no significant developmental activities "since independence." The first priority is literacy, he points out, "backed by a framework of vocational curriculum to suit the local needs and requirements, a curriculum to enable residents to earn their daily living." Ghosh continues: The failure to provide basic, then vocational, education—a failure of our learned politicians, educational planners, and administrators—is costing India too much: the loss of human lives first of all, and also the destruction of national properties by the almost daily violent and disruptive activities of the Naxals[56] often sympathized with by our disgruntled Maoist intellectuals and political leaders.

To reiterate: Historical (dis)continuities, cultural conflict, economic globalization, and political tension characterize the present circumstances of curriculum studies in India.

What is the state of the schools? It is, Poonam Batra cautions, "a fallacy to talk of school curriculum in India as a homogenous entity. We could perhaps talk of a wide set of curricula that operate across different parts of the country." That complexity acknowledged, Batra does posit an "essential aim of education in each of these traditions." That is "to develop the inner self along with the ability to reason, acquire other mental faculties and skills—the focus being the whole person." This emphasis upon the "inner self" distinguishes this view from those elsewhere. The juxtaposition, indeed, synthesis, of inner reflection, intellectuality, practicality—all personified in "the whole person"—provides a powerful perspective on what is possible in schools, a distinctive and important contribution to curriculum studies worldwide.

From the colonial to the contemporary period, there is a tradition of "alternative curriculum frameworks" enacted in schools that institutionalize the concepts Poonam Batra has so succinctly summarized. Meenakshi Thapan provided a strong example of one but, as she emphasized, "schools like Rishi Valley are few and far between in the vast educational landscape of India. The mix of academic excellence, co-curricular development, and the presence of a culture that is oriented towards students' psychological needs and processes, a concern for nature and the environment, the presence of a rural health and education program that involves students, and other activities make it an alternative [with] a unique quality." Unique, important, and worthy of study worldwide, I would say.

Thapan also provides a compelling portrait of singularity, heterogeneity, and complexity, concluding that "education for all is thus imparted in very different kinds of educational institutions and what goes on in these institutions therefore also varies depending on the kind of institution it is. While such complexities prevail and characterize educational practices across schools in India, curriculum in India further shaped by the characteristics of 'secular' schools, or those that are identified with a particular religious or cultural identity." Added to these religious and cultural complexities are the consequences of economic globalization. "The problems facing government and government-aided schools," Mary Ann Chacko pointed out, "range from de-professionalization of teachers, cost cutting by central and state governments, frequent policy and curricular interventions by government that leave parents and teachers apprehensive and uncertain, and the increasing tendency to equate quality with English-medium private schools."

Despite these difficult circumstances, the scholars published here remain clear that what is at stake is simultaneously the child, the nation, the world. Referencing his recent revised work[57]—*What Is Worth Teaching?*—Batra notes that Kumar associates curriculum with questions of the "society and people we are, and to…the kind of society we want to be." These panoramic questions crystallize in the concept of the citizen. "In my view," Thapan explains, "the good citizen is one who *engages with* social issues, norms and values, practices and policies, and is concerned with the meaning and intent of all action." To do so, the inner self becomes engaged in the public sphere, in my phrase reconstructing passionate lives into public service. In India, these aspirations are enacted within a long history—as Ghosh emphasizes—of occupation by colonizing powers.[58]

Recall that the first textbook of civics in colonial India (1897), *The Citizen of India*, authored by William Lee-Warner, underscored, in Jain's words, "the shortcomings of the native personality, society and institutions." In this textbook, Jain points out, "reason and loyalty to colonial state became the marker of a citizen's identity, as opposed to that of native who governed by uncontrolled emotions and passions could rebel against the colonial state."[59] He suggests that the colonial legacy persists, even "after independence until 2005 when the National Curriculum Framework (NCF) replaced civics by politics at the elementary level classes." Such curricular history—inaugurated by Ivor F. Goodson (2014)[60] and recontextualized in Brazil and elsewhere—may prove pivotal in the future formation of curriculum studies, a countersocializing opportunity for deliberation in an era characterized by presentism, even historical amnesia.

Becoming historical enables study of the present. Jain calls for research focused on "the enactment of textbooks in the classroom, e.g. the pedagogic interaction between the teacher and the student." He also endorses studies that examine relationships among "policies, research and school practices" as well "the development of curriculum in school or the strategies used by teachers and students to negotiate with the official curriculum." In his chapter Jain referred appreciatively to studies of schools and learning, concluding with an endorsement of research that investigates "the daily enactment of the school curriculum" especially structured by "social marginalization," including barriers of gender, caste, poverty, and ethnicity. Also on the agenda of curriculum studies in India, Jain suggests, are sustained studies of "teacher's work and its various spaces and time schedules within the school such as morning assembly, play grounds, library, canteen, lobby, club spaces, teacher's staff room and staff meetings."[61]

As in China—and in contrast to the United States—the future of curriculum studies in India looks promising. Jain reports growing interest in the subject among scholars from disciplines other than education as well as the appearance of new journals in English and Hindi. Despite the problems he outlines in his chapter, evidently there is sufficient scholarly activity—this volume is one testimony to that fact—to express confidence that (as Jain suggests) "we can expect that the conventional ideas…may get increasingly challenged within the academic field and practices of curriculum and textbooks." In addition to "increasing interest in curriculum issues," and "a larger community of scholars," there are new degree programs, one important example of which Poonam Batra outlined in her chapter and discussed in exchanges with Lesley Le Grange and Hongyu Wang. "This interdisciplinary reflection on and engagement with curriculum," Jain concludes, "may lead to emergence of a distinct field of curriculum studies." There must be adequate institutional support, he adds.

The character of the emerging field will be distinctive, this project promises us. While its scars may remain, the traces of not just British (as Ghosh makes clear) colonialism but others as well may morph into new forms, including apparently progressive ones like globalization, progressive against (again as Ghosh specifies) traditions no longer in touch with the present. "Once we understand that students are keen and active participants in the processes in which they are inserted," Thapan reminds, "our views about schooling, curriculum and its possible outcomes should change." Writing here against the determinism embedded in structuralism and ideology critique, Thapan's positioning of students as "keen and active participants" is significant. We saw this positioning in Batra's depiction of the University of Delhi's program of teacher education, in Thapan's portrait of the Rishi Valley School, and in Chacko's rendering of the imprinting research of Krishna Kumar.

"If we accept the view that students at school are not mute subjects, but thinking, acting, feeling actors," Thapan emphasizes, "it is possible for schools to also consciously engage students in other practices that move away from inculcating and reproducing hatred, violence and difference." This insight seems crucial, if vulnerable, to a globalizing neoliberalism that depersonalizes students into numbers on standardized tests. Not only associated with standardized testing, such (sometimes ancient) practices, Thapan worries, "have numbed the minds of children." The effort to inculcate "a culture of questioning, doubt and criticism" is crucial, Thapan allows, but such a culture is "not enough to allow for...understanding difference, heterogeneity and complexity in social and cultural life." That curricular question of "transfer" remains compelling.

Also compelling are those questions accompanying social "reconstruction" in a postcolonial space. "Is it possible to imagine the postcolonial space without the referent of lack,'" Jain asks. And can this "lack"—the Western construction of India as "irrational, superstitious, communal, casteist and patriarchal"—be filled through "a modern, progressive and secular education"? Such a construction of the problem and its inevitable "solution," Jain points out, "reproduces the colonial binaries." What is at stake, he appreciates, is the "agency" of the people. This "peculiarity of the postcolonial state," he notes, "is a question that rarely gets discussed in discussions on curriculum by those who are located in the discipline of education." Surely the postcolonial condition is a central theoretical—and existential—question the field faces. Addressing this, Batra reminds, would require the engendering of "curricular experiences that enable a dialectical engagement between social construction and inner reflection." As resounding as the answers are[62]—or will be—for Indian scholars, students, and teachers alike, they will also reverberate around the world, for the question of the postcolonial curriculum is compelling to former colonies— and colonizers—everywhere.[63] It is this scale of the curriculum question—*what knowledge is of most worth?*[64]—and the distinctive answers to it these scholars provide that render curriculum studies in India of worldwide significance.

# Notes

A special note of thanks especially to Professor Poonam Batra for her exceptionally close reading of—and suggested revisions of—this chapter.

1. Manish Jain also references this divide between school and everyday life in the context of his discussion of the Secondary Education Commission, convened after Indian independence. Batra also references this commission. See their chapters, this volume.
2. The centrality of the state in the education of children, Meenakshi Thapan asserts, confers "power to the textbook as the most effective tool of state policy on education and the goals it seeks to achieve." Thapan referenced Kumar, who has suggested that textbooks are linked to the "value-system entrenched in the school time-table" as "aspects of an industrial culture" that acculturates students to systems of "punctuality, specialization and obedience that characterizes the precision and rigidity of industrial societies." Thapan herself, however, is unconvinced, sharing the view of Marjorie Sykes that the significance of textbooks has been overstated. There are other influences, Thapan notes, including "the role children themselves play in the reception of knowledge, even in authoritarian and controlled settings. Textbooks are not sacrosanct to the young in school; students understand that they have to be mastered for purposes of evaluation and

discarded soon after, as only one aspect of a life at school that encompasses more than mere written or oral knowledge." In her reply to Hongyu Wang, Mary Ann Chacko also cited India's oral traditions; they are an important instance of "hybrid" resources upon which teachers and students can draw to bridge the gap between academic knowledge and everyday life. Chacko pointed particularly to stories, as these "promote good listening, give training in prediction, extend our world, and give meaning to words." For Kumar, she continued, orality can be a vital asset for countering "the homogenizing effects of modern education and media."

3. "In the context of amnesia about the colonial legacy of education," Jain points out, "the significance of such work for curriculum studies in India cannot be overemphasized." As Jain and other scholar-participants acknowledge—see the Ghosh chapter, for instance—"colonialism" itself was no monolith. "Colonial officials, missionaries, representatives of religious communities," Jain explains, "were no homogenous group.... Whether education should present colonial ideals of manliness and promote imitation of English manners and history did not evoke a common answer." History also emerges as a crucial discipline, Jain notes, when there were (in 1977 and 2000) "Hindutva attempts to rewrite history textbooks."

4. Jain identifies "nation-building" as one of the "two overlapping axes" by which to understand the present circumstances of curriculum studies in India. His study of colonial civics curriculum since late nineteenth century—see his chapter—showed that in the period after the First World War, a "nationalist elite" emerged as the "new speaking voice of the nation," challenging the colonial state in civics textbooks, which also served as sites of "contestation" over "the idea of India." Suresh Ghosh also registered colonialism and Indian struggle against it as structuring present circumstances. Recall that Ghosh suggests that the failure to "adjust the curriculum inherited from the British Raj (Administration) in 1947 was one of the major factors in the socio-economic and political disorder of our country."

5. Not only Western readers will associate this term first with Joseph Schwab, as we will see. As noted in the preceding chapter, Lesley Le Grange asked Mary Ann Chacko about the genesis of the term. I will reiterate the main points of this issue, suggesting as it does questions of "recontextualization."

6. These verbs are mine. "Inhabit" implies occupation of that "divide" between curriculum and everyday life on which Batra and Thapan dwell, and in ways that enable "reconstructing" the colonial past and globalizing present in more economically equitable, socially just, historically informed, and culturally distinctive ways.

7. Colonial education also cut two ways, Jain tells us, as it "also introduced idioms of individual rights, equality and universality." He adds: "but in the context of the limited availability of mass education, the process of emergence of vernacular public spheres and individuated selves was severely limited."

8. See Tröhler 2011.

9. "The British 'essentialist' view of knowledge of the 19th century," Batra explained, "emphasized the individual, scientific, universal and moral aims of education ahead of the social and cultural." The curriculum remained focused on "colonial objectives."

10. For "many thinkers" in India, Batra explained, "reflecting on the material reality—including oneself—is a process that draws from within. In this sense, there are no dualities, only processes that coexist but are seen as dichotomies in the circumscribed view of the logical 'mind,' which several scholars of the West have also challenged, including John Dewey and George Herbert Mead."

11. Gandhi's "Nai Talim" was adopted by several states in 1937.

12. "The social profile of the person who seemed to approximate and personify this 'scientific attitude' was," Jain argues, that of the "postcolonial bureaucrat."

13. Personal note, February 15, 2014.

14. The Kothari Commission is also discussed by Suresh Ghosh in his chapter and referenced by Chacko in her exchange with Wang, as she pointed out that the member-secretary of this commission—J. P. Naik—was Kumar's mentor. It was to Naik, Chacko points out, that Kumar dedicated his seminal work, *Political Agenda of Education* (1991).

15. Regarding the situation in the United States, see Pinar 2013, 28. Ghosh tells us that the 1986 program "imagined as outcomes…international co-operation and peaceful co-existence," lofty aspirations indeed, ones even religious institutions have failed to achieve.

16. Including, as Manish Jain points out, in higher education, how will the determination to make "quick profit" impact the quality of the curriculum? he rightly asks.

17. The KFI runs five schools in India based on the educational thought of J. Krishnamurti (1895–1986), Thapan notes.

18. "Clearly," Thapan acknowledges, "private education is not the most appropriate solution to the vast problems that beset education in India, but schooling for all under government auspices alone is unable to deliver quality education, e.g. with trained teachers and adequate infrastructure."

19. "Central to the educational vision of Krishnamurti," Batra emphasized, "is the idea of transformation of individual consciousness through an education that regards 'relationship' as the basis of human existence." See Thapan (this volume) and Kumar 2013.

20. Thapan tells us that "there is a recognition that, in general, government and private schools sorely lack the potential to enable children to grow to their full potential as a result of stunted and irrelevant curricular practices, limited teaching skills or commitment, lack of good quality textbooks and learning material, and several other problems such as student dropouts, teacher absenteeism, parental apathy, and so on."

21. Recall that Thapan studies the latter.

22. An unintended, unanticipated consequence of these efforts "to indoctrinate Hindu children with an ideology that is one that laments the decline of morals and values in Indian society, propagates pride in the being Hindu, and in the Hindu *rashtra* (nation) as well as hatred for other communities and people," Thapan points out, has been students' (and presumably their families') preoccupation with upward mobility. This translates into vocationalism, choosing "career *over* creating a Hindu nation" (Thapan, this volume).

23. Likewise, Thapan advises that "we must also endeavor to stay free of ideological commitments of one kind or another in our search for the best answers to India's problem of *quality* education for all." Since the latter half of the nineteenth century, Jain reports in his chapter, there has been in India a "recurring uneasiness" over religion and its accommodation within modernity.

24. The "religious fanaticism" of the BJP continues to be felt in the school curriculum, Batra notes, as their textbooks continued to be used by schools of the BJP-ruled states.

25. Thapan would seem to concur, decrying the "hegemonic control" of the school curriculum by "the state and its functionaries," circumstances that leave "very little space for schools, teachers, and students to be flexible with even the modes of transaction, as all schools are also affiliated to one or to the other schoolboards for examination and certification purposes."

26. A concept integral to understanding "internationalization," "recontextualization" is articulated in theoretical terms in Brazil (see Pinar 2011a, 13).

27. Not only in India of course, as "child-centeredness" in the United States also challenged the centrality of academic knowledge in school curriculum. See Pinar 2010.

28. As Poonam Batra pointed out in her review of this chapter, the exclusive emphasis on "how" is revised in Kumar's later work: see note 63.

29. As did Huebner (1999) in the United States, Batra associates the prominence of educational psychology in teacher education with the emphasis on the child as "learner," a decontextualized concept that sidesteps the key curriculum question of what knowledge is of most worth.

30. Its 1919 recommendations, Ghosh suggested, also represent the genesis of "curriculum" as a specialization taught in universities.

31. The commission encouraged the education of Muslims generally, Ghosh notes.

32. How an institution whose practitioners are primarily female could become "patriarchal" can be puzzling; Madeleine Grumet (1988, 34–58) explains what was in play in late nineteenth-century America.

33. Now many states, Batra noted, teach English from grade one. She added that many state schools now have a separate English medium section even in primary schools.

34. The very existence of these market-driven schools, Thapan insightfully points out, "depends upon developing a vocabulary of change." That once progressive concept—*change*—has now been converted to the catechism of the corporate-government alliance to end public education in the United States (Pinar 2013).

35. Malayalam is the regional language of the state of Kerala, Chacko notes.

36. In contrast, in the United States the nongovernmental sector is dominated by the private sector—specifically corporations such as Apple, Microsoft, and Pearson as well as the Bill and Melinda Gates Foundation—invested in replacing teachers with their products: "interactive" curricula moved online. See Pinar 2013, 24–34.

37. Thapan also cited the significance of the NGO sector, discussing (like Batra and Jain) the Hoshangabad Science Teaching Program (HSTP).

38. Recall that, in his chapter, Jain discusses civics as well.

39. Batra noted that "during the World Bank funded DPEP, Eklavya was involved in a spate of educational activity across several states."

40. Wherein the textbook is seen as the only source of legitimate knowledge (see note 2). Post NCF, 2005, knowledge remains central, but is viewed as residing in textbooks as well as in the quotidian of classroom life (Batra's note). This insight is also evident in Brazil (see Pinar 2011a, 206).

41. Chacko also references these trends, especially as they imprint Krishna Kumar's intellectual trajectory. In an exchange with Wang, Chacko also cites the Nambissan (2013, 99) critique of the sociology of education: "Though sociologists in India have made significant contribution to the study of inequality in education, there has been a lack of serious attention to opening up the 'black box' of schooling and understanding the context and processes of learning. This has resulted in a narrow and distorted discourse on what happens within schools." Chacko concludes: "I would like to note that while the field of Sociology of Education is India is plagued by various institutional, methodological, and theoretical concerns (Nambissan and Rao, 2013), it would not be erroneous to say that sociology of education and the work of sociologists like Krishna Kumar, Geeta Nambissan, Padma Sarangapani, and Meenakshi Thapan continue to be the major force in educational research in India."

42. Jain too references the emergence of this neoliberal discourse of "choice," "management," "accountability."

43. Referencing Gandhi's "Nai Talim," Batra writes that "the 'problem' of curriculum was to become an act of "deliberation" rather than one based on 'an intrinsic view of knowledge.' This powerful idea of Gandhi was much ahead of its time, when Western debates on curriculum of the 1950s and 1960s were circumscribed to either articulating the 'scientific principles' of developing curriculum or turning towards the philosophers' claim of identifying knowledge that had intrinsic worth. Gandhi's basic education was

an attempt to make curriculum democratically accessible by making it socially and economically relevant." Chacko too acknowledges that Kumar's work is "deeply inspired by Gandhian values."

44. Another unacknowledged source of Schwab's conception of deliberation was Judaism. See Block 2004.

45. Chacko lists "childhood, globalization, universalization, quality, equality" as well as "counter-socialization."

46. Perhaps the most notorious was the Carlisle Indian Industrial School; one of its most famous graduates would also seem to have undermined any simple school-society "dualism." See Pinar 2009, 23–25.

47. "I would suggest," Chacko continued, "that 'counter-socialization' does not imply a school-society 'dualism' but rather reminds us of the nature of schools as intentionally created institutions. In other words, counter-socialization gestures towards the 'intentionality' that must structure the curricular experiences in schools as opposed to viewing schooling and curriculum as reflections of society."

48. "It is when schools, textbooks, and teachers keep the world out of the school," Chacko asserted, "that we establish a dualism between school and society."

49. Thapan specifies three types of schools in India: "government, aided, and private (recognized and unrecognized). Those that are run by central, state or local governments are referred to as government schools; aided schools are those that are run by private management but are funded by government grants-in-aid; and private schools that receive no aid are referred to as private schools, although there is an important subdivision among those that are recognized by the government (i.e. they fulfill certain criteria) or are unrecognized. The most significant distinction between schools is that between the government and private schools."

50. "The term 'Hindu(s)' in contemporary India," Batra commented, "is associated with specific connotations of 'cultural nationalists'; although its genesis lies in Alexander's expression for the people who lived beyond the river Indus (read as 'Hindu')."

51. Questions of dependency—cultural and otherwise—linger in other former colonies, including Canada: see Pinar 2011b.

52. "Studies on the gendered character of textbooks," Jain reported, "have pointed to lower representation of women in textbooks, their portrayal as inactive and located in home in contrast to males characterized in positions of power."As was the case in South Africa, Brazil, Mexico, and China, scholarly attention to curricular questions of gender were not at the forefront of LGBT issues. In mid-December 2013, the Indian Supreme Court reinstated a colonial-era law banning gay sex. The 1861 law imposed a 10-year sentence for "carnal intercourse against the order of nature with man, woman or animal." That law had been ruled unconstitutional in a 2009 decision. But the Supreme Court held that only Parliament had the authority to alter the law, a position it has not tended to take on other issues. Despite a "rich history of eunuchs and transgendered people who serve critical roles in important social functions and whose blessings are eagerly sought," Gardiner Harris (2013, A6) reported, "Indians are in the main deeply conservative about issues of sexuality and personal morality." He suggested that the social sphere, not the legal apparatus, structures LGBT life in India, as many gay men and women are "forced" to lead "double lives" (2013, A6). The law banning homosexuality is rarely enforced, although police sometimes use it to "bully" and "intimidate" gay men and women (2013, A6).

53. Batra too had argued that, in its failure to engage schoolteachers enough with processes of curriculum design, the NCF, 2005 "could well have sown the seeds of its own capture by political and sectarian interests at state level within India's complex federal polity, where education is primarily a state jurisdiction" (Batra, 2005, 4349).

54. See Pinar 2013, 30.
55. "The forces of globalization," Ghosh reports, "have forced the development of new curriculum in information technology, engineering, management and the allied sciences, and without any help from our educational planners and leaders. The new curriculum now seems to answer to the needs and aspirations of the young people."
56. The Naxal Movement began in the early 1960s. It owes its name to the name of the birthplace of its deceased founder, Charu Majumdar, who was born in Naxalbari in North Bengal. Ghosh's note.
57. Kumar, Batra points out, associated the conception of curriculum as "received knowledge" with the uncritical importation of Tyler and Bloom. (Jain notes that students were also sent from India to study with Bloom in Chicago.) Recall that in Mexico the importation of US concepts was less "uncritical" than simply "forced" (see Pinar 2011c, 233). Chacko too referenced Kumar's critique of curriculum as "received knowledge," his contrasting characterization of curriculum as "constructed," and "resultant of particular choices and decisions, which in turn can be challenged."
58. The history of education, Ghosh pointed out to me, is a relatively recent—and extremely important—addition to those specializations comprising the broad academic field of education.
59. There were objections to Lee-Warner's textbook; see Jain's chapter.
60. For an overview see Goodson 2014.
61. As noted, everyday life studies are important in Brazil; studies of school life have also been conducted in Israel: see Ben-Peretz 2000.
62. I write "are" because there are answers already. Thapan and Batra—as well as Ghosh and Jain—describe historical and contemporary efforts to address questions of colonialism at both theoretical and practical levels.
63. Including, for example, South Korea: see Kim et al. 2014.
64. As Mary Ann Chacko points out in a reply to question from Hongyu Wang, Kumar conceptualizes the "problem" of curriculum in three basic questions: "What is worth teaching? How it should be taught? and How are the opportunities for education distributed?" (Kumar 2009, 2).

# References

Batra, Poonam. 2005. "Voice and Agency of Teachers: A Missing Link in the National Curriculum Framework." *Economic and Political Weekly*.

Ben-Peretz, Miriam. 2000. *Behind Closed Doors*. Albany: State University of New York Press.

Block, Alan A. 2004. *Talmud, Curriculum, and the Practical*. New York: Peter Lang.

Goodson, Ivor F. 2014. "Developing Curriculum History. A British Perspective." In *The International Handbook of Curriculum Research*, edited by William F. Pinar, 2nd ed. 515–20. New York: Routledge.

Grumet, Madeleine R. 1988. *Bitter Milk: Women and Teaching*. Amherst: University of Massachusetts Press.

Harris, Gardiner. 2013. "India's Supreme Court Restores an 1861 Law Banning Gay Sex." *The New York Times* 163 (56348): A6.

Huebner, Dwayne E. 1999. *The Lure of the Transcendent*. New York: Routledge.

Kim, Young Chun, Dong Sun Lee, and Je Hong Joo. 2014. "Curriculum Studies as Reconceptualization Discourse: A Tale of South Korea." In *International Handbook of Curriculum Research*, edited by William F. Pinar, 2nd ed. 299–314. New York: Routledge.

Kumar, Ashwani. 2013. *Curriculum as Meditative Inquiry*. New York: Palgrave Macmillan.

Kumar, Krishna. 1989. *Social Character of Learning*. New Delhi, India: Sage Publications.

Kumar, Krishna. 1991. *Political Agenda of Education: A Study of Colonialist and Nationalist Ideas*. New Delhi: Sage Publications.

Kumar, Krishna. 1992. *What Is Worth Teaching?* New Delhi: Orient BlackSwan.

Nambissan, Geetha B. 2013. "Opening up the Black Box? Sociologists and the Study of Schooling in India." In *Sociology of Education in India: Changing Contours and Emerging Concerns*, edited by Geetha B. Nambissan and S. Srinivasa Rao, 83–102. New Delhi: Oxford University Press.

Nambissan, Geetha B., and S. Srinivasa Rao. 2013. "Introduction: Sociology of Education in India—Trajectory, Location, and Concerns." In *Sociology of Education in India: Changing Contours and Emerging Concerns*, edited by Geetha B. Nambissan and S. Srinivasa Rao, 1–24. New Delhi: Oxford University Press.

NCERT. 2005. *National Curriculum Framework 2005*. New Delhi. http://www.ncert.nic.in/rightside/links/pdf/framework/english/nf2005.pdf.

Pinar, William F. 2009. *The Worldliness of a Cosmopolitan Education: Passionate Lives in Public Service*. New York: Routledge.

Pinar, William F. 2010. "The Eight-Year Study." *Curriculum Inquiry* 40 (2): 295–316.

Pinar, William F., ed. 2011a. *Curriculum Studies in Brazil*. New York: Palgrave Macmillan.

Pinar, William F., ed. 2011b. *Curriculum Studies in Mexico*. New York: Palgrave Macmillan.

Pinar, William F. 2011c. "Nationalism, Anti-Americanism, Canadian Identity." In *Curriculum in Today's World: Configuring Knowledge, Identities, Work and Politics*, edited by Lyn Yates and Madeleine Grumet, 31–43. London: Routledge.

Pinar, William F. 2013. *Curriculum Studies in the United States: Present Circumstances, Intellectual Histories*. New York: Palgrave Macmillan.

SCERT. 2007. "Kerala Curriculum Framework 2007." http://www.scert.kerala.gov.in/images/docs/kcf_englishfinal.pdf.

Tröhler, Daniel. 2011. *Languages of Education: Protestant Legacies, National Identities, and Global Aspirations*. New York: Routledge.

# Epilogue

## Meenakshi Thapan and Poonam Batra*

## Do We Know Where We Are Going?

Youth in India stand at the edge of an uncertain modernity that seeks to take them, by leaps and bounds, into a "modern" throbbing world of fast movement, flashing images, and imagined opportunities amid political upheavals and an uncertain future. Bollywood cinema, and endless television "serials," ceaselessly enumerate the virtues of a life of wealth, luxury, and social status. They thus play a crucial role in the communication of this modernity and fuel aspirations for a life that appears to be close at hand, within reach, and as accessible as to the actors on the screen. At the same time, this so-called modernity constrains youth by its very condition as India's youth-in-waiting, mired in poverty, trapped by caste, class, and gender prejudice, inhibited by lack of social capital, face unemployment and further deprivation, marginalization, and exclusion. These two dimensions simultaneously represent the social reality of India with an enormous youth population (41 percent in 2001) including those who never manage to complete secondary education, or if they do, rarely find employment after secondary or tertiary education. What then we may ask has been the benefit of reaching out to India's millions through the recent initiatives of the state such as the Right to Education Act (2009)? And other state-driven and civil-society initiatives over the past two decades? We may wonder whether or not there been a substantial difference in the opportunities that education has opened up to its beneficiaries. The real question that remains however is whether education has enabled youth to shape their futures differently from the past.

There is no doubt that when young children do not have equitable access to education, or are unable to stay in school due to multiple factors that are grounded in a nexus of power relations, it is imperative to interrogate what keeps education out of their reach. At the same time, it is essential to focus on the content of education and its outcomes in other than utilitarian terms. Instead of focusing on the instrumental aspects of education, we need to bring to the forefront those other, often neglected, and seemingly less important aspects of being educated that are to do with "an education" per se. In the race to "catching up" with the material success of the rest of the developed world, we seem to think that high grades and material success are the most crucial components of a "good" education. To this end, the government-directed curriculum is not only by and large accepted as the most legitimate but also craved for and endured as the one most suited to our children. This is perhaps why ruthless middle-class parents, hiding behind their children's "ambitions," dole out thousands of rupees for "coaching " of different kinds, whether for improving school grades, passing various entrance examination, or to secure a place for their wards in institutions of higher learning. David Sancho (2013) refers to these ambitious strivings as "aspirational regimes" that fuel educational goals in particular directions. Education is therefore prized, not in and for itself, but for the gains and dividends it is viewed as providing in an increasingly competitive and exclusionary world.

The question that concerns us is whether it is possible to reconsider the value of education to not only provide skills, resources, and decision-making abilities, but in addition, and in fact, to first seek to cultivate individuals as humane and socially responsible adults? An education built on Gandhian ethics, empty of religious content, seems to be a rather old-fashioned idea, located in the past, that surely can have no place in this "modern" Indian reality that is hurtling toward the chaos that is so well accepted as the norm in the Western world. Societies, and relationships within them, are not impermeable, bounded systems; the possibilities for change are ever present and the potential for exercising moral choice lies within each individual. The role of "moral imagination," it has been argued, "is to keep the choice open, allow various contending potentialities to be tempered so that the possibility of right conduct remains available at all times" (Suhrud 2013). By inculcating the ability to exercise choice, based on a kind of moral rationality, schools pave the way for developing new modes of becoming citizens. It is to this aim that I implore educators to turn their attention, not as some new age gobbledygook, but as reflective educators who seek a better world for future generations. The world of scholasticism and enterprise will find itself, and education will remain a conduit for ambitions to flourish, but if we keep the soul of education intact in the curriculum, we will restore humanity in social relationships. This does not mean that the curriculum adds on "co-curricular" or "extra-curricular" forms of activities or modules for civic participation and engagement. The idea is for the school curriculum to incorporate such forms within its core so that it becomes germane to every single disciplinary frame and activity content. Only then would we have evolved a truly egalitarian and humanitarian curriculum, without the trappings of an unbalanced development of the human being as "machine" and as "human," worshipping technology and the nation-state, and failing to pay attention to the uncertain, the unique, and the inexplicable. We need to first pause, take a step back, and then ask the question: Do we know where we are headed in educating our children and the young in this country?

\* \* \*

In his analysis of what characterizes the field of curriculum studies in contemporary India, William Pinar foregrounds "echoes" of the colonial past and its reconstruction in the neoliberal version of globalization. While globalization and its effects are seen in the several challenges of a new modernity, its complex impact in the everyday spaces of schooling and society is the subject of nuanced enquiry. It is evident that curriculum studies in contemporary India are encumbered by the convergence between forces of economic globalization and conservative ideological forces that have relentlessly attempted to capture the curricular space. "Cultural revivalism," coupled with liberalization of the economy, has led to the intensification of patriarchy and glossing over persistent social differences based on caste, community, and religion. Plural identities of the Indian citizen are being homogenized every day, challenging the very "idea of India." This is despite a national curricular discourse that has, over a decade, created space for meaningful integration and interrogation of local narratives and local knowledge, stressing the role of the teacher in this process of contextualization.

Two reasons could explain why this is so. The first explanation lies in the wedge in the educational discourse, created during the first wave of liberalization in India in the early 1990s that divorced questions of quality education from processes of teaching and learning. Market-based reforms during the second wave of liberalization in the 2000s took this logic further. As an example, large-scale testing of learning outcomes that sought to standardize school education was seen as the way forward. A consonance between a neoliberal framework and the behavioristic outcome–based model of education driven by an international policy discourse was established. The second explanation lies in the subversion of ideas and spaces created by school and teacher education via an attempted ideological capture of curriculum, aided by the states' indifference toward structures and mechanisms required to nurture its own constructivist national curriculum.

Curriculum scholars have taken cognizance of the everyday world of contemporary India in which culture is conflated both with religion and politics. In their view, this can be countered through a process of "social dialogue." The challenge before curriculum scholars is to reposition knowledge at the center of such dialogue. Even as policy enforcement of large-scale assessments, teacher efficiency, and accountability measures turn the trajectory of educational practice, the national curricular discourse establishes the need to recontextualize knowledge in curriculum. This is the more difficult task, as marginalization of knowledge has characterized the Indian educational project since colonial times. First, via the colonial imposition of its forms of "essentialist education" through an alien language, later through the "importation" of concepts of educational practice that failed to take root in a culturally diverse and locally rooted Indian society. Capitalizing on the post-Enlightenment social-subjective split, the moral ideals of cultural nationalism aligned with a neoliberal thrust on learning outcomes and teacher performance threaten to marginalize the role of knowledge and learning, mirroring the colonial experience.

As indicated by Pinar, the question raised by Krishna Kumar, "what knowledge is most worth" needs greater deepening to contribute to contemporary debates in curriculum studies. A critical engagement with this is likely to provide conditions for "recontextualization." If curriculum is to be a deliberative act of initiating social dialogue, then we would need to give expression to processes of engagement that promise to be emancipatory and transformative, reflected in the examples cited in this volume. This would require rethinking about educational process "not only in terms of cultures of learning and teaching but also dissenting against that which is learnt and taught by dominant cultural practices" (Rege 2010, 93). It is the democratization of methods of knowledge creation via simultaneous intellectual processes and inner reflection that allows clarity of purpose rarely witnessed and experienced through reason alone.

# Note

*The first section of the epilogue is by Meenakshi Thapan and the second section is by Poonam Batra.

# References

Rege, Sharmila. 2010. "Education as Trutiya Ratna: Towards Phule-Ambedkarite Feminist Pedagogical Pratice." *Economic and Political Weekly*, 45 (40): 88–98.
Sancho, David. 2013. "Aspirational Regimes: Parental Educational Practice and the New Indian Youth Discourse." In *Enterprise Culture in Neoliberal India: Studies on Youth, Class, Work and Media*, edited by Nandini Gooptu. London and New York: Routledge, Taylor and Francis.
Suhrud, Tridip. 2013. "The Crumbling Ground." *The Open Magazine*, 9 February. Retrieved online at http://www.openthemagazine.com/article/arts-letters/the- crumbling-ground. Accessed on December 10, 2013.

# Appendix: Interview Questions

1. Please describe the genesis of your present intellectual preoccupations and research agenda. To what extent do you regard these as consequences of your individuality and specific life history, to what extent were they structured by historical and political events within and outside of India? Regarding the former, did specific professors inspire your choice of fields (and specialization within the field) and/or did the intellectual content of the field draw you into participation? Regarding the latter, did political or social convictions influence your choice of field or, within the field of curriculum studies, structure your research?

2. As you reflect on your intellectual life history and specifically the paper you are preparing for this project, to what extent were and are your choices of what to study informed by the intellectual history of the discipline? How "independent" can your work be, given institutional and larger political circumstances?

3. Please provide a sketch of the academic field of curriculum studies in India, including how you position your research within it. How has your work been positioned by others? How has your work contributed to the intellectual advancement of your field?

4. How have global initiatives, influences (macropolitical events as well as global conflicts and cultural imports), aspirations (global citizenship issues, such as ecological sustainability and women's rights, for instance), and geopolitical realities (historical, regional, or colonial relationships, for instance) influenced the research you have conducted and plan to conduct?

5. What is, in your judgment, the "state of the field" in India and how does that state of affairs influence your own research and scholarship? What "next steps" might the field take in order to advance intellectually? What do you imagine your own "next steps"?

# Contributors

**Poonam Batra** is a professor in the Department of Education at University of Delhi. Her research interests are educational policy, teacher education, curriculum and pedagogy, comparative education, psychology, and gender studies. Her recent publications have focused on teacher education and teacher's agency.

**Mary Ann Chacko** is a doctoral student in Teacher's College at Columbia University. Her research interests are concerningpoststructural and postcolonial frameworks in education, globalization, and curriculum in transnational contexts, policing schools, qualitative research methods. Her latest publication is "Post-colonialism, Impact on Women" in *The Multimedia Encyclopedia of Women in Today's World*.

**Suresh C. Ghosh** was born in 1937 at Chandernagore. He studied history at the Calcutta Presidency College, the London School of Oriental and African Studies, and obtained a postdoctoral fellowship from the University of Edinburgh. Ghosh retired from the Chair of History at the Zakir Husain Centre for Educational Studies, JNU, in August 2002.

**Manish Jain** is an assistant professor in the School of Educational Studies at Ambedkar University, Delhi. His research interests are comparative education, educational history of the colonial India, gender and education, and new social movements in India.

**William F. Pinar** is Professor and Canada Research Chair at the University of British Columbia, Vancouver, Canada. He is the author, most recently, of *Educational Experience as Lived: Knowledge, History, Alterity*.

**Meenakshi Thapan** is a professor in the Department of Sociology at University of Delhi. Her research interests are sociology of education, sociology of migration, and gender studies. She is the author of *Life at School: An Ethnographic Study* (1991, 2nd ed., 2006) and *Living the Body: Embodiment, Womanhood, and Identity in Contemporary India* (2009).

# Index

Calcutta, 11, 12, 14, 27, 29, 84–6, 88–90,
    108, 115
  Hindu College, 86
  Madrasah, 85, 86
  University, 11, 89, 90, 193
  University Commission, 92, 93, 95, 214
calm, 152
Cambridge Board, 199
Cambridge University, 27, 145
Canada, 19, 23, 30, 34, 65, 109, 193, 194,
    231
capital(ism), 17, 19, 88, 125, 184, 209,
    222
  cultural, 15, 74, 75, 123
  human, 178
  social, 235
CARE India, 27
career, 4–6, 10, 28, 91, 93, 105, 145, 148,
    189, 198, 200, 229
Carlisle Industrial School, 231
caste(s), 5, 15–19, 28, 44, 49, 50, 52, 59,
    60, 77, 96, 112, 114, 116, 118, 120,
    124, 125, 128, 143, 157, 177, 178,
    187, 198, 200, 209, 218, 221, 226,
    227, 235, 237
  anti, 117, 130
  dominant, 36
  highest, 5
  Hindu, 69, 132, 146
  lower, 5, 116, 117, 132, 146, 165, 177,
    195, 215
  Other Backward, 17
  out, 165
  scheduled, 69, 96, 132, 174, 189, 195
  untouchable, 70
  upper, 15, 27, 35, 37, 40, 59, 117, 146,
    165, 209, 215
catharsis, 56, 212
Central Advisory Board of Education
    (CABE), 44, 93
Central Board for Secondary Education
    (CBSE), 94, 105, 145, 157, 158
Central Bureau of Textbook Research, 131
Central Colleges, 87
Central Institute of Education (CIE), 5, 65
Central Vigilance Commission, 104
Centre for Learning (CFL), 149, 158, 210
Ceylon, 89

Chacko, Mary Ann, 1, 8, 9, 10, 11, 23, 27,
    65–80, 163, 173–88, 203, 204,
    208, 213–17, 219–23, 225, 226,
    228–32, 241
Chacko, P. I., 80
Chagla, M. C., 103
Chakarabarti, Dipesh, 20
Chanana, Karuna, 158
Chandernagore, 107, 241
Chandernagore College, 12, 14
Chandra Gupta II Vikramaditya, 84
character, 41, 54, 88, 117, 118, 146
Chatterjee, Bankim Chandra, 90
Chatterjee, Partha, 115
Chattisgarh, 147
chauvinism, 39, 43, 105, 211, 215
chemistry, 86, 169
Chennai, 21
chess, 153
Chicago, 98, 122, 232
  University of, 12
child (the), 7–8, 28, 36, 37, 39–42, 45–8,
    51, 52, 57, 59, 67, 68, 70–2, 75,
    76, 79, 112, 121, 131, 146, 149,
    151, 158, 167, 168, 172, 174, 184,
    186, 203, 204, 210, 212, 214, 220,
    225, 230
  centered(ness), 26, 40–2, 46, 52, 53, 61,
    70, 78, 128, 164, 167, 168, 172,
    191, 201, 203, 212–14, 229
  marriage, 85
  rearing, 215
  rights, 197
childhood, 9, 115, 133, 167, 175, 231
children, 2, 5, 21, 26–8, 36, 38, 42, 47–9,
    51–8, 61, 66, 69, 71–6, 79, 94, 102,
    105, 109, 117, 118, 124–8, 132,
    133, 141–4, 146–51, 153–8, 166,
    168, 173, 176, 179–85, 188, 194,
    197, 198, 200–3, 207–10, 212, 214,
    216–18, 221, 223, 224, 227, 229,
    235, 236
China, 20, 191, 193, 199, 205, 226, 231
choice(s), 66, 117, 120, 129, 145, 155,
    173, 176, 184–6, 215, 230,
    232, 236
Christian(ity), 29, 29, 43, 85, 96, 147, 156
cinema, 175, 235

CPSIA information can be obtained
at www.ICGtesting.com
Printed in the USA
LVOW13*2137220318
570894LV00007B/145/P

9 781137 477170